W9-BSA-594

NEW WRITING
FROM THE
MIDDLE EAST

NEW WRITING FROM THE MIDDLE EAST

Edited, with an introduction
and commentary, by

Leo Hamalian and John D. Yohannan

FREDERICK UNGAR PUBLISHING CO. NEW YORK

Published by arrangement with The New American Library, Inc., New York, N.Y.

Printed in the United States of America

Library of Congress Cataloging in Publication Data
Main entry under title:

New writing from the Middle East.

(A Mentor book)
Bibliography: p.
1. Near Eastern literature—Translations into
English. 2. English literature—Translations
from Near Eastern languages. I. Hamalian, Leo.
II. Yohannan, John D.
PJ909.N4   808.8′004   78-4411
ISBN 0-8044-2338-5

PERMISSIONS and ACKNOWLEDGMENTS

Arabic section

Baalabaki, Laila: "A Space Ship of Tenderness to the Moon." From *Modern Arabic Stories*, ed. by Denys Johnson-Davies. Copyright © 1967 by Denys Johnson-Davies. Used by permission of Heineman Educational Books, Ltd.

Cossery, Albert: "The Girl and the Hashish Smoker." From *Men God Forgot* by Albert Cossery. Copyright © 1963 by City Light Books. Reprinted by permission of City Light Books.

Idriss, Yussef: "A House of Flesh." Copyright © 1978 by Mona N. Mikhail. Used by permission of Mona N. Mikhail.

Ikhlassi, Walid: "The Dead Afternoon." From *Modern Arabic Stories*, ed. by Denys Johnson-Davies. Copyright © 1967 by Denys Johnson-Davies. Used by permission of Heineman Educational Books, Ltd.

(The following pages constitute an extension of this copyright page.)

[iv]

[v]

Armenian section

ACKNOWLEDGMENTS

We wish to acknowledge with gratitude the special help received from Talat S. Halman, Vahe Oshegan, Rachel Eytan, and G. M. Wickens, but they are not to be held responsible for any errors of fact or judgment that we may have made.

CONTENTS

II. ARMENIAN LITERATURE 115

III. ISRAELI LITERATURE 187

IV. PERSIAN LITERATURE 271

GENERAL INTRODUCTION

All of the five contemporary Middle Eastern literatures represented in this anthology have ancient antecedents. Arab literature originated during the sixth century A.D. in the pre-Islamic poetry of the desert. Iranian literature in Farsi (modern Persian) is more than a thousand years old, and its roots in Middle and Old Persian go back to earlier Sassanian and Achaemenian times. The Turkish literary heritage antedates the appearance of the Seljuqs and the Ottomans on the world historical scene, reaching back to an older nomadic existence on the Asian steppes. Israeli literature is certainly nourished at its ultimate source by the Biblical writings. In its oral form, Armenian literature predates the creation of the Armenian alphabet, and its national epic was composed more than a millennium ago. The survival of these classical literatures in their modern phases testifies eloquently to the remarkable resiliency of Middle Eastern civilizations.

The modern phases have derived their character from contact with European civilization, at first in a colonial and subservient relationship, but since the Second World War, in a more nearly mutual one. The colonial relationship, though it began in the era of navigation and exploration by the Western powers, is mainly a nineteenth-century phenomenon. It was Napoleon's thrust into Egypt in 1789 to get at British imperial holdings in India that opened the Middle East to European influences and precipitated the modern renaissance that has so transformed the cultural life of all the peoples in the area. Franco-British rivalry produced both military and civilian schools, a popular press, the translation of European classics into the languages of the Middle East (Shakespeare is enormously popular in all the five language groups here represented), and ultimately the rise of a middle class and an intelligentsia oriented to the West and unwilling to patronize the traditional literature supported by, or supportive of, a court elite. In the twentieth century, constitutional movements in Iran and Turkey early wrested some democratic rights from the Qajar and Ottoman rulers. National aspirations produced an Arab rebellion against the Ottomans and at the same time laid the foundations for a future state of Israel. French influence focused the diaspora literature of the so-called Western branch of the Armenian cultural movement, while Soviet revolutionary doctrines dominated the development of the Eastern after the Armenian Republic collapsed in 1919.

Western readers have already been introduced to the writings that emerged from this colonial era of Middle Eastern history. There have been anthologies of modern Islamic literature; anthologies of modern poetry, drama, fiction by Arab, Persian, and Turkish writers; collections of Hebrew and Armenian poetry or fiction. As a result, Taha Hussein and Tewfiq al-Hakim, Bahar and Hedayat, Halide Edib and Nazim Hikmet, Bialik and Agnon, Raffi and Toumanian have become familiar, if not household, names in the West.

The purpose of this anthology is to present writers who for the most part have made their mark since the Second World War, when the "contemporary" phase of modern Middle Eastern literature may be said to have taken shape. Moreover, instead of limiting itself to a single nation or religion or genre—as the "modern" anthologies have generally done—this book employs a geographic frame. For, regardless of the conflicting claims of a multiplicity of ethnic, religious, and linguistic groups, the Middle East represents a geographic entity, and it exercises a peculiar power over the mind and the heart of the 100 million people who occupy the lands touching the eastern Mediterranean and the Caspian seas. This greater importance assigned here to a sense of place accounts for our inclusion of Moslem, Jewish, or Christian writers composing in Arabic, Persian, Turkish, Hebrew, Armenian, Russian, French, German, or English.

Although this anthology concentrates on authors who flourished in the era after the Second World War, it does not hesitate to include certain writers whose work appeared earlier. In some instances, for example Hedayat and Alavi from Iran, this is because their full impact was not felt until later and because they have not yet been brought to the full attention of readers of English. We include Tewfiq al-Hakim of Egypt and Nazim Hikmet of Turkey because, even after their deaths, their literary stature overshadows the work of their younger contemporaries.

On the other hand, no attempt is made to represent all forms of literature produced in the years under survey. Long fiction could not possibly be represented in any case—though Yashar Kemal's story is a novella and Reza Baraheni's piece is the prologue to a long novel. Even some outstanding poets and short-story writers have been left out because they were available in other recent English-language publications and it seemed advisable to offer some new voices in their stead. We have been able to represent, however inadequately, the drama of each literature except the Armenian; there is a flourishing theater in Soviet Armenia, but nearly all the plays are too long for inclusion here.

The modern contact between the Middle East and the West produced the orientalist vogue that tinged most of the great literatures of Europe in the nineteenth century. (Goethe's *West-Östlicher Divan* and Arnold's "Sohrab and Rustum" are but two examples chosen at random.) Middle Eastern literature felt the influence of the contact somewhat later, in the shape of the widespread adoption of Western forms and techniques and the imitation of Western authors. In general, the movement was from French, Russian, and German to British and American influences. "There is only one civilization in the world," a prominent Turkish intellectual could write sixty years ago, "and that is Western civilization."

Now, after decades of envious imitation, the literature of the Middle East is returning to its national or ethnic roots, but with an awareness of new possibilities: The dialectical process is producing a synthesis in which native and foreign, ancient and modern elements are blended. Eminent writers, like Egypt's Taha Hussein, have spoken in favor of bringing about a confluence of cultures rather than either remaining within the confines of the indigenous tradition or relying on Western inspiration alone. So far, drastic movements in either of the latter directions have produced only pyrrhic victories of East over West, or West over East.

What particularly characterizes the current literary synthesis is increased attention to the role of women and a greater interest in English and American authors. Hemingway, Faulkner, and Lawrence have their admirers and imitators in Iran, Turkey, and Egypt. The international vogue of Pound, Eliot, Yeats, Auden, and even Allen Ginsberg and Sylvia

Plath has affected Middle Eastern poets also. Writers in Soviet Armenia of course tend to respond to Russian influences, but through American émigrés they have kept abreast of John Dos Passos, William Saroyan, Bernard Malamud, and John Updike. Israeli writers, often despite linguistic affinity with Eastern Europe or Germany, and a devotion to West European models, are now more sensitive to American trends in both fiction and poetry.

The fact that many Middle Eastern writers are truly bilingual and often trilingual, in a way that few of their European and American counterparts can hope to be, assures a greater degree of cross-fertilization in their work. Adopting Western literary forms such as the novel, the short story, the drama of character, and free verse does not preclude the continued—or modified—use of traditional forms of dramatization, narration, and lyrical expression. The result is a complexity and sophistication perhaps insufficiently appreciated by most Western readers—and maybe impossible to appreciate fully in the language of translation.

As to translations in this book, the editors have sought out the most readable and have had them vouched for by reputable scholars. The translators are professionals, most of them associated with prominent universities here or abroad. Though a number of the selections have been taken from specialized journals of small circulation, many have been prepared especially for this anthology. A few were published in books now out of print or generally unavailable. Each of the five sections of this book has been provided with its own background essay surveying in broad outline the literary movements of the period. We have also supplied, in an appendix, brief biographical notes, and, in the text, such other notes as are necessary for a meaningful reading of the selections. The authors range from comparative unknowns in the West to the world-renowned, at least two of whom (Hedayat and Yashar Kemal) have been candidates for the Nobel Prize in literature. The selections that follow should constitute an illuminating experience in the literatures of an area that has a special importance in the world today.

PART I

ARABIC
LITERATURE

THE ARAB
BACKGROUND

The modern renaissance in Arab culture (called *nahda* or resurgence) took contrary directions at first: on one side was a
desire to revive the classical tradition, then moribund; on the
other, the attempt to shape a wholly new tradition based on
Western ideas. Eventually, an accommodation between these
two opposing tendencies became the prevailing trend. In the
world of letters, this course of compromise had its leading ad-
vocate in Taha Hussein (1889–1973), the grand old man of
modern Arabic literature. He was prolific and his influence
was immense—in scholarship, in educational theory, in history and religion, and in the establishment of canons of taste
through critical, autobiographical, and imaginative writing. In
An Egyptian Childhood and *The Stream of Days* (the English titles of two portions of his autobiographical *The Days*),
he described his early years in an Upper Egyptian village and
his period of adolescence at al-Azhar University in Cairo.
The Calling of a Bird is praised for its visual imagery, a
rather surprising virtue since Hussein was blind from childhood.

Early in the twentieth century, he and such writers as Hussein Haykal and Tewfiq al-Hakim gave world status to Arabic literature. Haykal's *Zaynab*, a sensitive study of an
Egyptian girl's life in a peasant village, is much admired.
Tewfiq al-Hakim is the outstanding Arab dramatist of our
time, rivaled only by the older Ahmad Shauqi (who wrote in
verse; al-Hakim chose prose as his medium). Through his
fifty or so plays on social themes, al-Hakim introduced the
"theater of ideas" to Egypt, and through his novels (such as
Bird of the Orient) he gave voice to the great silent majority
of his native country. All contemporary Arab writers, even
those who quarrel with the above three, have had to compose
in their shadow.

Although poetry had been the dominant medium of the

golden age of Arabic literature, prose became the chief language of the modern literary revolution. Of course, the Arabs always had their native (originally oral) forms of narration, of which *A Thousand and One Nights* and the romance of *Antar and Ab'lah* are perhaps the most famous examples; but it was the European novel and the short story—the latter particularly as practiced by Chekhov and Maupassant—that became the favorite literary genres in the early twentieth century. Even before the First World War, translations of short stories from abroad were accorded the peculiar hospitality of publication in newspapers devoted exclusively to French, Russian, or English literature.

The first notable writer of short stories was the Egyptian Mohammed Taymour, who before his death in 1921 enjoyed a huge success also in drama, poetry, and memoir writing. His younger brother, Mahmoud Taymour, has been even more popular, some half dozen collections of his stories being available to the Arab reading public. In the novel form, the greatest acclaim has been reserved for Najib Mahfuz (1911–), especially for a monumental trilogy of Egyptian middle class life between the two wars.

The great watershed in the development of Arab fiction, as indeed of all Middle Eastern literature of the modern period, was of course the Second World War. It was then that Taha Hussein's collected tales from the earlier years were published and fresh winds from abroad began to blow in. The use of the short story as a vehicle for social commentary, a tendency present from the very beginning, was now given further encouragement by the examples of Sartre and Camus in France, and of Caldwell, Steinbeck, Hemingway, and Faulkner in America. This social consciousness on the part of writers of fiction, often frankly Marxist, did not prevent their learning from Kafka, Joyce, and Huxley such stylistic innovations as the stream of consciousness, the interior monologue, and the syntax of surreal expression; and from D.H. Lawrence and others a new candor in the treatment of sexual themes. Hassan Abdul Kudus scored a notable success in 1959 with *A Man in our House* by writing openly of sexual intercourse. Yussef Idriss, a Cairo physician by profession, has combined the mood of Kafka with the spirit of Lawrence to create shocking and original stories about shifting planes of erotic reality, as in "A House of Flesh." A woman novelist from Lebanon, Laila Baalabaki, made a deep impression with her frank account of a woman's life in a patriarchal society in *I Live!* Her story in this collection, "A Space Ship of Tenderness to the Moon," explores, without the restraint of a previous decade, the erotic relationship between an Arab couple.

The Arab writer has been brought face to face with the universal problem of the artist anywhere: the reconciliation of his commitment to art with his concern for the social order, his sense of decorum and responsibility with his need to express his thoughts and passions without restraint. The problem is made more poignant by the continuous political struggles that have diverted the creative energies of the Arab artist. Considering the circumstances in which he has been forced to work, the level of excellence that the Arab writer has achieved is remarkable.

In 1958, Mahmoud Taymour, looking at the work of his contemporaries, offered a piece of aesthetic counsel worthy of Henry James. He warned writers of fiction to fight unrelentingly against

> . . . over-direct moralism, . . . an over-generalization that ignores specific truths, a tendency to neglect the contradictions in a single person's make-up, a wavering between excessive condemnation and excessive condoning of human weaknesses, the intrusion of the author's voice where his characters' voices should be heard, a neglect of image and atmosphere in favor of a bare narrative of information.

Arab fiction had clearly come of age and increasingly would heed this advice. The question of language would still be debated as writers sought that middle ground between the various colloquial idioms of the Arab world and the formal prose of the traditional past. But as the language of the writer became increasingly flexible, that most attractive of imported forms, the short story, continued on its popular career.

Modern Arabic poetry, too, has felt the influence of European and American models, both in form and in content, and it has also responded in a variety of ways to the tug between tradition and modernity. Hafiz Ibrahim (1871-1932) used classical forms to treat modern themes, Khalil Mutran (1872-1949) hoped to end for all time the tyranny of the long classical Arab poem, the *qasida,* by himself writing the longest one ever conceived, a mono-rhymed, mono-metered epic about Nero. The so-called Diwan group of poets, seeking a sincerity of expression they found lacking in their own past, reflected the practice of the English Romantics. The same Romantic leaning was prevalent in the Arab poets of the American migration, notably in the prose-poems of Gibran Khalil Gibran, who added the qualities of American Transcendentalism and Blakean mysticism to the rather vague Arab sentimentality of his work. In contrast to the optimism of Gibran was the disillusioned, melancholy romanticism of the French school of the Middle East. It would thus appear that Arab poetry in the first half of the present century was recapitulating the history of European poetry of the previous century. Again, World War II brought about the social changes that radically altered poetic perception and expression.

It was after the war that the free verse movement, led by Lewis Adad and advanced by the woman poet Nazik al-Malaikah, produced the ascendency of contemporary foreign influences—of the American cosmopolitan poets T.S. Eliot and Ezra Pound, of Mayakovsky, Garcia Lorca, Allen Ginsberg, and Neruda (the last read in English). Tewfiq Zayyad, who studied in Moscow, became acquainted with the work of the Turkish Marxist poet Nazim Hikmet in Russian translation. Other Arab writers involved in the necessary work of translation and adaptation were Adonis, Sayigh, M. Badawi, and Abd al-Sabur,. all represented in this anthology either as contributors or as translators.

The Arab intellectual of the era after the Second World War, when not devoted to Marxist social realism, was likely to be experiencing the same spiritual ennui that had been felt by Eliot and his contemporaries of the West in the backwash of the First World War. The debilitating political scene led many writers to search for values beyond the bounds of nationalism; and the Arab vogue of Eliot was immense, says Jabra I. Jabra. He himself responded to *The Waste Land* by translating a section of Frazer's *The Golden Bough* and later, his contemporary, Tewfiq Sayigh, put the *Four Quartets* of Eliot into Arabic. There was a longing for spiritual revivification among Syrian and Palestinian writers, who naturally turned to the Tammuz-Adonis myth native to their area. It is significant that the Syrian poet Ali Ahmad Saed took "Adonis" as his *nom de plume,* and that he edited an all-Eliot number of the journal *Sh'ir* (Poetry) in 1958. In Jabra's words, the Arab poets were seeking a more complex structure for their meaning and a multiplicity of levels for their effects. Another factor that may have led the Arab poets to prefer myth, symbol, and mystery over more direct techniques may have been, as Salih J. Altoma has suggested, "the restrictive nature of the poets' traditions and the risk involved in openly violating them." In a rapidly changing social order, the Arab poet is less and less likely to be the voice of the Establishment, as his counterpart, the *sha'ir,* was in ancient times. Arieh Loya has described this transformation of roles very well:

> For man in the Arab world today is no longer the uniform member of a monolithic tribal society whose poetry was, on the whole, a declamatory speech addressed to an audience. Rather, he is a member of a pluralistic society with a multiplicity of social, intellectual, political and moral shades of beliefs and tastes in which the individual is involved with his personal crisis.

Into this pattern fit a number of the poets here represented. But the smouldering Palestine question has given the poet as propagandist a new lease on life in the Arab world. Not only Palestinian poets such as Jabra I. Jabra and Mahmud Darwish, but also their cousins at several removes in Iraq, Syria, Lebanon, and Egypt have been stirred to intense poetical utterance in behalf of a perceived political injustice. Nizar Qabbani, a Syrian diplomat, has turned away from the love poetry at which he so excelled towards political concerns, expressing these in a free verse both direct and effective. Like Qabbani and others, the Jordanian Abu-Risha is a diplomat who writes poetry. His *Roving Along* (1960) expresses what the Arabs call "classical patriotism." Unfortunately, there is a very thin line between patriotic Arab poetry and Arab propaganda, and much of this poetry may seem naive to the Western reader.

Arab drama is among the most subtle and sophisticated of the Middle East. To some extent it remains faithful to a tradition of satirical writing for a puppet theater related to the Karagöz of Turkey, as in Yussef Idriss' popular *Farafoors.*

But the European sources of inspiration are not far to seek. Molière in translation was an early favorite in the Arab world, and since the revival of the theater in the 1950's and 1960's, the examples of Chekhov, Brecht, and Ionesco have served a number of writers for the stage. The most notable is Tewfiq al-Hakim, whose plays of absurdity have a wit and charm worthy of Ionesco, who perhaps inspired them. A sample of his shorter plays is here offered, together with a more recent play by a lesser known author, the latter revealing the sentiments generated by the Arab-Israeli struggle.

Whether in drama, poetry, or fiction, Arab authors in recent years have been creating works of genuine originality both in theme and form. They demonstrate a developing sense of professionalism just as their readers seem to be growing in sophistication. It is hoped that the following selections will give evidence of this.

FICTION

A Space Ship of Tenderness to the Moon

by LAILA BAALABAKI

When I closed my eyes I was able to see everything around
me, the long settee which fills one vast wall in the room from
corner to corner; the shelves on the remaining walls; the
small table; the coloured cushions on the carpet; the white
lamp, in the shape of a large kerosene one, that dangled from
a hole in the wall and rested on the tiled floor. Even the windows we had left curtainless. In the second room was a wide
sofa; a table supporting a mirror; a wall-cupboard and two
chairs upholstered in velvet. Since our marriage we hadn't
changed a thing in the little house, and I refused to remove
anything from it.

I opened my eyelids a little as I heard my husband
mumble, 'It's light and we alone are awake in the city.' I saw
him rising up in front of the window as the silver light of
dawn spread over his face and naked body. I love his naked
body.

Once again I closed my eyes; I was able to see every little
bit of him, every minute hidden detail: his soft hair, his
forehead, nose, chin, the veins of his neck, the hair on his
chest, his stomach, his feet, his nails. I called to him to come
back and stretch out beside me, that I wanted to kiss him. He
didn't move and I knew, from the way he had withdrawn
from me and stood far off, that he was preparing himself to
say something important. In this way he becomes cruel and
stubborn, capable of taking and carrying through decisions. I
am the exact opposite: in order to talk things over with him I
must take hold of his hand or touch his clothes. I therefore
opened my eyes, threw aside the cushion I was hugging and

[9]

seized hold of his shirt, spreading it across my chest. Fixing
my gaze on the ceiling I asked him if he saw the sea.

'I see the sea,' he answered.

I asked him what colour it was.

'Dark blue on one side,' he said, 'and on the other a grey-
ish white.'

I asked him if the cypress trees were still there.

'They are still there among the houses that cling close together,' he answered, 'and there's water lying on the roofs of
the buildings.'

I said I loved the solitary date-palm which looked, from
where we were, as though it had been planted in the sea and
that the cypress trees put me in mind of white cemeteries.

For a long while he was silent and I remained staring up at
the ceiling. Then he said, 'The cocks are calling,' and I
quickly told him I didn't like chickens because they couldn't
fly and that when I was a child I used to carry them up to
the roof of our home and throw them out into space in an attempt to teach them to fly, and both cocks and hens would
always land in a motionless heap on the ground.

Again he was silent for a while, after which he said that he
saw a light come on at the window of a building opposite. I
said that even so we were still the only two people awake in
the city, the only two who had spent the night entwined in
each other's arms. He said that he had drunk too much last
night. I quickly interrupted him by saying I hated that
phrase—I drank too much—as though he regretted the yearning frenzy with which he had made love to me. Sensing that I
was beginning to get annoyed he changed the subject, saying:
'The city looks like a mound of sparkling precious stones of
all colours and sizes.'

I answered that I now imagined the city as coloured card-
board boxes which would fall down if you blew on them; our
house alone, with its two rooms, was suspended from a cloud
and rode in space. He said that his mouth was dry and he
wanted an orange. I concluded what I had been saying by
stating that though I had never lived in any other city, I
hated this one and that had I not dreamt that I would one
day meet a man who would take me far far away from it I
would have died of dejection long long ago. Pretending that
he had not heard my last remark he repeated: 'I want an
orange, my throat's dry'. I disregarded his request and went
on to say that with him I paid no heed to where I was: the

earth with its trees, its mountains, rivers, animals and human beings just vanished. Unable to wait further, he burst out at me, 'Why do you refuse to have children?'

I was sad, my heart was wrung, the tears welled up into my eyes, but I didn't open my mouth.

'How long is it since we married?' he asked. I uttered not a word as I followed him round with my eyes. He stiffened and continued, 'It's a year and several months since we married and you've been refusing and refusing, though you were crazy about children before we married; you were dying for them.'

He swerved and struck the settee with his hands as he burst out, 'Hey chair, don't you remember her entreaties? And you lamp, didn't you hear the sound of her wailing? And you cushions, did she not make of you tiny bodies that she hugged to herself and snuggled up to as she slept? Speak, o things inanimate. Speak. Give back to her her voice which is sunk into you.'

Quietly I said that inanimate things don't feel, don't talk, don't move. Angrily he enquired: 'How do you know they're dead?' I replied that things weren't dead, but that they drew their pulse beats from people. He interrupted me by saying that he wouldn't argue about things now and wouldn't allow me to escape solving the problem as I always did. Absent-mindedly I explained to him that the things around me, these very things—this settee, this carpet, this wall, this lamp, this vase, the shelves and the ceiling—are all a vast mirror that reflects for me the outside world: the houses, the sea, the trees, the sky, the sun, the stars and the clouds. In them I see my past with him, the hours of misery and dejection, the moments of meeting and of tenderness, of bliss and of happiness, and from them I now deduce the shapes of the days to come. I would not give them up.

He became angry and shouted, 'We're back again with things. I want to understand here and now why you refuse to have children.' No longer able to bear it, I shouted that he too at one time refused to have them. He was silent for a while, then he said, 'I refused before we were married, when it would have been foolish to have had one.' Sarcastically I told him that he was afraid of them, those others, those buffoons in the city. He used to beg for their assent, their blessing, their agreement, so that he might see me and I him, so that he might embrace me and I him, so that we might each drown the other in our love. They used to determine for us our places of meeting, the number of steps to be taken to get there, the time, the degree to which our voices could be raised, the number of breaths we took. And I would watch them as they secretly scoffed at us, shamelessly slept with the bodies they loved, ate three meals a day, smoked cigarettes with the cups of coffee and carafes of arak, and guffawed as they vulgarly chewed over stories about us and thought up patterns of behaviour for us to put into effect the following day. His voice was choked as he mumbled: 'I don't pay attention to others. I was tied to another woman.'

Ah, how can I bear all this torture, all this passionate love for him? He used to be incapable of confessing the bitter truth to her, that he didn't love her, wouldn't love her. Choking, he said that it wasn't easy, he wasn't callous enough to be able to stare into another human being's face and say to her, after nine years of getting up each and every day and finding her there, 'Now the show's over,' and turn his back and walk off. I told him to look at my right hand and asked him if my blood was still dripping from it hot on to the floor? 'You were mad,' he mumbled, 'mad when you carried out the idea. I opened this door, entered this room and saw you stretched out on this settee, the veins of your hand slashed, your fingers trailing in a sea of blood. You were mad. I might have lost you.' I smiled sadly as I pulled the shirt up to my chest, my face breathing in the smell of it. I said that my part in the play required that I should take myself off at the end, and the form of absence possible for me, the form I could accept and bear, was a quick death rather than a slow, cruel crawling, like that of the turtle in the film *Mondo Cane* that lost its way in the sands, held in the sun's disc, as it searched for the river-bank. He repeated sadly that he didn't know I was serious about him. I asked him sarcastically whether he was waiting for me to kill myself in order to be sure that I was telling the truth. I told him that I had lost myself in my love for him; oblivious to all else, I slipped unseen, like a gust of wind, through people's fingers, scorching their faces as I passed through the street. All I was conscious of was the weight of bodies, the height of buildings and of his hands. I asked him to draw closer and give me his hand which I craved to hold. He remained standing far off, inflexible, and at once accused me that after all that misery and triumph I was refusing to become pregnant from him, had re-

fused again and again and again, and that from my refusal
he understood I no longer loved him.

What? I cried out that he could never accuse me of that.
Only yesterday I was stretched out beside him and he gave
himself up to deep sleep while I was open-eyed, rubbing my
cheeks against his chin, kissing his chest, snuggling up under
his arm, searching in vain for sleep. I told him frankly that I
was upset by the speed with which he got to sleep, and by my
being left alone and awake at his side. He hastened to deny
this, saying that he had never been aware of my having remained sleepless. He believed that I dozed off the moment he
did. I revealed maliciously that it wasn't the first time he had
left me alone. I then related in full yesterday's incident, telling of how he had been asleep breathing quietly, with me
stretched close up against him smoking a cigarette, when suddenly in the emptiness of the room through the smoke, I had
seen a foot fleeing from under the sheets. I moved my own
but it didn't move and a coldness ran through the whole of
my body. I moved it but it didn't move. It occurred to me to
shout. I moved it but it didn't move. I hurriedly hid my face
in his hair. I was afraid. He moved and the foot moved. I
cried silently. I had imagined, had felt, had been unable to
tell the difference between his foot and mine. In a faint voice
he said: 'In this age people don't die of love'. Quickly seizing
the opportunity I said that in this age people didn't beget
children. In olden times they knew where the child would be
born, who it would be likely to resemble, whether it would be
male or female; they would knit it woollen vests and socks,
would embroider the hems, pockets and collars of its dresses
with coloured birds and flowers. They would amass presents
of gold crucifixes for it and medallions with 'Allah bless him'
on them, opened palms studded with blue stones, and pen-
dants with its name engraved on them. They would reserve a
midwife for it, would fix the day of the delivery, and the
child would launch out from the darkness and be flung into
the light at the precise time estimated. They would register a
piece of land in the child's name, would rent it a house,
choose companions for it, decide which school it would be
sent to, the profession it would study for, the person it could
love and to whom it could bind its destiny. That was a long,
long time ago, in the time of your father and my father. He
asked, 'Do you believe that twenty years ago was such an age
away? What has changed since? What has changed? Can't

you and can't I provide everything that is required for a child?' To soften the blow I explained that before I married I was like a child that lies down on its back in front of the window, gazes up at the stars and stretches out its tiny arm in a desire to pluck them. I used to amuse myself with this dream, with this impossibility, would cling to it and wish it would happen. He asked me: 'Then you were deceiving me?'

Discovering he had changed the conversation into an attack on me so as to win the battle, I quickly told him that only the woman who is unfulfilled with her man eagerly demands a child so that she can withdraw, enjoy being with her child and so be freed. He quickly interrupted me: 'And were you unsatisfied?' I answered him that we had been afraid, had not travelled to the last sweet unexplored regions of experience; we had trembled in terror, had continually bumped against the faces of others and listened to their voices. For his sake, for my own, I had defied death in order to live. He was wrong, wrong, to doubt my being madly in love with him.

'I'm at a loss. I don't understand you', he muttered. I attacked him by saying that was just it, that he also wouldn't understand me if I told him I didn't dare become pregnant, that I would not perpetrate such a mistake.

'Mistake?' he shrieked. 'Mistake?' I clung closer to his shirt, deriving strength from it, and slowly, in a low voice, I told him how scared I was about the fate of any child we might cast into this world. How could I imagine a child of mine, a being nourished on my blood, embraced within my entrails, sharing my breathing, the pulsations of my heart and my daily food, a being to whom I give my features and the earth, how can I bear the thought that in the future he will leave me and go off in a rocket to settle on the moon? And who knows whether or not he'll be happy there. I imagine my child with white ribbons, his fresh face flushed; I imagine him strapped to a chair inside a glass ball fixed to the top of a long shaft of khaki-coloured metal ending in folds resembling the skirt of my Charleston dress. He presses the button, a cloud of dust rises up and an arrow hurls itself into space. No, I can't face it. I can't face it.

He was silent a long, long time while the light of dawn crept in by his face to the corners of the room, his face absent-minded and searching in the sky for an arrow and a child's face. The vein between his eyebrows was knotted; perplexity and strain showed in his mouth. I, too, remained silent and closed my eyes.

When he was near me, standing like a massive tower at a rocket-firing station, my heart throbbed and I muttered to him that I adored his naked body. When he puts on his clothes, especially when he ties his tie, I feel he's some stranger come to pay a visit to the head of the house. He opened his arms and leaned over me. I rushed into his embrace, mumbling crazily: 'I love you, I love you, I love you, I love you, I love you.' He whispered into my hair: 'You're my pearl.' Then he spread the palm of his hand over my lips, drawing me to him with the other hand, and ordered: 'Let us take off, you and I, for the moon.'

(TRANSLATED BY DENYS JOHNSON-DAVIES)

The Girl and the Hashish-Smoker

by ALBERT COSSERY

Faiza was completely carried away by the sudden tumult of her senses in delirium. She felt herself growing, multiplying to infinity. It seemed to her that her life was increasing while that of the man rolled in boundless absence. It was like a city stretching, stirring idly within her; an oriental city with its palaces and its lights.

Her passion moulded itself to the rhythm of a barbaric music. Like the jerking haunches of a frenzied dancer, pleasure seized her in a succession of nervous bounds. The sound of castanets tightened in a deafening circle about her. She heard the shrieking of a crowd of gesticulating women, as in those feasts when the demon is exorcised. All this went on in an extreme and painful point of her being. Her tension was against a wall. The man's virility penetrated her like a blade. His impetuosity was like that of a river. What river?

The enormous Nile with its treacherous currents flowed in her. She saw herself welcomed to the bosom of its immensity. And the holy flood fertilized the land of her joy. Her joy swelled, rose as a wave rises. She was confounded with joy, became joy itself.

They moved, both drawn into the unreflecting cadence of lust. Like the *sakieh,* the waterwheel, turning with its many scoops, they too turned about the center of their desires.

Faiza was shaken with a madness which did nothing but grow. The exorcism seemed to her to reach a unique violence. It was in her that the demon was panting, ready to succumb and about to cry alone. She was stupid and really thought herself the prey of a maleficent spirit. This was also the opinion of all her relatives and above all of her father, Abou Affan Effendi, the customs official. And the girl believed that the demon was this flame in the depths of her body, which consumed her night and day, and which she came to appease, every time, in the fierce clasp of this strange, sleeping man.

Mahmoud retreated slowly to free himself. The embrace broken, he fell into his accustomed lethargy. His emptied flesh was silent. There was nothing more in him than sleep and a queer stupefaction. Never had he felt himself so tired as after this struggle. He still kept his feeling of remorse at having disturbed his dream for these fatiguing attitudes. His whole body was, so to speak, in rebellion against them. He was hot. And this girl at his side who prevented him from sleeping. There she was now, sighing. Ah, how useless it all seemed to him!

'Sons of whores, sons of whores,' he murmured in the void.

But feeble as was his voice, the girl heard the insult. She had always heard him murmuring it, as in a dream. It was the favourite refrain which he brought back from his frequent absences. She believed that he left each time for a journey in hell.

'What sons of whores? Who are you insulting like that all the time?'

He threw an oblique glance at her, dull, almost dead, and seemed to be thinking. The girl's question had disturbed the plenitude of his stupor. He was not fond of questions, not even the simple words which ask for a reply.

'How do I know?' he said, and his far-off voice seemed to

come out of a deep pit. 'Creatures, people, animals, who knows? They're sons of whores, I tell you.'

'But where are they? Tell me that,' asked the girl again, troubled.

She was pale, upset to hear him talk so vaguely. She never succeeded in getting anything out of him. His conversation was formless and unsewn like the rags of a beggar. She could never reach the point of fitting them together.

'Well, answer me. You're asleep already,' she said, stretching out a fearful hand towards his inert body.

Yes, he was already asleep. And she knew that he could no longer keep awake, now. So she left him in peace and remained pensive for a moment. Strange, she felt no fear at being alone like this with this man, in this queerly horrible room on the roof. She thought neither of the present moment nor of the place she was in. She was thinking of all the time she had spent in his bed, sweating with heat and quivering. The afternoon had been endless; endless too the evening meal with the united family. She had escaped as soon as her parents were asleep, had tottered for an eternity up the gloomy staircase to reach this roof-top. And he, at first, had not wanted to wake up. She had to light the candle herself. Then on the fibre mattress, stinking and repugnant, she had let herself slip in beside him. Submissively she had waited for him to take her; for him to really want to deliver her. To seduce him from his lassitude she had ventured on caresses unknown to her before that day, caresses drawn from the depths of her carnal consciousness, under the inspiration of some maleficence.

Faiza thought she was dreaming. Everything about her seemed to encourage it. For if she was not dreaming, how could she be there without fear? One is only so far outside time in dreams. She was not able to fix reality except in the narrow frame in which she had developed up to now. But outside this family circle, everything was dreams. And this is precisely what attracted her, what gave her the courage to do all these impossible things.

And this stifling heat, was that a dream, too? No, she could no longer believe that. Despite herself, her obtuse spirit refused to cling any longer to the unreal. She thought of waking Mahmoud.

Shaken, the man allowed his voice to be heard again, languid, far away as if it had traversed whole worlds.

'Sons of whores, sons of whores!'

'Again? So you haven't finished blaspheming yet. Come, wake up, by the prophet! Why do you sleep all the time? I'm afraid of staying all alone.'

'All these sons of whores,' announced Mahmoud slowly, and he passed a hand over his face. 'No, they're gone . . . I was just dreaming that I was being chased by a pack of dogs. There were white ones and black ones and others with red hair. It was those that frightened me most . . . I was dodging through the lanes and losing myself in deadends, but they were always behind me with their long, long teeth. Perhaps they were wolves; I don't know. Listen, girl; off you go.'

He was in a hurry to see her go so as to take up again without a witness his dizzy race through sleep. This girl who offered herself to him had no interest for him at all. What did interest him was the little ball of hashish that one chews deliciously to draw out all the juice or that one disperses in the intoxicating smoke of a *goza*.[1] Through having taken her once when he was under the influence of the divine drug, he had never succeeded in getting rid of her. And if she would only keep quiet. But no, she had frightened and ridiculous manners which irritated him. He had wanted to teach her to sleep, to respect slumber, that brother to death which he himself loved so, but alas! she understoood nothing of it. She was obstinate, like all girls of her sort.

Poor Mahmoud had been five days without the least bit of hashish. It was a performance without parallel, which had been taken for the beginning of repentance but was in fact due to nothing more than a lack of that extraordinary metal called silver.

He could not understand the importance one gave to this cursed metal, nor why it existed. This morning, even, he had vainly explained to Maitre Darwiche, the proprietor of a joint in Abdine, the inhumanity of demanding money from people who could not get any and the almost terrible necessity there was that he, Mahmoud, should not be without the fatal drug. But the son of a whore did not want to listen. He just shook his head and caressed a little boy seated beside him. All narrow-minded people who prevented him from living the only real enchantment he had found in this world of miseries. There were thousands perhaps like that, who got in his way,

---

[1] A pipe made out of the wood of the pecan tree.—Ed.

obstructed his path, without leaving him in peace for an instant. When he walked in the street he looked at nobody, so much did he hate all of them. All these busy people around him were carrying out a pointless labour which he felt weighing on his own shoulders, crushing down on him.

'Why do you stay like that, looking at nothing?' said the girl who did not yet feel the need for going. 'Black and white dogs, and others which are red: what does all that mean? I will ask Om Hanafy, she interprets dreams very well. But do you dream all the time? Really, are you a man or a demon? By the prophet how do you live?'

Mahmoud did not wish to reply, but the last question stirred him imperceptibly. How did he live? A truly extravagant question. He realised that it ought to receive an answer, but he could not give it all the same. No, he didn't know how he lived. And it was very well thus. He was very happy not to know.

'How do I live? And what does that matter to you? Yes, I dream all the time. Your Om Hanafy is a whore. She knows nothing at all. All women know nothing at all. It's not only in my dreams that there are dogs; the dogs are always behind me; I can't go out of this room without their spying me and rushing at my heels; they take a thousand forms and change into vehicles of all kinds. One day I shall die, run over. They will bury me in a native oven . . .'

To be buried in a native oven was not one of those hashish jokes which were common with him. No, he knew it; and his mouth smiled in the drab and somnolent landscape of his face. The fact is that he used frequently, under the influence of hashish, to dream that he was in a great native oven. Its walls were crusted with soot and its ceiling was lost in a cloudy sky. On the floor twenty-piastre pieces glittered pleasantly, quite new; he was reluctant to pick them up. In a corner from which ascended white clouds of vapour, a little girl of four mimicked the *danse du ventre,* with the obscene gestures of an old stage crock. In another corner were dwarf palmtrees from which, instead of dates, hung all kinds of precious jewels. Mahmoud found himself squatting beside an apple-seller who kept on repeating incessantly: 'I sell young girls' breasts!' From his place he saw the master-baker putting the great loaves of maize in rows, after having taken them out of the oven. And then happened the loveliest and most astounding thing of all. These great loaves that the master-baker had just arranged took on the appearance of living flesh, swelled and swelled until they were moving like the fat and polished buttocks of women. Mahmoud was amazed at this lascivious blossoming. Then all of a sudden, without knowing how, he found himself in a great deserted field where hashish grew in profusion.

'A native oven? Why do they bury in a native oven? It's not true, they don't bury anyone there. Why do you always tell such stories? By the prophet, you are ill. Someone was saying the other day that you smoked a dirty drug that will make you mad. No, I don't remember who it was now. But they say all sorts of things against you in the quarter. And I shiver when I hear them. I would really like to die.'

'Shut up, you idiot,' said Mahmoud impatiently. 'Have you finished dinning my ears with your blasted gossip? What does it matter to me what they say about me? Am I a virgin that has to get married? All the people who live in this quarter are imbeciles. As for the women, they are all whores. The only thing they can do is gossip, when there's no man about to sleep with. How I should like to piss on all their heads! As for the drug that's going to make me mad, it's five days since I've had a smell of it. The world will soon come to an end. If this keeps on a few more days, there won't be any more world.'

'Why won't there be any more world?' asked the girl. She was naively intrigued.

'Yes, girl, I tell you there won't be any more world. How do you want there to be a world without hashish? And hashish is going to disappear from the earth. God doesn't want to allow hashish any more. It's Kaabour who told me. Don't you know Kaabour? He's an amazing fellow. Do you know what he's begun doing since he learnt this news? He's collecting all the hashish he can lay hands on and hiding it carefully in the shop of his uncle the shoemaker. But he's the son of a whore. How can he hide it? Does one hide hashish?'

Mahmoud had never believed the strange news reported by Kaabour. The idea of the total disappearance of hashish had exercised him for several nights without his being able to find in it the least trace of reality. But now that he had not succeeded in procuring the drug he desired so much, he imagined that the fatal decree had come into force, and took pleasure in believing himself one victim among thousands of others. In this way the catastrophe seemed more supportable to him, granted its universal character.

'Does one hide hashish?' he repeated. 'Cursed be his father! It must be mud that he's hiding, otherwise he'd have smoked it. One cannot have hashish without smoking it. Allah change them into pigs, all these sons of whores! I want to smoke, girl; I must smoke.'

'Is it true that you must smoke?' said the girl slowly. And she began to weary of all these mysteries. 'Why smoke?'

'Why smoke? So as to forget, girl.'

'Forget what?'

'You don't understand? To forget all these sons of whores. All these dogs who never stop chasing me with their long, long teeth. To forget, to get away from cars, from trams, from carriages and all the sellers who are always asking for money. Ah, to escape into the native oven! Then into the enormous meadow where hashish grows freely . . . like clover.'

He stopped, surprised at having talked so much. As after a hashish debauch, he had a sudden hunger for fruit and tidbits. The air in the room was heavy, on account of the closed door. In its bottle-neck the bit of candle was coming slowly to an end. Mahmoud had the girl's limbs pressed against him and in this contact he felt his desire revive. As if under the laws of a fatality, he caressed her abundant hips down to her thighs.

Faiza no longer felt pleasure in the man's caress. Nothing troubled her flesh, satisfied at last. The demon was dead this time, really dead. And, feeling this, she was stupefied by it. Repose entered into her from all sides like a fresh breeze, fanned her, rocked her, lulled her to sleep. Everything around her took on a distant, incomprehensible air. She half rose, searched on the mattress for her dress, all crumpled now, and put it on without haste. Definitely, she wanted to go.

'Come along, go down now and leave me in peace,' again came the bizarre voice of the man. 'Because of you I shan't be able to sleep any more. By Allah, I don't know who flung me on this roof-top. Cursed be the day I came to live here . . . But it's just my luck, which is sheer disgust. Before, I used to live in the basement of a house belonging to the *Wakfs;* nobody came to ask me for the rent. Next door lived a newly married lamplighter. But that son of a dog, when the desire came over him, used to go off and use his wife leaving the streets of the government abandoned to obscurity. He was dismissed after a few weeks. Then his wife began to cry night and day, and prevented me from sleeping. That's why I left. They never leave me in peace anywhere. Ah, if only I had some hashish! But no, there is no more hashish, and the world is coming to an end . . .'

For the first time she had been here, Faiza was really frightened. She wanted to go away but she couldn't. A superb stupor held her motionless, her gaze lost on everything and on nothing. The flame of the candle, nearly out, produced a black smoke which rose to the ceiling like a fine tress. Near a pile of rubbish a water-cooler stood upright, tragic with filth and like a growing menace. Faiza remembered the kitchen tap which was worn out and the sink which must now be overflowing on to the tiles.

She tried to get up to go and stop this water, which was in danger of flooding the whole house. But how could she tear herself away from this sleeping man? How leave him there, all alone in the dangerous presence of things? As long as he was asleep she could not abandon him to his fate. She felt herself bound to him even in his sleep.

The man's naked body rippled under the flickering brightness of the candle. The girl looked at this meagre, wiry body dancing with violet reflections, and the sight brought her an unheard of, complete satisfaction. She stretched out a hand to touch him; she found him hot as a city in high summer. He carried in him the heat of all hot days. It was burning sand. She was leaning over him as if over a desert.

She stayed, attached to this body whence escaped the whiff of an animal and primitive tenderness. She felt his presence in every corner of her flesh. It was stronger than everything. It was stronger than the house with its foundations buried solidly in the ground. It was stronger than the wind sweeping through the doors. It was stronger than the mad current of the river at the season of flood.

She was thirsty. She didn't know what kind of thirst it was. She leaned over the naked body of the man and kissed him. Now she understood what this man represented for her. No, it was not he, the demon. The demon was all that separated her from him. The demon was the hours passed away from him; it was the sad room she lived in; it was her parents with their idiotic superstitions and their ignoble prejudices, who kept her prisoner. No, this man was certainly not the demon.

On the contrary, he was the death of the demon. He was joy, the supreme joy of the free and living flesh.

She became comprehensive and real. Thus she discovered the powerful truth of the flesh. At present the man seemed to her a little child, ill, that she wished to caress and handle like a mother. Ah, to be able to give him everything, to make him happy.

'The world will never come to an end,' she said. 'Don't be afraid. Only keep me near you. And since you cannot live without hashish, I will bring you some. Allah pardon you!'

He did not hear her. He was far away.

He was in the enormous meadow where hashish grows freely like clover.

(TRANSLATED BY HAROLD EDWARDS)

A House of Flesh

by YUSSEF IDRISS

The ring beside the lamp . . . silence hangs heavy, ears grow blind. Fingers move stealthily, in silence grasp the ring and put out the light. Darkness reigns and in darkness eyes grow blind. The woman, her three daughters, and their house, a mere room.

The beginning is silence. The widow is tall, fair-skinned, willowy, about thirty-five. Her daughters are also tall and full-bodied. They continue to wear their long black mourning dresses. The youngest is sixteen, the eldest in her twenties, all three unattractive, having inherited the father's dark, badly proportioned body, corpulent and flabby; retaining their mother's build. The room, in spite of its size, holds them during the daytime. Despite its extreme poverty, the room is neatly arranged in an intimate, cozy atmosphere which reflects a feminine touch. When night falls, their bodies are scattered all over the room. Huge piles of warm throbbing flesh, sprawled on the single bed or on the couch: breathing, heaving, deeply insomniac.

Silence has hovered over the home since the man's death two years ago after a long illness. The mourning period was over, but the habits of those in mourning remained, most predominantly the habit of silence. It was in fact a silence of waiting, for the girls were growing older and the period of waiting was weighing upon them. No suitors were knocking on their doors. What man would dare to knock on the door of poor unattractive girls, particularly if they happened to be fatherless? But hope still lived of course (wine can remain in the barrels until the right buyer comes along), and each girl believed her luck would change. (No matter how poor one may be, there will always be someone else yet poorer, and if ugliness prevails there will always be someone even uglier . . . and dreams are fulfilled if one has enough patience. . . .)

That silence was occasionally interrupted by the sound of a voice reciting the Koran, a voice rising monotonously, emotionless. A recitation by a *muqri*.[1] The *muqri* is blind, but the prayers are for the soul of the deceased, always delivered at the same time. Every Friday afternoon, he comes poking his stick at their door. He abandons himself to the extended hand that leads him inside. There he sits cross-legged on the mat and recites. When it is over, he gropes for his sandals and pronounces a greeting that no one bothers to reciprocate, and then leaves. Out of habit he comes, out of habit he recites, and out of habit he leaves. No one notices him any more.

Forever this silence . . . even when the Friday afternoon recitation disturbs it. It is as if silence is broken only with silence. Waiting is forever, like hope, little hope but constant hope, for there is hope for every insignificant being, there is somewhere one who is even more insignificant. And they do not aspire to much, no, they do not aspire.

Silence persisted until something happened, until one Friday when the *muqri* did not show up. Every agreement comes to an end, no matter how long it has lasted, and it seemed this agreement had come to its end. Only then did the

---

[1] *muqri*: reader of Koranic verses.

widow and her daughters realize that not only was he the sole male voice that broke their silence once a week, but also that he was the only man who ever knocked at their door. Other things began to dawn upon them. True, he was as poor as they were, but his outfits were always clean, his sandals always shone, his headdress was wrapped meticulously (putting to shame any man with eyes), and above all, his voice was strong, deep and melodious. The proposition hovered in the air: why not renew the agreement, and why not summon him immediately? Could he be busy elsewhere? They could wait, for waiting was an old game they were very good at.

Evening was drawing to its end, and he recited as if for the first time. Then the proposition came up: why shouldn't one of them marry a man whose voice would fill the house?

He was a bachelor with a sprouting moustache, a young man. Words generate words, and he too was looking for the right woman. The girls confer about the matter and the mother scans their faces trying to figure who the lucky one would be. But their faces evade her searching looks and seem to say: Is this how we are to be rewarded for our long wait? Shall we break our fast with a blind man? For they still dreamt of suitors, and suitors are usually young men with eyes. Poor things, they have yet to know the world of men. Impossible for them to perceive at this stage in their lives that a man is not to be judged by sight alone.

"Mother, you marry him . . . marry him."

"Me? What shame, what will people say!"

"Let them say what they will, no matter what. It will be better than living in a house without a man, the resounding voice of a man."

"Do you want me to marry before you? Never . . ."

"Wouldn't it be better if you marry before us, so that our house becomes a treading ground for men? Then we can marry after you."

"Marry him, mother. O marry him . . ."

And she married him . . . and one more breath was added to the air and their income grew just a little bit more, and a much greater problem arose. True, they survived their first night, but they didn't dare come close to each other, even inadvertently. The girls were sleeping, or pretending to do so, but the mother could feel pairs of searching beams inspecting the space that lay between them, searching lights of human eyes, prospecting antennas. The girls are old enough to understand, and the room is suddenly transformed into sentient throbbing presences, vibrating in the light of day.

One by one, each left the house when morning set in, only to return by sunset, hesitant, embarrassed. Dragging their feet, they came back to a house filled with laughter, occasionally interrupted by faint noises of a woman. It must be the mother laughing, and the dignified *muqri* they had known was now laughing too. Their mother greeted them, bareheaded, hair wet and with a comb in hand, still laughing. They looked at her face and realized that it had been for all those years like an unlit lamp in whose corners spiders and cobwebs had taken refuge. Now suddenly that face had burst into light, electrified, glistening tearful eyes, with laughter lodged there instead. The silence dissipated completely. Suppertime bustled with loud voices, jokes, highlighted by the *muqri's* imitation of Umm Kulthum and Abd al-Wahab in his gushing, whining, beautiful voice.

Well done, mother. Soon this gaiety and laughter will draw more men to the house, for the presence of men attracts other men.

Be confident, girls. Soon men will be coming and suitors will make their calls. But in fact what was preoccupying her was that young man, not the suitors. True, he was blind, but how often are we blinded ourselves from seeing others, just because they happen to be blind? Yes, she was seeing this healthy young man. His overflowing vitality had made up for those years of sickness, impotence, and early old age.

The silence was gone, never to return, and the beat of life was there to stay. The man is her legal husband; she married him according to the law of God and his Prophet, and according to his Sunna.[2] No, nothing will make her feel ashamed, for all that she does is legitimate, even when she makes no effort to hide or keep the secret, or when night creeps up and they are all huddled together, and the power of the body and soul takes over, even with the girls there aware and awake in their observation posts, fighting to control sighs and groans.

Her mornings were spent washing clothes in rich people's homes, and his days were whiled away by reciting the Quran in homes of the poor.

At the beginning, he didn't return home for a break during

---

[2] Sunna: traditional teachings of Islam, according to the Prophet.

the day, but as his nights grew longer, he started coming home to rest his exhausted body, to regain strength for the night to come.

And once, after they had had their fill of the night, and the night had had its fill of them, he suddenly asked her what had been the matter with her during the lunch hour. Why was it that she was now so voluble and eager to talk, but then had adopted total silence? Why was she now wearing his cherished ring, the ring that was all he had given her in form of dowry, gift, wedding band? Why hadn't she been wearing it during the lunch hour?

She could have torn herself away distraught, screaming. She could have lost her senses. He could have gotten himself killed. For there could be but one meaning to what he was saying, a horrible, atrocious meaning. A choking sob kept everything back. She held her breath and kept her peace. With her ears, which she transformed into noses, eyes, and other organs of sense, she strained her every fibre to find out who the culprit was. For some reason she was positive it was the middle one, because in her eyes had grown a certain daring look that only a bullet could check. But she listened. The breathing of the three grew louder, deeper and feverish, flaming hot, hesitant and intermittent, growling in youthful dreams which would be sinful to interrupt!

Heavings turn into burning flames, into lava vomited by thirsty lands. The knots in her throat deepen and choke her. There are hungry breaths. With all her straining she cannot differentiate between one vibrant, hot pile of flesh and another. All are hungry. All groan and scream. And the groans are not just groans. They are pleas, supplications perhaps, perhaps something more.

She has totally immersed herself in her second legitimate right, and forgotten all about her first legitimate duty, her girls. Patience has become myrrh. Even the mirage of suitors is no more. Suddenly, as if bitten, as though awakened to a secret call, the girls are hungry. The food is forbidden, but hunger is yet more sinful. There exists nothing more sinful than this hunger. How well she has known it. And how well it has known her, freed her spirit, searched her bones. She has known it. Now that she has had her fill, it is impossible for her to forget.

Hungry ones! She who took the bread from her own mouth to feed them, she whose only preoccupation was to feed them even if she were to go hungry, she the mother—has she forgotten?

And no matter how insistent his demands, her pain was changed into silence. The mother became silent, and from that moment onwards, silence never left her. At breakfast, just as she had thought, the middle girl was silent and was to remain silent from then onwards. At suppertime, the young man was gay and jovial, blind and happy, singing and laughing, with only the youngest and eldest tuning in.

Patience is tried and its bitterness becomes a sickness and no one comes knocking on their door. One day the eldest looks at the mother's ring and expresses her admiration, and the mother's heart sinks; and its beating grows louder when the daughter begs to wear the ring just for the day. In silence the mother takes it off her finger, and in silence the girl slips it onto her own.

And that evening the eldest girl keeps silent, refusing to utter a word.

And the blind man is singing and laughing boisterously with only the youngest tuning in.

With unrewarded patience, and luck that has never turned with her worrying, the youngest grows older, and asks for her turn in the ring game, and in silence her turn comes.

The ring lies beside the lamp and silence sets in and ears become blind, and in silence the finger whose turn comes gropes stealthily for the ring and turns off the light.

Darkness prevails, and in darkness eyes grow blind. Only the blind young man remains happy. Yet behind his loudness and happiness he is tormented by this silence, he is tortured by uncertainty. At the beginning he would say to himself, it must be a woman's nature to be ever-changing. One time she is fresh as the morning dew, at another time she is worn out, exhausted like swampy waters. At times satiny like rose leaves, at others prickly like cacti. True, the ring is always there, but each time the finger it encircles seems to be different. He was almost positive that they knew for sure. So why doesn't silence speak, why doesn't it speak? The mere thought made him choke on his bread. And from that moment on, he never uttered a word. He lived in fear of the violation of that collapse. This time the silence was different, respected by all.

A conscious silence, not caused by poverty, nor patience, nor despair, but the most profound kind of silence, the most binding of all, a silence implemented without formal agreement. The widow and her three daughters, and the house which was a room. This was a new kind of silence. The blind reciter brought along this silence, with silence convincing himself that his companion in bed was always his legitimate wife, bearer of his ring, ever changing, unpredictable. Young and old, silken soft or callous and scaly, sometimes fat, at other times thin, whatever, this really was her business. Actually, all this was the business of those with sight and their sole responsibility.

For *they* alone possess the grace of certainty; *they* are capable of discernment; but the most *he* can know is doubt, doubt that can be removed only through the blessing of sight. So long as he is deprived of it, he will be denied certainty, for he is the one who is blind and there is no shame for the blind.

Or is there shame for the blind?

(TRANSLATED BY MONA MIKHAIL)

The Dead Afternoon

by WALID IKHLASSI

The wall-clock struck five, filling the house with its ringing.

I was watching the swallows from my window as they crossed the city sky; thousands of swallows, black moving specks.

The evening, meanwhile, prepared to occupy its place in a new day.

'May they find favour with God,' I said to my grandmother, who had finished her prayers.

'I was late performing the afternoon prayer,' she answered sadly.

'Never mind, there will be other afternoons.'

My grandmother did not hear me.

I looked at an enormous fly squatting on the outside of the window-pane: it seemed to be defying me, sitting there so close to my nose.

'This fly has annoyed me all day,' I said, 'and I haven't been able to kill it.'

My grandmother did not reply: she had started on a new prayer.

I was not conscious of the passage of time: the fly had taken up so much of it. I had threatened it by tapping on the glass, but it had not stirred. Looking at my finger-nails and seeing that they were long, I produced a pair of scissors and began to pare them.

The sky was being engulfed in soft darkness, and the only sound to cut across my grandmother's voice as she recited her prayers, seated in her gazelle-skin chair, was the clock striking six.

My young sister came in from the other room.

'Today we'll be eating *kunafa*[1] with walnuts,' she announced.

'I don't like it.'

My sister laughed. 'This morning you said you wanted *kunafa*.'

'I just don't like it.'

Turning again to the window, I was surprised to find that the fly was still asleep.

My grandmother, caressing my young sister, said to her:

'Turn on the radio so we can listen to Feiruz.'

'We listened to her at midday,' I said firmly. The darkness outside prevented me from seeing the swallows. Even so, though, I liked Feiruz's voice.

'We'll listen to her again,' said my grandmother.

I did not reply: I was contemplating the sleeping fly.

A frightening thought occurred to me: what if one of them should watch me as I lay sound asleep?

I heard my sister asking my grandmother to tell us the story of *The Singing Nightingale* this evening and my grandmother saying, 'Didn't we finish it yesterday?'

The little girl cried out petulantly:

[1] A jellied sweet, rolled flat, made from the juice of grapes.—Ed.

'Yesterday! Yesterday's over.'

'You won't hear the story of the singing nightingale any more,' I whispered to myself and I was filled with sadness.

'I'll tell you a new one today,' said my grandmother.

'We don't want a new story,' exclaimed my sister.

'But the old one's finished.'

'It's *not* finished,' shouted my sister.

I tried to excuse my sister, as she jumped off my grandmother's lap and hurried out of the room, but I too felt annoyed; I too wanted the old story.

After a while I complied with my grandmother's request to switch on the radio, and searched round for a station. I found one as the clock struck seven.

'This is Aleppo.'

I drew a veil of silence over the voice.

'Let's hear the news,' protested my grandmother.

Flicking through the pages of the morning paper, I said:

'It's stale news.'

'New things may happen, my son,' exclaimed the old lady, suddenly conscious of her age.

I began reading the headlines: having already done so at midday, they did not affect me.

All at once I wanted to get out of that room, but I had nowhere particular to go, so I changed my mind and stayed where I was.

The little girl returned with her large doll.

'Will you tell Suzanne a story?' she asked, looking at her grandmother with a challenge in her eyes.

The old lady laughed.

I went back to the window: the darkness had settled down completely in the vastness of the sky.

I felt a great desire to tease the sleeping fly coming over me. I no longer felt any resentment against it and had forgotten its impudence.

'Won't you tell Suzanne a new story?' asked my sister.

The fact was that I did not know any story. Then I remembered one I had heard on the radio at noon.

'I'll tell you the story of *The Bear and the Honey*,' I replied.

'But it's an old one,' cried my sister.

Confused, I returned to observing the fly.

'What is it?' asked the little girl, coming towards me as I sat by the window.

'A sleeping fly.'

'A sleeping fly?' my sister asked, knitting her brows. 'Is that a new story?'

'It's asleep, it's tired.'

'Will you tell it to Suzanne?' she said.

'All right, I'll tell it.'

My sister drew close to me.

'What are you looking at?' she demanded.

'I'm looking at the fly.'

She climbed on to a chair and stared at it. Then she proclaimed triumphantly in her shrill voice:

'But it's dead!'

I felt uneasy as I looked at the girl who was suddenly as tall as I was.

'It's asleep.'

'It's dead!' said my sister, amazed at my ignorance.

I opened the window cautiously and blew softly on the fly: it fell off like a wisp of paper.

I remembered it flying around me, remembered that I had hated it and then loved it.

'Won't you tell Suzanne the story of *The Sleeping Fly?*'

I didn't answer her: I was listening to the striking of the clock which reverberated through the house.

(TRANSLATED BY DENYS JOHNSON-DAVIES)

The Death of Bed Number 12

by GHASSAN KANAFANI

Dear Ahmed,

I have chosen you in particular to be the recipient of this letter for a reason which may appear to you commonplace, yet since yesterday my every thought has been centred on it. I chose you in particular because when I saw him yesterday dying on the high white bed I remembered how you used to use the word 'die' to express anything extreme. Many is the time I've heard you use such expressions as 'I almost died laughing', 'I was dead tired', 'Death itself couldn't quench my love', and so on. While it is true that we all use such words, you use them more than anybody. Thus it was that I remembered you as I saw him sinking down in the bed and clutching at the coverlet with his long, emaciated fingers, giving a convulsive shiver and then staring out at me with dead eyes.

But why have I not begun at the beginning? You know, no doubt, that I am now in my second month at the hospital. I have been suffering from a stomach ulcer, but no sooner had the surgeon plugged up the hole in my stomach than a new one appeared in my head, about which the surgeon could do nothing. Believe me, Ahmed, that an 'ulcer' on the brain is a lot more stubborn than one in the stomach. My room leads on to the main corridor of the Internal Diseases Wing, while the window overlooks the small hospital garden. Thus, propped up by a pillow, I can observe both the continuous flow of patients passing the door as well as the birds which fly past the window incessantly. Amidst this hubbub of people who come here to die in the serene shadow of the scalpel and whom I see, having arrived on their own two feet, leaving after days or hours on the death trolley, wrapped round in a covering of white; in this hubbub I find myself quite unable to make good those holes that have begun to open up in my head, quite incapable of stopping the flow of questions that mercilessly demand an answer of me.

I shall be leaving the hospital in a few days, for they have patched up my insides as best they can. I am now able to walk leaning on the arm of an old and ugly nurse and on my own powers of resistance. The hospital, however, has done little more than transfer the ulcer from my stomach to my head, for in this place, as the ugly old woman remarked, medicine may be able to plug up a hole in the stomach but it can never find the answers required to plug up holes in one's thinking. The day she said this the old woman gave a toothless laugh as she quietly led me off to the scales.

What, though, is such talk to do with us? What I want to talk to you about is death. Death that takes place in front of you, not about that death of which one merely hears. The difference between the two types of death is immeasurable and cannot be appreciated by someone who has not been a witness to a human being clutching at the coverlet of his bed with all the strength of his trembling fingers in order to resist that terrible slipping into extinction, as though the coverlet can pull him back from that colossus who, little by little, wrests from his eyes this life about which we know scarcely anything.

As the doctors waited around him, I examined the card that hung at the foot of his bed. I had slipped out of my room and was standing there, unseen by the doctors, who were engaged in a hopeless attempt to save the dying man. I read: 'Name: Mohamed Ali Akbar. Age: 25. Nationality: Omani.' I turned the card over and this time read: 'Leukaemia.' Again I stared into the thin brown face, the wide frightened eyes and the lips that trembled like a ripple of purple water. As his eyes turned and came to rest on my face it seemed that he was appealing to me for help. Why? Because I used to give to him a casual greeting every morning? Or was it that he saw in my face some understanding of the terror that he was undergoing? He went on staring at me and then—quite simply—he died.

It was only then that the doctor discovered me and dragged me off angrily to my room. But he would never be able to banish from my mind the scene that is ever-present there. As I got on to my bed I heard the voice of the male nurse in the corridor alongside my door saying in a matter-of-fact voice:

'Bed number 12 has died!'

I said to myself: 'Mohamed Ali Akbar has lost his name, he is Bed number 12.' What do I mean now when I talk of a human being whose name was Mohamed Ali Akbar? What does it matter to him whether he still retains his name or whether it has been replaced by a number? Then I remembered how he wouldn't allow anyone to omit any part of his name. Every morning the nurse would ask him, 'And how are you, Mohamed Ali?' and he would not reply, for he regarded his name as being Mohamed Ali Akbar—just like that, all in one—and that this Mohamed Ali to whom the nurse was speaking was some other person.

Though the nurses found a subject for mirth in this insistence on his whole name being used, Mohamed Ali Akbar continued to demand it; perhaps he regarded his right to possessing his name in full as being an insistence that he at least owned something, for he was poor, extremely poor, a great deal more so than you with your fertile imagination could conceive as you lounge around in the café; poverty was something engraved in his face, his forearms, his chest, the way he ate, into everything that surrounded him.

When I was able to walk for the first time after they had patched me up, I paid him a visit. The back of his bed was raised and he was sitting up, lost in thought. I sat on the side of the bed for a short while, and we exchanged a few brief, banal words. I noticed that alongside his pillow was an old wooden box with his name carved on it in semi-Persian style writing; it was securely tied with twine. Apart from this he owned nothing except his clothes, which were kept in the hospital cupboard. I remembered that on that day I had asked the nurse:

'What's in the old box?'

'No one knows,' she answered, laughing. 'He refuses to be parted from the box for a single instant.'

Then she bent over me and whispered:

'These people who look so poor are generally hiding some treasure or other—perhaps this is his!'

During my stay here no one visited him at the hospital. As he knew no one I used to send him some of the sweets with which my visitors inundated me. He accepted everything without enthusiasm. He was not good at expressing gratitude and his behaviour over this caused a certain fleeting resentment in me.

I did not concern myself with the mysterious box. Though Mohamed Ali Akbar's condition steadily worsened, his attitude towards the box did not change, which caused the nurse to remark to me that if there had been some treasure in it he would surely have given it away or willed it to someone, seeing that he was heading for death at such speed. Like some petty philosopher I had laughed that day saying to myself that the stupidity of this nurse scarcely knew any bounds, for how did she expect Mohamed Ali Akbar to persuade himself that he was inevitably dying, that there was not a hope of his pulling through? His insistence on keeping the box was tantamount to hanging on to his hope of pulling through and being reunited with his box.

When Mohamed Ali Akbar died I saw the box at his side, where it had always been, and it occurred to me that the box ought to be buried unopened with him. On going to my room that night I was quite unable to sleep. While Mohamed Ali Akbar had been deposited in the autopsy room, wrapped up in a white covering, he was, at the same time, sitting in my room and staring at me, passing through the hospital wards and searching about in his bed; I could almost hear the way he would gasp for breath before going to sleep. When day dawned across the trees of the hospital garden, I had created a complete story about him for myself.

Mohamed Ali Akbar was a poor man from the western quarter of the village of Abkha in Oman; a thin, dark-skinned young man, with aspirations burning in his eyes that could find no release. True he was poor, but what does poverty matter to a man if he has never known anything else? The whole of Abkha suffered from being poor, a poverty identical to Mohamed Ali Akbar's; it was, however, a contented poverty, a poverty that was deep-seated and devoid of anything that prompted one to feel that it was wrong and that there was something called 'riches'. And so it was that the two water-skins Mohamed Ali Akbar carried across his shoulders as he knocked on people's doors to sell them water, were the two scales which set the balance of his daily round. Mohamed Ali Akbar was aware of a certain dizziness when he laid down the water-skins, but when taking them up again the next morning he would feel that his existence was progressing tranquilly and that he had ensured for himself a balanced, undeviating journey through life.

Mohamed Ali Akbar's life could have continued in this quiet and ordered fashion, had fate emulated civilization—in not reaching faraway Oman. But fate was present even in far-off Oman and it was inevitable that Mohamed Ali Akbar should suffer a little from its capricious ways.

It happened on a scorchingly hot morning. Though the sun was not yet at the meridian, the surface of the road was hot and the desert blew gusts of dust-laden wind into his face. He knocked at a door which was answered by a young, brown-skinned girl with wide black eyes, and everything happened with the utmost speed. Like some clumsy oaf who has lost his way, he stood in front of the door, the water-skins swinging to and fro on his lean shoulders. Abstractedly he stared at her, hoping like someone overcome with a mild attack of sunstroke that his eyes would miraculously be capable of clasping her to him. She stared back at him in sheer astonishment, and, unable to utter a word, he turned his back on her and went off home with his water-skins.

Though Mohamed Ali Akbar was exceptionally shy even with his own family, he found himself forced to pour out his heart to his elder sister. As his mother had died of smallpox a long time ago and his father was helplessly bedridden, it was to his sister that he turned for help, for he had unswerving confidence that Sabika possessed the necessary intelligence and judgement for solving a problem of this sort. Seated before him on the rush mat, shrouded in her coarse black dress, she did not break her silence till Mohamed Ali Akbar had gasped out the last of his story.

'I shall seek her hand in marriage,' she then said. 'Isn't that what you want?'

'Yes, yes, is it possible?'

Removing a straw from the old rush mat, his sister replied:

'Why not? You are now a young man and we are all equal in Abkha.'

Mohamed Ali Akbar spent a most disturbed night. When morning came he found that his sister was even more eager than himself to set off on her mission. They agreed to meet up at noon when she would tell him of the results of her efforts, and from there they would both make the necessary arrangements for bringing the matter to completion.

Mohamed Ali Akbar did not know how to pass the time wandering through the lanes with the water-skins on his shoulders. He kept looking at his shadow and beseeching God to make it into a circle round his feet so that he might hurry back home. After what seemed an eternity, he made his way back and was met at the door by his sister.

'It seems that her mother is agreeable. But it must all be put to her father, who will give his answer in five days.'

Deep down within him Mohamed Ali Akbar felt that he was going to be successful in making the girl his wife. As far as he was able to imagine he began from henceforth to build up images of his future with this young and beautiful brown-skinned girl. His sister Sabika looked at the matter with a wise and experienced eye, but she too was sure they would be successful, for she was convinced that her brother's name was without blemish among the people of Abkha; she had, in addition, given a lot of attention to gaining the approval of the girl's mother, knowing as she did how a woman was able to put over an idea to her husband and make him believe that it was his own. Sabika, therefore, awaited the outcome of the matter with complete composure.

On the fifth day Sabika went to the girl's house in order to receive the answer. When she returned, however, her disconsolate face showed that she had failed. She stood in a corner of the room, unable to look Mohamed Ali Akbar in the eye, not knowing how to begin recounting what had happened.

'You must forget her, Mohamed Ali,' she said when she had managed to pluck up her courage.

Not knowing what to say, he waited for his sister to finish.

'Her father died two days ago,' continued Sabika, finding an opportunity in his silence to continue. 'His dying wish to his family was that they should not give her to you in marriage.'

Mohamed Ali Akbar heard these words as though they were addressed to someone else.

'But why, Sabika—why?' was all he could ask.

'He was told that you were a scoundrel, that you lived by stealing sheep on the mountain road, trading what you steal with the foreigners.'

'I?'

'They think you are Mohamed Ali,' said Sabika in a trembling voice she was unable to control. 'You know—the scoundrel Mohamed Ali? Her father thought that you were he . . .'

'But I am not Mohamed Ali,' he replied, palms outstretched like a child excusing himself for some misdeed he has not committed. 'I'm Mohamed Ali Akbar.'

'There's been a mistake—I told them at the beginning that your name was Mohamed Ali. I didn't say Mohamed Ali Akbar because I saw no necessity for doing so.'

Mohamed Ali Akbar felt his chest being crushed under the weight of the blow. However, he remained standing where he was, staring at his sister Sabika without fully seeing her. Blinded by anger, he let fly a final arrow:

'Did you tell her mother that I'm not Mohamed Ali but Mohamed Ali Akbar?'

'Yes, but the father's last wish was that they shouldn't marry her to you.'

'But I'm Mohamed Ali Akbar the water-seller, aren't I?'

What was the use, though, of being so stricken? Everything had, quite simply, come to an end, a single word had lodged itself in the gullet of his romance and it had died. Mohamed

Ali Akbar, however, was unable to forget the girl so easily and spent his time roaming about near her house in the hope of seeing her once again. Why? He did not know. His failure brought in its wake a savage anger which turned to hate; soon he was no longer able to pass along that road for fear that his fury would overcome him and he would pelt the window of her house with stones.

From that day onwards he refused to be called by anything but his name in full: Mohamed Ali Akbar, all in one. He refused to answer to anyone who called him Mohamed or Mohamed Ali and this soon became a habit with him. Even his sister Sabika did not dare to use a contracted form of his name. No longer did he experience his former contentment, and Abkha gradually changed to a forbidding graveyard in his eyes. Refusing to give in to his sister's insistence that he should marry, a worm called 'wealth' began to eat its way into his brain. He wanted to take revenge on everything, to marry a woman with whom he could challenge the whole of Abkha, all those who did not believe that he was Mohamed Ali Akbar but Mohamed Ali the scoundrel. Where, though, to find wealth? Thus he decided to sail away to Kuwait.

The distance between Abkha and Ras al-Khaima is two hours by foot, and from Ras al-Khaima to Kuwait by sea is a journey of three days, the fare for which, on an antiquated boat, was seventy rupees. After a year or two he would be able to return to Oman and strut about proudly in the alleyways of Abkha wearing a snow-white *aba* trimmed with gold, like the one he had seen round the shoulders of a notable from Ras al-Khaima who had come to his village to take the hand of a girl the fame of whose beauty had reached all the way there.

The journey was a hard one. The boat which took that eager throng across the south and then made its way northwards to the corner of the Gulf was continually exposed to a variety of dangers. But ebullient souls accustomed to life's hardships paid no heed to such matters; all hands co-operated in the task of delivering safely that small wooden boat floating on the waves of the great sea. And when the sails of the ships lying in Kuwait's quiet harbour came into view, Mohamed Ali Akbar experienced a strange feeling: the dream had now fallen from the coloured world of fantasy into the realm of reality and he had to search around for a starting-point, for a beginning to his dream. It seemed to him that the fantasies nourished by his hate for Abkha and for which he now sought vengeance were not of sufficient moment. As the frail craft approached, threading its way among the anchored boats, he was slowly drained of his feeling and it appeared to him that his long dreams of wealth were merely a solace for his sudden failure and that they were quite irrational. The packed streets, the buildings with their massive walls, the grey sky, the scorching heat, the warm air of the north wind, the roads crammed with cars, the serious faces, all these things appeared to him as barriers standing between him and his dream. He hurried aimlessly through this ocean of people, conscious of a deep feeling of loss which resembled vertigo, almost convinced that these many faces which did not glance at him were his first enemy, that all these people were the walls obstructing the very beginning of the road to his dream. The story was not as simple as in Abkha. Here it was without beginning, without end, without landmarks. It seemed to him that all the roads along which he walked were endless, that they circuited a rampart that held everything—every single thing—within its embrace. When, at sunset, a road led him to the sea-shore and he once again saw the sea, he stood staring across at the far horizon that joined up with the water: out there was Abkha, enveloped in tranquillity. It existed, every quarter had its beginning and its end, every wall carried its own particular lineaments; despite everything it was close to his heart. He felt lost in a rush of scalding water and for the first time he had no sense of shame as he lifted his hand to wipe salty tears from his cheeks.

Mohamed Ali Akbar wept without embarrassment, perhaps for the first time since he grew up; involuntarily, he had been overcome by a ferocious yearning for the two water-skins he used to carry across his shoulders. He was still staring out at the horizon while night gradually settled down around him. It made him feel in a way that he was present in a certain place at a certain time and that this night was like night in Abkha: people were sleeping behind their walls, the streets bore the lineaments of fatigue and silence, the sea rumbled heavily under the light of the moon. He felt relief. Wanting to laugh and yet unable to, he wept once again.

Dawn brought him an upsurge of fresh hope. He rose and went running through the streets. He realized that he must find someone from Oman with whom he could talk and that he would, sooner or later, find such a person, and from there he would learn where he was destined to proceed, from where to make a start.

And so Mohamed Ali Akbar attained his position as errand boy at a shop and was provided with a bicycle on which to carry out his duties. It was from this bicycle that the features of the streets, the qualities of the walls, registered themselves in his head. He felt a certain intimacy with them, but it was an intimacy imposed upon a background of a forbidding impression that he was being dogged by the eyes of his sister Sabika, the chinks in the girl's window, and Mohamed Ali the scoundrel who, unwittingly, had caused such dire disaster.

Months passed with the speed of a bicycle's wheels passing over the surface of a road. The wealth he had dreamed of began to come in and Mohamed Ali Akbar clung to this tiny fortune with all his strength, lest some passing whim should sweep it away or some scoundrel lay his hands on it. Thus it was that it occurred to him to make a sturdy wooden box in which to keep his fortune.

But what did Mohamed Ali Akbar's fortune consist of? Something that could not be reckoned in terms of money. When he had collected a certain amount of money he had bought himself a diaphanous white *aba* with gold edging. Every evening, alone with his box, he would take out the carefully folded *aba,* pass his thin brown fingers tenderly over it and spread it before his eyes; on it he would spill out his modest dreams, tracing along its borders all the streets of his village, the low, latticed windows from behind which peeped the eyes of young girls. There, in a corner of the *aba,* reposed the past which he could not bring himself to return to but whose existence was necessary in order to give the *aba* its true value. The thin fingers would fold it gently once again. put it safely back in its wooden box, and tie strong cord round the box. Then, and only then, did sleep taste sweet.

The box also contained a pair of china ear-rings for his sister Sabika, which he would give her on his return to Abkha, a bottle of pungent perfume, and a white purse holding such money as God in His bounty had given him and which he hoped would increase day by day.

As for the end, it began one evening. He was returning his bicycle to the shop when he felt a burning sensation in his limbs. He was alarmed at the thought that he had grown so weak, and with such speed, but did not take a great deal of

notice, having had spells of trembling whenever he felt exceptionally homesick for Sabika and Abkha; he had already experienced just such a sensation of weakness when savagely
yearning for all those things he hated and loved and had left
behind, those things that made up the whole of his past. And
so Mohamed Ali Akbar hastened along the road to his home
with these thoughts in mind. But his feeling of weakness and
nostalgia stayed with him till the following midday. When he
made the effort to get up from bed, he was amazed to find
that he had slept right through to noon instead of waking up
at his usual early hour. What alarmed him even more was
that he was still conscious of the feeling of weakness boring
into his bones. Slightly afraid, he thought for a while and
imagined himself all at once standing on the sea-shore with
the glaring sun reflected off the water almost blinding him,
the two water-skins on his shoulders, conscious of a sensation
of intense exhaustion. The reflection of the sun increased in
violence, yet he was unable to shut his eyes—they were
aflame. Abruptly he slid back into sleep.

Here time as usually understood came to an end for Mohamed Ali Akbar. From now on everything happened as
though he were raised above the ground, as though his legs
were dangling in mid-air: like a man on a gallows, he was
moving in front of Time's screen, a screen as inert as a rock
of basalt. His part as a practising human had been played
out; his part as a mere spectator had come. He felt that there
was no bond tying him to anything, that he was somewhere
far away and that the things that moved before his eyes were
no more than fish inside a large glass tumbler; his own eyes,
too, were open and staring as though made of glass.

When he woke up again he realized that he was being carried by his arms and legs. Though he felt exhausted, he found
the energy to recall that there was something which continued to be necessary to him and called out in a faint voice:

'The box . . . the box!'

No one, however, paid him any attention. With a frenzied
movement he rose so as to get back to his box. His chest panting with the effort of getting to his feet, he called out:

'The box!'

But once again no one heard him. As he reached the door
he clung to it and again gasped out in a lifeless voice:

'The box . . .'

Overcome by his exertions, he fell into a trance that was of

the sea-shore itself. This time he felt that the tide was rising little by little over his feet and that the water was intensely cold. His hands were grasping a square-shaped rock with which he plunged downwards. When he awoke again he found himself clasping his old box tied round with cord. While spectres passed to and fro in front of him, a needle was plunged into his arm, and a face bent over him.

Long days passed. But for Mohamed Ali Akbar nothing really happened at all. The mercilessness of the pain continued on its way, and he was not conscious of its passing. He was conscious only of its constant presence. The sea became dissolved into windows behind wooden shutters low against the side of the street, a pair of china ear-rings, an *aba* wet with salt water, a ship suspended motionless above the waves, and an old wooden box.

Only once was he aware of any contact with the world. This was when he heard a voice beside him say:

'What's in the old box?'

He looked at the source of the voice and saw, as in a dream, the face of a young, clean-shaven man with fair hair who was pointing at the box and looking at something.

The moment of recollection was short. He returned to gazing silently at the sea, though the face of the clean-shaven, blond young man also remained in front of him. After this he felt a sudden upsurge of energy; for no particular reason things had become clear to him. He distinctly saw, for the first time since he had collapsed, the rising of the sun. It seemed to him that he was capable of getting up from his bed and returning to his bicycle. Everything had grown clear to him: the box was alongside him, bound round as it had always been. Feeling at peace, he moved so as to get up, when a crowd of men in white clothes suddenly descended upon him, standing round him and regarding him with curiosity. Mohamed Ali Akbar tried to say something but was unable to. Suddenly he felt that the tide had risen right up to his waist and that the water was unbearably cold. He could feel nothing. He stretched out his arms to seize hold of something lest he should drown, but everything slid away from under his fingers. Suddenly he saw the clean-shaven face of the blond young man again; he stared at him, somewhat frightened of him on account of his box, while the water continued to rise higher and higher until it had screened off that fair, clean-shaven face from his gaze.

'Bed number 12 has died.'

As the male nurse called out I was unable to free myself from Mohamed Ali Akbar's eyes staring out at me before he died. I imagined that Mohamed Ali Akbar, who refused to have his name mutilated, would now be satisfied at being merely 'Bed number 12' if only he could be assured about the fate of his box.

This, my dear Ahmed, is the story of Mohamed Ali Akbar, Bed number 12, who died yesterday evening and is now lying wrapped round in a white cloth in the autopsy room—the thin brown face that shifted an ulcer from my intestines to my brain and who caused me to write to you, so you don't again repeat your famous phrase 'I almost died laughing' in my presence.

Ever yours,

I haven't yet left the hospital. My health is gradually getting back to normal and the method by which I gauge this amuses me. Do you know how I measure my strength? I stand smoking on the balcony and throw the cigarette end with all my strength so that it falls along the strips of green grass in the garden. In past weeks the cigarette would fall just within the fourth strip, but today it was much nearer the sixth.

From your letter I understand you to say that you were in no need of being a witness to Mohamed Ali Akbar's death to know what death is. You wrote saying that the experience of death does not require the tragic prologues with which I described Mohamed Ali Akbar's life and that people die with far greater matter-of-factness: the man who fell down on the pavement and so let off the loaded pistol he had with him, whose bullet ripped open his neck (he was in the company of a strikingly beautiful girl), or the one who had a heart attack in the street one April evening, having become engaged to be married only a week before. Yes, that's all very true, my dear Ahmed, all very true, but the problem doesn't lie here at all, the problem of death is in no way that of the dead man, it is the problem of those who remain, those who bitterly await their turn so that they too may serve as a humble lesson to the eyes of the living. Of all the things I wrote in my last letter what I want to say now is that we must transfer our thinking from the starting-point to the end. All thinking must set forth from the point of death, whether it be, as you say,

that of a man who dies contemplating the charms of the body of a wonderfully beautiful girl, or whether he dies staring into a newly-shaven face which frightens him because of an old wooden box tied round with string. The unsolved question remains that of the end; the question of non-existence, of eternal life—or what? Or what, my dear Ahmed?

Anyway, let's stop pouring water into a sack with a hole in it. Do you know what happened after I sent you my last letter? I went to the doctor's room and found them writing a report about Mohamed Ali Akbar. And they were on the point of opening the box. Oh, Ahmed, how imprisoned we are in our bodies and minds! We are always endowing others with our own attributes, always looking at them through a narrow fissure of our own views and way of thinking, wanting them, as far as we can, to become 'us'. We want to squeeze them into our skins, to give them our eyes to see with, to clothe them in our past and our own way of facing up to life. We place them within a framework outlined by our present understanding of time and place.

Mohamed Ali Akbar was none of the things I imagined. He was the father of three boys and two girls. We have forgotten that over there men marry early. Also, Mohamed Ali Akbar was not a water-seller, water being plentiful in Oman, but had been a sailor on one of the sailing ships that ply between the ports of the south and the Gulf, before settling down here quite a time ago.

It was in fact four years ago that Mohamed Ali Akbar arrived in Kuwait. After unimaginably hard effort he managed—only two months ago—to open what passed for a shop on one of the pavements of New Street. As to how he provided for his children in Oman, we simply don't know.

I read in the doctor's report that the patient had lost his sight six hours before death and so it would seem that Mohamed Ali Akbar had not in fact been staring into my face at the moment of his death as he was then blind. The doctor also wrote that as the address of the patient's family was not known, his burial would be attended solely by the hospital grave-diggers.

The doctor read out the report to his colleague. It was concise and extremely condensed, merely dealing in technical terms with the man's illness. The doctor's voice was lugubrious and colourless. When he had finished reading he proceeded to untie the string round the box. At this point I thought of leaving the room, for it was none of my business: the Mohamed Ali Akbar I knew had died and this person they had written about was someone else; this box, too, was some other box. I knew for certain what Mohamed Ali Akbar's box contained. Why should I bother myself about some new problem?

And yet I was unable to go to the door, but stood in the corner, trembling slightly.

The box was soon opened and the doctor quickly ran his fingers through the contents. Then he pushed it to one side.

Fearfully I looked into the box: it was filled with recent invoices for sums owed by the shop to the stores which supplied it; in one corner was an old photo of a bearded face, an old watch strap, some string, a small candle and several rupees among the papers.

I must be truthful and say that I was sadly disappointed. Before leaving the room, though, I saw something that stunned me: the nurse had pushed aside Mohamed Ali Akbar's invoices and revealed a long china ear-ring that glittered. In a daze I went to the box and picked up the ear-ring. I don't know why it was that I looked at the nurse and said:

'He bought this ear-ring for his sister Sabika—I happen to know that.'

For a brief instant she stared at me in some surprise—then she laughed uproariously. The doctor, too, laughed at the joke.

You are no doubt aware that nurses are required to humour patients with stomach ulcers in case they should suffer a relapse.

Yours ever—

(TRANSLATED BY DENYS JOHNSON-DAVIES)

The Price of Freedom

by JAFAR AL-KHALILI

We had made a bad estimate of both distance and time when we set out from the Lebanese village of Jabā with only a small quantity of supplies, to scale this monstrous, lofty mountain on our way to the tomb of a holy man, Ṣāfī by name. He was said to be one of God's saints, able to confer a blessing on his visitors, and send them back—after the labor of climbing this mountain—rejoicing, believing, reassured. And if this was not due to the action of the faith he left in the soul, then it must have been the effect of such delightful views, which Ṣāfī's mountain brought together on all sides and laid out beneath your eyes and feet in beautiful, bright colors, over all the valleys and plains around.

I had begun to feel hunger and fatigue at the same time. In former days the great divine Shaikh Muhammad al-Husain Kāshif al-Ghiṭā' had felt the same way while scaling the mountain; and a saying of his has been handed down, which is always recalled by anyone proposing to climb this mighty peak or happening to think of the name of Ṣāfī the saint: "O Ṣāfī! What great fatigues you impose for such small rewards!" Anyway, we reached Ṣāfī after a mighty effort and after using up the last of our provisions. But my companions realized I was not up to returning, even to the nearest inhabited spot, or of enduring hunger, even for a few hours; so they began to face the issue with considerable concern. Before long, we glimpsed a man in the distance, scaling the jagged rocks halfway up the mountain, aiding himself with a stick along a twisting path on which a monkey might fear to slip, and preceded by a goat which he urged forward and upward. The distance was such that no voice would reach his ears but for those echoes which, in the mountains, make a

[47]

voice heavy, rich, and powerful; so one of my companions
set about hailing him: "Hello there, you! Hey, there! Hello!"

After a while, back came the answer, drawn out and mag-
nified by the echo: Aye! Aye! Aye! —Come over this way!
—I can't, caaan't, what would I do with the goat? —Never
mind, for God's sake come over here, over here! After an exchange of shouts lasting several minutes (and consisting of
such phrases as "Come here!" "I can't!" "It's all right!" "No,
it's not!") the fellow left his goat—God knows where!—and
made toward us along a path concealed from us by rocks;
and in a short while he was among us in 'Ṣāfī' territory.

He did not spend much time in talking, and my companions found no difficulty in making him understand that I was
a guest and a stranger, hungry and tired, and that he had an
obligation to discharge the duties of hospitality with all speed.
It was quickly agreed that we should all move to his home,
which not many people had ever seen, but which he said was
only five minutes' distance away.

So we set off, preceded by this fellow, who had very gener-
ously offered me his stick. Following him, we ascended amid
the lofty peaks and descended through the twisting defiles;
scarcely traversing one of those swelling, gigantic, upthrust
rocks before we were on the lip of a crevice, dropping down,
deep down, to the farthest point our sight could reach. So we
continued, climbing and dropping, scaling and descending,
turning and twisting, in dread and fear of a slip (something
not to be spoken of!) that might take us neither we nor anyone else knew whither. For these were tracks—it now seemed
very likely—never trodden by any man before our friend
Abū Riḍà, retreats which (given their difficulty of access)
were but rarely beheld, even by animals. Finally, I refused to
go on walking, and implored my companions to return; but
the road back, as they said, might be more difficult than what
remained ahead of us, apart from the fact that (as Abū Riḍà
averred) we had almost reached his dwelling.

Exactly two hours passed, not to be forgotten, though life-
times might be. During the course of these hours every one of
us came close to falling from on high into the mouth of one
of those gaping abysses, or breaking his neck with one slip of
his weakened, exhausted feet. The path grew still more
twisted and rugged, so that movement along it would have

been difficult even for athletes and mountaineers, able though they might be to get around the whole length and breadth of the Alps themselves.

What could have brought Abū Riḍà thither? Why had he chosen to live in this secluded, remote spot in such an arid quarter, so bereft of water as not to be coveted even by frugal birds or ascetic monks? Why all this effort? Why such excess of striving to get away from mankind?

These were thoughts that rambled around within my head, questions that passed across my mind, while I looked for an appropriate occasion that might clarify this mystery and reveal this secret to me.

Beside me was a companion with whom I was on closer terms than with the others, and I addressed these questions to him, but he answered me no more than to say that Abū Riḍà had dwelt here from birth; that there was nothing untoward in his doing so, since here he was beyond the reach of thieves and predatory animals; and that a solitary existence was preferred by some people, as better assuring happiness and peace of mind than life in the cities. Thus my companion continued to discourse on the reclusive and monastic life and the habitations it required, ascribing Abū Riḍà's choice of this rugged, remote spot for his swelling to a sheer philosophy of abstention and asceticism such as had long taken possession of many minds.

We had by now worked our way round a great hill formed by one solid rock of granite, when the barking of dogs suddenly filled our cars. Immediately, Abū Riḍà uttered a few words and some noises, which had a magical effect on these barking dogs, so that they withdrew with a low whine that soon ceased. There were three of them, tall beasts, thick-coated and shaggy, of a breed whose glaring eyes suggested viciousness and lionlike ferocity. There we were, in front of Abū Riḍà's house.

It was composed of three rooms, carved into the mountain, and it looked as though it had once been a large cave on which the builders had worked to make a house with all amenities and serving all needs. Beside it was an enclosure for the goats, one half of which penetrated deep into the interior of the mountain, while the other half—devoid of any sort of roof—looked up to the sky. Next to this enclosure was a

spacious run for the chickens, and then came two large cisterns for water. One of these was set aside for chickens, dogs,
and livestock, the other for the people of the house themselves. They had been built in such a way that not a drop of
rain, or of the floodwater running down from the mountaintop, could fail to flow into them; and whenever they were
filled, the water was free to pass along a rock conduit,
whence (after the household had taken its annual sufficiency)
it dropped to the valley, roaring and surging on its way.
More than anything else, the house resembled a fortified
castle, and it may well have been more impregnable and
unassailable, by virtue of the very difficulty of reaching it,
than were the castles of the Middle Ages. It was as though
made from this barren land itself, this land that held nothing
but rocks and a few miserable little outgrowths, scattered
here and there up to a mile or more from the house—or, if
you will, from this impregnable castle.

Abū Riḍà's family consisted of his wife, two daughters,
and a son who was the eldest child; and of a flock of goats
not exceeding thirty head, some chickens and three dogs. Every so often he would take his produce—without the dogs, of
course—down to the nearest market, enlisting the aid of a
few hired hands, and selling cooking butter, yoghurt, goat's
hair, eggs and chicks. Then he would return, laden with what
he needed in the way of seeds, vegetables, cloth, and anything
he could stow away against a time of necessity or shortage.

Now Abū Riḍà had become accustomed in recent years to
pass by Sāfī's tomb, watching over it and taking a special interest in it. He had even begun to avail himself of some of
the votive offerings, returning home sometimes with more
than a little food or cash or a few candles. On the present occasion, however, he could not know that fate would present
him with such guests as those who now accompanied him
home. Indeed, this was doubtless the first occasion of its kind
that visitors to the shrine had accompanied him to his house
and sought his hospitality.

So we sat, discussing the reasons why Abū Riḍà had
pushed his way so far away from mankind and chosen this
remote house in this barren place, when he himself spoke up:
"It was not I who chose to dwell in this remote spot. Indeed,

I was not even born at that time, on the day my father came
with some masons and workmen, who should carve him from
out of this mountain a complete house, thus enabling him to
dispense with life in a village or the cultivated countryside.
He had already moved my mother, who was pregnant with
me, along with my spinster aunt and a little sister of mine;
and his dog, Jadd, to keep watch before the house. My father
was a young man, so bursting with youth and vitality that his
strength and dash had become a general byword. His prowess
at all sorts of sports, such as horse-riding, swimming, shooting
and hunting, had made him a model for all the "free spirits"
of this vast region. Indeed, his name occupied first place in
the records of those who had been on the run from military
service for five years or more. But who could get a sight of
my father, let alone arrest him? And who could get close to
him, let alone drag him into the city? Sometimes he would be
here, sometimes there, now in this village, now in that—with
the army in constant pursuit of him, continuously on his
tracks, but unavailingly and to no effect. My father knew
well enough that if they succeeded in catching him it would
be the end of his days in Syria and Lebanon; for few of those
conscripted in those times ever returned to their homelands,
if indeed one ever heard anything of them again once they
had been enlisted. This father of mine had a blazing affection, a passionate love for his country, a great enthusiasm for
its valleys and mountains, its olive groves and oak trees. This
was the very reason why he contrived to escape the military
with such ease, laughing hugely at his pursuers' expense.

"Eventually, my father was married to my mother, and the
marriage consummated; and she conceived my elder sister.
He was still on the run from the army, still the cynosure of
those who watched for him and those who envied; and his
marriage had only inflamed his feelings the more. But while
love bound him in attachment to his spouse, it made him less
cautious, less watchful of those who pursued and harried
him; so one night the military caught him unawares as he
was about to leave his house, and he was led under guard to
Beirut. Thus he left my mother pregnant with me and went
away.

"Some days passed and my father became one of those to
embark on a steamer bound from Beirut to Constantinople,
whence they would be finally distributed as soldiers over the
vast dominions of the Ottoman Empire; and none would

again have any word of them. But my father, who knew what freedom meant and what it was worth, and whom nature had richly endowed with many gifts of body and mind, was oppressed by the idea of submission or resignation to such a fate while still in possession of such powers and such gifts. Night had scarcely descended, and the steamer had been under way for little more than an hour, when he came across a stout wooden plank in one of the latrines. He wrenched it away, cast it into the sea, jumped in after it, and began swimming until he reached it and could support himself by it. But the wind was contrary and the sea rough, and it took him some ten hours to reach the coast—ten hours in which he put forth enormous effort, growing ever more tired and weak, for all his heroic strength and energy.

"My father returned to his bride after an absence of two months. The first thing he did was to bully a party of workmen into climbing this haughty mountain to hew him out this house, at a distance of twenty miles from the nearest inhabited village.

"Anyone who listened to my father or talked with him would hear a discourse on freedom such as none had ever heard before, and would see in his every movement a remarkable grasp of that freedom about which he spoke. He had chosen to live in this rugged, remote spot, with its limited horizon of ideas, in his concern to get away from the military uniform, the fetters of drill, and the rigorous training of those days.

"Gradually my mother and my aunt became acclimated to this life. Indeed, in the course of time, they came to prefer it to any other sort of life in the comfort of cities; and this, despite the fact that they knew nothing of the bitterness of military service, or the full price of freedom, in the same sense as did the conscript soldier of the Ottoman period.

"One day my mother, being pregnant at the time, stumbled on a rock and fell; and when she tried to get up, her foot slipped and she fell again; and suddenly she began to roll so far that it cost my father a great effort to rescue her. And not just my father, but my aunt and my sister as well. As for my mother herself, it cost her a miscarriage and the breaking of the femur in her right leg. For several months she continued to suffer the aftereffects of losing her unborn child and breaking her leg, and then she got up from her couch with a limp and a deformity. My aunt too, on one occasion, was stricken with typhoid, and spent more than two months in a state of sickness that disorganized the whole life of the household.

"Another night, as my father was returning home shortly before sunset, he had the impression that a man was following in his footsteps, keeping close on his tracks so as to be led to his house. Wild ideas whirled in his mind, and he allowed his fancy to conceive that the military's concern with him had induced them to pursue him even into these winding defiles and beyond these towering rocks. So he turned aside from the road home, making an enormous detour. The sun disappeared while he was still climbing and descending endlessly. Realizing he would be unable to reach his house that night, he spent it sheltering in one of the many caves thereabouts, protected by great stones. It was a night to be recalled in legend: neither my mother nor my aunt at home closed their eyelids for a moment in their anxious expectation of my father's return and their fear on his account. For him too, it was a long, dark night, weakened as he was by fatigue and dread, yet on his guard against pursuit.

"Many such troubles came our way. Yet life hereabouts— and particularly in this hermitage, withdrawn from mankind—was pleasant enough, even happy and comfortable, so long as freedom cast its protective shade over the house; and so long as my father came and went, and came and went again, as his heart desired—and not according to the will of his Turkish officer, telling him to halt or to march whenever the officer wanted him to do so.

"Yes, life in this spot was pleasant, sweet, fragrant, even for the dogs, even for the goats, even for the chickens. But when a *person* knows the meaning of "freedom" as it ought to be known, he can really enjoy its fruits to the extent of his full capacity, answering no call save that of his own dear heart."

Then Abū Riḍà said abruptly: "If you can now manage to climb around this monstrous great rock, you will find the grave of my father; and beside it, that of my aunt and my elder sister. And at my father's feet is buried the dog who caught two of the wolves that were attacking the goats one cold winter's night."

Two years later I passed through Jabā on my summer vacation, and asked after Abū Riḍà. I was told he had died and been buried beside his father, his aunt, his sister, and Jadd, their first dog. Left to run his house was his son Riḍà, and he may die without ever knowing his grandfather's secret, or the reason for the choice of this house as a dwelling in such a rugged, remote spot. Equally, events may come to pass that will sweep all the inhabitants of this hermitage into their graves or to other parts of the world, obliterating all memories and killing off all thoughts of the past. But the one thing that will remain as a symbol of freedom is that house: its inhabitants will pass away, the military will pass away, but it will remain, enduring, under the protective shadows of this haughty peak—a true symbol of freedom.

(TRANSLATED BY G. M. WICKENS)

A Handful of Dates

by TAIEB SALEH

I must have been very young at the time. While I don't remember exactly how old I was, I do remember that when people saw me with my grandfather they would pat me on the head and give my cheek a pinch—things they didn't do to my grandfather. The strange thing was that I never used to go out with my father, rather it was my grandfather who would take me with him wherever he went, except for the mornings when I would go to the mosque to learn the Koran. The mosque, the river and the fields—these were the landmarks in our life. While most of the children of my age grumbled at having to go to the mosque to learn the Koran, I used to love it. The reason was, no doubt, that I was quick at learning by heart and the Sheikh always asked me to stand up and recite the *Chapter of the Merciful* whenever we had visitors, who would pat me on my head and cheek just as people did when they saw me with my grandfather.

Yes, I used to love the mosque, and I loved the river too.

Directly we finished our Koran reading in the morning I would throw down my wooden slate and dart off, quick as a genie, to my mother, hurriedly swallow down my breakfast, and run off for a plunge in the river. When tired of swimming about I would sit on the bank and gaze at the strip of water that wound away eastwards and hid behind a thick wood of acacia trees. I loved to give rein to my imagination and picture to myself a tribe of giants living behind that wood, a people tall and thin with white beards and sharp noses, like my grandfather. Before my grandfather ever replied to my many questions he would rub the tip of his nose with his forefinger; as for his beard, it was soft and luxuriant and as white as cotton-wool—never in my life have I seen anything of a purer whiteness or greater beauty. My grandfather must also have been extremely tall, for I never saw anyone in the whole area address him without having to look up at him, nor did I see him enter a house without having to bend so low that I was put in mind of the way the river wound round behind the wood of acacia trees. I loved him and would imagine myself, when I grew to be a man, tall and slender like him, walking along with great strides.

I believe I was his favourite grandchild: no wonder, for my cousins were a stupid bunch and I—so they say—was an intelligent child. I used to know when my grandfather wanted me to laugh, when to be silent; also I would remember the times for his prayers and would bring him his prayer-rug and fill the ewer for his ablutions without his having to ask me. When he had nothing else to do he enjoyed listening to me reciting to him from the Koran in a lilting voice, and I could tell from his face that he was moved.

One day I asked him about our neighbour Masood. I said to my grandfather: 'I fancy you don't like our neighbour Masood?'

To which he answered, having rubbed the tip of his nose: 'He's an indolent man and I don't like such people.'

I said to him: 'What's an indolent man?'

My grandfather lowered his head for a moment, then looking across at the wide expanse of field, he said: 'Do you see it stretching out from the edge of the desert up to the Nile bank? A hundred feddans. Do you see all those date palms? And those trees—*sant*, acacia, and *sayal*? All this fell into Masood's lap, was inherited by him from his father.'

Taking advantage of the silence that had descended upon my grandfather, I turned my gaze from him to the vast area defined by his words. 'I don't care,' I told myself, 'who owns those date palms, those trees or this black, cracked earth—all I know is that it's the arena for my dreams and my playground.'

My grandfather then continued: 'Yes, my boy, forty years ago all this belonged to Masood—two-thirds of it is now mine.'

This was news to me, for I had imagined that the land had belonged to my grandfather ever since God's Creation.

'I didn't own a single feddan when I first set foot in this village. Masood was then the owner of all these riches. The position has changed now, though, and I think that before Allah calls me to Him I shall have bought the remaining third as well.'

I do not know why it was I felt fear at my grandfather's words—and pity for our neighbour Masood. How I wished my grandfather wouldn't do what he'd said! I remembered Masood's singing, his beautiful voice and powerful laugh that resembled the gurgling of water. My grandfather never used to laugh.

I asked my grandfather why Masood had sold his land.

'Women,' and from the way my grandfather pronounced the word I felt that 'women' was something terrible. 'Masood, my boy, was a much-married man. Each time he married he sold me a feddan or two.' I made the quick calculation that Masood must have married some ninety women. Then I remembered his three wives, his shabby appearance, his lame donkey and its dilapidated saddle, his *galabia* with the torn sleeves. I had all but rid my mind of the thoughts that jostled in it when I saw the man approaching us, and my grandfather and I exchanged glances.

'We'll be harvesting the dates today,' said Masood. 'Don't you want to be there?'

I felt, though, that he did not really want my grandfather to attend. My grandfather, however, jumped to his feet and I saw that his eyes sparkled momentarily with an intense brightness. He pulled me by the hand and we went off to the harvesting of Masood's dates.

Someone brought my grandfather a stool covered with an ox-hide, while I remained standing. There was a vast number of people there, but though I knew them all, I found myself for some reason watching Masood: aloof from that great gathering of people he stood as though it were no concern of his, despite the fact that the date palms to be harvested were his own. Sometimes his attention would be caught by the sound of a huge clump of dates crashing down from on high. Once he shouted up at the boy perched on the very summit of the date palm who had begun hacking at a clump with his long, sharp sickle: 'Be careful you don't cut the heart of the palm.'

No one paid any attention to what he said and the boy seated at the very summit of the date palm continued, quickly and energetically, to work away at the branch with his sickle till the clump of dates began to drop like something descending from the heavens.

I, however, had begun to think about Masood's phrase 'the heart of the palm.' I pictured the palm tree as something with feeling, something possessed of a heart that throbbed. I remembered Masood's remark to me when he had once seen me playing about with the branch of a young palm tree: 'Palm trees, my boy, like humans, experience joy and suffering.' And I had felt an inward and unreasoned embarrassment.

When I again looked at the expanse of ground stretching before me I saw my young companions swarming like ants around the trunks of the palm trees, gathering up dates and eating most of them. The dates were collected into high mounds. I saw people coming along and weighing them into measuring bins and pouring them into sacks, of which I counted thirty. The crowd of people broke up, except for Hussein the merchant, Mousa the owner of the field next to ours on the east, and two men I'd never seen before.

I heard a low whistling sound and saw that my grandfather had fallen asleep. Then I noticed that Masood had not changed his stance, except that he had placed a stalk in his mouth and was munching at it like someone surfeited with food who doesn't know what to do with the mouthful he still has.

Suddenly my grandfather woke up, jumped to his feet and walked towards the sacks of dates. He was followed by Hussein the merchant, Mousa the owner of the field next to ours, and the two strangers. I glanced at Masood and saw that he was making his way towards us with extreme slowness, like a man who wants to retreat but whose feet insist on going forward. They formed a circle round the sacks of dates and began examining them, some taking a date or two to eat. My grandfather gave me a fistful, which I began munching. I saw Masood filling the palms of both hands with dates and bringing them up close to his nose, then returning them.

Then I saw them dividing up the sacks between them. Hussein the merchant took ten; each of the strangers took five. Mousa the owner of the field next to ours on the eastern side took five, and my grandfather took five. Understanding nothing, I looked at Masood and saw that his eyes were darting about to left and right like two mice that have lost their way home.

'You're still fifty pounds in debt to me,' said my grandfather to Masood. 'We'll talk about it later.'

Hussein called his assistants and they brought along donkeys, the two strangers produced camels, and the sacks of dates were loaded on to them. One of the donkeys let out a braying which set the camels frothing at the mouth and complaining noisily. I felt myself drawing close to Masood, felt my hand stretch out towards him as though I wanted to touch the hem of his garment. I heard him make a noise in his throat like the rasping of a lamb being slaughtered. For some unknown reason, I experienced a sharp sensation of pain in my chest.

I ran off into the distance. Hearing my grandfather call after me, I hesitated a little, then continued on my way. I felt at that moment that I hated him. Quickening my pace, it was as though I carried within me a secret I wanted to rid myself of. I reached the river bank near the bend it made behind the wood of acacia trees. Then, without knowing why, I put my finger into my throat and spewed up the dates I'd eaten.

(TRANSLATED BY DENYS JOHNSON-DAVIES)

The Face of the Moon

by ZAKARIA TAMIR

The wood-cutter's axe fell with monotonous regularity on the trunk of the lemon tree which stood in the courtyard of the house, as Samīha sat near the window overlooking the alley, from which every now and then the cries of a mad young man rose and mingled with the noise of the axe. The scent of the lemon tree wafted into the room and penetrated its atmosphere like a blind beggar woman knocking on every door in humble supplication.

The madman's shouts came up from the alley and reached Samīha's ears, harsh and disjointed. An angry savage animal lurked in them calling out to a mysterious creature lying dormant in her veins. She could see the madman leaping in the alley, while around him a group of boys shouted and threw orange peel at him. Samīha thought his eyes were like two sick tigers drowsing on the grass of some thick jungle.

Samīha's father was a very old man, tortured by illness. The scent of the lemon tree distressed him, and he had decided to get rid of it. He had called in the wood-cutter regardless of Samīha's entreaties—for the lemon tree had been her friend since the days of her childhood. With the approach of winter its beauty always increased and rain drops glittered like pearls upon its leaves. Then its green coat seemed to shine and glow, as though it were about to burst into flame.

The sound of the madman's cries rose again as though it were the weeping of the lemon tree which would so soon be destroyed. A vague fear grew in Samīha's flesh. It seemed to her that she possessed a sky full of pale-fired stars which were nothing but her dead dreams; for at that moment Samīha was just an ordinary woman in the prime of her life, whose husband had divorced her several months ago. She

might have been a good wife: cooking the food, washing the
clothes, cleaning the rooms, surrendering herself to the man
who was her husband, with simulated ecstasy and joy and
warmth. When she was ten years old her father had slapped
her cruelly because he had seen her dress uncovering her
thighs. Then, on the eve of her marriage, those of her female
relations who were already married had taught her how she
should move her body when it was joined with the man's and
become an answering voice full of responsive harmonies, full
of passionate yearning and desire for the man. And her husband had been angry with her, for, at night when she lay
stretched out beside him, she would panic and flinch whenever his hands touched her. She would then become passive
flesh, motionlessly submissive to the weight of a man. The
husband had not been able to go on living with her; he
wanted a woman who moaned in ecstasy, whose flesh would
tremble when it sensed a man near.

So Samīha had gone back to her parent's home to live
abandoned, helping her mother with the housework and idling away the rest of the day sitting by the window watching
the passers-by in the alley. And the madman was always
there, screaming and leaping about trying to drive away the
boys.

The axe was still wounding the trunk of the lemon tree
with its blade and penetrating its body further and further.
The sound of the axe made Samīha feel that she was losing
her childhood little by little. In the old days Samīha had
been a child who laughed with no reason; she had been
frightened of the moon and could never be reconciled to the
fact that it was only a solid disc which shone with white light.

Samīha heard a strange shrill scream. She realised immediately that it must have come from the madman. She looked
out of the window: there was the madman, sitting on the
ground, holding his head with his hands, while the blood
gushed out between his fingers. The boys had fled for safety
after one of them had thrown a stone at him.

Seized by a mysterious terror, Samīha turned away from
the window and lay down on the couch. The scent of the
lemon tree and the noise of the axe mingled with the cries of
the madman. Samīha shut her eyes and succumbed to a
severe fit of trembling. She imagined that there were fingers
pressing into her throat preventing her from breathing, and
she wanted to cry out for help before she was strangled. She

felt a painful weight creeping over her whole body and then drawing away leaving her calm and able to breathe once more. She began to pant with happiness mixed with apprehension. And suddenly she saw the mysterious man who used to come bursting into her dreams at night. He was a tall man, completely naked, and his skin was covered with a thick layer of coarse black hair. She always longed to touch him but she was unable to move.

The axe beat away maliciously at the trunk of the lemon tree. The mysterious man smiled; he was standing near the door, his eyes gleaming. Samīha said in a hoarse voice: "Go away."

His lips split open into a broad smile. His teeth were very white, and his lips were like frozen scarlet blood. If only he would say something! She wanted desperately to hear his voice—surely it would be like the roaring of the waves as they beat against the rocks of a far distant shore.

As the man began to come nearer she tried to run away and said again: "Go away."

The man paid no attention and continued to approach her. He stretched out a hand, and the five fingers stroked her flowing hair. His lips moved and no sound came from them; but Samīha was certain that he was saying to her: "My darling."

The madman's screams grew louder, and the mysterious man took hold of Samīha's hand and began to pull her after him. Samīha followed him unresisting. A feeling of sweet reassurance calmed her; she knew his hand, knew it well. Where had she seen it before? She could not remember, however hard she tried. The man led her onwards. Together they crossed the vast plain where the snows of winter, the summer sun, and the flowers of spring all meet together. They arrived at the front of a crumbling house. Samīha thought she had known this house. Where had she seen it before? Where? Where? The darkness began to clear, and she had the sudden fleeting impression that it was the same old deserted house which had squatted like a ghostly figure at the entrance to the alley in the days when she had been a little girl.

She looked at the man, and saw that he had changed. He was no longer young but had become middle-aged. She recognised him immediately. One day, when she was not yet twelve years old, she had been returning to her house. Dusk had fallen and she had begun to run along the streets. When she reached the old deserted house, a middle-aged man had blocked her way. He had grabbed her little hand in a cruel grip, and said roughly: "I will kill you if you scream."

Then he had dragged her quickly inside the house and stripped off her clothes. Her breasts were not fully developed in those days, but their flesh was smooth and firm. The body of the middle-aged man smelt like an extinguished fire. Samīha looked with anxious longing at the middle-aged man who was returning to her after she had waited long for him. She wanted to rush towards him and bury her head in his breast. But she had heard him say: "I will kill you if you scream." And she made no attempt to resist him. She was fascinated by the strange feeling of desire which surged deep inside her, and remained lying on her back waiting for the body of a middle-aged man who smelt of burnt-out fire.

The madman's cries rose again. Samīha tried to lie on the couch and ignore them; but the screams continued to grow louder and more savage, until she could not bear it any longer. She jumped to her feet, ran over to the window, and looked down into the alley. She saw that the madman was still sitting on the ground and was fighting off the barber and the greengrocer, who were trying to bandage his head with a piece of white cloth, while his screams changed to the savage howls of a wild animal.

Samīha did not try to go back and lie down on the couch, though at this moment she could have gone back and hidden in the old deserted house with the evening darkness and the middle-aged man.

Instead she looked at the madman who was rolling on the ground agitating his arms and legs. She felt that the middle-aged man had departed and was breathing his last in a distant place. She longed for the madman to turn into a vast flood of knives which would sweep through her body slowly tearing her flesh apart, and then leave her face to face with her old terror.

Samīha went back to the couch, lay down, and shut her eyes. One day she would be alone in the house, she would lure the madman inside, strip off her clothes without any shyness and give her breast to the madman's mouth. She would laugh as he tried to nibble the teat, she would beg him in a voice heavy with panting to bite her flesh, to sink his teeth into it until the blood spurted out and stained his lips.

Then she would lick his lips with her tongue greedily and compassionately.

The beating of the axe stopped for a moment; and there came the sound of the lemon tree falling, crashing to the ground in the courtyard with a sound which soon faded away.

Samīha smiled when she thought of the moon. It would never frighten her again—now that she had seen its face unveiled.

(TRANSLATED BY H. AL-KHATEEB)

POETRY

ADONIS (ALI AHMAD SAED)

The Frontiers of Despair

On the frontiers of despair my house stands,
Its walls like yellow foam,
Hollow and disjointed like clouds.

My house is lattice work of dough.
My house consists of holes.
It is shaken by the wind until the wind grows tired,
And is then relieved by the gale.
My house is deserted by the sun, despite its nearness;
It is deserted even by sparrows.

My house has been turned by its convulsions
Into something invisible, transcendental,
Fixed beyond the invisible world.
In it I sleep and around me the morning
Lies asleep, with voice muted and choked.

You Have No Choice

What? You will then have to destroy the face
Of the earth and form another.

What? You will then have no choice
Other than the path of fire,
Other than the hell of denial—

When the earth becomes
A dumb guillotine or a god.

The City

Our fire is approaching the city,
To destroy the throne of the city.

We shall destroy the throne of the city,
We shall live and, through the arrows, cross over
To the land of troubled transparency,
Behind that mask hanging on the revolving stone,
Around the whirlpool of terror,
Around speech and echo;
And we shall wash clean the bowels of day, its intestines
    and its child,
And burn that patched-up being called the city.

(TRANSLATED BY M. M. BADAWI)

A Mirror for Autumn

Have you seen a woman
Carrying the corpse of Autumn?
Have you seen a woman
Rubbing her face on the pavement,
Weaving her dress
With threads of rain?
People
Are burnt-out coals
On the pavement.

(TRANSLATED BY ABDULLAH AL-UDHARI)

ADBUL WAHAB AL-BAYATI

Why Are We in Exile the Refugees Ask

Why do we die
In silence
And I had a house
And I had . . .
And here you are
Without a heart, without a voice
Wailing, and here you are
Why are we in exile?
We die
We die in silence
Why are we not crying?
On fire,
On thorns
We walked
And my people walked
Why are we Lord
Without a country, without love
We die
We die in terror
Why are we in exile
Why are we Lord?

(TRANSLATED BY ABDULLAH AL-UDHARI)

The Wall

I shall curse the love
which breeds in our desert cactus
I shall curse the day
if I can't find in its light a guitar
if I can't find flowers.
Our wells are poisoned,
my darling, where shall we escape to?
Our friends died
nothing remained but the wall
mocking our dead,
our cracked
night!

(TRANSLATED BY M. B. ALWAN)

MAHMUD DARWISH

Pride and Fury

O homeland! O eagle,
Plunging, through the bars of my cell,
Your fiery beak in my eyes!
All I possess in the presence of death
Is pride and fury.
I have willed that my heart be planted as a tree,
That my forehead become an abode for skylarks.
O eagle,
I am unworthy of your lofty wing,
I prefer a crown of flame.
O homeland!
We were born and raised in your wound,
And ate the fruit of your trees,
To witness the birth of your daybreak.
O eagle unjustly languishing in chains,
O legendary death which once was sought,
Your fiery beak is still plunged in my eye,
Like a sword of flame.

Unworthy of your lofty wing,
All I possess in the presence of death
Is pride and fury.

(TRANSLATED BY MOUNA A. KHOURI AND HAMID ALGAR)

BULAND AL-HAIDARI

The Dead Witness

Who killed the last commando . . . ?
I know who
I know who blinded him and who
Cut his hands and who,
Your highness, shattered
His great dream
I know who
Because I looked after that child for years
Before he was born in our dreams
     In our longing
Before he lay in ambush at the bend in the road
Before love became his world
And the earth his dreams
Ah,
Before this young man
Became
A bleeding wound,
The blood of vengeance on the knife
I know who
I know who killed
The last commando, your highness

I know who
For a thousand, thousand nights I stayed at his door
Stayed awake in the blackness of his eyelashes

I was part of his bitter night
A glimpse of light in his exile
. . . . . .
And a thousand thousand times
I was the mud-spattered blood in his skin

I know who
—— Who killed the last commando
—— Who killed the . . .
—— I know who
—— Say who
—— Who's who
—— If I said who
I would become, your highness,
The dead witness of the last commando

You and I, your highness,
You and I

The Parcel

I was born behind the door
I grew up
Behind the door
And behind the door
Many times love turned in my body
To talons
And fangs
Many times, you were spilt, my blood, on the ground,
Present in absence,
I was the murderer
And the murdered, I was the wound and the flies
Many times
I closed the door behind me
And slept, but did not dream,
Did not ask questions
Nor searched for an answer

Because I am . . .
Don't worry
The wolves will return

The wolves will return
And for the second time
And the third
And the fourth
Man will be born behind the door
And we . . .
Don't worry . . .
We will remain in the small feast present in absence

(TRANSLATED BY ABDULLAH AL-UDHARI)

RASHID HUSAIN

Lessons in Parsing

I—The First Lesson

He was in his sixties . . .
                    Still teaching;
Once he came into the class and said:
                    "Parse: 'The teacher came.' "
We thought he was joking
So we laughed and answered:
                    " 'came'   : verb
                      'teacher' : . . ."

                    Suddenly we understood . . . in a flash
                    We fell silent, and heard him muttering:
                    " 'came'   : verb
                      'teacher' :
                                    He didn't come!
                                    The police brought him . . .
                                              But he will teach."

II—The Second Lesson

We grew up together until he was nearly seventy but
Still teaching;
For example: The teacher said:
" 'My master dreams of the revolution but won't fight'
A sentence complete in itself—a thousand times.
And he who parses that will become a fighter!"
We were silent. We didn't say a word but
Our silence in itself was fighting
Our silence was . . . but:

In the class there was a boy who nourished the earth with his
hands
Its olives ran over his mouth
His name was Adnan . . . a peasant with no land but
He was not silent . . . no, he was every inch a fighter.

That day I saw him disregarding the rules of grammar
And teaching:

" 'My master'	: is not a subject
'dreams'	: is not a verb
'of'	: governed by a preposition
'revolution'	: is not governed by a preposition
'but won't fight'	: that is correct."

III—The Lesson Before The Last

A day later the teacher came into the class
As cheerful and as lively as the zest of an orange,
Although in his seventies, he was a child . . . he greeted
us and said:
" 'They put Adnan in prison.'
Parse that, girls
Parse that, boys."
We were overjoyed . . . we wept . . . and we cried out:
" 'Adnan   : subject
'prison'   : object."
Suddenly we were women
Suddenly we were men.

(TRANSLATED BY ABDULLAH AL-UDHARI)

JABRA IBRAHIM JABRA

In the Deserts of Exile

Spring after spring,
In the deserts of exile,
What are we doing with our love,
When our eyes are full of frost and dust?

Our Palestine, green land of ours;
Its flowers as if embroidered of women's gowns;
March adorns its hills
With the jewel-like peony and narcissus;
April bursts open in its plains
With flowers and bride-like blossoms;
May is our rustic song
Which we sing at noon,
In the blue shadows,
Among the olive-trees of our valleys,
And in the ripeness of the fields
We wait for the promise of July
And the joyous dance amidst the harvest.

O land of ours where our childhood passed
Like dreams in the shade of the orange-grove
Among the almond-trees in the valleys—
Remember us now wandering
Among the thorns of the desert,
Wandering in the rocky mountains;
Remember us now
In the tumult of cities beyond deserts and seas;
Remember us
With our eyes full of dust
That never clears in our ceaseless wandering.
They crushed the flowers on the hills around us,

Destroyed the houses over our heads,
Scattered our torn remains,
Then unfolded the desert before us,
With valleys writhing in hunger
And blue shadows shattered into red thorns
Bent over corpses left as prey for falcon and crow.

Is it from your hills that the angels sang to the shepherds
Of peace on earth and goodwill among men?
Only death laughed when it saw
Among the entrails of beasts
The ribs of men,
And through the guffaw of bullets
It went dancing a joyous dance
On the heads of weeping women.

Our land is an emerald,
But in the deserts of exile,
Spring after spring,
Only the dust hisses in our face.
What then, what are we doing with our love?
When our eyes and our mouths are full of frost and
    dust?

(TRANSLATED BY MOUNA A. KHOURI AND HAMID ALGAR)

NIZAR QABBANI

Comments on the Notebook of Decadence

Friends:
I deplore our old language, our old books,
our speech, punctured like battered shoes,
our words of profanity, of slander, of insult;
I deplore
the demise of intellect which has brought about defeat.

Bitter to our mouth is poetry;
bitter to our eyes is plaited hair,
the veils, the thighs, the night;
bitter to us are the things we see.

Oh, my grieved Homeland,
you have changed me overnight
from a poet of love
to one who writes with blood.

Since our feelings surpass our words,
our poetry must shame us.

No wonder we lose the war,
for we enter it
with the Oriental's oratory,
with the display of buzzing heroism;
we enter it
with the logic of the drum and the lute.

Our tragedy is no secret,
for clamor, not action, is our gift,
the sword is mightier than our word.
Our tragedy has come to this:
we wear the facade of civilization
with antique disposition.

The flute and the lute
do not secure victory;
our pompous speechifying
has cost us 50,000 new tents.

Blame not circumstances, no,
blame not heaven if it forsakes you;
for God, who grants victory to whomsoever He wishes,
is no smith forging spears for you.
It pains me to hear the news in the morning,
to hear the dogs bark.
The Israelis conquer not our borders,
but thrive on our shortcomings.
5000 years we have lived in dark vaults—
our beards unshaven, our currency unknown,
our eyes festering nests of flies.
Friends:
Break the doors, purify the thoughts, cleanse the gar-
    ments.

Friends:
Read a book, write a book,
plant letters, pomegranates, grapes,
sail to the land of snow and fog;
for you are unknown without your dark vaults,
you are a species of wolves.

We are stones, we are senseless things,
our souls are barren, destitute.
Chess, sleep, shrine are such stuff as our life is made on.
Are we, then, the best of all people?

Our oil which floods the desert
could have been a burning spear.
But—to the embarrassment of the Nobles of Qureish[1]
and those of Nizar and Awse[2]—
we spill it at the maidens' feet.

We run in the streets with ropes under arms,
climbing without discernment,
breaking the glass and the locks,
praising like frogs, or cursing like frogs.
We make heroes of our dwarfs
and scoundrels of our nobles.
Nay, we sit in the Mosque indolently,
composing verses, reciting proverbs—
supplicating God for victory over the enemy.

If I could with impunity meet the Sultan,
I would say to him, Sire:
your fierce dogs have torn my suit,
your spies—their eyes, noses, feet—haunt me,
weaving their snares of doom around me.
They interrogate my wife
and write down my friends' names.
Sire: I have come within your invincible walls
to express my grief and my affliction;
but your henchmen beat me with their shoes
and forced me, unwilling, to eat my shoes.
Sire, and my Master:
twice you have lost the war,
because half of our people's minds are suppressed

---

[1] Qureish is the tribe from which the prophet Mohammad came.
[2] Nizar and Awse are famous Arab tribes.

and live in close confinement with ants and rats;
indeed, Sire, Can a people survive without expression?

If—free from the henchmen's cruelty—
I could meet the Sultan,
I would say to him, Sire:
twice you have lost the war
because you are ignorant of human rights

Had we not buried the Unity in the sand,[3]
had we not torn its tender body with the spear,
had we kept it secure in our hearts,
our bodies would not have been prey to wild dogs.

We want a new generation
to plough ahead into the horizon,
to search the roots of history
and penetrate the annals of thought.
We want a generation with new features,
unforgiving, unwilling to overlook mistakes,
unbending, unaccustomed to dissembling.
We want a lofty generation—with imposing height.

Oh children—from the Ocean to the Gulf,[4]
you are the blossom of hope,
the new generation which shall break the chains,
destroy the opium of our people,
and rid us of our sluggishness.
Oh children,
you are innocent and pure,
clean-handed as the dew or snow.
Do not read the history of this generation,
for we are the vanquished;
we are insignificant as the watermelon rind,
decayed like old shoes.
Do not read our news;
do not follow in our footsteps;
do not accept our thoughts.
We are the generation of sickness, of consumption,
of deceit, of acrobatics.
Oh children,

[3] The reference here is to the political Unity concluded between Syria and Egypt in 1958; it lasted three years.
[4] The circumference of the Arab World.

you are the spring rain, the blossom of hope,
the seed of fertility in our sterile life.
You are the generation which shall conquer defeat.

(TRANSLATED BY CHRISTOPHER NOURYEH)

Bread, Hashish, and Moon . . .

When the moon is born in the East. . .
The white roofs doze,
Under stacks of flowers. . .
People leave their shops and walk in groups,
To meet the moon. . .
Carrying bread, and record-players to mountain tops,
And narcotic utensils
And they sell and buy fancies,
And images. . .
And they die when the moon lives,
What does a bright disc do
To my country?
The country of prophets. . .
The country of simple people,
Tobacco chewers and dope peddlers.
What is the moon doing to us
That we lose our pride
And live to importune heaven?
What does heaven have
For the lazy and weak. . .
Who turn into dead men when the moon lives,
And shake the saints' graves,
That they might provide them with rice and children,
And they spread out beautiful embroidered carpets
Enjoying an opium we call fate
And divine decree?
In my country . . . in the country of simple people,
What feebleness and laxity
Seize us when light pours
Then carpets, and thousands of baskets
And tea-cups and children fill the hills. . .
In my country,

Where the innocent weep
And live on light they do not see
In my country,
Where people live without eyes
Where the innocent weep
And pray
And fornicate
And live on fatalism
Since eternity they lived on fatalism
Calling to the crescent:
"O, crescent!
O, spring which rains diamonds,
And Hashish and slumber!
O, suspended marble god
You unbelievable thing
May you live for the East, for us
A cluster of diamond!
For the millions whose senses are numbed."

On nights in the East when
The moon is full
The East strips off all dignity,
And strife. . .
The millions who run without shoes,
And believe in four wives
And the day of resurrection,
The millions who do not find bread
Save in fancy. . .
Living, at night, in houses
Of coughs
Never knowing medicine!
Bodies dying under the moonlight,
In my country. . .
While the stupid weep
Dying of tears
Whenever the moon's face rises over them.
They weep more
Whenever a soft lute excites them . . . and "Layali"[1]
That death we call in the East
"Layalis" . . . and songs.
In my country
In the country of the simple people!

[1] "O, Night": a long-drawn and endlessly repeated word in Arab popular songs.

While we regurgitate long tawashih[2]
This disease which ravishes the East:
The long tawashih. . .
Our East that regurgitates its history
Lazy dreams
And past myths
Our East, that seeks all heroism:
In Abu-Zayd al-Hilali[3]

(TRANSLATED BY ZVI GABAY)

I Am the Train of Sadness

I travel on thousands of trains
I saddle my despair
I mount the clouds of my cigarette
In my suitcase
I carry the addresses of my lovers
Who were my lovers of yesterday?

The train's travelling
Faster . . . faster
Chewing on its way
The flesh of distances
Ravaging the fields on its way
Gulping the trees on its way
Licking the feet of the lakes

The inspector asks for my ticket
And my destination
Is there a destination?
No hotel on the earth knows who I am
Nor does it know the addresses of my lovers

I am the train of sadness
I have no platform
To stop at . . . In all my journeys
My platforms slip away
My stations
Slip away from me

[2] Postclassical form of Arab poetry, arranged in stanzas.
[3] A legendary figure of fantasy and supernatural heroic feats.

A Personal Letter to the Month of June

Month of June, explode in our antique skulls
Sweep away thousands of synonyms
Sweep away maxims and ancient wisdom
Rip up our old dirty linen
Slash the skin of our ugly faces,
Change, turn extremist and rebel against conventions,
Shoot the past
Be the gun and the crime;
After the hanging of God on the gate of the city
Prayers lost their value
Belief and unbelief lost their value.

(TRANSLATED BY ABDULLAH AL-UDHARI)

SALAH ABD AL-SABUR

The Tartars Have Struck

The Tartars have struck
Casting destruction on our ancient city
Our divisions returned torn . . . in the scorching heat of
the day
The black banner, the wounded, the caravan of death
And the hollow drum, the humble march, looking
straight ahead,
The hands of a soldier beating on the wood
The tune of starvation.
The trumpet, out of breath,
The air stifled with dust.
There is a chariot broken, moving on the road,

Its horses looking defeated.
The soldiers marching with their arms hanging down
    close to their feet,
Their shirts creased and stained with spattered blood,
The nose running, defeated
The eye shedding tears of defeat
The ear stung by dust.

Mothers took refuge in the dark hill from the terror of
    fire
Or the horror of debris
Or the Tartars' loathsome gaze into their faces
Or their hands stretching towards the flesh with loath-
    some greed.
Destruction and defeat have crawled upon us
The Tartars have struck, O my city!

In the outlying prisoners' camp
The night, the barbed wire and the armed guard,
The senseless dark, the wounded and the smell of pus,
And the laughter of the drunken Tartar soldiers
Gloating over their victory
And the end of their happy journey—
I embraced my defeat and dug my feet in the sand.
I remembered our long happy evenings, mother,
And shed many tears at a memory as soft as the breeze
And the clouds of old familiar words.

I wonder if on that hill among those who have fled
When night summons terror for children beneath their
    eyelids
Hunger and flimsy clothes
Disaster and demons, and darkness lurking in dungeons
I wonder if you cried, mother, because our village lay in
    ruins
And our loved days have gone never to return?
But we shall not die
For I can hear a friend from our time-honoured alley,
The coughing of some one defeated, who cannot walk,
And lips murmuring threateningly from a distance.
I and all my comrades when the daylight faded
Swore that in the forenoon we would shout with hatred
    and spill the blood of the Tartars.

Mother, tell the children:
At the break of day we shall peer round our dark houses
And rebuild what the Tartars have destroyed.

People in My Country

People in my country are predatory like hawks,
Their singing is like the winter wind blowing through the
　　trees,
Their laughter like the hissing of wood consuming fire.
When they walk their feet wish to sink into the earth,
They murder and steal, they belch when they drink
And yet they are human
When they have a handful of money they are good
And they believe in Fate.

At the gate of my village uncle Mustafa sits
—He adores Mustafa, the chosen prophet,—
Whiling away an hour between sunset and night
Around him the men are sitting silently
Listening to him telling them a tale, the fruit of life's ex-
　　perience,
A tale that filled them with pain,
And made them sob and bend their heads down, gazing
　　into the stillness,
Into the deep waves of terror, void and stillness,
'What is the end of man's toil? What is the end of life?
O Lord!
The sun is Thy forehead, the moon is Thy forehead
And these firm mountains are Thy powerful throne.
Thy decree is unalterable, O Lord!'
Mr. X had erected high buildings, built castles and as-
　　cended his throne.
He owned forty rooms filled with glittering gold
And on a night with faint echoes, there came to him the
　　Angel of Death
Holding a little book, a list at the head of which was the
　　name of that man.
The Messenger of Death pointed his stick
—with the secret of the words: 'be' and 'was'—

And into the depths of Hell the man's soul was sent rolling down
(How inscrutable and ruthless thou art, O Lord)

Yesterday I revisited my village . . . Uncle Mustafa had
 died,
And his head had been laid in the dust.
He never owned castles (his hut had been built with un-
 burned brick)
Behind his old coffin there walked
Those who, like him, possessed only one old linen gown.
They mentioned neither God nor the Angel of Death,
 nor the mysterious words
For it was a year of hunger.
At the mouth of the grave stood my friend Khalil,
The grandson of uncle Mustafa,
Lifting his muscular arm to the sky
And a look of scorn surged in his eyes
For it was a year of hunger.

(TRANSLATED BY M. M. BADAWI)

TEWFIQ SAYIGH

The Sermon on the Mount

I too have followed Him,
Feeding His strength with my weakness
And helping Him realize His very Being.

On the tongue-tied hill—
Long awaited by two limp arms
Of our drowsing Lake
(Like a tear, yearned for by the cheek,
While yet it hangs within an eye)—

I have eaten with the eaters,
Seeing them hail Him, God-wise, when sated,
And tumbling in his track.
Alone I've lingered on the hill,
Watching Him listening to the waters that, in silence,
    proclaimed fellowship;
His chosen ones around him, chirping.
Alone I've lingered, awaiting His return.

I knew He would return:
For the stale loaves and the fish crumbs
(Even had a mother's hands wrapped them,
And they been salted with a mother's blessing)
Left me griped for hunger;
And the waters, turned once to wine,
Were water again upon my lips;
And the mud with which He cleansed the eyes of Barti-
    maeus
Turned mine disgusted while refreshed by it;
The cry He brought the Nain lad to life with
Left my mother in blackness.
    On the hill of fecundity,
Amid the hyacinths that rise like candles,
Their cheeks acolour when ogled
With languid eyes
By fish who do not sleep,
I'm griped for hunger.
    I too have been tried,
In more than one land, tried.
But He returned.

From waters spring the gods of love.
He returned, and opened His mouth
(Some said He sang,
And some that it was prayer);
Did any hear Him but me? I thought
He spoke to me alone.
He called me not, but I came forth;
No loaves He broke, no wine-jars touched,
But the baskets were filled anew,
And I saw those summoned, all unaware, savouring
    again awareness.
He did not spit upon the earth renewed,

But lo! the seven citadels were seventy—
   When He opened His mouth.
Upon the hill I lie;
And when the sun wheels over it,
And its heat increases,
Though the brightness does not increase—
I rush to meet the wave
That comes to me, oarless.
   At home, to home I make my pilgrimage.

I know He will return,
And I await His returning
(Our burying-ground is now upon the hill).
To it He will return, leaving the crowds behind,
To seek where a head may be pillowed.
Maybe He will open His mouth,
And I hear "Blessed . . ."

(TRANSLATED BY G. M. WICKENS)

BADR SHAKIR AL-SAYYAB

For I Am a Stranger

For I am a stranger
Beloved Iraq
Far distant, and I here in my longing
For it, for her . . . I cry out: Iraq
And from my cry a lament returns

An echo bursts forth
I feel I have crossed the expanse
To a world of decay that responds not
To my cry

If I shake the branches
Only decay will drop from them
Stones
Stones—no fruit
Even the springs
Are stones, even the fresh breeze
Stones moistened with blood
My cry a stone, my mouth a rock
My legs a wind straying in the wastes

Burning

And even when I smelt your body of stone in my fire
And wrest the ice from your hands, between our eyes
Persist whole wastes of snow that devour the night-traveller
As if you saw me through mist and moonlight
As if we had never met in hope and longing
Hope for love is a meeting . . . where then did we meet?
Your naked body is torn open
Your breasts, beneath the roof of night, are torn by my nails
My ardor has torn apart all but the veils
Which hide within you what I desire
As if the blood I drink from you were salt
Whole draughts of it still not my thirst
Where is your passion? Where is your unbared heart?
I bolt on you the gate of night, then embrace the gate
Conceal within it my shadow, memories and secrets
Then search for you within my fire
And find you not, find not your ashes in the burning flame
I will cast myself into the flame, if it burns or not
Kill me, that I may feel you
   Kill the stone
With a shedding of blood, with a spark of fire
. . . . or burn then without fire

(TRANSLATED BY MOUNA A. KHOURI AND
HAMID ALGAR)

DRAMA

The Song of the Bullet

by Amin Bakir

Characters

AN ISRAELI SOLDIER
CORPORAL YAKOV
YUSEF (*known as the entertainment boy*)
THE RABBI, *Shadi the Palestinian in disguise*
1ST MAN
2ND MAN
3RD MAN
4TH MAN
THE OLD MAN, *a Palestinian*

TIME: Evening

A *frontier area in the Gaza Sector, the outskirts of the village of Ain Galut. At the front of stage right is a pavement about a foot high. At the front of stage left is a nice clean kiosk, with some climbing plants and wild flowers on its walls. This is an occupied area, and a signpost in Arabic and Hebrew says "Inspection Point." There is a lamp post at the front stage right. A modern telephone can be seen inside the kiosk. In the background, old and simple houses and some refugee tents.*

At curtain rise, regular drumbeats (tympani and tremolo), that change to a different tempo, rapid staccato beat, while a searchlight in a watch-tower sweeps the area from time to time. The light now moves slowly from the depths of the stage out over the audience, while the drums beat ominously. There is a sound of wind, and a blue spot lights an area in front of the kiosk. Yakov, the sentry, is on duty at the post. He has a modern automatic weapon, and he surveys the area round the kiosk carefully for a few moments, then goes in-

*side and disappears. A roll of drums heralds the entry of a
soldier from stage left, accompanied by a workman carrying
a pail of paste with a brush in it and a roll of paper under his
arm. It is a poster with the picture of a wanted man, wanted
by the Israelis as being dangerous to their security. The soldier
indicates to the workman to paste up the poster where the
audience can see it well. The worker does so.*

SOLDIER: Stick up the rest of the posters where I told you
. . . and hurry up. *(He comes up to the kiosk and looks
inside it.)* Hello there.

YAKOV: Shalom.

SOLDIER: Good evening. Is everything all right?

YAKOV: So-so. *(Pointing at the poster.)* What's that?

SOLDIER: Oh, a newcomer.

YAKOV: You mean a new rebel?

SOLDIER: This is really lousy weather. *(Blows on his hands.)*

YAKOV *(Yawns and looks at his watch)*: I've still got three
hours to go before I can go off duty.

SOLDIER: Madame Pompadour . . . here, have some . . . it's
a good drink and it'll warm you up quicker than you
think. Cheers. *(He takes a couple of steps away.)*

YAKOV: Isn't it difficult to find a bottle of this stuff
nowadays? *(The soldier stops.)*

SOLDIER: I just finished a quarter of a bottle of Dewars a few
minutes ago, that's why I feel so energetic. If only it
wasn't for him *(He points at the poster)*, I'd have been
sleeping peacefully in my bed right now.

YAKOV: Why's he so important?

SOLDIER: We had an urgent radio call. He's dangerous to security. He's an explosives and demolition expert, and
helped with a lot of killings. That's why he's wanted
. . . there's a reward of two thousand dollars for his
capture. And don't forget what it says there in red Hebrew: Duty and Survival . . . For our New State.

YAKOV: From the country of death.

SOLDIER *(Turns)*: What was that? *(Looks sharply at Yakov.)* What did you say?

YAKOV: Nothing . . .

SOLDIER: I'd prefer to have a shot of brandy to going hunting for him, that's what I think. They've lots of these
sabotaging rebels around. Now, I'm an Oriental Jew like
you, and you know as well as I do that the Western

Jews get all the high positions and the good jobs, while
we . . . well, you can see what we are. We get to look
for the saboteurs, and kill or get killed.

YOKOV: You're right.

SOLDIER: Maybe someone else will have the honour of
catching him and getting the reward. Oh, it's so cold, excuse me, I've got to leave you and supervise the posters
being put up in the other places. Good luck. (*He waves
and exits at stage left.*)

YAKOV: Good luck, and goodbye. (*The searchlight sweeps
the area from right to left, and sweeps over the audience. Yakov walks slowly round the area. The muzzle of
his weapon can be seen protruding through the front of
his coat. He adjusts his helmet, looks over the area and
goes back into the kiosk. As he reaches the edge of the
pavement, the sound of a bicycle bell is heard approaching, and the entertainment boy comes onstage
from stage right. He has a number of thermos flasks of
tea and coffee on his bike, and he also has cigarettes and
newspapers. Yakov looks in the direction of the entry of
Yusef. An explosion is heard, the searchlight sweeps the
area.*)

YAKOV: Another explosion. (*Yusef looks fearfully in the
direction of the explosion.*) Don't be afraid.

YUSEF: I'm not afraid, just sad. Good evening.

YAKOV: There's a lot in your bag, boy. What's the news in
the paper tonight?

YUSEF: Mostly about our friend there disguised as a rabbi.
(*He points at the poster.*) That fellow there in the picture.

YAKOV: Forget it. What do you have besides newspapers?

YUSEF: Tea . . . coffee . . . cigarettes . . . here's a flask of
nice strong tea.

YAKOV: I don't want a hot drink.

YUSEF: You must be joking. Surely you don't want a cold
drink on a night like this?

YAKOV (*Laughs*): As a matter of fact, I do want a cold
drink, but one that'll warm me up.

YUSEF (*Laughs*): You funny Oriental.

YAKOV: Do you have anything like that?

YUSEF: Liquor? No, I just drink it, I don't carry it. (*They
both laugh.*) Here, friend, take this, it's the best thing
for you.

YAKOV: What is it?

YUSEF: Strong sweet tea, the kind you like and always ask for. Would you like a paper?

YAKOV: No, I don't think so . . . but why not . . . something to keep me entertained . . . to stop me yawning. *(Yusef hands him a paper.)*

YUSEF: Cigarettes?

YAKOV: Something other than Kents?

YUSEF: No, just Kents. How about an orange?

YAKOV: No thanks.

YUSEF *(Turns and sees the picture of the wanted man)*: They've got his picture here too. This is his last hurdle. If he makes it through here he's a free man.

YAKOV *(Snaps his fingers)*: Oh yes, give me a cheese sandwich.

YUSEF *(Hands it to him)*: Maybe you'll get the reward if you catch him here.

YAKOV: And then again, he may not even come this way at all. They know the settlement better than we do.

YUSEF: Good looking, isn't he? Looks Jewish, don't you think?

YAKOV *(Eating his sandwich and sipping the tea)*: I had a friend who looked very much like him. *(He stops eating.)* We come here to face death thousands of times every night, and others get all the easy jobs. But we get tossed out here to these inspection posts.

YUSEF: Eat and don't worry yourself about it. Have you heard the latest joke?

YAKOV *(Sound of explosion, Yakov starts)*: Oh . . . another explosion.

The searchlight sweeps the area, there is a sound of running, which slows down to a walk. Sound of machine gun fire. The steps quicken again. Shadi comes on stage. He is a member of the Palestinian resistance, and is disguised as a rabbi. He shows signs of fatigue. He stops, panting, by the lamp post, and is spotted by Yakov, who hurries over to him, followed by Yusef. Shadi tries to look natural.

YUSEF: Good evening.

SHADI *(The drums roll loudly and he appears hesitant)*: Sh . . . Shalom.

YAKOV *(Slows down)*: Shalom. What's going on over there?

SHADI: It seems the saboteurs are trying to get away from a

police force that's pursuing them. You'd better keep your eyes and ears open.

YAKOV *(Caressing his weapon)*: They haven't got a hope.

YUSEF: Has anything happened to you, rabbi? *(Yakov peers at Shadi's face.)*

SHADI *(Trying to avoid Yakov's gaze by turning away)*: No . . . no . . . listen!

YAKOV: What's your destination, rabbi?

SHADI: I'm going to the kibbutz, then I'm going to the synagogue at Bal Hanis.

YUSEF: Do you want anything else, Yakov?

YAKOV: No thanks.

SHADI *(Aside, when he hears the name)*: Yakov . . . it's him . . . no, how could it be? He seemed to be trying to remember something as he looked at me.

YUSEF: Do you want anything, rabbi?

SHADI: A newspaper. *(Looks at the poster on the kiosk.)* No . . . I don't want one . . . I can already see what's in it.

YUSEF: True . . . nothing new. I'm here risking my life for another new risk, and there's a severe shortage of good news these days, isn't that so, rabbi?

SHADI *(Coming back from his thoughts)*: Huh? What? Oh yes . . . that's right. *(Yakov walks around Shadi, scrutinizing him.)*

YUSEF: I've got to go to the kibbutz to deliver some papers. I've got some cigarettes too, rabbi, are you sure there's nothing you want?

SHADI: No, thank you, my son.

YUSEF: Well, goodbye. *(He waves and wheels away his bicycle and exits stage right.)*

YAKOV: Where did you say you were going?

SHADI: To the temple.

YAKOV: Oh yes, that's right . . . I forgot . . . the synagogue.

SHADI *(Looks in the direction of Yusef's exit)*: Nice young man.

YAKOV: Yes, he is. We call him the number one entertainment boy. He can sing and dance and write poems. Have you never heard of him?

SHADI: No, son, I never had that opportunity. You know, we have other things to keep us busy.

YAKOV: Is that so? *(He moves away from him, stroking his weapon.)*

SHADI *(Comes slowly towards him)*: We're only interested in

the religious matters. All we have to do in the outside
world is a little military duty as regards praying for the
dead.

YAKOV: Oh! The dead.

SHADI: I swear by the Sabbath I haven't even seen the streets
of the kibbutz for three weeks. Would you believe it?

YAKOV: Oh yes, I believe you, rabbi.

SHADI: It appears to me you're an Oriental. Could I be mistaken?

YAKOV: How do you know? Does it show on me?

SHADI: I can tell by the warmth of your voice.

YAKOV: Amazing! Are you an expert on voices, rabbi?

SHADI: We men of religion know about such things, Yakov.

YAKOV: And how do you know my name?

SHADI: That was not difficult. The entertainment boy called
you by your name.

YAKOV: Oh, I'd forgotten that. And apart from the voice,
what does an Oriental look like, in your opinion?

SHADI: First of all, permit me to call you by your name . . .
(Sound of explosion.)

YAKOV: But of course. *(He looks all around him, covering
the whole area.)* But . . . *(he looks closely at Shadi
again)* do you own a farm, rabbi?

SHADI: A farm? No.

YAKOV: It seems to me I've seen you somewhere before.
You've a determined face—a military face.

SHADI: People often imagine things that really have no basis.
(A sharp look from Yakov.) Why didn't you answer my
question? I asked you if I could call you by your first
name.

YAKOV: And I said you could. But honestly, rabbi, I feel very
afraid. A mixture of fear and death . . . and . . .

SHADI: I'm sorry, I didn't hear you. Age, my son. What were
you saying?

YAKOV: Oh . . . nothing much.

SHADI: I'm a Palestinian, a Jewish Palestinian like you. You
can tell me what's troubling you, and I'll help you if it's
in my power to do so.

YAKOV: Forgive me, but I keep thinking I've seen you before,
or at least that you look like someone else very much
. . . someone who was my childhood friend. We went to
the same school, and played in the same house. Forgive
me, it's just my imagination.

SHADI: You're very intelligent. Tell me, did you ever live in Cairo?

YAKOV: Of course.

SHADI: In Khan Abu Takia?

YAKOV *(Happily)*: Oh yes indeed.

SHADI: And your father was a jeweller working for . . . ?

YAKOV: Lito Murad!

SHADI: And during vacations you used to come to visit your relatives in Haifa?

YAKOV: Precisely, rabbi, precisely. *(Shadi embraces him.)* How did you know all this?

SHADI: Because I know you, and you know me.

YAKOV: But I've never known a rabbi in all my life.

SHADI: Ah . . . memories, memories . . . but then there's also fear . . .

YAKOV: Fear . . . fear of what?

SHADI: That I'm a rabbi . . . I travel around the occupied land in the clear evenings . . . it's nice to talk of memories.

YAKOV: I don't understand.

SHADI: Every evening I'm carried away for hours on the wings of rosy dreams. I dream that I shall return . . . I dream.

YAKOV: You dream?

SHADI: And I imagine. I imagine that I'm still . . . I dream, dream that I'm before the door of my home . . . and here, over here is its princess, the princess of my inspiration . . . and over there is the window of the house which gathered us together, you and I, when we were children. And in the window there are blue curtains, embroidered by a loving artist. You may recall him, Leisha the Crosseyed? Ah, he was an artist. Now he's with the New York Times.

YAKOV: What do you mean by the princess of your inspiration?

SHADI: The orange tree which we planted together.

YAKOV: Who . . . who planted it together?

SHADI: You and I . . . do you remember?

YAKOV: Take off your beard, you old sinner. *(Laughs.)*

SHADI *(Takes off his headgear and laughs)*: I risk a great deal, and I always laugh at danger, and for the sake of your old friendship and our old love I'll solve the mystery for you, the mystery that has puzzled you and

frightened you. *(He removes his beard.)* Now do you
know me? You sucked at my mother's breast.

YAKOV *(Shouts with joy)*: Shadi! Impossible . . . it's you,
Shadi! *(He rushes at him and they embrace, dancing in
a full circle.)* How are you, my brother?

SHADI *(They let go of one another)*: As you can see, I'm a
rabbi. *(They laugh.)*

YAKOV: I can't believe it! Shadi himself in the flesh! But why
are you dressed up as a rabbi?

SHADI *(Points at the poster)*: Because that's me.

YAKOV *(Laughs, then suddenly his expression changes and he
leaps back, bringing up his weapon and aiming it at
Shadi)*: Shadi, watch out! I'm dead serious. Raise your
hands above your head. *(He walks backwards to the kiosk, picks up the telephone.)* Hello, hello, give me head-
quarters. Hello . . . send a car right away . . . yes, the
last post . . . he almost got away, a guerilla we're looking for. *(Replaces the receiver.)*

SHADI: What? What are you doing? Why did you do that,
Yakov? My . . . *(bitterly)* brother.

YAKOV: Silence, keep your hands up. I'm sorry, but our orders are very strict, and the reward is generous . . . and
it's my duty. *(Shadi comes slowly towards him.)* Stop
where you are, Shadi . . . and forget all that about
mother.

SHADI *(Laughs and continues to advance slowly)*: I don't believe that you're serious. Can one be betrayed by his
dearest friend? Say that what you're doing now is simply
a routine job. *(He advances, smiling.)* You'll straighten
things out afterwards, won't you?

YAKOV *(His eyes spit evil as his finger tightens on the trigger)*: Don't you believe it. Be careful, Shadi, my trigger
finger's ready. Stop where you are and surrender!

SHADI: Surrender! Oh . . . what a word!

YAKOV: Raise your hands high, Arab!

SHADI: Surrender? Raise your hands high, Arab? I must have
made a mistake. You cannot be Yakov. What happened
to those childhood dreams and memories? To hear you
now telling me to surrender, telling me to raise my
hands, Arab, just as they used to say. *(Yakov hurries
back to the telephone and picks it up.)* Now, what
more?

YAKOV *(Sharply)*: You'll see! *(Into the phone.)* An order to all

police kiosks . . . an order to all the villagers . . . Every
Arab is to come out of his house or tent with his hands
high, immediately! *(Replaces receiver. A loudspeaker is
heard immediately.)*

VOICE ONE *(From offstage)*: Order to all the villagers. If you
have any guerrillas, give them up. Come out of your
houses and tents with your hands high. We're going to
open fire in three minutes.

VOICE TWO *(Offstage)*: Police notice. Police notice. Every
Arab and every armed guerrilla in hiding is to come out
right away with his hands above his head.

SHADI: You really aren't joking, Yakov.

YAKOV: I'm in deadly earnest. Keep your hands above your
head. Was it you who blew up the patrol car?

SHADI: I? *(Tries to explain his point of view.)*

YAKOV: Saboteur! Keep your hands above your head, and
quick march over to the lamp post. Move it! *(Picks up
the phone again.)* Hello, what's keeping you? He's a
dangerous guerrilla. What? Road blocked? Now what?
How many soldiers were in it? Fifteen? Please, not longer
than ten minutes.

SHADI: Again, so you really mean it.

YAKOV: I definitely do. A truck with fifteen soldiers in it has
just been blown up. It was blown up by one of you.

SHADI: One of us?

YAKOV: Yes, one of you. Don't think for a moment that
we're friends. I work for Israel. I have no emotions.

SHADI: Well, in that case, God help me. Yakov, I give you
permission to shoot me. Go ahead. Shoot me.

YAKOV: A different tune . . . the tune of fear.

SHADI: No, not of fear, just the truth. I would prefer to die
at the hands of my childhood friend.

YAKOV: And I'd prefer to hand you in alive and get the reward.

SHADI: Training overcomes nature. The Israeli machine really
knows how to mould its men. What are you waiting for,
Yakov? I thought you'd still be honest and innocent.
You always believed in fair play. But what are you now?
I'll tell you, you're a Zionist soldier. Come on, what are
you waiting for, you Nazi murderer of your own people?
Squeeze the trigger. Let your bullets tear apart the chest
you used to hug when you came to the village from

Egypt for your vacations. The chest that holds a heart
that loved you up till now.

YAKOV: More tears?

SHADI: I don't hope to change the situation by talking. We're
enemies. I know that as well as you do. All we have to
do is wait for ten minutes for the police car.

YAKOV: Are you afraid?

SHADI: I want you to know I'm not alone.

YAKOV *(Starts)*: What do you mean? Are there others? Here?

SHADI: Don't worry, they'll show up in good time. I just want
to give you a history lesson, in case you're not aware I
have the right to kill, destroy, and blow up. I've been
driven from my home, and your people are living in it
now.

YAKOV: The fable of the return. You declared war against
our Jewish state twenty-five years ago. It's up to us to
see the State of Israel survives.

SHADI: This won't happen.

YAKOV: Why not?

SHADI: Because of your slogan, "Pay a dollar and kill an
Arab."

YAKOV: You have a similar one, "Sow a million mines in their
path." And who wants to drive us all into the sea, with
our hopes and dreams? You've declared you'll do this
. . . on every possible occasion. You Arabs aren't logical.

SHADI: You know nothing of the Arabs' point of view, so
don't talk of it so stupidly!

YAKOV: I . . . ?

SHADI: It's ironical and laughable that you consider the basic
issues to be illogical.

YAKOV: Laughable?

SHADI: Yes, laughable! There's such a thing as international
law, and you claim there's a state of truce. But the truth
is we Arabs live in an uncertain and incomprehensible
situation . . . neither war nor peace . . . neither here
nor there. What now, Yakov?

YAKOV *(To himself, but still aiming the weapon)*: The police
are late. I hope this devil isn't starting something. I'm
afraid he's planted a time bomb somewhere.

SHADI *(Playfully, as if to scare Yakov)*: Stand where you
are! *(He points his hand at him, simulating a revolver.)*

YAKOV: That's what I was afraid of! *(He fires several rounds,*

but misses, as Shadi throws himself on the ground.)
What's that. . . . you don't have a gun?

SHADI: How could I? How could I pull a gun on my friend?
But I'm angry with you. What do you mean by that?
(He points at Yakov's weapon and imitates the sound of firing.)

YAKOV: I'm sorry . . . but it's war.

SHADI: That's the complication.

YAKOV *(Sorry)*: What?

SHADI *(Aside)*: The complicated situation . . . no peace, no
war. Well, now I know you're in earnest and that you
meant to kill me. What's happened to the love you had
in your heart?

YAKOV *(Sarcastically)*: Love?

SHADI: Yes, Yakov, love.

YAKOV: Don't get me into useless talk. We're enemies. I'm
serious, Shadi.

SHADI: That's to say if I move away from here now?

YAKOV: You'll move over my dead body.

SHADI: Would you get a reward for my body? What's my
dead body worth, Yakov? Ah, the evils of war!

YAKOV *(To himself)*: I wonder what his mother's name was?
What was she like? I remember her as tall and fair. My
older sister told me she breast-fed me when our own
mother died giving birth to my little brother Farag. She
died and he lived, and his mother looked after me and
Farag after my sister got married.

SHADI: I said, ah, the hell of war!

YAKOV *(Snaps out of his reverie)*: What, you're afraid?

SHADI: No . . . just sad.

YAKOV: What sort of sadness?

SHADI: The same as Hamlet. "To be or not to be, that is the
question." The unknown land, where none have set foot
. . . unexplored. I, the Palestinian Hamlet say: slavery
won't disappear with a miracle. I face death every moment so as not to fall into fear and submission.

YAKOV: How's your mother? Is she all right?

SHADI: She's dead. She was shot to death.

YAKOV *(Angrily)*: That's war!

SHADI: Oppression won't be wiped out from our world by a
miracle. Some Zionists think we got rid of the United
Nations peace-keeping setup when it suited us. You all
believe this.

YAKOV: That's true.

SHADI: No, it isn't. Now look, my childhood friend, I'm in a jam. But if I could escape, you could plant another tree in a new land. For a new person being born now in the new Palestine.

YAKOV: Damn you, the new Palestine and the old Palestine! Who do you think you are? Jesus Christ? Listen, I'll turn you in. But I guarantee you'll live, if you do what I tell you.

SHADI: And what's that?

YAKOV: I'll get the reward, and you'll be jailed. Then I'll intervene, and you can switch sides. It can be done, seeing you're my brother in a way. I'll get you settled in a house, and you'll get a good salary from . . .

SHADI *(Interrupts)*: From your Israeli secret service . . . I get it.

YAKOV: What do you say to that?

SHADI: Now, I've completely lost hope, Yakov.

YAKOV: Hope for what?

SHADI: Hope that you'd be a decent human being.

YAKOV: But . . . I like . . .

SHADI *(Interrupts)*: Shut up!

YAKOV: What you're doing now is decent and humane?

SHADI: What I'm doing now is honourable, just, and humane.

YAKOV: It's just to blow up our homes with their occupants?

SHADI: Every Israeli living in Israel at this moment is living in an Arab's home. *(With great bitterness.)* I never thought I'd live to see the day when I'd blow up houses that had seen the birth of children who would become homeless.

YAKOV: How could you?

SHADI: How? What can compensate us? If every Israeli living in Israel today is only there because an Arab was driven out of his homeland.

YAKOV: Don't try and get the better of me! Israel exists! You understand? It exists!

SHADI: It exists because Palestine was prevented from existing! The existence of Israel is a result of the nonexistence of Palestine!

YAKOV: Please! Forget that! And listen to reason.

SHADI: Listen to unreason! Who can accept the nonexistence of an Arab country called Palestine?

YAKOV: Why be so stubborn and hold onto this dream, you poor fool?

SHADI: We can never recognize you if it means not being recognized as well.

YAKOV: Rubbish . . . listen to me.

SHADI: I'm shedding my blood drop by drop for the sake of Arab Palestine.

YAKOV: Honestly, Shadi, what's worth this ambition for what you call Palestine? Live your life, agree with me. Accept my offer and let me take care of things.

SHADI: You?

YAKOV: It's better than futile hopes. *(The police car's siren is heard in the distance.)*

YAKOV: You blockhead . . . think fast . . . that's the police car. Think fast and let me fix things for you.

SHADI: I've thought.

YAKOV: And?

SHADI: Press the trigger. I want to die at your hands. That's the very best service you could do for me.

YAKOV: You fool. *(Four policemen enter brandishing their weapons, driving before them an old decrepit Arab.)*

OLD MAN: Don't push me like that! I told you I'm a grain merchant, don't you believe me?

1ST MAN: Move forward. Keep your hands above your head.

SHADI *(Sees the man)*: Uncle Ghassan?

1ST MAN: So you know him? *(To Yakov.)* Is this the guerrilla?

YAKOV: I don't know yet.

2ND MAN: Keep your hands over your head, you grain merchant. I swear you're a guerrilla saboteur.

3RD MAN *(Goes around Shadi with his weapon pointed at his chest)*: What are these clothes?

2ND MAN: How dare you wear a rabbi's clothes?

1ST MAN: A rabbi's clothes, you filthy bastard!

2ND MAN *(To the old man)*: I said keep your hands above your head.

SHADI: Why not, sir? We're at war, as he says. *(Points at Yakov.)*

2ND MAN: Silence! You know what's in store for you, you fool.

SHADI: I'm ready for anything. I'm not here to play around with my people's murderers.

2ND MAN: Don't move . . . guerrilla!

1ST MAN: What's your name?

2ND MAN: Speak up. What's your name?

3RD MAN *(Kicks him)*: Speak!

SHADI: Oh Cain. Why dost thou kill thy brother? *(Approaches Yakov.)* Why dost thou kill thy brother?

YAKOV: I haven't asked his name.

SHADI: Love . . . *(Bitterly.)* Ah, love, and memories!

YAKOV: Leave him with me for a moment. *(He tries to take him aside but Shadi refuses.)* You refuse?

SHADI: Let the old man go.

4TH MAN: He's going all right . . . to jail, then to court.

SHADI: And then to jail . . . or to be shot without a trial. That's the way you do it.

4TH MAN: Mind your own business.

SHADI: How can you ask me to keep out of it when it's rightfully my business?

3RD MAN: Rightfully yours, eh? And him? *(He slaps the old man.)*

SHADI: The conscience of Zionists living in Israel will awaken. They'll realise they wrongfully took the land of another people. This will happen, old man. Don't be afraid! Don't be sad!

4TH MAN: An intellectual too . . . shut him up!

SHADI: You stole the land of another people. *(1st man advances to hit him, but is restrained by 3rd man, who laughs.)*

3RD MAN: If he's an intellectual, let him talk. It'll be fun to hear him. What next, Arab intellectual? What happens after the conscience of Zionists awakens?

SHADI: You want to know . . .

3RD MAN: I can't wait . . .

SHADI: One day there'll be a democratic Palestine, where all of us may have our homes, instead of only a Zionist state, here at the expense of the true owners of the land.

3RD MAN: An intellectual.

4TH MAN *(Laughs)*: And a dreamer too.

1ST MAN: You mean we would drop the present structure of the state? Is that what you mean?

SHADI: Better than lose everything.

3RD MAN: What you're trying to say to us is, "We're in the right . . . Don't die." *(Derisive laughter.)*

4TH MAN *(Laughing)*: Yes. Don't die. Just leave.

2ND MAN *(Collapsing with laughter)*: Crazy . . . that's crazy.

SHADI: There's no need for such sarcasm. *(Their laughter builds.)*

YAKOV *(Interferes)*: He . . .

4TH MAN: No, no *(Laughs)*. Let him be . . . he's real entertaining.

YAKOV: But . . .

3RD MAN: Let's have some fun . . . and what else, intellectual? Go ahead. Feel free. How's that for democracy?

SHADI: Through all history, we've taken care of you, you who now make fun of me. I'm deeply aware of a just cause, I who had to leave all the family and possessions I had. *(The old man takes the opportunity of the policemen's mirth to steal quietly away.)* Don't forget! The Arab countries were the only place in the world where Jews could go when they fled the persecutions of Christian Europe.

3RD MAN: What a sad sight! What moving words! By the Sabbath, saboteur, you've moved me. You'd make a good tragic actor on Broadway.

SHADI: My role is only good for fighting . . . for dark nights. The only instrument I play is the machine gun.

3RD MAN: Stop it! Christian Europe and persecution . . . rubbish! Play the machine gun, hah.

4TH MAN: We shouldn't have had all this useless talk. Let's go . . . move, saboteur . . . and you too, old man. *(Looks around, but does not find the old man. Shouts angrily at his comrades.)* Where's he gone? How'd he get away? We've got to find him. *(Distant sounds of firing are heard, violent and merciless.)*

SHADI: Unless I'm mistaken, those bullets were meant for the old man. They'll be in his heart now . . . or in his back.

4TH MAN *(To one of the Policemen)*: Go and see what's happening. *(2nd man exits running.)*

YAKOV: Stop. *(Tries to halt the man.)*

4TH MAN: No emotions now . . . that's not allowed. *(He faces him brusquely.)*

2ND MAN *(Returns)*: He's dead. The sentry at the post shot him when he saw him running so fast. Shall we get someone to replace him, Sergeant?

YAKOV: Stop it.

4TH MAN: Are you upset? I'll deal with you later. I said emotions weren't allowed here.

YAKOV: What happened to the old man means . . .

4TH MAN: It means that he tricked us. He shouldn't have done that. It's a betrayal.

3RD MAN: It's happened, and that's all. *(Imitates sound of machine gun.)* See, that's all.

SHADI: May his blood not be in vain.

3RD MAN: Huh?

4TH MAN: What's that?

2ND MAN: No time for discussions. Let's go. All right, move, and keep your hands above your head.

SHADI: I'm not moving from here.

2ND MAN: Scared, you coward?

SHADI: I, a coward? No coward even talks of peace . . . I'm standing firm here on this spot. I cherish this piece of ground . . . I give all I have for it. Freedom is what I worship, and peace is what I believe.

2ND MAN: Zapata.

4TH MAN: A new Lumumba.

SHADI: No, I'm Shadi . . . a Palestinian trying to find himself. I put my dream before everything. This is Palestine! All you wise people. This is Palestine! You followers of Guevara . . you rebels everywhere . . . in Angola, Mozambique, and Jerusalem. Let's finish singing of hope and find deliverance! You murderers and shedders of innocent blood, wake up and listen to the new tune . . . the song of the guns. *(He takes out a machine gun from beneath the folds of his gown and takes a few steps back to cover them all.)* Drop your weapons.

YAKOV: Shadi, you're mad . . . You had a gun all the time?

SHADI: Yes, and bombs too.

YAKOV: You can't get away from me. Listen to me. I'll give you safety. Let's talk this over.

SHADI: You can't give what you don't have.

4TH MAN: I can torture you to death. Throw down your gun and surrender.

SHADI: Don't be so stupid, you animal.

3RD MAN: He swore at the Sergeant. Swear at the Sergeant, would you?

SHADI: We've learned that what you did in sixty-seven doesn't have to happen again.

4TH MAN *(Sarcastically)*: Is that so? Why not, you intellectual philosopher?

SHADI: We've seen many conquerors come into our land. We've also seen them leaving, beaten, with their tails between their legs. *(The soldiers laugh.)*

4TH MAN: You never saw anyone conquer your land as quickly as we did! *(He laughs.)*

SHADI: I'll see you leaving. Believe me, I will.

3RD MAN *(As they laugh)*: It won't be for a long, long time.

SHADI: No. *(They stop laughing as they see that Shadi really does mean to kill them and that his finger has already tightened on the trigger.)* No. See, I'm ready to squeeze the trigger. Back, all of you. *(To Yakov.)* You, too, Judas, get back.

YAKOV *(Hurt by this reference)*: Judas? Me?

SHADI *(To 3rd soldier)*: Not for a long time, eh? You think we expect to wait homeless for long? No. I'll be there to see you leave our homes. If I don't, my one-year-old daughter will see you go. Or my brother in the army. Get back.

YAKOV: If you kill us you'll be killed too.

SHADI: I'm wanted. If I give myself up, if I'm killed, it makes no difference. Get back! *(They back up as far as the lamp post. Shadi picks up the telephone.)* Hello. Ain Galout station. This is Corporal Yakov Shadmy. That saboteur that was wanted . . yes . . . he's been snatched from us by guerrillas . . . They've taken him to the kibbutz . . . They're dressed as our soldiers. Set up road blocks and mine the roads.

Yes, a military lorry. Send police and army reinforcements; there are many of them. *(He replaces the receiver.)*

4TH MAN: Fire, men, fire. *(1st man raises his weapon. Shadi shoots him and he falls. 4th man does not know what to do; Yakov is biting his nails.)*

YAKOV: He's dead, he's dead.

SHADI: It's war. Drop your guns, all of you . . . hands above your heads. *(He walks backwards, preparatory to leaving.)*

YAKOV: What about us? . . .

SHADI: I spit on our friendship . . . It's down, Yakov. We'll both die if you try to kill me. Let the Israeli generals fix coloured pins on the new map of their stolen territories.

I and my gun speak for the survival of the new Palestine
. . . our new state. *(He fires at them. Some fall dead,
others are wounded. The wounded fire at Shadi, and he
too falls. The stage is darkened completely.)*
VOICE: You who follow me. Our dream is in the air. Fight.
Don't let another Christ be crucified. Fight. Swallow
your words and drink your tears. They are useless. The
dream is in the air. You who follow me, I beg you, hold
fast. Enough has happened to your land.

CURTAIN

Not a Thing Out of Place
by TEWFIQ AL-HAKIM

Characters

BARBER   YOUNG MAN
CUSTOMER   YOUNG LADY
POSTMAN   MAN IN EUROPEAN DRESS
                                VILLAGERS

*A village square near the station. A barber has set up by
a wall; he has a customer and is sharpening his razor.*

BARBER *(Taking hold of the customer's bald head)*: When
there's a water-melon right there in front of you all nice
and shiny, how can you find out whether it's red inside
or unripe except by splitting it open with a knife?
CUSTOMER *(Disturbed)*: What's the connection?
BARBER: Nothing at all, just that certain things remind one
of others.
CUSTOMER: What things? What reminds you?
BARBER: Tell me, can you know what's inside this head of
yours?

CUSTOMER: What are you getting at? Do you mean in the way of ideas?

BARBER: What ideas are you talking about, man? Who mentioned ideas? We're talking about water-melons.

CUSTOMER: I don't get it at all.

BARBER: Just let me explain. It's something that can be perfectly well understood. If you've got a water-melon in your hand, what do you do with it? Play football with it?

CUSTOMER: Of course not.

BARBER: Quite so. That's just what happened—my brother wasn't wrong then.

CUSTOMER: Your brother?

BARBER: Yes, my full brother. God bless him, he was a real fine barber like myself.

CUSTOMER: What about the water-melon?

BARBER: A customer's head—and not a wit better than that of your good self.

CUSTOMER (*With a cry of alarm*): Customer's head?

BARBER: And so what? Slice it.

CUSTOMER: What do you mean 'so what'? Slice the customer's head?

BARBER: Isn't that the way to see whether it's red inside or unripe?

CUSTOMER (*Looking in fear at the razor*): With a razor?

BARBER: You see, at the time he happened to have the razor in his hand and the soap was on the customer's chin.

CUSTOMER (*Fearfully*): And what happened after that?

BARBER: I swear to you, they carted him off to hospital.

CUSTOMER: The customer?

BARBER: My brother.

CUSTOMER: Your brother? It was *he* they carted off? But why?

BARBER: What d'you think they said? They said he was mad. Can you believe it? Can you credit it?

CUSTOMER: I really can't. So they carted him off to the lunatic asylum?

BARBER: That's right, sir. Can you imagine such a thing?

CUSTOMER: And the customer?

BARBER: He was carted off by ambulance.

CUSTOMER: God Almighty! The good Lord preserve us!

BARBER (*Sharpening his razor on the palm of his hand*): Just put yourself in my brother's place. In front of you there's a water-melon and you're holding a knife. What would you do?

CUSTOMER: And have you ever done it?

BARBER: God be my witness—up until now, no.

CUSTOMER: Any intention of doing so?

BARBER: Maybe. After all, is there anything wrong about slicing a water-melon with a razor?

CUSTOMER (*Tearing the towel from his neck*): I'm off!

BARBER: Where to? There's still the other side to be done.

CUSTOMER: One side's quite enough. 'Bye. (*The customer makes his escape at a run.*)

A postman appears carrying a handful of letters.

POSTMAN: What's that customer of yours running off for with the soap still on his chin?

BARBER: Mad, God spare you.

POSTMAN (*Holding out the handful of letters*): Take delivery of today's post.

BARBER: Just throw them down in the old basin as usual.

POSTMAN (*Hands him the letters*): Take them and throw them in yourself, then come along and let's have a game.

BARBER (*Taking the letters and throwing them down into a nearby basin on the floor*): What shall we play today?

A young man in European dress appears.

YOUNG MAN (*To the postman*): Is there a letter for me? My name's . . .

POSTMAN (*Interrupting him*): There are plenty of letters for you. Just choose yourself the letter you fancy.

YOUNG MAN: But I want a letter addressed to me.

POSTMAN: Are you new to the village?

YOUNG MAN: I arrived here only yesterday. I came for my cousin's wedding.

POSTMAN: You don't know how naïve you're being. In this village, son, we don't have the time to deliver letters to people. The whole postbag's in the basket . . .

BARBER: In the basin . . .

POSTMAN: In the master barber's basin—and what a blessed and auspicious basin it is! Everyone comes along and simply takes his pick—be it addressed to him, to someone else, it's no concern of ours. The great thing is to get rid of the post day by day.

YOUNG MAN: You mean you take a letter that doesn't belong to you?

POSTMAN: One letter, two—just as your fancy takes you.

YOUNG MAN: My fancy? What's my fancy to do with it? I want a letter that's mine.

POSTMAN: Every letter you have here is yours. Open any letter and you'll find it contains amusing things. Don't you want to be amused?

YOUNG MAN: Whatever are you saying? Is this how you're dealing with people's letters?

POSTMAN: Every day—and the people like it this way. In a couple of hours they've swiped the lot.

YOUNG MAN: But this is what's called chaos.

POSTMAN: Not at all. That chaos you're talking about is something altogether different.

BARBER: That sort of chaos doesn't happen here, my dear sir—thank God! Like me to give you a shave?

YOUNG MAN: No thanks, I've just shaved.

BARBER: I'll crop a bit of the fur off the water-melon?

YOUNG MAN: Water-melon?

POSTMAN: What he means, begging your pardon, is that he'll shave your head for you.

YOUNG MAN: No—thanks.

POSTMAN: Then grab yourself a couple of letters from the basin and take yourself off. The fact is we just haven't got the time.

YOUNG MAN (*Goes up to the basin and searches for a letter addressed to him*): No letters for me. 'Bye. (*He is about to depart.*)

POSTMAN (*Stopping him*): Going away empty-handed like that? Man, take yourself a letter from those in front of you. Like me to choose you one? (*He goes up to the basin and chooses a letter.*) Take this one—it's in a woman's handwriting. You'll enjoy it.

YOUNG MAN (*Hesitating*): Yes, but . . .

POSTMAN: But what? Don't say 'but'. Go on—don't embarrass me. Really, don't embarrass me.

BARBER: Go on and take it. Don't embarrass him. Put your trust in God and off you go. We just haven't got the time to attend to you.

YOUNG MAN (*Takes the letter from the postman*): Hope it's all right! What an extraordinary thing! (*He goes off with the letter.*)

POSTMAN: What were we talking about before that asinine young fellow came along?

BARBER: We were saying what would we play today.

POSTMAN: Yes, quite right—what shall we play? I'll tell you what—we'll play the game of the donkey and the philosopher.

BARBER: What's a philosopher?

POSTMAN: Someone with a big brain.

BARBER: That'll be me.

POSTMAN: No, you're the donkey.

BARBER: Why?

POSTMAN: Because a donkey's got a bigger brain.

BARBER: How's that?

POSTMAN: I'll tell you: Ever seen a donkey having a shave at a barber's?

BARBER: No.

POSTMAN: Is that clever of him or not?

BARBER: Yes.

POSTMAN: Right, then I'll be the donkey.

BARBER: Just now you said I'd be the donkey.

POSTMAN: I've changed my mind.

BARBER: What about me—who'll I be?

POSTMAN: You'll be the philosopher.

BARBER: No thanks, I don't want to be no philosopher.

POSTMAN: You silly man, a philosopher's more intelligent.

BARBER: Do you take me for a fool? Do you think I'm so gaga I don't know?

POSTMAN: Don't you believe me? All right, go and ask anyone: Is a donkey more intelligent than a philosopher? He'll tell you . . .

BARBER: I'll tell you myself. Ever seen a donkey going off to post a letter?

POSTMAN: No.

BARBER: Is that intelligent or not?

POSTMAN: Yes.

BARBER: Right, then I'll be the donkey.

POSTMAN: But, my dear fellow, I want to be the donkey.

BARBER: You be a donkey as well—then we'll both be donkeys. What's wrong with that?

POSTMAN: It's no good, one of us must be a philosopher. That's how the game's played.

BARBER: I'm no good for a philosopher—I've got a big brain.

POSTMAN: And I'm the empty-headed one?

BARBER: No, not at all, I just meant that. . . .

The young man reappears, the opened letter in his hand.

YOUNG MAN: This letter's from a girl to her fiancé. She tells him to meet her off the noon train.
POSTMAN: There's the noon train giving a whistle—it's inside the station.
YOUNG MAN: What's to be done now?
POSTMAN: Very simple—go and meet her at the station.
YOUNG MAN: Who shall I meet?
POSTMAN: Man, the girl who sent you the letter.
YOUNG MAN: She didn't send it to me.
POSTMAN: Isn't that it in your hand?
YOUNG MAN: But it isn't for me, it isn't mine.
POSTMAN: What did you open it for then?
YOUNG MAN: You handed it to me.
POSTMAN: And you took it and opened it and read it. It's therefore yours. Off you go and meet the lady at the station.
YOUNG MAN: And how shall I recognize her?
POSTMAN: You'll recognize her all right if she's pretty.
YOUNG MAN: Pretty?
POSTMAN: Pretty and on her own and getting off the train looking to right and left.
BARBER (*To the young man*): Man, go and meet her. Don't be so gormless.[1]
YOUNG MAN: How extraordinary! Hope it's all right! (*He goes off in the direction of the station.*)
POSTMAN: Now take this young fellow: Is he a donkey or a philosopher?
BARBER: If he gets off with the lady he'll be a donkey.
POSTMAN: He'll be a philosopher, fool!
BARBER: How's that?

The customer, half his face in lather, reappears.

CUSTOMER: D'you like the idea of me walking around half shaved?
BARBER: Is that my fault?—it's you who ran off like a madman.

---

[1] British slang for stupid. —Ed.

CUSTOMER: So it's I who's mad?

BARBER: Well, I then?

CUSTOMER: And what about your brother—you well know the one I mean?

BARBER: And what about my brother?

CUSTOMER: The water-melon . . .

BARBER: Man, have some sense—is this the season for water-melons?

CUSTOMER: Thanks be to God—you've put my mind at rest. So you had no intention . . .

BARBER: To do what?

CUSTOMER: To slice the water-melon?

BARBER: Man, talk sense, can't you. Where's this water-melon you're talking of?

CUSTOMER: My head.

BARBER: This head of yours a water-melon?

CUSTOMER: You mean it's not a water-melon?

BARBER: You asking me?

CUSTOMER: Then what you said was a joke?

BARBER: What d'you mean 'joke', man? Why should I joke with customers? All I say is dead serious.

CUSTOMER: You mean then that the story of the water-melon was serious?

BARBER: Of course it was serious.

CUSTOMER: Meaning that you were seriously intending to slice the water-melon?

BARBER: D'you think I was going to play football with it or just sit down and look at it?

CUSTOMER: Good God! 'Bye. (*He makes off hurriedly.*)

BARBER: Why's he run away again? What would you say about him too—a philosopher or a donkey?

POSTMAN: It seems there are a lot of philosophers around these days.

BARBER: Then why not ask him to play with us?

POSTMAN: A stranger wouldn't fit in with us.

BARBER (*Looking in the direction of the station*): Good heavens! Just look—the young fellow's coming along with the lady.

POSTMAN: She must have turned out to be pretty!

The young man and the lady—a young and beautiful girl—approach. He is carrying her suitcase for her.

YOUNG LADY: But where is he? Why wasn't he waiting for me at the station?

YOUNG MAN: After all, *I* was waiting for you.

YOUNG LADY: But you're not he.

YOUNG MAN: Who am I then?

YOUNG LADY: How should I know who you might be?

YOUNG MAN: How don't you know—wasn't it you who wrote this letter and posted it to me? (*He shows her the letter.*)

YOUNG LADY: Yes, it was I who wrote and posted it, but . . .

YOUNG MAN: Fine, then I'm he.

YOUNG LADY: But you're not he.

YOUNG MAN: Was he old?

YOUNG LADY: No, young.

YOUNG MAN: And what am I—old or young?

YOUNG LADY: Young of course.

YOUNG MAN: That settles it—I'm he.

YOUNG LADY: How do you work that out?

YOUNG MAN: Don't you believe me? Come along and we'll ask some of the locals. (*He moves towards the postman and the barber.*) Please tell us, gentlemen: am I he or not?

POSTMAN: You are.

BARBER: The very same.

YOUNG MAN: You've heard for yourself.

YOUNG LADY: That's crazy talk.

POSTMAN: Tomorrow you'll come to your senses.

BARBER: In the same way as the gentleman has. (*He points at the young man.*)

YOUNG MAN (*To the young lady*): The most important people in the village have ruled that I am he—so I *am* he. Come on, let's go off to the registrar.

YOUNG LADY: Registrar?

YOUNG MAN: Of course. Aren't we engaged to be married? All that remains therefore is the registrar.

YOUNG LADY: But that's impossible.

YOUNG MAN: Why impossible? Everything's possible.

YOUNG LADY: Hey—and what about my fiancé?

YOUNG MAN: But, my dear lady, I'm your fiancé. It's I who received your letter and it was I who met you at the station. The villagers have borne witness to it.

YOUNG LADY: What an odd sort of village this is!

YOUNG MAN: What's wrong with this village? It's the very

best; it's the one you arrived at to meet up with your fiancé and—Allah be praised—I've done just that.

YOUNG LADY: But that's absolutely impossible.

YOUNG MAN: Only too possible. Everything's possible here.

YOUNG LADY: But it's not reasonable.

YOUNG MAN: Everything's reasonable here. God be my witness—I am now absolutely convinced.

POSTMAN: Convinced that this village of ours is not chaotic?

YOUNG MAN: Absolutely so—in this place of yours not a thing is out of place.

BARBER: Put your trust in God then and off you go to the registrar's.

YOUNG MAN: And the village registrar, is he like your good selves, with never a thing out of place?

BARBER: Have no fear—put a summer water-melon in your stomach and relax!

POSTMAN: Let's do without the water-melon—this is not the place for it!

YOUNG MAN: What are you driving at?

POSTMAN: Relax—we're talking about some other water-melon.

YOUNG MAN: Then you're agreed about our being engaged and going off to the registrar's?

BARBER: Agreed.

POSTMAN: Absolutely agreed.

YOUNG LADY: But I'm not agreed.

YOUNG MAN: That's something to be said in front of the registrar—he'll deal with it.

YOUNG LADY: How'll he deal with it?

YOUNG MAN: Just as our good friend the postman dealt with matters—and he did so very soundly.

YOUNG LADY: It's extraordinary!

YOUNG MAN: I said that before you did. Come on, let's go off to the registrar's.

YOUNG LADY: Heaven knows how all this is going to end!
(*The young man leads her away by the hand.*)

POSTMAN: The end will be like the beginning—all one and the same!

BARBER: And half a shave's like a whole one—all one and the same!

POSTMAN: And a letter of yours turns out not to be yours—all one and the same!

BARBER: And a head you think is a water-melon, and a

water-melon you think is a head—all one and the same!

POSTMAN: And where the village registrar is concerned . . .

BARBER: All's one and the same.

POSTMAN: Let's give them a send-off.

BARBER: Bring the drum!

POSTMAN: Where's the flute?

BARBER: And let the village folk gather round—they're great ones for fun and gaiety.

POSTMAN: Yes, they never miss a chance for making merry. Go on, give them a call!

BARBER (*Together with the postman he calls out*): Villagers! Villagers! Bring your drums and flutes! (*Some of the villagers begin to gather together.*)

A man in European dress with twirled moustaches appears.

MAN IN EUROPEAN DRESS: What's happening around here? Why are you calling to the villagers?

POSTMAN: What's it to you?

MAN IN EUROPEAN DRESS: What are you talking to me like that for?

BARBER: And who twirled your moustaches like that for you? What d'you reckon to have standing on them?

MAN IN EUROPEAN DRESS: And what are you being so rude for?

BARBER: And if I'm rude, who d'you think you are?

MAN IN EUROPEAN DRESS: And why would you be asking me that?

POSTMAN: In order to learn the reason for your honouring this place with your presence.

MAN IN EUROPEAN DRESS: And you still don't know why I'm here in this village?

POSTMAN: No, why?

MAN IN EUROPEAN DRESS: Why?

BARBER: Yes, why?

MAN IN EUROPEAN DRESS: I'm an Inspector . . .

POSTMAN (*In alarm*): Good God! We're in a real mess now! You're an Inspector? A Police Inspector?

MAN IN EUROPEAN DRESS: No . . .

BARBER: A Special Branch Inspector?

MAN IN EUROPEAN DRESS: An Inspector of Music in the band

of the world-famous singer Nabawiya Santawiya, otherwise known far and wide as Naboubou!

BARBER: The Devil take you far and wide! You scared the life out of us.

POSTMAN: Yes, why didn't you say so right from the beginning? And what brought you here?

MAN IN EUROPEAN DRESS: We came for a wedding feast being held in the village.

BARBER: It must be the wedding of that fellow over there with the young lady.

POSTMAN: We were just about to give them a send-off.

MAN IN EUROPEAN DRESS: Why, are you two working in Madame Shakaa Bakaa's band?

BARBER: Shakaa Bakaa?

MAN IN EUROPEAN DRESS: That dead-beat singer who's competing with us wherever we go.

POSTMAN: No, sir, we don't work in any band.

MAN IN EUROPEAN DRESS: Amateurs?

BARBER: No, sir, we're respectable and sensible people. My honoured friend is the Grand Bey, Director of the District Post Office, while I myself am the owner of the hairdressing establishments in the district.

MAN IN EUROPEAN DRESS (*Looking at the corner of the barber's stall and the basinful of letters*): Just the place for them! Honoured to have made your acquaintance.

POSTMAN: Come on, let's give the young man and his lady a real send-off all the way up to the registrar's! Villagers! Villagers! Where are your drums? Where your flutes! Where the dancers among you?

The people of the village gather together with excited shouting, with singing and mad dancing, while chanting.

> Dancing to sound of drum and flute
> Into reverse the world we'll put—
> And yet it's going right we'll find.
> Whether sane or out of mind
> It really matters not at all.
> Come step it out now, one and all.

CURTAIN

(TRANSLATED BY DENYS JOHNSON-DAVIES)

PART II

ARMENIAN
LITERATURE

THE ARMENIAN
BACKGROUND

Numerically and geographically the smallest nation represented in this collection, Armenia exists today as one of the Soviet Socialist Republics, the Caucasian remnant of a once-mighty empire that stretched from the shores of the Caspian Sea down to the mid-Mediterranean. Outside Soviet Armenia, Armenians constitute a significant cultural minority in Egypt, Lebanon, Iran, Iraq, Israel, Jordan, and Syria. And beyond geography, Armenia is a state of mind for millions of people who fled the Turkish terror to Europe and the Americas. Fragmented by history, the Armenian people have remained cohesive through their literature.

Armenian literature has a long and impressive heritage. Its content was more or less determined when the Armenians adopted Christianity in 301 A.D. (the first nation of people to do so), and its form of expression was established when the monk Mashtots invented the Armenian alphabet a century later. This early tradition was given impetus by another monk, Agathangelos, in his sprawling *History of the Armenians* (c. 460), recently translated into English. Subsequently, in the golden age of Armenian literature, the strongly Christian tradition was developed by translations from Greek and Syriac texts, especially of the Bible, and by the tenth-century *Book of Lamentations* of Gregory of Narek, a series of ninety-five canticles lauding the redemptive power of Christ (also newly rendered into English).

Following the political collapse of Greater Armenia in the eleventh century and the shift southward of the cultural center to Little Armenia or Cilician Armenia, governed by a French king (from 1343 to 1375), the literature divided itself into a Western and an Eastern branch. This split has persisted into modern times. After the destructive conquests of the Mamelukes (1375) and the Mongols (1385) there was a period of literary decadence, but recovery began in the sixteenth century with the rise of popular bards or troubadours, of whom the most famous was Sayat Nova, through whose poetry of pagan love ancestral voices spoke. By the eighteenth century, the spoken language—and secular themes—had begun to gain ascendency over the church language (*grapar*) and classical and religious subjects. Thereafter, Armenian writers looked to Europe rather than to their historic roots for their models and values—the writers of the West to France, and those of the East to Russia. The secularization of Armenian literature was quite complete by the first decade of the twentieth century.

In 1915, the rulers of the Ottoman Empire, fearful of "fifth-column" activity, decided to deport the entire Armenian population of western Turkey to the deserts of Syria. In the ensuing catastrophe, countless Armenians lost their lives, among them the writers responsible for a brief renaissance in letters at the turn of the century. Thereafter Constantinople (now Istanbul) declined rapidly as the center of Armenian culture, though the poets Kambuskan and Zahrad (Zareh Yaldizciyan) still raise their voices among the fifty thousand descendants of the Armenians who survived. Other writers, forced to flee for their lives, were scattered abroad but continued to write in Paris (Shahnour), England (Michael Arlen), the United States (Constant Zarian), and in the Middle East, especially Lebanon (Antranik Zaroukian).

Among those writers who survived were Gourgen Mahari, born and raised near Lake Van, and Hagop Oshagan, who escaped capture by the Turkish police in 1915 by fleeing to Bulgaria disguised as a German officer. He spent the rest of his life in various Middle Eastern countries as a teacher and writer (his son Vahe, a distinguished writer himself, teaches at the University of Pennsylvania).

Thus, Armenian literature of the contemporary period is, for our purposes, synonymous with the writing that came out of the Soviet Armenian Republic after World War II. The uprooted Armenian writers, while superior on many counts, sometimes inevitably lost touch with the continuing reality of the Armenian experience.

The novel was strongly represented in Russian and eastern Armenia, where it became the vehicle for moral, social, and political aspirations. Khachadour Abovian had created the modern Armenian literary language in *The Wounds of Ar-*

menia (1858), and his promotion of the rich and complex idiomatic language was continued in the twentieth century by several less talented novelists such as Constant Zarian, who wrote about the short-lived Armenian Republic created out of the ashes of the First World War in *The Boat on the Mountaintop*.

During the Stalinist purges of the 1930s, Isabel Essayan, Vahan Totoventz, Yegheshe Charentz, Axel Bakuntz, and a number of other writers were arrested for alleged political "deviationism" and either jailed or deported to Siberia (Osip Mandelstam and Isaac Babel shared similar fates). Gourgen Mahari, a novelist and poet who had escaped to Russia during the Turkish massacres of 1915, was sent into Siberian exile some thirty years later. The selection from his work in this book was published in the Armenian literary weekly *Gragan Tert*, on April 19, 1964, before Solzhenitsyn's account of the Gulag Archipelago (the editor of the magazine was relieved of his position the day after the account appeared).

Despite such adversities, Armenian literature rose again. Vakhtang Ananyan created deceptively simple stories of hunting adventures, and Rachia Kochar's *The Children of the Great House* was inspired by the gallantry of the Armenian troops who repelled the invaders during the Second World War—as was Derenik Demerjian's *Vartanunk*. Drawing upon an early history of the Mamikonian dynasty, Demerjian wove these events into an epic novel about Vartan the Great, who with a small band of warriors stunned the invading armies of the Persian king. His *Mesrop Mashtots* is a novel dealing with the life of the founder of the Armenian literary language.

At the other end of the spectrum, the explorers of space have fired the Armenian imagination no less than history. A. Shiabon's *The Captains of the Oceans of Space* and Sero Khanzadian's *The Country* achieved some popularity. Khanzadian, a very prolific prose writer, is represented in this collection with a story, "The White Lamb," which depicts the changing moral and ethical values in Armenia through an ironic treatment of the Prodigal Son theme.

Two women writers have attained prominence if not popularity (Armenians regard them as too "Russified"). Nora Adamian dramatizes the daily life of the "liberated" Armenian woman in the Soviet system, and Marietta Shaginian has brought out novels, stories, criticism (she is quoted extensively in the preface to Patricia Blake's *Halfway to the Moon*), and travelogues over a long distinguished career culminated by the recent award of the Lenin Prize for Literature.

Among the most talented writers of fiction is Hrant (or Grant, in Russian) Matevosian, who is represented here by a story from his most recent collection, *The Orange Herd*. One of his stories, a sketch of village life entitled "Akhnidzor," published in 1961, is regarded as a landmark in Armenian literature. Never before had Armenian village life been shown with such honesty, and the whole work is permeated with broad spiritual overtones despite its satirical tone. Matevosian is the editor of an anthology of Armenian stories in English entitled *We of the Mountains*, a good sampling of contemporary writing from that land.

The tradition of the Armenian bards was given contemporary modulation after World War II by two powerful yet lyrical voices—those of Sylva Gaboudikian and Gevorg Emin. Though Gaboudikian is sometimes accused of "superpartriotism," her roots go deep into the Armenian tradition, and her love of the language and the very soil of her mountainous birthplace is unrivaled in its intensity. Emin, an engineer by training, is also blazingly responsive to his blood, but his poetry appears to be more open to influences from places beyond the world of his small republic. Both of them, during their recent visits to the United States as guests of the State Department, illustrated how smallness can seem great and the particular seem universal.

The recent generation of poets, including the late Paruir Sevag, contributed notably to the revitalization of the lyric tradition in Armenian letters. Antranik Zaroukian, now living in Beirut where he taught for years, has achieved status as one of the outstanding contemporary writers of the Diaspora. His poems in this collection, like those of Sevag, testify to the vigor and relevancy of recent poetry in Armenian. Another poet of great promise, Krikor Belidian, is not included in this volume because his poems are so difficult to translate without a more than ordinary loss of meaning.

What might be considered the folk poetry of Armenia has been gathered together and put into idiomatic English by a young poet and translator from Paris, Garig Basmadjian.

Created in the past, the proverbs carry conviction into the present. One can discern their influence on some of the poets included in this section.

A national drama began to develop towards the end of the nineteenth century, realistic in tone and mode. Its founder and most important figure was Gabriel Sundukian, after whom the national theater of Armenia is named. The success of his comedy, *Pepo*, translated into both Turkish and Russian, was rivaled only by Shirvandzade's *For the Sake of Honor* and Hagop Baronian's *The Oriental Merchant*. These plays are still performed enthusiastically wherever Armenians congregate, but very little of interest or significance aside from the folk operas and ballets has emerged from the contemporary theater of Armenia. The troubled career of Serj Paradjanov, the Armenian film maker whose motion picture based on the life of Sayat Nova was censored, suggests the nature of the obstacles facing any playwright of originality.

In the past ten years, the publication of books in Soviet Armenia has flourished, and perhaps as never before, Armenian artists, especially the obedient writers, are prophets with honor in their own country. However, even with the encouragement that the Soviet government gives to ethnic literature, it is doubtful that the republic of Armenia can hope for a literature that is free in the Western sense of that term. Armenians in the Diaspora, recalling their Middle Eastern roots, have created a small renaissance away from their homeland, much as the Jews did, but English or French is gradually becoming the language of the writer who honors his ancient Armenian heritage of free expression.

FICTION

◆

Revenge

by VAKHTANG ANANYAN

There wasn't a man, woman, or child in all the small villages scattered over the southern slope of the Mount Alagyoz who did not know the Kurd hunter Davot. He was as strong as an ancient oak and as keen-eyed as an eagle, and had a huge head and a powerful chest like an old lion's.

Half a century before, he had escaped from Turkey, evading the Cossack frontier guards at the foot of the Ararat, and had come to live in one of the mountain villages.

It became a custom in those parts that whoever came there to hunt had to go to Davot's house first, share a meal with him, and ask his advice about where to go in order not to come back empty-handed from the hunt. On their return the guests would stay with Davot overnight and listen to his stories of times long past.

One day, when my friend and I, loaded with our hunting spoils, were heading for Karaburun railway station, hoping to catch a train there, we were caught in a snowstorm. The sky turned livid and merged with the earth, the paths became indistinguishable under the snow, and wolves left their lairs to look for such as us, lost in the snowstorm.

Driven by the blizzard, we reached a hamlet crouching under high cliffs and knocked at the door of the first cottage we came across. The master of the house asked us to come in, but the next moment, catching sight of the hare slung to my belt, stopped short, asked, "Hunters, eh?" and without waiting for an answer said to us, "Come with me."

He led us to the other end of the village to a ramshackle hut that stood a little apart, all by itself. At the door we were met by several wolf-hounds which were so hostile that we were forced to defend ourselves with the butt ends of our rifles. But the door opened and an old man with white bushy

[122]

eyebrows on a shrunken face, a broad chest and short legs called back the dogs and asked us to come in.

In the middle of a spacious room, close to the fire-place, stood an old grandfather *kursi*,[1] around which his old wife, two daughters-in-law, and three children sat with their feet in the warm *tonir*. They all wore Kurd clothes with beads and silver coins on their breasts and sleeves, and some even on their forehead.

"See, Uncle," said our guide, "I've brought you some visitors."

"I wish you health a thousand times, dear guests, you've brought joy to me and my old eyes. My poor house is yours, and all I have you can use as your own," the old man said warmly and bowed to us with Eastern courtesy; then he shook hands with us and asked us to take seats round the *kursi*.

His daughters-in-law got up and stepped aside, and we took their places.

There is nothing that can compare with sitting round a *kursi*, on a cold January evening after coming back from the hunt, when the blizzard is howling outside and blowing snow through the *yerdik*[2] and the cracks in the door.

We were soon warm and cheerful, especially when one of the old man's daughters-in-law brought in supper—mutton *khaurma*, pickles, crumbling Kurd cheese, cream and—the dream of a man caught in a snow-storm—a bottle of famous mulberry vodka.

"Goat feels more for goat than for a herd of sheep," the old man said, pushing towards us the choice bits and the biggest glasses.

"He's a hunter himself, you know," said our guide, "that's why you're so welcome here."

"You aren't hunter Davot, are you?" I cried joyfully, jumping to my feet.

The old man's dim eyes kindled up for a moment.

"Yes, he is," the guide said. "You've heard of him, of course?"

My joy knew no bounds. I talked animatedly, and, unable

[1] *kursi*: a small table on short legs standing over a hole in the floor—*tonir*, where fire is kindled. After the fire has burnt out, people sit around this table, which is covered with a big carpet reaching to the floor, and put their feet into the *tonir*.
[2] *yerdik*: the smoke-hole in the ceiling.

to hear enough of the old man's stories, kept urging him to tell more.

We heard many fascinating things that evening about the life of the Kurds in Turkey, but one story moved me particularly and I promised the old man to write it down and tell it to the world. Now I'm keeping my promise.

When summer comes, Davot began his story, I drive my sheep herd into the mountains. Up there on the beautiful Alagyoz I sit on a piece of rock by a murmuring stream and my eyes turn sadly to Mount Masis. Past troubles are revived in my memory and sadness grips my heart. Fifty years ago I left those I loved at the foot of that mountain. I remember my bride-to-be, my betrothed, slender like a plane-tree. Yusuf-bek took her away from me and gave her to his son for a wife. On a dark night I killed my rival and fled here. I remember the gorgeous crimson flowers that grew on the Artos mountain, and the bright frocks of the girls, as lovely as those flowers—the girls that came in summer from Diarbekir and brought youth and merriness to the old mountain.

Those were beautiful places, but my memories of my life there are mostly sad. Two images stand out among them, two images that haunt me always, that torment me day and night. One of them is that of my beloved, with tears flowing from her eyes, and the other—that of a poor she-bear I'm going to tell you about for you to tell the world. Let people know that, though a hunter may be constantly shedding blood, he has a heart and soul and warm feelings, the same as anybody else. Let people know that a dumb beast may have a heart too, and a heart a thousand times gentler than the hearts of those who took Davot's sweetheart away by force and doomed him to a life of exile, far from his beautiful native land.

Davot filled his pipe unhurriedly and went on after a pensive silence to tell of the events of fifty years back.

You townsfolk will find it hard to understand me. A Kurd lives all his life side by side with animals, and becomes attached to them with all his heart, so that the death of a favorite dog, sheep, or ox causes him nearly as much grief as the death of one of his dear ones. And no wonder, because the animals come into the world under our very eyes, we warm them with our bodies, protecting them from rain and hail, we nurse them as our own children and they have their place in our hearts. That is why I mourn at the thought of my Lame Mokhnatka,[3] whom I nursed like a child of my own, who grew up in my house, and whose great sorrow I witnessed with my own eyes.

But, as they say, you won't be understood unless you start at the very beginning.

I was once hunting on the Artos Mountain. Opposite it is Mount Sipan, and on the other side spreads the majestic Van Lake. I used to sit for hours on the bluff slope of the Artos and, forgetful of everything else, admire the proud beauty of Van Lake. Down below, the mountain was encircled by the sparkling silver belt of the Semiramis River, that had fed the villages on the mountain slopes and on the shores of the lake with their fields and pastures for three thousand years. When the sun sank behind the tops of the distant ranges I would wake from my dreams, take my flintlock and start out in search of bears.

I killed many bears among those rocks. Often enough, too, a bear got hold of me or flung me down a steep cliff so that I barely escaped with my life. I know the ways of bears as well as those of my sheep and dogs. I know that a bear feels strongly. A female won't be daunted even by fire when its cub is in danger; it will face a gun without fear.

On one occasion, however, I came upon a cruel mother bear. Actually, it was I who was cruel if anyone, shooting at a bear that was dozing tranquilly among the rocks. She jumped up with a furious roar, spitting madly, and finding no suitable object picked up her cub and hurled it in my face.

The next moment, recovering from my astonishment, I shot again—right into the maddened beast's muzzle. That quieted her. The cub lay at my feet whining with pain.

I wrapped it up in my coat and took it home. We offered it some milk—it would not touch it, neither did it take any interest in bread. Then we gave it to one of our dogs to nurse. She was a very clever dog and she adopted the bear cub and brought it up together with her own puppy.

The cub proved to be a source of unending delight for the children. Those were happy days indeed. From morning till night a living tangle of bear, children, and dogs rolled hilariously about the yard. Or else the children would climb a nut-

---

[3] *Mokhnatka* means a "shaggy one."

tree and the cub would follow them there. Its fur was so long and fluffy that the kids called it Mokhnatka.

In August, when the fruit season began, the cub hardly ever left the fruit-trees—all day long it would hang onto the branches like a monkey, stuffing itself with fruit.

Once, when I thought it had been there far too long, I got annoyed and shook the tree (may my arm wither for this cruel deed): the poor beast fell down from the top of that tall tree and broke a leg. You should've heard the wailing of the kids! I set the bone, bandaged the leg, and looked after the cub until it was well again. While nursing it I came to love the little thing like a child of my own. It always limped afterwards and came to be called Lame Mokhnatka.

By the winter Mokhnatka was the size of a biggish calf. When she was in a playful mood she would hoist the dog, her foster-mother, on her back and carry it about with her peculiar bear's waddle.

In the autumn I started taking Mokhnatka with me when I went hunting. She was more useful to me than a donkey and a dog together. I'd strap a *khurjin*[4] with food onto Mokhnatka's back and off we'd go. You should know, being hunters yourselves, what a strain it is to carry the catch back home when one is tired out by a whole day's tramp. Mokhnatka relieved me of this burden. I'd load the roe, gazelle, or mountain sheep on Mokhnatka and she'd follow me home waddling unhurriedly behind.

She was remarkably intelligent. I went hunting with her all through the winter and she got accustomed to this sort of life and learned to help me just like a man. When she saw me, for instance, squatting over a heap of dry leaves and twigs, striking my flint with steel, she'd go off to collect firewood and would bring it to me, walking on her hind legs and hugging the wood to her breast—just like a man. By the time I had got the fire going she would be dragging an enormous tree-stump along, snorting with the exertion.

When I spoke to her, I used special words that she understood. If I said "bokh," it meant: "Stand aside, I'm going to shoot," she would then walk aside, sit under a tree or behind a rock, and stop her ears with her paws. When I said "gech," she walked ahead, when I said "osh," she stopped, and if I shouted "ai, khavar," she hurried along to beat off the dogs.

---

[4] *khurjin*: two carpet-bags joined together, thrown across the back of a horse, donkey or some other pack animal.

During the hunt, if she saw me crouch and put my finger to my lips, she lay flat and remained motionless.

The only thing she feared was my gun. She knew by experience that this thing that looked like a club let off fire and smoke and produced a deafening noise carrying death with it, for immediately afterward either a goat tumbled from a rock or a deer dropped to the ground, its legs jerking in the air.

One day, as I was having my lunch by the fire, Mokhnatka suddenly took my gun from the branch I had hung it on and handed it to me. I noticed her gaze was fixed on something below in the gorge. I looked, too, saw some roes hurrying to the watering-place and fired. This convinced me that Mokhnatka understood what a gun was for and knew that it was this thing that felled animals to the ground to be later skinned and carved. Remember this well, otherwise the end of my story may sound like a fairy-tale to you.

So a year passed. Mokhnatka grew into a huge bear and became cleverer still. Often I went to hunt riding astride her along mountain paths.

Mokhnatka was the favorite of the whole village. She won particular admiration during summer when I took her into the mountains to help me watch the herds. Wolves made several attacks on the herd, but stopped bothering us after Mokhnatka taught them a good lesson: she caught one of them and whacked it against a rock so that it breathed its last there and then. After that we had no fear of wolves, thieves, or robbers.

Mokhnatka's fame spread as far as the Van Lake district. Many traders offered me handfuls of gold for her; cattle-breeders wanted to buy her for thirty or forty sheep, but I would not part with my pet for anything. How could I! Apart from being worth at least ten dogs and two donkeys for me, she was a helper during the hunt, a powerful defender in moments of danger, and a beloved friend. Even if I yielded to temptation and gave her away, she would never go of her own accord, and, if they took her by force, she would escape and come back to me.

Once something of the kind actually happened.

In summer, tribes of Kurds came to our pastures from the banks of the Tigris with their numerous herds. That year one of the best grazing grounds in our parts—on Mount Artos—was taken up by Yusuf-bek, who pitched his luxurious tent there and housed the pink-faced wives he had brought with him on richly adorned camels.

My heart sank when I heard this.

"No good will come to me from this bandit," I thought. "He'll take my bear away."

I moved to an out-of-the-way pasture, but there was no getting away from Yusuf-bek. No sooner had he heard of my bear, than he sent armed men to me with instructions to buy the bear or to take it by force if I refused to sell it.

They ignored my indignant protests and even compelled me to gag and tie up Mokhnatka with my own hands. Then they loaded her on a two-wheeled *arba* and drove away.

Gloom descended on our house. Crying disconsolately, the children saw our beloved Mokhnatka off to the place outside the village where the road topped a hill, while I went off into the mountains, sought refuge in one of the deeper gorges, and spent hours looking at Van Lake and singing mournful songs.

One night I felt something wet and hot touch my face. I jumped up—a huge bear was licking my face. My brain clouded by sleep, I did not at once recognize Mokhnatka and stretched my hand for the gun. But the bear hurled the gun away and lay at my feet. Then I knew who it was, hugged Mokhnatka's head, kissed her wet muzzle, and broke out sobbing. So we finally went to sleep, lying close together.

When it became light I saw that the neck of the poor beast had been bleeding. I cleaned the wound. It had been made by a bullet. Then it dawned on me that something out of the ordinary must have happened in Yusuf-bek's camp. I burned a bit of cloth and putting the ashes to the wound bandaged Mokhnatka's neck with a silk kerchief.

The next day some shepherds told me that Mokhnatka had mauled one of Yusuf-bek's guards. The news spread over all the camps on the Artos. The bek's people organized a hunt, but Mokhnatka and I fled to places where the devil himself would not have discovered us.

In August, when the nomads went away, we returned home. You can't imagine the welcome we got. All the people of the village poured out to meet us. The kids climbed on the bear's back or hung to its neck and tail screaming with joy. Mokhnatka bore the scamps' pranks patiently, grunting amiably. She was overjoyed to meet her foster-mother, whom she had not seen for two months and had missed badly. But she expressed her joy in a true bear-like fashion—standing on her hind legs, she picked the dog up and tossed her onto the roof of the house. The poor dog started running helplessly to and fro, unable to come down.

Autumn came. Mokhnatka accompanied me on my hunting trips as before, and in her free time sat perched on the trees eating fruit.

Towards spring Mokhnatka became thoughtful and irritable. Neither her foster-mother nor the children dared to approach her when she was in a black mood. After wandering in the mountains and fields she came home depressed—all her thoughts, it seemed, remained in the gorges of the Artos. Mokhnatka to love and to have children. And so, with her kinsfolk. She was particularly gloomy in the evenings. With the last rays of the setting sun she would walk out of the village, climb the top of the hill, sniff the air, and, feeling the nearness of the bears, whine wistfully.

Nature was taking its course, and an urge had developed in Mokhnatka to love and to have children. And so, with her blood boiling with desire and her thoughts in a state of commotion, she moved about restlessly, longing to join those wild animals she had never seen and could not remember, but to whom she was tied by bonds of blood.

One evening, plodding along the Tigris gorge, I heard the roaring of bears behind. I looked around. Two bears stood at the entrance of a cave a short distance away and looked after us sniffing the air. Without waiting for me to say "Gech," Mokhnatka walked towards them.

"Osh, Mokhnatka, osh!" I cried. She stopped and looked back hesitantly. I could see there was a struggle going on inside her. But Nature got the upper hand.

I knew that even a human being has not the power to resist the call of Nature and let her go. Besides, June was approaching and I was eaten up by anxiety lest Yusuf-bek, who was coming again soon, would take Mokhnatka away and harass me on her account into the bargain. This consideration strengthened my determination to give Mokhnatka her freedom. I turned to go, but suddenly heard the stamping of feet behind. Mokhnatka! She came to me, licked my hands, and let out a sorrowful howl. I understood that she loved me so much that she did not want to leave me against my will. I stroked her head pointing with my finger at the bears and said, "Gech!"

So Mokhnatka joined her own kind and started a new life, while I walked home overcome with melancholy.

As time went on, we began to forget Mokhnatka. I went hunting as before, only no longer to the Tigris gorge—I did not like the idea of meeting Mokhnatka.

The southern slopes of the Artos are practically bare during summer. The sun burns out the young grass as early as June, and all that remains is an ash-grey mass of rocks, pebbles, withered bushes, and brambles. Only in the gorge by the springs is the eye relieved by green signs of life. An old leafy oak-tree stands on one of those denuded slopes, providing shade for travelers exhausted by the heat of the day and for herds of sheep. Even from some distance one can make out a narrow dark-green hollow somewhat below the tree, pointing to the presence of a life-giving spring.

One day I stopped under this tree for a rest on the way out to one of my hunting grounds. I unwrapped my *bashlyk*,[5] had something to eat, and then just sat leaning against the tree.

Sleep crept on me unawares. It's easy enough to doze off in cool shade after a tiring walk.

God only knows how long I slept, but when I opened my eyes the sun was dipping towards the mountains. I stretched out my hand for the gun but it wasn't there. I looked around—it was gone. There were no people to be seen, either. If it was a robber, I reflected, why had he left me alive and not even tried to take my money? And, if not, what could have happened to the gun?

No sooner had that thought crossed my mind than I heard a heavy tread behind me. I turned round, and cold sweat stood on my brow. An enormous bear was coming towards me! Woe to me, I thought, if I had my flint-lock I could smash its head, but what can I do with a dagger alone? I wrapped my left hand in the tail of my *boorka*,[6] put it out like a shield and waited.

The cursed beast was coming on so fearlessly one might have thought I wasn't there. I was numb with fright. This is the end of me, I thought.

I thought of climbing the tree, but remembered that bears

---

[5] *bashlyk*: a cloth hood with long ends used as a scarf.
[6] *boorka*: a sleeveless felt coat.

are far better hands at that sport than myself. At that desperate moment I noticed that the bear had a lame right hind leg. My heart danced with joy.

"Mokhnatka, my pet, my own lame darling," I shouted and stretching out my arms ran towards her and hugged her head.

Mokhnatka grunted and licked me in the face as in days gone by. Then she looked at me so sadly, so forlornly, as if she had just buried a child.

"Why are you so sad, my darling?" I asked her. "Why are you alone? Did I send you to your folk to have you unhappy? Where is your husband? Where are your little ones?"

She listened to me with drooping head, like a bereft widow, sighing softly. Then she walked aside, looked under a big stone and came back on her hind legs carrying my gun in her arms.

"Now, can you imagine that!" I thought. "What did she hide my gun for? Miraculous are thy deeds, oh Almighty Lord. Just imagine—she knows that a gun sends death and feared lest I killed her offhand before I was properly awake and recognized her."

Yes, Mokhnatka knew all that. . . . I made to take the gun but she would not give it to me. Instead she turned and walked uphill, towards some rocks. She went a few steps, then stopped and looked back at me, made another few steps and looked back at me again and then at the rock in front as though to say that there was something there and that I was to follow her.

I walked after her bewildered, my legs feeling wooden under me as if they weren't my own. I wondered whether I was bewitched or dealing with the devil himself or whether it was the will of the Prophet that a bear should take my gun and I should follow it empty-handed. I knew that there was a steep cliff on the other side of the hill. Reaching the top Mokhnatka lay flat on her belly and crawled towards the edge of the cliff. She peered cautiously down, then crawled back, handed me the gun and looked now at me, now to the edge of the cliff.

Following her bidding, I called on Allah, and moved forward on all fours. When I was near the edge I lay flat and looked back. Mokhnatka followed me and pressed herself to the ground at my feet.

I bent over the edge. The face of the rock was as steep as a wall. There was a cave at the foot of it. The sight that met my eye made my heart well nigh jump out of my breast. A gigantic cat, the size of a cow, slept sprawling at the entrance of the cave. Sheaves of rays from the setting sun falling on its orange and black striped coat made it glint and sparkle like the silk garments of the shah himself. I have never seen such a beast before—only heard about them from my father. It was sleeping peacefully, now and then chasing tiresome flies away, as a cat does.

When the fit of trembling that overcame me had subsided and I was again able to think coolly, I picked up my gun and steadied it on the rock. But to aim it was devilishly difficult, because the wall slanted inwards and the tiger was lying at the very entrance into the cave. I could only sight its head by leaning out over the precipice at the risk of tumbling down headlong.

At last I summoned up my courage, leaned out, aimed and pressed the trigger. The roar of the shot echoed through the gorge, and the smoke hid the tiger from view. Mokhnatka jumped up and raced off. At the foot of the hill there was a hollow in the ground washed out by the heavy rains. She hid in the hollow under the dog-rose and bramble bushes. I jumped in after her. A few minutes passed without a sign of the tiger; we crept out from our place of concealment and climbed the rock again, looking around cautiously. I peeped warily over the edge and sighed with relief—the tiger was still sprawled out—the bullet must've hit it exactly where I had wanted, in the head.

When Mokhnatka had made sure that the tiger was dead, the sadness in her eyes was allayed a little as though a healing lotion had been applied to her wounded heart. She licked my hands, grunted, and went down.

It took us some time to get round to the other side of the hill, but finally we found ourselves at the entrance of the cave. In my exultation I sang and shouted loud enough to be heard all down the gorge. This was a cause for joy indeed! There had been only one other tiger killed in our region before and that was by the famous Armenian hunter Akop. It had happened twenty years before, when I was a mere child. They had sent the skin to the *kaimakam*[7] that time, to soften his heart towards us. As I skinned the tiger, I thought that I'd present the skin to Yusuf-bek—perhaps, he would then for-

---

[7] *kaimakam*: the administrative head of a district.

give Mokhnatka and would even give me something in return.

Then this idea was driven out of my mind by another one, quite different. To hell with beks and sultans! I knew what I'd do—I'd marry Match, Slo's daughter, and present the skin to my Match, my beloved who was as beautiful as a gazelle, and for whose sake I later killed a man and had to flee to Russia.

"I'll tell Match tonight that for love of her I braved a ferocious tiger and her heart may warm up towards me, and Slo, her father, will praise me for my courage. The whole village will sing the bravery of Davot the shepherd, and Match will become my betrothed."

The thought made me so happy that my heart began to beat faster and my face flushed hot. I burst into my favorite song that I had made up in honor of Match, and all the gorges around joined in.

I went on skinning the tiger, overwhelmed with joy, when I suddenly heard a low groan. I glanced towards Mokhnatka, and a shiver ran down my spine—it was as though cold water had been poured on a flaming fire.

I felt as if my heart had been pierced by a bullet. Freshly chewn bones were scattered about the cave—two little heads, thin legs resembling a sheep's ribs, small hairy paws. Mokhnatka was gathering them in a heap and whining woefully. Only now did I understand what a terrible misfortune had befallen poor Mokhnatka. The tiger had devoured her cubs and so, unable to deal with him herself, she had chosen me as the weapon of her revenge.

Petrified with pity, I watched the movements of the bereft mother. She collected the bones, hunched over them, and with dull whines and sorrowful sighs began to sniff and lick the remains of her cubs. Even now I can hear the sad dirge that her heart sang over her dead children. When I finished skinning the tiger and loaded the skin onto my back, Mokhnatka seemed to have woken up; she sighed dismally, and rose too. She scraped some earth together and buried the little bones under it, heaping leaves, twigs, and stones over the grave.

By sunset we reached the hill on the outskirts of our village. From there we could hear the barking of dogs. Mokhnatka stopped. I bent down, kissed her on the forehead and the eyes, and, a stony-hearted hunter though I am, sobbed like a child, mourning our parting, mourning Mokhnatka's children and her boundless grief.

Wiping my eyes dry, I went on towards the village.

The sun was setting. Mokhnatka stood on the hill, silhouetted against the red sky, and followed me with her eyes. When I entered the village, she turned and shambled off—back towards the Tigris gorge, towards the grave of her little ones.

I never met her again.

Fifty springs and fifty autumns have passed since those days. I've grown old, my hair has turned white, the events of later years have become dim in the fog of my memory, and only two images still make the heart of the old hunter throb—one is that of a girl, slender like a gazelle, and the other is of a woe-stricken she-bear, hunched over the grave of her cubs.

(TRANSLATED BY RAISA BOBROVA)

Night

by GOURGEN MAHARI

I was again gripped by the illness and once again it resolved the question of my being and non-being. Since that day, when in one night I became a criminal, it has always accompanied me. It gradually changed my behavior and altered my features and with it altered my very self. And this time it convinced me that I wasn't an exception and that in this cold and dark underground mortuary, its benefits and inconveniences concerned me too.

But the illness in no way resembled that prevalent and ordinary sickness all the prisoners dreamt of—the type they loved to cling to. In the evening after work when you enter the camp, spent and tired, your face burning, and you feel a slight spasm within, you feel sure you are on the threshold of happiness. You are separated from your group and taken to the hospital. The small and squarish waiting room is where Dr. Merpert looking like a pharoah with his snow white beard treats all those who fell ill during work. To some he gives a liquid medicine which he has concocted himself from various herbs—its effectiveness and quality a secret known only to him. Into most patients he would slip a thermometer. If the temperature registered above 99.5°, he would write down the patient's name. This meant the man was excused from work the following day. Glowing with happiness the patient would head for his barracks to tell his friends about it. They would compliment and envy him at the same time.

The more clever prisoners raised their temperatures artificially by rubbing garlic under their left armpits. Others coaxed the mercury upwards with their thumbs after having tapped the thermometer. Michael Zingayev, a Jew from Tiflis, ruined it for everyone. Once when he took the thermometer out from under his armpit and handed it to Dr. Merpert, he stunned the doctor because it read 113°. Zingayev had over-manipulated it, having lost his usual finesse. After a discussion among the authorities, it was decided that a guard would be posted in the waiting room to make sure the patients used their thermometers properly.

So this time it hadn't been a pleasant illness for me—the kind that I desired.

All those both totally and partially unfit for manual labor were transferred to the newly constructed and less comfortable barracks Number 4. My only consolation was that two Jewish students, Aidlemann and Bevzner, had also been assigned to the new barracks. My relationship with both of them became a close one. They could recite Nadson and Yessenin by heart—and both ranked Yessenin above Nadson.

But no matter how much warmth these friendships generated, it didn't affect the cold in barracks Number 4. When you came in from outside, only the bitter smell of *makhorka*[1] would remind you that you were inside, not outside.

In the midst of this kind of grim routine, the illness finally gripped me as if it had been waiting all along to settle its accounts with me. First my feet grew numb—then my teeth started rattling. Eventually my entire body began to shiver, racked by fever and buffeted by the freezing weather.

---

[1] *makhorka*: cigarettes.

I see Aidlemann and Bevzner. They look worried and their lips seem to be moving, but I cannot hear their voices clearly. As the fever takes deeper hold of me, I feel as though I am being lowered into a dark well where it's hot yet cold, narrow and yet wide, and where in the darkness I sense dusk.

—Call Ashod Dayi, I shout in Armenian, and they seem to understand.

—Soon, soon, Bevzner assures me, his triangular nose hovering over me. He really has a triangular nose and until now I had never noticed it.

—Bevzner, I say almost breathless with fever,—you have a triangular nose.

—You better not talk about noses, he replies in a hurt but still reconciliatory tone as he stares at my face—no—my nose.

—In any case my nose is not triangular, I say defending myself as I catch his glance. At that moment Dr. Merpert enters.

—He's turning blue, he says looking at me, and it sounds to me as if he's talking about noses too. It all seems so funny I want to laugh, but instead I feel hot tears running down my cheeks knowing they have nothing to do with either crying or laughing—they are neutral tears.

Ashod Dayi appears, then disappears. Then he reappears. I also see two hospital attendants wearing rumpled, dirty coats.

Next Ashod Dayi helps me remove my clothing before he wraps my body in a handmade blanket and . . .

And I'm standing stark naked on the cold floor of the bathroom dancing with rare and delicate steps, keeping in rhythm with my shivering and writhing body—a standstill against the elements. After taking off his winter coat, Ashod Dayi lurches for a pail which he fills with hot water and immerses his hand in before shouting:

—Stand still, you crook.

I always know when he'll call me that—at a time when I'm the farthest thing from one.

He splashes the entire contents of the pail over me and then for a second, third, fourth and fifth time refills it and pours it over me. Vanya, the Chinaman, is silhouetted against the wall in the misty bathroom. He lunges at Ashod Dayi and grabs his hands.

—*Khvat, khvat,* he says meaning that's enough considering the fact that the water rations of five other prisoners were used on me. But Ashod Dayi undaunted breaks loose and splashes a decisive sixth pailful over me and I feel as though I am in seventh heaven. I feel as though my bones are melting, becoming soft. Cotton clouds form a cocoon around me and I feel weightless. Then I have an uncontrollable desire to lie down on the cement floor and sleep. Just as I am about to give in to the urge, I feel Ashod Dayi's powerful hands around my body. He carries me out of the bathroom as my feet barely touch the floor. Outside with Vanya's help he dresses me and wraps a blanket around me. Then, joined by a hospital attendant, Ashod Dayi guides me into the courtyard where the freezing sleet beats against the exposed parts of my face and I breathe slowly and carefully as if to hoard the warmth inside of me.

Soon we're at the hospital. To the left of the door of the main building is another door which leads into a cell where there are two narrow, iron beds—both empty.

—Here, Dr. Merpert says arranging one of the beds.

—Why can't he stay in the main building? grumbles Ashod Dayi.

—Of course he can, Dr. Merpert mutters—but it is better here, right here.

It surprised me that Ashod Dayi seemed gloomy about my staying in the cell where the air is purer and where I won't have to see or hear other patients.

They laid me down on the bed—the one on the left.

—Be firm, you crook, I'll see you in the morning, said Ashod Dayi smiling sadly as he went out into the corridor where he spoke first with Dr. Merpert then with the hospital attendant before leaving. The doctor returned to place a thermometer under my armpit.

I fell asleep and while I was sleeping someone removed the thermometer. Noise had woken me up and when I looked around I noticed that on a small square table-cupboard between the beds there was a lit lantern. I saw the door swing open and I was aware of a stretcher being carried in although I didn't seem to see any attendants at first. After I saw a man lying on the stretcher I finally noticed the attendants. They were propping him up into a sitting position—then one held the patient by the arms and the other grabbed his feet and they placed him in bed.

He is young and his yellowish face is marked with bronze spots. He moves his head as he struggles to rest it somewhere while the rest of his body remains immobile. His eyes suddenly jump out of their sockets as if straining to see something. He utters exclamations in German, but I can tell he is a German who lived in Russia because otherwise he wouldn't have spoken the broken Russian I heard.

—Oh Mein Gott, Oh Mein Gott, he says breathlessly while beating the bed with a hand.

—My bowl, he pleads.

An attendant places a clay bowl, made in the hospital pottery, on the table. The prisoner almost assaults the bowl with his long, trembling fingers, and after he secures it, places it on his chest.

—The spoon, he groans with difficulty. As the attendant hands it to him, he grabs it away, but then gently puts it in the bowl.

—I had some bread, he reminds the attendant uncertainly and weaves his head back and forth.

—Yes, I had some bread, this time speaking with more conviction. The attendant slips him a battered piece of black bread. The German works it into the bowl with difficulty, pauses and then becomes completely still for what seems a few or more seconds or a whole eternity.

The door closes, muting the growl of an agitated dog. Now we are alone and he still hasn't noticed me and that's just fine. I have stopped shivering and feel a new sensation as if soft yet hot flames were burning inside of me. I am bundled in the blanket and crouching like a child tucked in its mother's womb. Wound like a ball of thread, I can see with one eye only through a small opening in the part of the blanket wrapped around my head.

—Oh Mein Gott, he says with a muffled voice. As if to test his strength he tries to move even as he firmly secures that treasure on his chest.

In walks Dr. Merpert with a thermometer in his hand. He gets close to the patient, bends over, and peers into his face, and changing his mind about taking his temperature, bolts out of the room just after the reflection of the thermometer plays on his white beard. I barely hear him whisper "Shh, shh" outside in the waiting room. When there is noise in the waiting room you hear his "Shh, shh." But who wants to hear "Shh, shh" here where silence dominates—an ironbound and stony silence—a silence emanating from the burden of living on Earth.

—O, Oh, I hear him groan, the sounds slipping through his lips from deep inside him. Oh, I reply, responding to this O—what are you? who are you O? . . . and I get an answer. You must know who I am. I am a ring, an enormous burning ring, so huge I can encircle all the world's prisons and camps where the innocent are condemned to die, these condemned who are all Pharaohs because their corpses do not rot in all the freezing tombs. O!

I know my neighbor is suffering. I don't hear any more O's. He sounds instead as if he is gargling water. As I hear the sounds, thick, coagulated saliva rises and fills his mouth then drips down his chin and onto his chest and pillow. After a while, he is completely motionless.

An eye peers through a crack in the door which closes and then reopens. Dr. Merpert enters and quickly leaves. Did I hear or did I imagine I heard "Sh, sh" again? I see a stretcher outside, then I see the stretcher-bearers. They come in and lower the German's body onto the stretcher, making sure the bowl doesn't overturn. They remove him from the room as the bowl rests firmly against his chest, holding the wooden spoon and the battered piece of black bread.

—The man died, I say to myself,—he died just now and they took him away. You will die too. Doesn't that bother you? I look at the empty bed—nonsense! The whole thing is due to my being feverish. I'm seeing things. The German died with a piece of bread on his chest. It's a lot of nonsense, just nonsense. But how come the pillow is wet? Perhaps this is how people go mad. And how can you prove to yourself you already haven't gone mad? "Sum ergo cogito" But it's clear I haven't lost my mind because I can even quote. Quotations! Quotations!

There is movement in the corridor and once again the door opens revealing another stretcher. O new ones O good ones—now who said that? Toumanian.[2] To whom? To the young writers. It's obvious that I'm either crazy or a clown. It's a comedy, perhaps a hospital comedy, no, a worldly comedy. Maybe it's a divine comedy. Why divine? What's that divine citizen doing out there? It's simply a human comedy, oh no, it's an antihuman comedy; that is, if we seriously consider why I'm here and what a long journey it turned out to be. It's been eight years since I've been cut off from my work. Why did I come here? I should be back

[2] A famous Armenian poet.

home. But I didn't come, they brought me here. I can't leave, only they can send me home.

I can see my new neighbor under a blanket. He is skinny and his eyes are glued to the ceiling. He has fair, unevenly cut hair. It looks like only the head on the pillow exists. But then a hand moves from out under the blanket, trying to make a full gesture for help. But who could he be calling for? There's nobody in here. Now I am aware of his long, white and narrow neck. And I realize he does have a body but that it is shriveled, very shriveled. When they put him in bed I shut my eyes hoping that he will have vanished when I reopen them. But there he goes signalling again with that hand, really there stretched out under the blanket.

He asks someone to come to him several times with a kind of deep groan. I am listening to him very attentively.

—I'm the famous photographer of my city's daily. I'm called Sarko Leskov or simply Seryoja. I'm happy to know you, he says and goes on muttering to himself.

He is flexing the muscles of his thin face perhaps in an effort to smile.

—O.K. boys, come closer towards me. That's it, all the way up front. There'll be editorials about your team. They'll appreciate this: (He drops his hands.) Ah—you all look well fed. But you—come closer, haven't you eaten? and you too, it doesn't look good. Did you walk out of a hospital? What's eating you? You're too slow and lazy. I wonder if everyone is so skinny. Are you all ready now—smile, all of you, smile.

He falls into silence and tries to raise his head from the pillow but can't. Smile! he orders again with a dying voice. It's not something only government officials do. So smile. Give me the biggest smile you can, smile, otherwise they'll print a picture of faces at a funeral. Then pleading he asks again, smile, please smile, just once . . .

He's crying like a little child as he pleads again—Smile. I'm begging you on my knees . . . I know it isn't easy these days but try anyway. Aha! that's better, that's it, just think of all the pictures in the papers, that's the way they all smile. . . . right? . . . the sons of bitches. . . . they've just forgotten how to smile. . . .

He stops talking and still feeling like a hurt child starts sniffling. I try to smile for his sake, a special smile for this helpless and hapless photographer, for the man who was once

Seryoja—but I can't. My face stutters. I try again but I can't,
I want to but I can't.

It appears I have been speaking and speaking loudly because someone is looking through a narrow opening in the
door—and then vanishes. And now what if that gloomy boss
of the Third Department walks in and smiles and commands
me to smile—says smile just once and I'll let you go free—
will I be able to smile? What if he starts coaxing me to smile
as if I were an idiot. (When could freedom be bought to such
a low price—all wrapped up in a smile?) What if he eggs me
on—smile, remember the noble race of cows in Stepanavan
and smile. . . . smile you fool! smile. . . .

And now he seems to be working up to a crisis, jumbling
his words.

—Me? start a revolt? are you kidding or something, don't
hit me—I'm not an animal. Me? Have I made fun of the Father of the People?[3] Me? I never took that picture, it was delivered to us. My retouching job was lousy—it came out
blurry. So beat me! beat me!

He tries to raise himself up but falls back on the pillow. Is
he laughing or crying? I can't tell but I don't want to hear
anymore—I just don't. I want to scream. I try but I can't.
My head is screaming, my heart is screaming—maybe my
soul is screaming . . . screaming. . . .

When I open my eyes the bed next to me is empty. I feel
as if I'm in flames without being reduced to ashes; maybe this
is what they call hell. I feel as heavy as a thousand mountains. It's so obvious I was drifting off in a nightmare. There
really was no German, no freedom given for a smile, no photographer with his retouching problem—hallucination. But do
I exist? Yes, I do—even if this I is only me.

This I is me—because the sound of a deep voice draws me
out of an oppressive unconsciousness: Boo . . . Boo. Nothing
else now enters my consciousness besides the word Boo. Is it
a sound ringing in my ears? Or am I just delirious? I open
my eyes with difficulty and there is only darkness; through it
only a shaft of light emerges—and I know that the link with
the world outside has been cut off. I pull down the blanket
from over my head and cannot believe my eyes. In the other
bed is a man who appears to be well-built with a flushed, fat,
ruddy face and a thick, curling black mustache. But as I
study him more closely I see that he is not well-built after

[3] A reference to Stalin.

all—maybe he once had been—only his face exudes a reminder of past strength and distinction. But even the face is deceiving—the fullness is merely swollenness and the reddish quality is a symptom of some illness—is sickly and unhealthy. I look at him as he sits wearing hospital underwear, his legs dangling over the side of the bed—his big, uneasy and restless eyes gazing out of a small, frosted window.

—The weather outside is terrible, he says with a deep voice apparently continuing a conversation he started a long time ago. It's a snow storm—I got up off the stretcher and could hardly (he paused—placed his left hand on his chest) toss my body in here; who knows when morning will come? Do you have a watch? That's a stupid question. I've never waited for dawn to break as much as I do tonight. What's wrong with you? Do you have a cold? My problem is my blood—it hoisted a white flag and surrendered; but that wasn't good enough, today I developed fever and they brought me in here. Just let me sleep. This place seems to be reserved for people with minor illnesses and foreign prisoners. Take me for example—I come from abroad—from Bulgaria, from Sofia.

He stops talking, turns over on his side, gazes at the window again as the snowstorm like a bird beats its wings against it, and, wounded, flies away. Outside the leaves flutter. Someone is walking down the corridor. It's a good thing there are other people in the world besides Dr. Merpert and the two attendants, besides the Bulgarian and myself. Through the wooden partition next to me I hear something groaning in the ward. It means there is someone else who couldn't sleep. It really doesn't matter why he wasn't sleeping. It's tough on a person to be awake and alone when everyone else is sleeping. Because then he thinks and suffers for everyone else. From out of this thought emerges a great philosophy: it's better to sleep for others than to stay awake, it's better that I should die than others . . . no; that one doesn't work out too well; I keep on wondering: didn't I die eight years ago instead of all the people who kept out of the camps? I died and ended up in this world where devils are dressed in military uniforms and angels . . . no, there aren't any angels here, angels are worthless in hell, they just never show up.

—I run Sofia. Yes, I run it! There's a big difference between a man and a city—when a man is beheaded he dies—

you can't screw a new head on his shoulders. But a city . . .
Sofia was beheaded, a new head was screwed on and it lives.
Yes, the cities go on living, and so do the people. Here in
your country (he lowers his voice) there's a sharply trimmed
mustache and a pair of iron boots.[4] That's all.

> *In the forest nothing of the sort has ever happened,*
>   *ever happened o best of men!*
> *that Jantakis may become king, become king*

He sang, but it didn't sound like a song; he tried to laugh
but couldn't.

—It's a children's song, he says, and I know that even in
prison you're afraid of it. Just a children's song.

He tries to fix his eyes on me as he is making an effort to
compose his thoughts.

—And I can't understand why you are afraid. Up to this
day I've passed through thirteen prisons in thirteen cities like
a tourist of sorts. It's been a long and difficult trip. There's a
lot of difference between all the prisons. In one they removed
the dead from their beds the day they died but a few days
later I was in a prison where they never removed anyone. We
set up a spot for them and called it death corner where we
piled them up in order to get a few inches of extra space. It
was a head-to-foot sleeping set-up. In all the dungeons I've
been in it was the same story—people maddened by hunger
and filth; and from standing in a line of five hundred waiting
to piss in one can. Men driven mad by the stench, who in-
voked their "Father's" name out of fear. I knew great men
including scientists and important politicians who had their
medals brutally torn off. I saw them with their shredded
tunics. But they still continued to believe in Him.[5] You get it.
I won't invoke his name myself and believe me that means
something to me. They searched for the "sinners" and found
them. They tried to make me believe that he didn't know
anything about this great tragedy and that if he ever found
out about it . . . ? If he ever heard anything about it . . . In
walked Dr. Merpert.

—Sleep! he orders, it's getting late and if you don't sleep
the wolf will steal you away, I think he smiled because I saw
his teeth bared between his lips.

---

[4] An allusion to Stalin.
[5] Stalin.

—If the wolf comes he won't ask who is awake and who is asleep, he said as he left.

I am swept out to sea on the crest of a wave and can no longer understand what my roommate was saying—only the resonance of his deep voice. Let him rant because I'm in Yerevan now. It was the last day of my youth and perhaps of my life. In a store window on Abovian Street[6] there were toys. I saw a large horse and decided to buy it for my son. But the store was closed. It was a beautiful, black-maned horse on four green wheels. But that night the "knights" of our republic, our capitol, who planned both days and nights for us, and displaying amazing foresight for our country's security, arrested me and took me to Cell Number 2 in the basement of that well-known tufa building. The wooden horse must have waited a very long time for me the next day and who knows maybe its mane turned blacker or maybe turned white overnight.

Since then I've bought the horse many times and walked up Abovian Street with it tucked under my arm. I have a recurring nightmare which has a different ending each time— either I am arrested carrying the horse under my arm or I have a bicycle accident and the horse breaks, or the saleswoman runs out the store after me and steals my horse without an explanation. I've never been able to give that spirited horse to my son, not once. But right now, as if for the first time, I am walking down Abovian Street with the horse under my arm and my heart is pounding with joy. Reaching our street I approach our house and I freeze on the spot: it is completely boxed in by columns linked together by thick barbed wire. In front of the house a tall, black-mustached soldier is pacing and he is armed with a pistol in his hand.

—What's going on, I ask him. Just then my eight-year-old son looks down from the window and shouts:

—Don't come near me, father. I'm a terrorist now, and a spy and a lot of other good things.

—Are you crazy? What's the matter with you? I told the soldier, don't you know he's just an innocent kid.

—So what? he tells me, they're all innocent, but after we harden their soft spots and soften their hard spots they start remembering all the crimes they haven't committed.

—Haven't you got a heart? I ask him.

—Don't come near me, he warns, we have no orders about

[6] The main street in Yerevan, the capital of Armenia.

that thing. So, I set the horse down on the ground and leapt at the miserable creature, grabbed his pistol and killed him.

—Get his keys, my son shouts, I'm behind seven locks.

I bend over to get the keys and I see someone else writhing on the ground dressed in white prison underwear—wait! I ask myself—where have I seen him before?

—I haven't got the keys, he cries, He's got them. A pair of blood-filled boots, yes a pair of them. Isn't it an awful night? When is it going to be morning? Do you have a watch?

It is my roommate. The iron bars of his bed rattle. It is still another time I can't take the horse to my son—What an absurd dream!

—It's morning, he whispers, I hope it ends soon. It's daytime in Sofia now. If morning arrived late in Sofia I'd send out an order from government house to double the street lights. Or has the sun just lost its way? Maybe they arrested the sun. I warn you not to threaten the sun. I'll give you one more warning, for the last time. Hey you, listen, why are you so quiet? Are you just dumb and charged with anti-government agitation? It's possible. I've known deaf spies, terrorists as frightened as rabbits, scientists who blow up their labs, crippled and near-sighted people who crossed the border . . . I've seen many things but never a night as long as this. O God, what a night. By now I could have eaten an entire goose as large as a sheep stuffed with rice and raisins. But right now if there was just a little black bread . . . listen, do you have any bread? Don't worry, I won't steal it. Maybe you slipped it under your pillow. Just give me a piece and I promise I'll return it to you in the morning. Maybe you think I'll be dead in the morning? I promise you I won't die, I'll give you my word of honor I won't.

He doesn't keep his promise. It is like emerging from a subjective oblivion when I open my eyes and see his face looking shrunken and blue, his frozen eyes fixed on me and the two forefingers of his right hand signalling a V.

I understand.

I had supposed that this time I had "slept" for a long time and that he hadn't liked the way I had acted toward him. I slept with a clear conscience without giving him a piece of my non-existent bread, or who knows, maybe I only pretended to be sleeping.

I turn my head towards the wall to ease the deep guilt I felt. Then from some unfathomable and distant place in me, from some well in me, I hear bells peeling a signal, distinct and clear, of my rebirth. It meant morning had come. That they had not arrested the sun after all. I turn my head to take another look at the man who wasn't able to see daybreak. But the bed is empty; it stands on its four legs looking innocent as though nothing happened. Nothing did happen. In a world of confusing mixed-up reality, dreams and imagination I don't know which is which. One thing is certain—I wouldn't tell Ashod Dayi anything about tonight. Was it real, just a dream, or my imagination? I can't say for sure. Cold air fills the cell and I see Ashod Dayi. He places his hand on my forehead and greets me, "Good morning."

—Is it morning? I ask him.

—It's morning, he says, but how would you know? Daytime reaches here late. How did you pass the night?

—Happily, I felt well, I reply. Listen:

In the forest nothing of the sort has ever happened,
ever happened o best of men!
that Jantakis became king, became king

—What is it? Ashod Dayi asks sounding disturbed.

—It's a children's poem, I reply.

He leaves. I can hear him. Maybe he's talking to Dr. Merpert. Then the door opens and I see them both coming in.

—In the first place there isn't any room in the main building. All the beds are occupied. Let him stay here another night, Dr. Merpert says, then leaves.

—I would have kept you out of this damned cell if I could but now you can understand there's no way I could manage it, he says, pausing, and then thinking out loud:

—Zamanov is in critical condition.

—Where's he? I ask him.

—In the main building. He can't even smoke anymore. He offered to give his tobacco to Sanasar but Sanasar turned him down. I've got it now.

—I feel fine here, I try to console Ashod Dayi.

—For God's sake I wish you really meant it, he answers. He very deftly wipes a tear drop from the corner of his right eye with the rough thumb of his glove; then he says:

—I have to leave now, take care of yourself you crook. I'll see you in the evening.

When he leaves I close my tired eyelids. Again the courtyard reverberates with the sound of the bell.

I feel happy and out of danger. I feel as if the entire world is sliding into a bottomless abyss and that I am safe. It's an awful catastrophe that doesn't concern me. When Dr. Merpert took my temperature it read 102°. There isn't a person in the world who could cure my feverish joy. If there is clay nobody could force me to dip my feet into it when my feet are already numb from its coldness and my shirt is soaked with perspiration. I dash to the oven in the pottery and place my feet in front of it trying to bring them back to life. After I dry out my shirt I sink my feet deep into the stubborn depths of the clay. I remember all the other workers in the pottery who are dead now. If I could cry I would weep for the German suffering from the ancient illness diagnosed as "private property"; for the miserable photographer, for the people of Sofia who never saw this black morning. I would have cried for all the living and dead; for the Pharaohs of both sexes, those decaying and those not yet decaying; for those who still flourish behind barbed wire, and for man, the world's most valuable capital, secured behind seven locks like diamond and gold. If I only had the tears.

An attendant comes in and removes the lantern after blowing it out. The frozen window panes turn blue. It's finally daybreak. The attendant comes in again this time carrying a clay bowl holding a wooden spoon and my daily bread. I have a strong urge to place it on my chest but the idea frightens me. And I know why I am frightened. But it's more than being frightened. It also concerns what Ashod Dayi often says: Wake up, you crook! the little morning is here and a person who sleeps through it will never see the big morning. Now I know the big morning will come. When Dr. Merpert took my temperature again it read 95.9°. He shook his head and murmured "Amazing" and I recalled Ashod Dayi's six pails of hot water back there in the bath.

Dr. Merpert is thinking out loud now:

—Hitler is retreating. The last German has left our land, if you don't include the prisoners.

I know I'll see the dawn break. It'll be great and I'll walk down Abovian Street with steadier steps and buy my son that beautiful, black-maned horse.

I will buy it.

(TRANSLATED BY GARIG BASMADJIAN AND
VAUGHN KOUMJIAN)

The White Lamb

by SERO KHANZADIAN

The old gardener Navasard went down to the spring that welled up under the nut tree to wash and to rest. No sooner had he bent down to let the cool water splash on his sun-burned face than he heard the team leader calling him. "Hey, Navasard! Hurry! Your son Arshak is back!"

"What?" the old man said excitedly and then straightened up with difficulty. He rushed back up to where the man was standing with an agility surprising for his years. "What did you say? When did he come? Where is he?"

"He's in the village. I saw him myself. He's driving a blue sedan, riding through the village. Lucky you, Navasard! God has blessed you with a fine son!"

The sun began to shine ten times as brightly as before. Navasard felt he was walking on air. His heart pounded from excitement.

Navasard seemed to be pondering over something as he looked in the direction of the village. But then he turned sharply and ran towards the winepress instead.

He had not seen Arshak for ten years. Each year he would look at the road hopefully, and wait. He had waited patiently. And now, at long last, he would see him. Arshak had come at a good time: the fruit in the orchards had ripened, and he was still hale and hearty.

Navasard had no living relatives left in the village. His had not been a happy life. He had never had any children of his own, and his wife had died many years before. His brother and sister-in-law had both died of hunger during the war, leaving an only son, Arshak.

Navasard picked up the spade that lay on the ground by the edge of the ditch and began to dig. The earth was moist and smelled of wine. He extracted a small jug he had buried ten years before and was pleased at the touch of the cold earthenware vessel. Sniffing the delicate aroma of the wine, he smiled and said to himself: "It's turned into lion's milk." Then he recalled that the largest of the watermelons had ripened under the huge mulberry tree by the river bank. He cut its stem, wiped the silvery dust from the melon with the hem of his long jacket and admired its shiny stripes.

"My Arshak loves watermelons," he mumbled. He got down on his knees, put his arms around the melon and squeezed hard, with his ear to the rind. He nodded approvingly at the sound. He then went over to the fig tree, climbed it with difficulty and began picking the honey-sweet fruit that had been pecked at here and there by birds. He chose the best figs and packed them gently into a bright woven basket.

Then Navasard set out along the bank to where a six-months-old white lamb was grazing. He was saving the lamb for a special occasion.

"Arshak has come home. I've finally lived to see the day," Navasard said to himself and untethered the lamb. It bleated loudly.

"Let's go, fellow," Navasard said. "Come on, Arshak's home."

He climbed the steep path to the village. The heavy basket pressed on his shoulders, the wine splashed in the jug, while the meek and gentle lamb either ran on ahead or fell behind him.

"Where are you going so early in the day?" the people he met on the way asked.

"Arshak has come home for a visit," the old man replied proudly.

On the way each tree and bush, each stone and spring reminded him of Arshak's childhood. Many were the times that he had carried the child up the steep path on his back. He would sit down to rest on this stone. Navasard would give Arshak a pear and would wipe his nose with the hem of his long jacket. There was the spring which Arshak liked to drink from. Navasard would cup his hands and Arshak would drink from them. Here was the small orchard. The trees still bore fruit abundantly and stayed green far into the autumn. When Arshak was seven he had fallen from that cherry tree and had broken his leg. Navasard had carried him the many miles to the doctor in the distant settlement.

Then Navasard thought of all the things he had sold to outfit Arshak for city life when he had sent the boy off to study. It had been a long stretch, but Arshak had graduated from the university and had then gone on to study in Moscow. He had risen high in the world.

Navasard would often tell his fellow-villagers about the very important work Arshak was doing in the capital, about his grand car and also that he lived in the biggest house in Moscow.

The old man was in a hurry to reach the village. The wine splashed in the jug, and the meek and timid lamb followed on his heels.

He finally reached his house, but did not see Arshak's car outside. "Why didn't he drive right up?" Navasard wondered. "Ah, what am I talking about. The gravel's too sharp here. He was probably afraid he'd ruin his tires. It's a good thing he didn't drive up to the house."

His one-storey flat-roofed house with a terrace and an earthen floor was like an eagle's nest stuck onto the mountain slope, one among many others.

Navasard entered the yard, set the jug and basket on the ground, tossed an armful of grass to the lamb and looked about. For the first time in his life the house looked pitiful and decrepit to him.

"Well, it's Arshak's house, too. This is where he grew up. He won't be ashamed of his own house," he said to console himself and began clearing the yard.

"Congratulations, Navasard. Arshak's come back." It was the old neighbour woman, looking over the fence.

Navasard flushed with joy. "Thank you. And may your wanderer return as well."

"I saw Arshak."

"Was he here?"

"No. I went to the shop for a package of needles and saw him standing out in front of the farm office. What a fine boy he is. You'd never say he wasn't a shah's son. I just couldn't take my eyes off him. May the Lord bless you."

"Thank you," the old man said in a voice that was thick from emotion. He went about tidying up the yard with zeal.

First he swept up the dirt: "I don't want my boy to dirty his shoes." Then he hammered in a protruding nail with a rock: "Arshak might catch his sleeve on it and tear his jacket."

Navasard opened the door. A cot stood forlornly against the bare wall. "I'll say, 'Remember how you slept on this bed, Arshak, and I slept here, on the floor?' " he was thinking aloud as he smoothed the cover. "I'll say: 'This is your old bowl, the one you ate from. Look, Arshak, this is your wooden spoon. Remember the day I bought it from the wood-carver Manas, and you were angry, because there was no design on it? And then I took it to the artist and had it painted for you?' "

Conversing thus in thought with Arshak, he set out for the spring, brought back some water and sprinkled the yard, the terrace and the floor inside. Then he began to sweep.

Once again the old neighbour woman's head appeared over the fence.

"Navasard, do you know that Arshak has gone over to the chairman's house?"

"No. When did he go there?"

"Just before you got back."

"He must have seen there was no one at home and gone over there to rest up. He'll be along, he won't get lost."

"Of course."

Navasard brought some kindling wood and stacked it by the outdoor fireplace. Then he took his knife from his belt and went over to the lamb. At the last moment he changed his mind. "I'll wait till Arshak comes," he decided and looked in the direction of the chairman's two-storey house. "What's keeping him? It'll be dark soon. The figs will spoil, the cornel will lose its taste."

He took the fruit from the basket and laid it on the windowsill. Then he borrowed a new tablecloth from the neighbours, covered the table, shook out the rug, covered the couch and put a pillow on it.

Everything was now ready. Still, Arshak had not come. "What's the matter! Why did he go to the chairman's house?" Navasard wondered irritably and a tremor passed through his hands. He hurried to console himself, however, saying, "Arshak is an important man. He had to drop by and ask the chairman about how things are in the village. And what's the rush, anyway? I'll have him all to myself for a couple of days. I won't let him out of my sight. We'll make up for lost time."

The sun was setting, but still Arshak had not come home. The old man's anxiety mounted. There was a moment when he was about to set out for the chairman's house, but then he changed his mind.

He went out into the yard and called to his neighbour's grandson.

"Run over and see what Arshak is doing. Tell him I'm at home and waiting for him," he said.

The boy was back in no time.

"Well? Did you see Arshak?"

"Yes."

"What's he doing?"

"Drinking wine."

"Did you tell him that I'm home?"

"Yes."

"What did he say?"

"He said, 'All right.' "

Navasard repeated the words to himself. "Well, then, that means he'll soon be home. I'll start the fire for the *shashlyk* meanwhile."

He soon had a good fire going in the fireplace. Then he set to cleaning the skewers. He went back into the house, wiped the dust off the lamp and sat down at the table to wait.

Time dragged on endlessly. The lights went on in the village, and the houses took on a cozy look. The street noises were dying down. Soon the only sound was that of dogs barking mournfully in the distance.

Arshak had still not returned. The fire died down, leaving a mound of ashes in the fireplace, while the lamb lay on the grass, chewing its cud. Navasard was all ears as he peered into the darkness. His eyes became strained and started to tear, his head felt heavy. He rose, but his feet refused to budge. "Why should I go begging to him? I'm older than he is. He should come to me," he began to grumble, but then consoled himself once again by saying, "Well, he's an important man. Maybe he has some important business to discuss with the chairman. He'll certainly come home in the morning."

But still, he waited. He waited far into the small hours. The autumn night was drawing to a close. The old man's eyes grew dim from peering intently into the darkness. He was gradually overcome by slumber. Navasard fell asleep as he was, sitting at the table.

He did not know how long he had slept. He was awakened

by the neighbour woman's voice calling from the yard. He
opened his eyes and was surprised to see the first rays of the
sun peeping into the window.

"Navasard! Hey, Navasard!" the neighbour called.

He rushed out of the house. His neighbour was looking
over the fence. "How come you've slept so late today?"

"What is it? Is Arshak on his way here?"

"No," she said and shook her head. "Your Arshak is leaving. Look at the road."

Navasard felt as if the roof had come down on his head.
He ran over to the low shed and climbed to the roof. Arshak's car was speeding along the road, glittering in the sun,
quickly becoming smaller and smaller.

His unsteady gait was that of an old man. Navasard was
making his way down the path to the orchards. His eyes that
stared at the ground seemed to have become sunken, his back
seemed more stooped than ever. The white lamb gamboled
after him.

(TRANSLATED BY FAINNA GLAGOLLVA)

The Orange Mare

by GRANT MATEVOSIAN

In 1945 our collective farm received seven pedigreed mares
and one insanely high-spirited stallion to fill out the herd that
had become miserably depleted during the war. I don't know
what eventually happened to them all, but I do know that a
year later there were only one mare of a strange orange color
left and the orange stallion. It was believed that the stallion
was the mare's son.

Mesrop, the groom, was ready to bet anything the stallion
was the orange mare's son and said that until there was another stallion she would never foal. The village was divided
on the matter. Some agreed with the groom, while others did
not. Naturally, Levon was among the dissidents. "That's just

like him, always complicating things," he said of Mesrop.

However, as long as the orange stallion was the leader, no other stallion dared approach the herd. The orange stallion was wickedly mean, and whenever he spotted a rival he would charge at him, no matter how far away the other might be. As he galloped towards a miserable dray-horse, bent double under a load, it seemed that the wind was blowing a flickering flame from one spot to another. His copper-colored tail would blow in the wind, barely keeping up with his body. His one white foreleg would flash and be gone, flash and be gone in the endless crossings and recrossings of his legs, while his fiery mane flowed over his back. One could hear his rapid breathing from one mountain to another. From afar the racing steed was breathtakingly beautiful. However, if you happened to be the owner of that other horse, your one desire was to shoot a barrel-full of lead into the broad chest of the orange stallion. You would wish he would trip and come crashing to the ground, shattering his spine under that orange coat of his.

A year later our bay herd became dotted with bright orange foals. They would tear down the slope and spread out in orange blobs across the broad green meadow. Their lazy mothers would whinny deeply, calling them back from the far edge of the valley, but these mad creatures, as wild as their father, would pay no attention to their mothers' summons and would race back up the mountain, dazzled by the wind.

In the spring of 1949 the collective farm was given three trucks and two tractors. One tractor was attached to the threshing machine, while the other, having completed all of the autumn sowing in a week, was set to pulling brushwood from the woods for nothing better to do. The oxen and horses were growing sleek and fat. Finally, the oxen were sent to the slaughter-house. They were soon followed by the aged mares, then the lame, undersized and oversized horses and, in the end, by those that were too slow, and those that were too nervous. However, there still remained a huge herd which would consume a staggering amount of feed during the coming winter. The price of a horse had dropped and nearly equalled the price of a sheep, and the horses were hastily offered for sale.

A dental technician bought the orange mare. That had been a lean year, with a poor wheat crop, but he had not been discouraged and had come to our mountains anyway.

There he made gold crowns for the shepherds and the milkmaids, and they began smiling crooked golden smiles, while he earned a pile of money in a month. He paid a moderate sum for the mare and said to Mesrop, "I'll throw in a gold crown free of charge if you need one."

The mare would not be caught. She remembered the feel of a saddle and knew the value of freedom. There were about twenty of us out to catch her, and she understood we were after her and that so many people would not be wasting their time on an ordinary nag. She regarded our efforts to make her join the herd as an evil omen, and it made her shiver. She would not let us drive her into the middle of the herd. As we tried to force her against the wall of heavy cruppers, she turned into a shivering bundle of nerves, circled round the herd and did not yet know whom she would trample when the time came to flee. She drew in her sides, arched her neck and circled, neighing ominously, barely touching the solid wall of bodies. Her copper tail fell in a waterfall, while her long mane rippled incessantly against her neck. Her alert, sensitive ears recorded our every move. Her forelegs kept veering off to the left, raising the eternal green covering of the earth up from under her hooves. She had charted a circle for herself at some distance from the herd and kept to it. The circle on the ground was becoming progressively darker. This went on for ten minutes, for twenty, for half an hour. Then we approached. She seemed to bunch up. We came closer. She tensed, then broke away from the circle and was off. The fact that she had fled only whetted our desire to catch her, not to let her go. We saw ourselves as the hunters and the mare as the treacherous fugitive.

The herd turned in her wake and she somehow became pressed in among the horses. Now the herd was her enemy. The inanimate circle was pressing closer and could crush her. She began biting until she had fought free of them and bolted. The herd flowed after her, while she raced away, and the number of legs under her kept multiplying. There were more and more legs until they disappeared completely, movement alone left to catch the eye. This movement was accomplished by some other means than legs, for they were absent. There was only the orange flame slipping across the earth. Alas! It could not break away from the ground, but dipped where there were ravines, rose where there were hills and turned where the road turned. Thus did she disappear completely, our orange mare, at the point where the road was lost to the eye in the distance.

Mesrop was ready to bet anything she wouldn't let herself be trapped. "I'll stake my life on it," he said.

"Leave your life out of it," the dental technician said as he pulled his wallet out of his inside breast pocket. "It's like this," he said and counted the money, then peeled off some bills and handed them to Mesrop. "Here." He was acting as if he couldn't manage the wallet in one hand, since he was holding the bills in the other. "Here, hold this and listen to me. Man to man, I want you to take this money and catch that mare for me."

"All right. But I won't take the money," Mesrop said as he crumpled the bills and proffered them hesitantly and regretfully to the dental technician.

Two days later I was sent to the village and back to school. The dental technician remained in the mountains for a while to collect his fees. He did not leave for the city until the middle of September. Then the others came down, too. Mesrop stayed up in the mountains with the herd for another twenty days or so. Since the mare was somewhere nearby, it made his heart beat faster. The mountains, clad in the last grass of the year, were still green beneath the rays of the warm-chill autumn sun. No smoke rose from any of the tents any more. The sun rolled across the sky in complete silence. Mesrop yearned for the voices of summer.

"Come here, girl," he would call to the mare. "Don't be afraid. They've all gone. There's only you and me here now."

Mesrop hoped fervently that the dark speck in the distance was a rider who was coming his way. "I know you're a rider and you're adjusting the horse's pack. I can see that. Do you need any help?" he said, addressing the dark speck.

But the minutes dragged on and the speck in the distance grew no bigger. Evening came, and he still sat there in the twilight, swaying gently.

"You're just a rock," Mesrop said to the speck. "I can go down to the village if I want to, but you'll always be stuck here. Poor old rock."

"I'll tell you what, girl," he said to the mare that stood on the crest of the hill, her head thrown back motionlessly so that she resembled nothing as much as the picture of a horse in a schoolbook. "The technician's gone. Hear me? He's gone. There's nobody here." At this he clapped one hand down

against the other as if to say: "See? It's empty. There's nobody here."

"Summer's over," he said sadly. "But you're only a horse,
you can't understand." He was all alone with the horses there
in the mountains. Then he added, "I mean, you can't really
understand. You understand more than any other animal,
that's a fact, but still, a person's different."

The mare did not leave the herd altogether, but always
kept within sight of it, following it down to the village early
in October and grazing nearby. When it began snowing in
December the horses were driven into the stable and fed hay
and oats. But she stayed beyond the village, gnawing at the
bushes and never letting anyone near. On the 17th of December a pack of wolves devoured Levon's cow near the river.
The wolves raided Artem's barn on the night of the 18th.
Some shots were fired, and they did not reappear on the 20th,
but they kept close to the village and howled all through the
night. Mesrop got up in the middle of the night and looked
out of the window. The mare was outside, pressing close to
the wall and shivering, but as soon as he approached her she
trotted off.

Four days later Mesrop went out about midnight, and by
the light of his flashlight he glimpsed the orange mare. That
very same night his dog disappeared. There was a noise, as if
something bumped against the door. Mesrop went outside.
He saw nothing. Neither the wolves nor his dog were in sight.
All he heard was a muffled crunching some distance away.
On the night of the 28th Mesrop was in the stable when he
heard a horse whinny outside. He went out and saw the
mare. She did not wait for an invitation, but shoved past him
and entered her stall haughtily, her hooves thudding on the
floorboards. It was warm in the stable. There were plenty of
oats, and the air was filled with the familiar sound of horses
snorting.

I took my children to the circus about five years ago and
suddenly saw our orange mare. She had a whole turn to herself in the show. Her mane was clipped, as was her tail, and
she was sleek and well-groomed, though she did seem a bit
stout. However, no village horse ever possessed such grace,
nary a one. She waltzed, and as she did, every part of her
large body—legs, ears, head, muzzle and back—was under
control. I held my breath, hoping she would not trip up in

any way. She did not. Everyone clapped. She did her dance again and then came to the center of the ring and bowed to the right and left. Everyone applauded still louder, but she did not deign to pamper the audience and dance again. Paying no attention to us any longer, she bowed to the band and the band bowed to her, while the M.C. nodded, signalling her to leave the ring and smiled as she did. The M.C. was also sleek and pomaded. I suddenly wished she would kick his fat mug just once.

"Narinj! Narinj!" I shouted, calling her by the name she was given in the village and which meant "Orange". The audience was waiting for the next turn, and here I was, shouting and disturbing the silence. "Narinj! Narinj!" Everyone heard me. People began looking for whoever it was that was shouting. Meanwhile, I stood up in my seat and called: "Narinj!" again.

"Sit down. People are looking at us," my wife said, tugging at my jacket.

"Wait! This is too much!" I yelled and climbed over the benches to get out of the hall as quickly as possible.

I was alone backstage. The laughter and breathing of those in the circus reached me from under the curtain as a warm, stifling wave. It was as heavy and slippery as the hippopotamus that was now performing out there and that did not want to leave the ring. It was sweaty here and unpleasant. There were some masks lying on the floor. The area was dimly lit by hundred-watt bulbs. It seemed that everything here was rotting. I opened door after door until I suddenly glimpsed her.

"Narinj? No, you're not Narinj."

She didn't even look my way. There was a strip of bronze paint down the length of her back. One leg had white paint on it and her clipped mane had a green tint.

"You're not Narinj, are you?" I asked, offering her a filled chocolate bar.

She didn't take it, didn't even sniff at it. For a second I felt that she didn't want the bar, because there was only a thin layer of chocolate on top, while inside was a sweet, sticky mass. I jerked my hand away and hid the chocolate, to be sure she would not see it. My grandfather's grandfather had probably treated his horse in this way when they had been out in the field. He would set out some sour milk gruel and boiled bindweed, or some other equally unappetizing mess.

Then I felt a loathing for the fat mare welling up in me. As I looked at her sleek body that was carefully groomed and brushed each day, I felt that I hated her, and that my heart belonged to another horse, one called a gelding, that was bitten by horse-flies, taunted by children, buffetted by grownups, despised by stallions, and whose lot was usually a clump of straw.

"You slut!" I said and smacked the glossy rump. "You slut! You never gave birth, you never carried a load, you never moaned under a heavy burden. You slut!"

The hippo had finally been led off, and a clown was now tumbling about and jesting in the ring. He wanted to tip his hat, but pulled off his beard instead. Then, when he wanted to put his beard back on again, he stuck it on his rear.

"I've had enough," I said to my wife as I sank down into my seat beside her. "I've had all I can take."

POETRY

GEVORG EMIN

Small

Yes, we are small
the smallest pebble
in a field of stones.
But have you felt the hurtle
of pebbles pitched
from a mountain top?

Small
as the smallest mountain stream
storing rapids, currents
unknown to wide and lazy valley rivers.

Small,
like the bullet in the bore
of the rifle;
small as the acorn waiting to sprout.

Small
as the pinch of salt
that seasons the table.

Small, yes
you have compressed us, world,
into a diamond.

Small,
you have dispersed us,
scattered us like stars.
We are everywhere in your vision.

Small,
but our borders stretch
from Pyuragan telescopes to the moon,
from Lousakan back to Urartu.[1]

[1] Towns in Armenia.

Small as the grain of marvelous Uranium which
cannot be broken down, put out, or consumed.

Ararat

We stand rooted
eyelashless, eye to eye
my mountain and I.

Faith, they say moves mountains
as Noah moved you into
sight.

I am filled with the same fanatic
flood. And still we are planted
stones.

I curse my own immobility.
Is it for nothing
this is Ararat, I am an Armenian
and we are apart.

For how long? Satan knows.
I am transient. I am mortal.
I shall pass.

And you, my mountain,
will you never walk toward me?

(TRANSLATED BY DIANA DER HOVANESSIAN)

In Granite

Something is going to happen.
I know it.
Each time I start to write I feel
the sharp foreboding of
something leaning forward:
the same feeling that comes before love,
when a glance or a touch on the arm

fills me with the pungence of a strange flower
or a new ointment
(or do I pour the fragrance into these?)

My nostrils flare
like the panther's
breathing in the shiver
of the unseen gazelle. But
I am bodiless. A fever.
A passion. A focus. A dot in time.
I wait for the silent deer, that drinking gazelle.
In whose eye will I drown? I do not know.

I only know I dread that perhaps
instead of love, a mocking flirtation;
instead of song, mocking sounds;
instead of deer, a rabbit
will spring upon me
ending my eagerness.

Yes or No

There are no shorter words to use
as simple as a yes or no
and yet some people live and die
before deciding which to use.

(TRANSLATED BY DIANA DER HOVANESSIAN)

Ballad of the Home

1
He couldn't remember his father's home—
Men come to this world born as men,
But as if marked with sin,
He came to the world . . . exiled.

He couldn't remember his father's home.
When in Alexandretta, the hammer

In his hand to build a house—his own—
Said his mother:
        "My son, don't torture yourself
Placing stone on stone in vain;
All you need is a shack to get by;
It's all the same,
Sooner or later you'll go away . . ."

His mother was killed, her words survived;
The Turks had reached Alexandretta,
And surrendering the half-built house
To the catastrophe, he left for Lebanon.

2

He couldn't remember his father's home—
But after he became a father,
In Beirut one day he picked up the hammer
To build a house—his own—
Said his wife:
        "In vain you make the walls solid,
Dig deep foundations, adorn the pillars;
Don't take the foreigner's land as yours.
Sooner or later you'll go away . . ."

The poor woman died, her words survived;
Then welcome news of the Return arrived,
And, leaving the half-built house behind,
He went back to his father's land.

3

He couldn't remember his father's home—
Already feeble, shaky and old,
When in Yerevan he picked up the hammer
To build a house—his own—
Death said to him:
        "Old man, heavy with sin,
What more do you want from this fleeting life?
Who cuts stone and mixes mortar
With one foot already in the grave?"

4

But already the old man was painting
The roof, and in front of the new home

On the slopes of Ararat,
The grandson stammering his first Armenian letters.

(TRANSLATED BY MARTIN ROBBINS)

SYLVA GABOUDIKIAN

Song About Our Stones

O, stones. . . .
You are history itself!
We lived in misfortune, in poverty,
and we built mournful buildings
as monuments to darkness.
The builders with doomed eyes
wiped the blood and sweat from their brows
and used black stones in the walls
that were like our black fate.
Black are the melancholy monasteries,
and the ancient temples are black.
The worn features
of my Armenia are revealed by them.
O, sad, black, mournful stones,
of the floors,
the ceilings,
the walls,
murky,
smoke-stoned,
dents hollowed out in floors
by kneeling supplicants!
But somewhere, colorful and varied,
hidden quietly in corners,
some stones of happiness were concealed in the earth,
like bits of coal under ashes.
O, stones that slept through all the centuries,
You who have known grim times,

O, stones, rose-colored,
lilac and violet stones!
You have come out of the depths,
which were so unfitting for you.
Come up, up,
onto the earth.
You have struggled up to the people—
and the earth has been gladdened!
The spring colors of the new walls
are like the color of our spring days,
And the full destiny of my Armenia
is like the destiny of her stones.
The new day has awakened them
with gentle hands.
O, stones, rose-colored,
lilac and violet stones!

(TRANSLATOR ANONYMOUS)

You Went Away

You went away . . .
        But I know, I know,
Wherever you go, I will be with you, I will come to you;
I am within you so very much already
That there is no room for others there . . .
Though a thousand eyes sparkle before you,
I will look through the eyes of every maiden;
Whoever speaks to you, my voice will reach you,
My whisper will cling to your ear.
When you walk in the streets lit with electricity,
My gaze will reflect from every lamp;
If the thick velvet of the trees should touch you,
They will stroke your tired face with my caress.
If you go home and submerge yourself in your books,
Again I will appear out of the pages,
I will turn into the tobacco-smoke at your lips,
I will come in through the window with the breeze.
If you close your window, I will turn into a storm,
Into a gale and smash your panes

And invade your room,
    and your world,
And I will stir up
    your papers,
      your life,
        and your soul . . . !
No, you cannot, you cannot forget me . . . !

(TRANSLATED BY MISCHA KUDIAN)

The Walnut Tree

There is a walnut tree
growing in the vineyard
at the very edge of the world.

My people, you are like
that huge ancient tree—
with branches blessed by the graces

but sprawling
over the small corner of land,
roots and arms spread out
and spilling your fruit
to nourish foreign soils.

(TRANSLATOR ANONYMOUS)

AVEDIK ISSAHAKIAN

A Mother's Heart

There is an old story
About a boy
An only son
Who fell in love with a girl.

"You don't love me,
You never did," said the girl.
"But if you do, go then
And bring me your mother's heart."

Downcast and distraught
The boy walked off
And after shedding many tears
Came back to his love.

The girl was angry
When she saw him thus
And said, "Don't you dare come back again
Without your mother's heart."

The boy went and killed
A mountain roe deer
And presented its heart
To the one he adored.

But again she was angry
And said, "Get out of my sight.
I told you what I want
Is your mother's heart."

The boy went and killed
His mother, and as he ran

With her heart in his hand
He slipped and fell.

"My dear child,
My poor child,"
Cried the mother's heart.
"Did you hurt yourself?"

Three Untitled Poems

Everything in this world
Fades and disappears
Even planets and stars.
What is man but nothingness
Dust unto dust;
And yet
In his sorrow
He can drown the universe.

* * *

I have suffered much in this world,
I have shed many tears in this world,
And eyes that have not shed tears
Have seen nothing in this world.

* * *

It is a mid-winter night, windy and cold.
There is warmth in the glittering hall
And singing, dancing, and merry-making.
But you, my comrade, you lie asleep
On the edge of town
Deep in the dark, heavy earth
As the wind howls like a hungry wolf
Over your snow-covered grave.

(TRANSLATED BY ARA BALIOZIAN)

PARUIR SEVAG

We Armenians

We don't class ourselves above anyone
We simply say:
   We and only we have the Ararat
   And the sky has found its true image
   In Lake Sevan in our highland.
It is simply that here
   David fought:
   Nareg was written:
We simply know how to carve cathedrals inside mountain-
     sized rocks,
   Turn stone into fish,
   Mould man out of clay,
   Study and serve
   That which is beautiful
   True
   Sublime
   And fine . . .
   We don't say we are better than anyone else:
It's simply that our luck has taken a different turn,—
   We have shed plenty of blood,
   And in centuries past
   When we were many and mighty,
   We never suppressed any people;
   No one got hurt from our might:
If we captivated
   It was with books only,
   If we conquered
   It was merely by our skill . . .
When we were driven away from our land
   Wherever we went, wherever we were

We strove for the good of all;
We built bridges,
Tied beams together,
We plowed, produced
And shared with others
Our ideas, stories, songs,
Protected them from freezing spiritually.—
Left the light of our eye everywhere
The spark of our soul
And the warmth of our heart . . .
We are few, yes, they call us Armenians—
We can groan from the pain of old unhealed wounds
Also rejoice with new joy;
We know how to fight our foe
And aid our friend;
To one kind deed
We return ten;
We will give our very life
For what is just and fair.
And if they force us to the stakes,
We know how to raise huge smoke and choke their fire
And when the time comes for the darkness to be lifted,
We can turn from charred ash to glowing embers.
We love each other with zeal, with passion
But always respecting others.
We don't consider ourselves above any nation,
We know ourselves too;
Armenians they call us.
And why shouldn't we be proud
We are.
We shall be:
And moreover . . . we shall multiply.

(TRANSLATED BY H. KELIKIAN)

Inside the Camel's Ear

At a certain time, anonymous people
have thought, created and decided
to do this, not to do that,

consider this true, reject the other
in the name of honour and duty.

And we pass at ease through this absurd museum,
wearing out not our clothes but our poor souls,
in whose depths lies a likewise unbearable thing
as sand in our shoes or a thorn under our nails.

While over a record's grooves
glides the needle of life
playing always that same tune
which has no author, though that author
has long been considered
an absolute authority.

And a strange, hot desire
haunts me also in daylight,
and I want not only to growl and grin
but to roar with my chin placed
on this stone or that table.
For I never pity, I disregard
all those miserable animals
who are considered tame.

You prefer the giant camel?
I seriously prefer the mouse,
even the rat that has not turned tame.

And if ever in your nightmares
rats gnaw your flesh with pleasure . . .
will you wake up and think seriously
once and for all:
is it worthwhile to sleep for ages
in the small ear of a big camel?

(TRANSLATED BY GARIG BASMADJIAN)

The Clown

I decided to amuse you.
Today I shan't eat flame,
swallow a dagger or produce

a handkerchief or a bird from my mouth
as very ordinary magicians do.
Nor shall I place a plank on my head
carrying pairs of pretty, half-naked girls
as they so often do at the circus.

I can turn a pumpkin into a sun,
or if you wish a head,
turn Saturn into a wide-brimmed hat
and present it on the spot to any girl
working in a cigarette-factory.
I can also turn the hat into a cardinal,
a field-marshal if you wish,
but friends, today
I won't waste my time doing such things.

Today I shall make you believe
(and make myself disbelieve)
that tomorrow, the prisoners in the zoo,
from the elephant down to the snake,
without any discrimination
will receive medals
in proportion to their patience.
Medals will be awarded to all
except the zebra, that old jackass
who (until now) hasn't become a decent citizen.

Allow me to continue making you believe
that telling the truth today
has become as ordinary an act as pissing.
So from now on
consider kidney troubles wholly abolished,
whatsoever they be called: stone or prostatitis.
And from now on do not sell lies,
but dangle a tail like me
to sweep away the biting flies,
be they called mind or sadness—
isn't it the same?

Finally
how can I make you believe
that exactly in this way
the yellow bull
I wanted to buy this autumn,
ate the vegetable

I wanted to plant this spring.
Greedy bull!
Anything else?
Nothing.
My nothing at your nostrils,
your nostrils at my tail
and
good bye.

(TRANSLATED BY GARIG BASMADJIAN)

ZAHRAD (ZARSH YALDIZCIYAN)

The Woman Cleaning Lentils

A lentil, a lentil, a lentil, a stone. A lentil, a lentil, a lentil,
   a stone.
A green one, a black one, a green one, a black. A stone.
A lentil, a lentil, a stone, a lentil, a lentil, a word.
Suddenly a word. A lentil.
A lentil, a word, a word next to another word. A sentence.
A word, a word, a word, a nonsense speech. Then an old
   song.
Then an old dream.
A life, another life, a hard life. A lentil. A life.
An easy life. A hard life. Why easy? Why hard?
Lives next to each other. A life. A word. A lentil.
A green one, a black one, a green one, a black one, pain.
A green song, a green lentil, a black one, a stone.
A lentil, a stone, a stone, a lentil.

(TRANSLATED BY DIANA DER HOVANESSIAN)

Words Words

Words words—you are my soldiers—
One by one I embrace you and regiment by regiment
I line you up with my own two hands—
And when I see that all's in order
—That not a single troop—not a single soldier marches out
    of step—
I send you to the front—

You are my valiant soldiers—
In my name you descend upon the death-dealing battlefield—
My poet's lofty banner
Flutters radiantly in your powerful hands—
You carry on the struggle—victoriously you storm castle and
    fortress—

Words words—my dauntless soldiers—
I a mad tactician of words—without you I don't exist

Heroic Struggle

        We too
Had our conflicts in the past we too—
        With those days
Which went by without a woman—without a friend or ac-
            quaintance
        Alone
        Unarmed
        Without artillery
    We experienced silent struggles
        And from their
    Muffled explosions
    From the flames which never burned
From the blood never spilled upon the earth

We bore our martial memories

We too
In our past waged a heroic struggle we too—
And wounded survived

Letter

City—I kiss the hands of your boulevards
I grew up in their lengths and breadths
—If my neck has remained bent it's not really my fault
Beauty used to run beautifully along your boulevards
    I couldn't catch up

City—I love the luminous face of your lamps
My first kiss was under a streetlight
She was a sweet girl with eyes full of dreams
If we have long since separated from one another
    How can the streetlight help it

City—of course one day I'll come and lay my cheek against
        one of your sidewalks
Satisfy my longing—weep over the loneliness of my days
        gone by
Allow the passersby to offer me pity as alms
    And stay like that having forgotten how to stand

City—in the night when your lights come on and above the
        roofs
A multicolored haze suffuses all—when everything slumbers
    Do not forget your vagabond son Zahrad
    Say he sent greetings to those who ask about him

Nine Celestial Poems

CELESTIAL WORDS

Together with the poet we set out to sing
He sings—we just go through the motions of singing

CELESTIAL LAUGHTER

Anchored high in the heavens
There is a naughty star
That has been looking at the earth for three million years
And dying of laughter

CELESTIAL FLIRTATION

A blue-tailed airplane wiggles his tail at a sparrow—
Raucous voice—metal flesh—unflapping wings—
Terrified Mr. Sparrow thinks
—I wonder what color the egg of this monstrous winged
    creature might be

CELESTIAL STONE

There aren't enough stones to stone each of us one by one
We gather together all in the same place on the world
And we await the tumultuous stone which doesn't come

CELESTIAL FLAME

I am
A tiny feeble lamp—
When the stars in sad autumn skies are extinguished by the
    wind
—Let them be extinguished—I shall burn

CELESTIAL HEIGHTS

He has indigestion—
From the top of the skyscraper
He vomits his grandeur downward
To forbearing mother earth

CELESTIAL POEM

A poem written
Your eyelashes the pen tip
The sky's azure the parchment
I the author

CELESTIAL BODY

And there was yet another that finally grew bored
Of the prescribed measured regular order—
He attempted to escape—in boundless space
He melted like an adolescent dream

It was a tranquil August night—peaceful—
And a new meteor fell

CELESTIAL INVITATION

Come all of you despairing and weary
Come all of you defeated and exhausted
This is the celestial realm that I a lowly poet
Dispense by the handful to alleviate your thirsts

The heavens a haven for star and sun
The heavens a haven for your dreams

(TRANSLATED BY RALPH SETIAN)

ANTRANIK ZAROUKIAN

Elegy for a Lynched Negro

Did the swallows part the skies
of that spring morning of your last breath
trailing wings and pulling life
across the nightmare of your death?
Did the swallows part the skies?

Did your old village lean against your eyes
with the light of sundipped huts
while the raging mob became a tide of hate?
Did your village shine across your eyes?

Did you call your mother, father, son
as the last breath bellowed from your lungs
when you fell on the sidewalk across the wall,
when you fell against their knives,
Did you call your mother, father, child?

Were there tropical leaves, shadows of Senegal
as a last impression in your eyes
or those tangled hands, the mob,
in the pupils of your eyes?

Was the magic totem on your chest
symbol of protection from
panther and the scorpion
worthless against the final beast,
your fellow man, the mighty totem of your race?

Where did the white soul of your black body go?
To the strange god who betrayed you?
Did he leave his heaven door ajar?
Where did the white soul of that body go?

Did the mob with frothing mouths
know the sidewalk stones

were not thirsty for your blood;
nor did the goddess, Liberty, who nurtured them, provide
venom, with her majestic breasts.
She had no poison for their lips.
Did the mob know? Did you know?

Let It Be Light

Let it rest lightly
if it can
this foreign soil.
Let it grow pity like a bloom.
Although once you said
even the air in a foreign land
is heavy and cuts the lungs.

Let it be light
this handful of earth
I throw against the coffin,
my last debt and your newest
wound.

Without a fatherland
the landless find
all brown earth an insult,
all soil rootless.
The exile is a stranger
even to his grave.

Yesterday you wrestled luck
boot to boot. The Armenian's lot
is to fight for his lost land.
Even after death. Now fight
this soil over you. Hold it
lightly and away from your face.

Excerpts from "Letter to Yerevan"

And who has not cheated us?
Who hasn't like a leech

clung to our wound to
quench a thirst for gold
with our red blood?
Who has not cheated us?

A handful of soil from home
is all these wanderers ask
now, a small handful
of native soil, barren even,
even in a dark cemetery
so that the dead
will not feel the cold
of this bleak foreign earth.

A handful of earth too
for the tottering children
so that our ancient speech
will not freeze
like a flower in the snow.

The brightness of our souls
is lost with the lost
incense, the breath
and clean rituals of our homes.

Wolves in disguise
who come speaking of paradise
and unreachable heaven
pluck the bloom from our flesh
as they smile
hypocritical smiles.
They speak of the cross
and nail us to it again
as they speak.
And here I am singing,
an insignificant poet,
mixing my breath with the words
of thousands in anguish.
Hear, in my song,
their uncollectable sadness,
the cry of the homesick,
the yearning called *garod*.
Hear in my song too,

regret and dismay
for battle's retreat.

And hear with me
an entire people's cries,
half of its number
destroyed in one day,
one pitiless massacre.
And remember Deir-Zors[1]
the other half scattered
and left to the luck of the winds
to call from Aleppo
from Paris
and California
to call to heaven
to God
and to Hell
to take them home.

My soul is the broken lyre
in which the grim past
sticks like an echo
like the resonant string,
the taut gut of a million
and more dead victims
rings and reverberates.
This is the century that pulsates
on these strings and throws its mourning
to the centuries that come.

And now we have reached
that awful moment
the last act of life and death.
That echoing moment
that tells us: For us now
there is no salvation
except through the black luck
of the dead, the dark road of hell
the road through the desert
that goes through our hearts
to reach toward you
our crimson-lit fatherland.

[1] *Deir-Zors*: a city on the Euphrates River, terminal point of death
march across the Syrian desert. —Ed.

I don't have a god now,
nor a fake golden calf.
I'm just a tired passer-by
passing, heart-bare and
threadbare
worn by abrasions
filed down to the quick.
And with no single magnet
pulling me now
but one bright pulsating star.

Dear Yerevan, I might become
dust before seeing you
but with the last shudder
of my breath
I will praise
your fields and the clear coffer of stars
that is Sevan.[1]
And I will celebrate the mass
of your factories,
the sweat of your workers,
dear Yerevan.

Stay green against winter
Stay in flower and victorious.
Let your fist be the scourge
against evil. And for faraway children
keep your arms, like a mother's,
open and wide.

Hold the flag firmly
Keep the vast dream intact.
Stay like a link between future and past,
burning away evil with the fire of your eyes.

Grow green, Yerevan,
let your ancient dust spring green
in one single moment
shining with glory.
Dear Yerevan see in our tears
your soul.
Erase old grieving

---

[1] A lake in Soviet Armenia. —Ed.

and sound the bugles
for returning the wanderers home,
jan[1] Yerevan.

(TRANSLATED BY DIANA DER HOVANESSIAN)

[1] *jan*: dear. —Ed.

GARIG BASMADJIAN

76 *Armenian Proverbs and Sayings*

1. The shepherd lamented all that was taken away, the wolf
   lamented all that was left behind.
2. Always tell the truth in the form of a joke.
3. Pass the horse by the head and the dog by the tail.
4. Nobody cuts off the nipple of his cow.
5. A full stomach will never learn.
6. When the donkey received a wedding invitation, he said:
   "You only invite me to carry the water."
7. Eat bad soup with a big spoon.
8. Better ruin a church than a girl's honor.
9. New nightwatchmen whistle even when they piss.
10. Cats in gloves cannot catch mice.
11. He makes dice out of his father's bones. (i.e.: cruel)
12. The rich man will have iced water even in hell.
13. A man and wife had a fight: they threw their cat into the
    fire.
14. An uninvited guest sits on a thorn.
15. An experienced devil is better than an inexperienced an-
    gel.
16. Better to be an ant's head than a lion's tail.
17. A new bride will show her husband only half her behind.
18. Spit against the wind and you spit in your own face.
19. A daughter is the light of another house.

20. Flee from hairy women, hairless men.
21. The blind do not care if candles are expensive.
22. A man's beard caught fire, another came to warm himself.
23. Don't eat with the wolf and mourn with the shepherd.
24. When the bear grows old, the cubs play with his balls.
25. The jackass has been forty times to Jerusalem but is still a jackass.
26. My cap looked dusty so he took me for a miller.
27. A meal before sleeping is a lost meal.
28. Law for the rich, punishment for the poor.
29. When the herd reversed direction, the lame became the leaders.
30. The donkey's tomb is the wolf's stomach.
31. Pigs never see the stars.
32. A man who picks up a big stone does not mean to throw it.
33. Pull a thread and a thousand patches will fall off.
34. Debt ends by paying, sin by weeping.
35. Bribe the saints with candles and incense.
36. Seven mother-in-laws walk together, they say there's nobody to talk to.
37. Slap according to the face.
38. Only when you beat a mule will he admit his father was a donkey.
39. The blacksmith's horse is always shoe-less.
40. Better die standing than live crouched.
41. The cat couldn't reach the meat: "It's Friday," she said.
42. The hen that lays most cackles most.
43. They read the Bible over the wolf, "Take that away," he said, "I'm off after the lamb."
44. Even if he were the sun he wouldn't dry your handkerchief.
45. Alive, he had no underwear; dead, he had a temple over his grave.
46. The sugar would eat itself if only it had teeth.
47. You can always find a blind smith for a lame donkey.
48. If eggs were good for the voice, the hen's asshole would sing like a nightingale.
49. Bribes give light even in hell.
50. Nobody will give a pauper bread, but everybody will give him advice.

51. The guest hates the other guest, the housewife hates them both.
52. When a donkey wants to spite his master, he dies.
53. A girl with beautiful hair is worth two girls.
54. When the head gets hot, the pocket gets cold; when the pocket gets hot, the head freezes.
55. He's so ugly, you couldn't eat an omelette fried on his face.
56. A purse filled by hard work, like a camel's tail, never gets any longer.
57. Cats don't have nightmares.
58. When bread is dear, death is cheap.
59. The face is the mirror of the heart.
60. A watermill profits from a mouse's piss.
61. When they want to kill a dog they say he has gone mad.
62. Don't burn the carpet to get rid of a flea.
63. Bad wood gives bad shavings.
64. They told the cat her shit was medicine, so she buried it deep in the earth.
65. Only the grave straightens a hunchback.
66. Do not promise a saint a candle or a child a sweet.
67. "Who's your father?" they asked the mule. "My mother's a horse," he said.
68. Believe a woman when she tells you good news.
69. When God wants to make a poor man happy, He makes him lose his donkey and then find it again.
70. Cover your eyes in the village where everyone else is blind.
71. When they gave the donkey flowers to smell, he ate them.
72. If you run after two rabbits you won't catch either.
73. Kiss a lovely woman on the cheek, an ugly one on the hand.
74. Had not there been the human donkeys, every donkey would have cost a fortune.
75. The wine you drink on credit makes you twice drunk: one when you drink it and one when you pay for it.
76. If a mother-in-law had been a good thing, God would have had one.

PART III

ISRAELI LITERATURE

THE ISRAELI
BACKGROUND

Israeli literature ought to be, of course, the literature written by the inhabitants of the state of Israel. And indeed a vital literature has already sprung from that beleaguered land in the short span of less than thirty years. Yet even before the state of Israel was established in 1948, there existed a body of writings that might properly be regarded as pre-Israeli, since it was produced by either immigrants into the Palestinian territories or their children born there (*sabras*). Ezra Spicehandler speaks of three periods of modern Hebrew poetry: the European (1880–1924), the Palestinian (1920–1947), and the Israeli (1948–   ). His divisions may aptly be applied to Israeli literature in general.

Some overlapping categories need to be made distinctive. Both Hebrew poetry and prose have been written outside Israel. The modern revival of the Hebrew language goes back to the European Enlightenment of the eighteenth century, although its general acceptance as a medium of literary expression is due to its status as the official language of the new state. But, for that matter, not all Israeli literature is written in Hebrew: Yiddish, the language of European Jewry (written in the Hebrew alphabet), is making a vigorous if last stand in the new homeland; and the European languages have always been accepted, with English at present replacing German and Russian as the second language of discourse among those with European roots.

The first great names in what was to become Israeli literature, if we disqualify from that category the incomparable poets of the Bible, were three writers who were born in Eastern Europe and came to Palestine by way of Germany. Russian was the mother tongue of Hayyim Bialik (1873–1934), a lyricist of passion, force, and impulsiveness who is revered as the greatest modern Hebrew poet in both content and form. His contemporary Saul Tchernikovsky

(1875–1943) decided to make himself fluent in Hebrew (which he had studied as a schoolboy in Russia) only after a civilian and military career as a physician in Russia and Germany. He wrote poetry unique for its sensuous beauty and its praise of the heathen gods; and he produced unrivaled Hebrew translations of Homer, *The Epic of Gilgamesh,* the *Kalevala,* and Goethe.

S. Y. Agnon (1888–1970) was born in Poland, migrated to Palestine in 1907, returned to Europe for the duration of the First World War, and then settled permanently in Palestine in 1924. Though one of his novels describes life in Jaffa and Jerusalem before 1940, the chief subject of his strongest fiction is the Jewish Diaspora in Eastern Europe. He became the doyen of Israeli literature and the recipient, in 1966, of the Nobel Prize. Even those writers of a later *aliyah* or immigration—such as Avram Shlonsky, Uri Greenberg, Nathan Alterman, and Aharon Megged—who led a rebellion against the "old guard," were themselves European-born. This international character still persists in Israeli letters.

Contemporary Israeli literature, then, can be said to begin with the foundation of the state in 1948. It is therefore coeval with the contemporary phases of the other Middle Eastern literatures represented in this collection. Like those other literatures, it too has felt the powerful impact of West European and American writers. In the 1950s, the poets were dominated by the examples of Rilke and Valéry; in the 1960s, by those of Yeats and Auden, Pound and Eliot. This influence inevitably imparted a cosmopolitan and perhaps even an existential ambiance to the poetry of the new nation. Naftali Brandwein, looking back from the time of the Six-Day War of 1967, saw these young writers of Israel as living in a "spiritual and idealistic vacuum, growing older in a world apparently empty of meaning and void of purpose, without goal, motivation, or direction." The pioneering spirit that had inspired the early settlers and the first generation of writers was transmuted into an attitude of ironic observation that many readers mistake as detachment. These writers remained engaged, but they forsook the language of the zealot. Indeed they were not running away from politics, according to novelist/critic Rachel Eytan; they simply took a subtler stance toward political questions.

If, however, as other critics argue, Israeli poetry today is less socially and politically engaged than it was in the earlier years, it nevertheless possesses remarkable energy and vitality. For instance, there is the modern treatment of Biblical themes in Dan Paggis (1930–) and Yehuda Amichai (1924–), the latter's sense of alienation expressed with marvelous skill in such different forms as the sonnet, the elegy, and even the Persian *rubaiyat*. T. Carmi, who was born Carmi Charney in the United States, but who spoke Hebrew as his first language, writes verses of *haiku* simplicity with the objectivity of the Japanese poet. In *The Brass Serpent,* thus far his best major work available in English, he manages to synthesize the Hebraic, Judaic, European, and American traditions which have nourished Israeli culture. Dahlia Ravikovitch, a *sabra,* composes quasi-realistic verses with a kind of sensitivity that belies her poetic apprenticeship during years of military service. Young David Avidan voices in striking poetry the "cool" attitudes and concerns of the "hip" generation in Israel, his stance skeptical and self-questioning. Raquel Chalfi's poetry carries women's declaration of independence to a ruthless conclusion. In her vision of sexual relationships, men and women are pitted against each other, perhaps by their natures, in the shape of prehistoric fish, one with a "need for endless wariness," the other "never afraid." Like most of the new poetry, her work achieves freedom by denying its heritage of authority.

Contemporary Israeli fiction, although much of it was created as it were under military siege, shares the self-questioning spirit absent in the earlier years. Adam Gillon, writing in 1972 about the new attitudes, sees little of the former chauvinism—only anxious writers trying to reconcile past and present, the religious and the secular, public idealism and private conscience. Perhaps the most influential figure of recent time is S. Yishar, the first *sabra* to write in English. His stories, such as the anthologized "The Prisoner," mark a turning point in Israeli fiction. A new sense of complex realities became apparent in place of propaganda. For instance, in Aharon Megged's *The Fortune of Fools* (1962), the first Israeli novel to win a wide readership in America, the hero realizes that Israel must conquer the enemy, but having conquered, he refuses to behave like a conqueror. The moral position of the victor seems very shaky to anyone willing to examine it. Elsewhere, Megged has said that all Israeli writers must suffer from a kind of inferiority complex because they write in the shadow of the world's greatest book. This self-consciousness, this inevitable comparison, perhaps has turned the writer in on himself and his craft as well, and in so doing, may have disengaged his interest from social reality outside his own imaginings.

Most representative of this recent trend toward withdrawal into a personal world and toward a critical view of the present reality is Abraham Yehoshua. In "Facing the Forests," a selection from his brilliant collection of novellas called *Three Days as a Child,* a scout entrusted with the security of the national forests does not believe that they exist. He is, in the words of Gillon, "an ironic conqueror of a land to which he does not truly belong." Whereas one Israeli critic calls this work "the most authentic expression of our self-destruction," Gillon maintains that Yehoshua merely expresses the "sense of alienation and restriction that reflects the tensions of people living in a garrison state . . . he does not typify or suggest a total rejection of Israeli reality by the Israelis." It is clear, however, that the sensitive Israeli writer can no longer be commanded by the Zionist Establishment to be its "official" spokesman, perhaps as much a tribute to the free spirit of Israeli democracy as to the growing spiritual maturity of her artists in quest of an identity consistent with a humane stance.

An equally powerful presence on the literary scene is Amos Oz, son of the writer Yehuda Arieh. In recent years he has emerged as one of the leading spokesmen for the generation of *sabras* who grew up along with the fledgling state. His social and literary essays brought him attention in Israel, but his stories and longer fiction have gained international popularity, even notoriety, for their controversial themes and bold presentation. In *My Michael,* the novel that introduced Oz to American readers, we watch the personal disintegration of a young housewife in Jerusalem, the author's native city. Many Israelis were disturbed by the suggestive violence of the heroine's erotic fantasies of abduction and rape by the Arab twins with whom she grew up. In *Elsewhere, Perhaps,* his second book in English (a truncated version of his first novel, published in Israel in 1966), a young soldier (Oz himself took part in the Sinai and Golan Heights campaigns) casts a critical glance at that most sacrosanct of Israeli institutions, the *kibbutz.* The selection in this book is a chapter from that novel. His next book, *Unto Death—Crusade,* led critic

Robert Alter to say that Oz had developed control over a "hallucinatory vision of spiritual and sexual unrest."

More palpably than in any other Middle Eastern country, the democratic atmosphere of the new cities and the egalitarian ambiance of the experimental settlements have helped to break down the barriers against women in the professions and in the arts. Even before statehood, two Lithuanian-born women had made their mark: Deborah Baron with her stories of Jewish life in Eastern Europe and Palestine (recently published as *The Thorny Path*) and Leah Goldberg for her full-bodied lyrics. More recently a number of other women have achieved recognition: Miriam Oren, Esther Rab, Miriam Schneid, Amalia Kahane-Carmon (who uses the stream of consciousness to reveal the intricate inner lives of quite ordinary people). The work of Dahlia Ravikovitch and Raquel Chalfi has already been noted.

Among these talented women are two novelists presently living in New York. Rebecca Rass was born in Tel Aviv, the daughter of a Polish pioneer who founded one of the key kibbutzim in Palestine. Her first novel, *From A to Z* (1959), is a parable about what happens when the prepositions decide to leave the language. Her second book, *From Moscow to Jerusalem* (1976), is autobiographical adventure, and *The Fairy Tale of My Mind* (1978) will return to the fictional form. The story included in this book is an excerpt from her novel in progress, *Count Me Out,* and reveals the profound changes Israel is undergoing in its social fabric as the idea of liberation from past customs reaches into all corners of the culture. Rachel Eytan, also born and educated in Tel Aviv, won the Brenner Literature Prize for her *The Fifth Heaven.* Her second novel, *And Pleasures of Man,* a controversial bestseller in 1975, provides another clue to the changing relationships between men and women in Israel.

Like the poetry and fiction, Israeli drama comes out of a variegated past. In its Ur-form, it may be said to have been born with the famous Yiddish play of Ansky, *The Dybbuk,* translated into Hebrew by the poet Hayyim N. Bialik, and staged in Moscow by the Habima Theater under the Armenian director Yevgheny Vakhtangov. The Habima moved to Palestine in 1928, and although it established a firm tradition of good theater in its new home, it did little to create an original dramatic literature. Of the six or seven hundred plays it produced in the first twenty years of the new state, only about one hundred were new, and few of these had any distinction. The remainder were revivals of Ibsen, Shaw, Brecht, and other European playwrights.

Even the founding of the Chamber Theater in 1944, and the subsequent contributions to it of such reputable writers as Yigal Mossenson and Moshe Shamir, did little to appreciably raise its level of dramatic composition. The new plays were not concerned with psychological subtlety in either language or character. They were content to deal with gut issues of the struggle for survival and to reveal the nobility and heroism of this struggle, often in the realistic language of military slang. Aharon Megged, a playwright as well as a novelist, placed more stock in his message than in his medium. His popular *I Like Mike* (1951) satirized the pseudo-patriot of the day. Other writers for the stage were interested in historical drama that patriotically glorified a past era or event, whether Biblical or modern Palestinian. The poetic drama received some attention from the distinguished poet Nathan Alterman in *Kineret* (1961) and from Yehudah Amichai in *Voyage to Nineveh* (1964), but these plays were more in the nature of experiments than substantive new forms. Realism has remained the dominant mode of the Israeli theater, in striking contrast to the trend both in the West and in the other Middle Eastern countries. Even the highly innovative play of actor/playwright Naftali Yavin, *Precious Moments* (1968), was staged in the realistic tradition. There are exceptions to our generalization about the weakness of Israeli theater: the thriving art of mime, and the Yehoshua play *A Night in May,* an Albee-like series of self-revelations by seven people gathered under one roof; but Israeli critics are agreed that serious drama is yet a fledgling form.

Israel has no native tradition of stage comedy similar to that of the Yiddish theater in the United States, but a genuinely gifted writer of the comic mode has appeared in the person of Ephraim Kishon, who has scored several notable successes with his film scripts (in particular, "Sallah"). The play included in this volume applies gentle irony to the treatment of a social problem of mounting concern to Israelis, namely the integration of non-Western Jews into the framework of a state conceived primarily along Western lines. Kishon, himself an émigré from Hungary, believes in the healing touch of humor for the displaced as well as for their hosts.

All Israeli writers seem to have one thing in common, according to Adam Gillon, and the reader of even this small representation of their work may find grounds to agree: ". . . they can show all kinds of *awareness,* seek out the grotesque, the ridiculous as well as the sublime in the Israeli experience," and perhaps that is eloquent testimony to the "vitality of their utterance and to the intellectual freedom in a country beset by many problems, not the least of which is that of physical survival."

FICTION

Leah Berlin

(from *The Richter File*)

by AHARON MEGGED

Over a five-month period I went back and forth to visit Leah Berlin at her home. For five months—until her disintegration and demise, until she was consumed in her own fire.

After Joseph and I had had our talk along the beach that night, I couldn't fall asleep. I kept churning in my mind all the things he had told me; the more I thought about what he had said, the more heartsick I felt. Putting two and two together, I concluded that if Joseph Richter had known Leah Berlin for three years, during which time, in all our long and frequent conversations, he had not so much as mentioned her name, it was obvious that their acquaintance was one based not purely on literary interests. But what point was there in his revealing all this now? Did he intend simply to throw off his yoke of responsibility toward her and fasten it upon my shoulders now that their relationship had become too burdensome for him or had reached a point of crisis? My entire being rose up against this: I had no desire to be either their go-between or a silent partner in some kind of conspiracy against Olga. But on the other hand: how could anyone abandon a woman like Leah Berlin? She might now be in serious straits with no one around to hear her cries for help. . . .

Contemplating the fate of this Yiddish poetess whose works I admired (what little I had heard about her endeared her to me even more) haunted me during the days that followed. At the same time, thinking of her helped to soothe my bitter feelings toward Joseph Richter. My attention was diverted away from all this, from his relationship with her.

I didn't dare visit her until one day I found a pretext: a

poem of hers had appeared in an issue of *Zukunft*[1] mailed to me from the United States. So, I said, I'll go show it to her and cheer her up.

To reach her apartment you had to walk down five steps. It was located in the basement of a building on Yosef Hanasi Street. There was a furniture workshop on the first floor. Since there was no electricity in the entrance, I had to grope my way down the stairs till I found the door to her apartment.

I knocked. I could hear a voice answer from inside: "Just a moment." I heard the squeaking of bedsprings, the brushing of houseshoes across the floor, the rustle of clothing. With the door open just a crack, I could see her large, frightened eyes, and her hand pressing the corners of a faded, woolen dressing-gown to her neck. She seemed to have been expecting someone else and was disappointed.

When I told her my name, her eyes lit up a bit. She said: "Yes, Joseph has told me about you."

I stepped in, and she asked me to have a seat on a stool next to a round table covered with a brown, embroidered, fringed tablecloth. On the table stood a pitcher containing long stalks of caladia. Leah Berlin sat down on the bed and apologized for the disorder. "I'm not in good health," she said. "I've been confined to bed for the past few weeks."

She had an oblong face with protruding cheek bones and large eyes that reflected both sorrow and Jewish nobility. Her hair, black and gathered into a bun, was interwoven with threads of gray. Even though illness and distress showed in her face, a great deal of beauty was still preserved there—a kind of dying light.

I handed her the copy of *Zukunft*. I told her I had come to show her the poem of hers which had been published there, for I was sure that she hadn't yet seen it. She paged through the journal, lingered at some headlines on the first few pages, paused a moment over her poem, and then laid it down upon the bed and said:

"Have you read Lisitzky's *Dying Campfires?*"[2]

I told her I had heard of the book but hadn't had a chance to read it yet.

---

[1] Socialist Yiddish monthly published since 1940 by the Central Yiddish Cultural Organization.
[2] *Dying Campfires* is a long poem dealing with the American Indian, by the Hebrew-American poet who died in 1962.

"You must read it," she said. "It's a really wonderful long poem." Then she got up and walked toward the bookstand. Richter's books were among the volumes I saw on the shelves. "Here. . . ." She handed me Lisitzky's book. "Take it with you. Read it."

I opened the book and said that I'd take it home for a few days and then return it.

"You don't have to return it," she said. "I love to give away books I like."

I thanked her. I was bewildered by this display of generosity; after all, she didn't even know me. "We're siblings in fate," she said after sitting back down on the bed. "Lisitzky writes in Hebrew in the United States, and I write in Yiddish in the land of Israel. Both of us are in exile. But exile in the land of Israel is more cruel. His eyes look toward this land, but where can my eyes look? Toward Poland? Is there a Poland anymore? It's a graveyard. And those of us who write in Yiddish—we chisel inscriptions into the tombstones."

Her voice was harsh and stood on guard against slipping into sentimentality or plaintiveness.

"I'm presently reading 'From the Land of Childhood' by Dov Shtok,"[3] she said. "It's very nice, of course: very rich. But strange for me! Our lives in Poland were certainly not rich! They were wretched! There was wretchedness in every step we took! How can one write about poverty in a language so rich as Hebrew? On poverty one should write only in Yiddish! The language of the poor! I read Hebrew, and I enjoy reading it; but I think to myself: How can you enjoy it? Enjoyment is forbidden! You are committing a sin! It's as if Dante had used his glorious language to write about some little town."

I said that even Dante was called a "poet of cobblers" by his contemporaries.

"Yes, but for us in our times he's exalted!"

I told her that I myself had come from Poland—from Galicia, to be exact, and that there we certainly did have a rich life—rich in scholarship and in enlightened Jews knowledgeable in Torah and quite clever, and for this reason Dov Shtok's Hebrew style seemed to fit into the scheme of things.

"Maybe," she said. "I'm from a small town in Congress

[3] Yiddish and Hebrew writer, critic, and colleague of Megged's on the staff of *Davar*, a newspaper published by the Histadrut General Federation of Labor.

Poland, and we ate the black bread of Yiddish. We didn't
know what white bread was."

"Do you have a cigarette?" she asked in the tone of a
starving prisoner being visited by someone from the outside
world.

I told her I didn't smoke.

"It's a good thing you don't have any," she said. "I
shouldn't be smoking. Joseph would have given me one. But
he doesn't care about me." A smile formed on her lips.

Suddenly she looked at me and said:

"Tell me, don't you think he's a genius?"

I chuckled. I said that I considered him an excellent writer.
But a genius—I'm not sure what that is.

"No, he's a genius!" she said. "You realize that he's doing
for Hebrew prose what Tchernichowsky did for Hebrew poetry . . .?"

When I asked what she meant, she said:

"He writes about the land of Israel as if the exile had
never existed! He writes as a proud Hebrew man who never
walked with a stoop, who never had to go awandering! He's
like a free man! Do you know who it is he writes like? Like
one of those early Jewish settlers who roamed the country on
horseback!"

"Do you think he wrote like that in 'Law of Blood' also?" I
asked.

"Yes! Also in 'Law of Blood'! He could, after all, have
chosen some Jew from Lithuania, Poland or Russia as his
hero! But instead he chose Prosper Marino, a Jew who isn't a
Jew at all in the usual sense: he's a butcher! a murderer! a
man about to topple a kingdom!"

"And build a Jewish kingdom!" I said.

"What 'Jewish kingdom?' A *chivalrous* Jewish kingdom!
The type of 'Jewish' our history has never seen before. . . ."

But she didn't have her heart set on arguing. Suddenly, her
eyes were aglow with a tinge of madness that would so often
astound me in the weeks to come.

"Tell me, do you know his wife Olga?"

What she said hit me with a jolt. I stammered. I was bewildered. I said that I knew her slightly.

"She's an evil woman!" Her eyes were aflame.

I was so startled I didn't know what to say. I began stammering again and told her I didn't think so.

"She's destroying him!" She spoke resolutely. But since I

was not echoing her words, she did not continue along these lines.

Before I left, I asked her if I could assist her in any way. "Thank you," she said, "but I've got a nice neighbor who regularly stops by to bring me everything I need." Then she added, halfway seriously, halfway in jest: "If only you could stop the awful noise from that sawmill upstairs. . . . From seven in the morning till four in the afternoon every day, every single day. . . . It's driving me out of my mind!"

I bade her farewell, but she shut the door behind me without saying a word.

After that I came and visited her once a week, and frequently more often than that. I first used various pretexts, such as to pay her back measure for measure for the books she had lent me, or to bring her some new periodicals; but these pretexts were superfluous after we had become closer friends.

It was amazing how aware she was of the things going on outside her room. Even though she was the one imprisoned in her house and I was the one who frequented the cafés and learned of all the goings-on of artists and writers, she was much more aware than I about the latest events in "the literary world": she knew about quarrels in the Writer's Association, disputes within the pages of *Moznayim*[4] and other journals—between the poets Jacob Fichman and Avigdor Hameiri and between the poet Lamdan and the critic Lachower;[5] about books on the verge of publication; about critical articles not even written yet, along with the reactions there would be toward them; and even about the relationships between men and women. From time to time she'd surprise me with news about someone who was traveling here or there, of someone else who had left home for some other place. She'd ask me the details of one incident or another, and she was astonished at my lack of information. Once she asked me if I knew that P. had a daughter in France from a woman other than his wife. I was stunned; never had I imagined that this unassuming man, who never leaves his wife's

---

[4] The literary journal of the Hebrew Writers' Association.
[5] Lachower, until his death in 1947, was the chief critic of the Hebrew literary world; Hameiri (d. 1970) was an expressionist poet; Lamdan (d. 1954) wrote about the life of immigrants of the Third Aliyah (1919–1923). Fichman (d. 1958) wrote poetry and prose based on Biblical themes.

side, had had it in him to be unfaithful even once. I was amazed at how she could have learned of all this. She read the newspapers—*Davar* daily, and on Friday *Ha'aretz*; and also the literary journals. But things of that ilk were never mentioned in such periodicals, and to the best of my knowledge, no other person but myself visited her during those months, save her doctors and that neighbor lady of hers, a simple woman who surely didn't know the first thing about what was going on in "the literary world."

She was fanatical about Joseph Richter's works. If I happened to praise a newly published story by someone, she would more often than not scorn my opinion; or at best, she'd make a minor concession and add: "Yes, how distant that story is from the true greatness that you find in Joseph Richter!" Or: "This is outright profanity as compared to the sacredness in Joseph's 'Road to Bethlehem'!" Or, for example, when we discussed Shofman's articles appearing in the newspaper: "They are sparks from the fire, but you well know the greatest of all fires is found in Joseph's stories!"

But it was not just admiration. She also had a deep comprehension of his stories; she presented diagnoses that others could not grasp. Once she told me:

"Not since Ibn-Gabirol has Hebrew literature seen a writer like Joseph."

I was flabbergasted. I asked her how she could even make a comparison between an eleventh-century poet from Spain and a contemporary writer of prose.

"One can be made," she said. "They both are aware of the infinite that exists within the finite and the metaphysical that exists within the mundane. When Ibn-Gabirol writes about a flower bed in a garden, he's writing about the relationship between heaven and earth. And when Joseph writes about a pool of water in a grove, he is actually writing about the reflection of death."

Or, on another occasion:

"Did you pay attention to the old man who stops Prosper along the road to Jerusalem and asks him what he's carrying? Whom does that old man remind you of?"

I thought but couldn't come up with anything.

"Why it's Satan who dresses up as an old man in the aggadic embellishment of the Binding of Isaac tale.

"Isn't that obvious?" Her eyes shone. "Prosper is carrying a bagful of sticks on his back, just as Isaac does in the tale. He is a child of God!"

And once she enlightened me to a great truth that no one had ever given thought to before: that the structure of Richter's tale follows that of a sonnet—two quatrains and two short stanzas.

The more we met, the more she revealed about herself, and thus I became aware of the secret love affair between her and Joseph. She had fallen in love with him, as she said, even before she first saw him. It happened when she came across his second book of short stories. She wrote him a letter expressing her opinion on the stories, and she asked if she could meet with him. (The irony of fate: without my knowing it, I was the one who brought them together. Since she didn't know his address, she sent her letter to the publisher. There they handed me the letter to give to Richter. . . . He, of course, never revealed any of this to me.) When she met with him, he was exactly as she had imagined him to be; his looks; his voice; everything! They then started meeting more frequently. First in the mornings at a little café on the waterfront. (Inspired by those meetings, she wrote the poem "Gulls.") Later on they started taking long walks together, to the German Templar village of Saronah, to Jaffa, to the Seven Mills, going as far east as Rosh Ha'ayin. Then they started meeting in the evenings at her house. They even took several trips together to Jerusalem; they stayed at the pension owned by Mrs. Lazarus. She never met Olga face-to-face; nor did Richter ever speak of her in her presence. But she did go to concerts to see her perform, "to torture herself." Every time she mentioned Olga's name to me, she spoke in a tone dark with enmity and with a spark of madness in her eyes. Olga was, as it were, not her enemy but rather Richter's, a kind of "whore to the Messiah," who seduces him into sin, who stands as an adversary in his path, who prevents him from bringing salvation.

All at once they broke off relations. By the time he stopped seeing her, her illness had already been detected. I never managed to find out whether it was he who abandoned her or whether it was she who dismissed him. Or perhaps it was a mutual decision. Even though she knew I frequently saw him, she never asked me how he was or what he was doing.

She never issued a word of complaint against him and never addressed a request to him. It was as if she had made a resolution to herself. As if she had, for his sake, come to terms with her fate and given justification to her sentence. I knew she was burning with desire and longing for him. Once, finding her feverish in torment, I implied that it might be well for me to call for Joseph. The spark flared up in her eyes, and she said:

"Heaven forbid! That cannot be done! Even if a snake is wrapped around his heel!"

She seemed to look upon him as the High Priest of old at the Day of Atonement, strictly forbidden to break off from divine service, no matter what the distraction.

Once she said to me about him:

"Joseph is much more than a writer, and what he writes transcends the realm of literature! It's the vision of the kingdom yet to come! . . . Some day they'll understand this!"

Her illness, an incurable blood disease, was untreatable; she knew that the end was near. During the final two weeks of her life, she was lost in a world of fantasy; her consciousness became obscured, and she would lie there murmuring, partly in Hebrew, partly in Yiddish. I came to see her every day after work, and I stayed by her bedside until late in the evening.

One evening she made a request:

"Read me some of the stories of Rabbi Nahman[6] of Bratslav. My sister used to read them to me when we were girls. There are marvelous dreams in them."

I searched through the books on the shelves but couldn't find the one by Rabbi Nahman.

"You can't find it?" she said. "I really don't know. Perhaps I left it in Poland. Maybe someone took it. Read me some poems then. Read me some of the poems of Rachel Bluwstein. I love her poems."

But I couldn't find a volume of Rachel's poems either. I picked up a book of her own verse and said I'd read to her from it. She didn't say yes or no, so I sat down and read poem after poem. I saw tears gather in her eyes.

"Who'll read them?" she said. "There are no more eyes to read them any more. They've all grown dim. Even the poems themselves have gone blind. Soon they'll wither and turn to ash."

---

[6] The founder of a school of Hassidism in Bratslav, he visited Jerusalem in 1798.

One evening she spoke while fully alert, as if a spirit had breathed new life into a wilting flower.

"There's a lovely biblical expression," she said. " 'He was gathered unto his people.' I too am being gathered unto my people. I'm not sorry about it. I'm even happy perhaps. I'll be there with everyone, with my sister, my mother—a large family. A very, very large family now. But in my heart, I think that I have one kind of people and Joseph—he has another. How different are his from mine! No similarity whatsoever! There's no similarity whatsoever between Joseph's people and mine! I think, then, that we'll never ever meet again. . . ." After growing silent, she spoke once more. "Maybe . . . maybe I'll get to meet him in one of his tales. . . ."

This was about a month before her death. When I saw Joseph, I told him about Leah's condition, and I even informed him—for the first time—of what she had said. I told him that perhaps he should go see her before she closed her eyes for all eternity. He listened to what I had to say but said nothing. I never found out if he went to see her or not.

The last words I heard from her mouth were spoken as she lay in a high fever; like a disembodied spirit, her eyes shut, her limbs withered.

"Why not? . . . He could have been the Messiah son of Joseph. . . ."[7]

Leah Berlin surrendered her spirit on September 19, 1941. Her funeral procession moved from the courtyard of Hadassah Hospital to the cemetery at Nahlat Isaac. The procession consisted of about ten persons. Richter was not there.

(TRANSLATED BY SAMUEL ROBERT WHITEHILL)

---

[7] According to Jewish eschatology, there will be two Messiahs. The first, the Messiah son of Joseph's tribe, will be killed attempting to overthrow the kingdom of the evil Armilus, who will have gained control of the entire world. The Messiah son of David will then arise and defeat Armilus and bring eternal peace and harmony to all mankind.

If There Is Justice

(from *Elsewhere, Perhaps*)

by AMOS OZ

Rami Rimon came home for the weekend on leave.

His face was thinner. His skin had shrunk a little. His jaws seemed more prominent. The lines on his face were sharper. His mother's face struggling to get out. Fine creases ringed his mouth. The sun had etched wrinkles round his eyes. Twin furrows ran from his nose to the corners of his mouth.

He was wearing an impeccable greenish uniform, with his beret tucked in his pocket. His stout boots were shod with steel at toe and heel. His sleeves were rolled up to reveal hairy forearms, and his hands were covered with little scars. He was conscious of his manly appearance as he strode slowly across the yard with an air of studied indifference. The men and women he met greeted him warmly. He responded with an offhand nod. There were traces of gun grease under his fingernails, and his left elbow was dressed with a grubby bandage.

When the first tumult of hugs and kisses, received by Rami with a wavering smile, had died down, Fruma said:

"Well, you won't believe it, but I was just thinking of you the moment before you turned up. Mother's intuition."

Rami thought there was nothing strange in that. He had said in his letter that he would come on Friday afternoon, and she knew perfectly well what time the bus came. As he spoke, he put down his shabby kit bag, pulled his shirt outside his trousers, lit a cigarette, and laid a heavy hand on Fruma's shoulder.

"It's good to see you, Mom. I wanted to tell you that I'm really glad to see you again."

Fruma glanced at his dusty boots and said:

"You've lost so much weight."

Rami drew on his cigarette and asked about her health.

"Come inside and have a shower before dinner. You're all sweaty. Would you like a cold drink first? No. A warm drink would be better for you. Wait, though, the first thing is to take you along to the surgery. I want the nurse to have a look at your elbow."

Rami started to explain about the wound. It happened during a bayonet practice; the clumsy oaf of a section commander . . . but Fruma did not let him finish the story.

"There you go dropping your ash on the floor. I've just washed it in your honor. There are four ash trays in the house, and you . . ."

Rami sat down in his filthy clothes on the clean white bedspread and kicked off his boots. Fruma rushed to fetch her husband's old slippers. Her eyes were dry, but she tried to turn her face away from her son to hide the look he disliked so much. Rami, however, pretended not to have seen that strained look, as of a dam about to burst. He lay back on the bed, looked up at the ceiling, drew the ash tray that Fruma had put in his hand closer to him and blew out a puff of smoke.

"The day before yesterday we crossed a river on a rope bridge. Two ropes stretched one above the other, one to walk on and the other to hold. With all our stuff on our backs, spade, blankets, gun, ammunition, the lot. Now, who do you suppose it was who lost his balance and fell in the water? The section commander! We all . . ."

Fruma eyed her son and exclaimed:

"You've lost at least ten pounds. Have you had any lunch? Where? No, you haven't. I'll dash across to the hall and get you something to eat. Just a snack—I'll make you a proper meal when you've had a rest. How about some raw carrot? It's very good for you. Are you sure? I can't force you. All right, then, have a shower and go to sleep. You can eat when you wake up. But perhaps I'd better take you to the surgery right away. Wait a minute. Here's a nice glass of orange juice. Don't argue, drink it."

"I jumped in the water and fished him out," Rami continued. "Then I had to dive in again to look for his rifle. Poor wretch! It was hilarious. It wasn't his first accident, though. Once, on an exercise . . ."

"You need some new socks. They're all falling apart," Fruma remarked as she pulled his dirty laundry out of the kit bag.

"Once, on an exercise, he fired his submachine gun by accident. Nearly killed the battalion commander. He's the clumsiest fool you can imagine. You can tell what he's like from his name. He's called Zalman Zulman. I've written a song about him, and we sing it all day long. Listen."

"But they don't feed you there. And you didn't write every other day, as you promised. But I saw in the letter box that you wrote to Noga Harish. That's life. Your mother works her fingers to the bone, and some child comes and collects the honey. It doesn't matter now. There's something I must know: Did she answer your letter? No? Just as I thought. You don't know what she's like. It was just as well you ditched her. Everybody knows what she is. The mistress of a man who's old enough to be her grandfather. It's disgusting. Disgusting. Have you got enough razor blades? It's disgusting, I tell you."

"Is it true they're starting to work the Camel's Field? That's going to cause a flare-up, all right. Provided, of course, the powers that be don't get cold feet. You know, Jewish sentimentality and all that. My buddies say . . ."

"Go and have a shower. The water's just right now. No, I heard every word. Test me. 'Jewish sentimentality.' There aren't many boys of your age with such an independent way of thinking. After your shower you can have a nap. Meanwhile, I'll ask the nurse to come here. That wound looks very nasty. You've got to have it seen to."

"By the way, Mom, did you just say that she . . ."

"Yes, son?"

"All right. Never mind. It doesn't matter now."

"Tell me, tell me what you need. I'm not tired. I can do anything you want me to."

"No, thanks, I don't need anything. I just wanted to say something, but it's not important. It's irrelevant. I've forgotten. Stop running around. I can't bear it. We'll talk this evening. Meanwhile, you must have a rest, too."

"Me! I'll rest in my grave. I don't need to rest. I'm not tired. When you were a baby, you had something wrong with your ears. A chronic infection. There weren't any antibiotics then. You cried all night, night after night. You were in pain. And you've always been a sensitive boy. I rocked your cradle all night, night after night, and sang you songs. One does everything for children, without counting the cost. You won't repay me. You'll repay it to your own children. I won't be here any more, but you'll be a good father, because you're so sensitive. You don't think about rest when you're doing something for your children. How old were you then? You've forgotten all about it. It was the time when Yoash started going to school, so it must have been when you were eighteen months old. You were always a delicate child. Here am I rambling on, and you need to sleep. Go to sleep now."

"By the way, Mom, if you're going to the surgery could you bring me some corn ointment. You won't forget, will you?"

At five o'clock Rami woke up, put on a clean white shirt and gray trousers, quietly helped himself to a snack, and then went to the basketball field. On the way he met Einav, limping awkwardly. She asked how he was. He said he was fine. She asked if it was a hard life. He said he was ready to face any hardship. She asked if his mother was pleased with him and answered her own question:

"Of course Fruma's pleased with you. You're so bronzed and handsome."

The field was floodlit, but the light was not noticeable in the bright twilight. The only living souls there were Oren's gang. Rami put his hands in his pockets and stood for a while without doing or saying anything. The Sabbath will go by. Empty. Without anything happening. With mother. Sticky. What do I need? A cigarette. That thin boy playing by himself over there in the corner is called Ido Zohar. Once I caught him sitting in the common room at night writing a poem. What was I saying? A cigarette.

Rami put the cigarette to his mouth and two planes roared by, shattering the Sabbatical calm, hidden in the twilight glow. The dying sun struck sparks off their fuselage. The metal shone back dazzlingly. In a flash Rami realized that they were not our planes. They had the enemy's markings on their wings. An excited shout burst from his throat.

"Theirs!"

Instinctively he looked down, just long enough to hear Oren's confused cry, but by the time he looked up again the drama was almost over. The enemy planes had turned tail and were fleeing from other planes that were approaching powerfully from the southwest, evidently trying to block their escape. Instantly, dark shapes fell through the air toward the orchards to the north. Both planes had jettisoned the spare fuel tanks fixed to their wings to speed their flight. Rami clenched his fists and growled through his teeth, "Let them have it." Before he had finished there was an answering burst of gunfire. Lightning flashed. After what seemed a long interval, there came a dull roll of thunder. The fate of the raid was settled in an instant. The enemy planes disappeared over the mountains, one of them trailing a cloud of white smoke mixed with gray. Their pursuers paused, circled the valley twice like angry hounds, then vanished into the darkening sky.

Oren shouted jubilantly:

"We hit one! We smashed one! We brought one down!"

And Rami Rimon, like a child, not like a soldier, hugged Oren Geva and exclaimed:

"I hope they burn! I hope they burn to death!"

He pounded Oren's ribs exultantly with his fists until Oren drew away groaning with pain. Rami was seized by demented joy.

His joy accompanied him to the dining hall, where a spirit of noisy excitement reigned. He made his way among the tables to where Noga Harish stood in her best dress, looking at the notice board. He put his hands on her shoulders and whispered in her ear:

"Well, silly girl, did you see or didn't you?"

Noga turned to face him with a condescending smile.

"Good Sabbath, Rami. You're very brown. It suits you. You look happy."

"I . . . I saw it all. From beginning to end. I was up at the basketball field. Suddenly I heard a noise to the east, and I realized at once that . . ."

"You're like my little brother. You're cute. You're happy."

These remarks encouraged Rami. He spoke up boldly:

"Shall we go outside? Will you come outside with me?"

Noga thought for a moment. Then she smiled inwardly, with her eyes, not with her mouth.

"Why not?" she said.

"Come on then," said Rami, and took hold of her arm. Almost at once he let it go.

When they were outside the dining hall, Noga said:

"Where shall we go?"

Strangely enough, at that moment Noga remembered something she had forgotten: Rami's full name was Avraham. Avraham Rominov.

"Anywhere," Rami said. "Let's go."

Noga suggested they sit down on the yellow bench, facing the door of the dining hall. Rami was embarrassed. People would see them there, he said. And stare at them. And talk.

Noga smiled again, and again she asked calmly, "Why not?"

Rami could find no answer to her question. He crossed his legs, took a cigarette out of his shirt pocket, tapped it three times on his matchbox, stuck it in the corner of his mouth, struck a match, shielded the flame with both hands even though there was no wind, inhaled deeply with half-closed eyes, blew out a long stream of smoke, and when all this was done, lowered his eyes to the ground once more. Finally, he gave her a sidelong glance and began:

"Well? What have you got to say for yourself?"

Noga replied that she hadn't been going to say anything. On the contrary, she thought it was he who was going to do the talking.

"Oh, nothing special. Just . . . What do you expect me to do?" he suddenly burst out violently. "Spend the whole evening, the whole Sabbath, my whole leave with my mother, like some mother's darling?"

"Why not? She's missed you badly."

"Why not? Because . . . All right. I can see I bore you. Don't think I can't live without you. I can get on quite well without you. Do you think I can't?"

Noga said she was sure he could manage perfectly well without her.

They fell silent.

Hasia Ramigolski and Esther Klieger-Isarov came toward them, chatting in Yiddish and laughing. When they caught sight of Noga and Rami their conversation stopped dead. As they walked past, Hasia said:

"Good evening. Shabbat Shalom." She dwelt suggestively on the stressed syllables.

Rami grunted, but Noga smiled and said gently:

"A very good evening to you both."

Rami said nothing for a while. Then he murmured:

"Well?"

"I'm listening."

"I hear they're going to start working on the hill," Rami said. "There's going to be trouble."

"It's so pointless."

Rami quickly changed the subject. He told the story of his section commander who had fallen in the water while trying to demonstrate how to cross a river on a rope bridge. He went on to say that it wasn't the poor fool's first accident. "Once, on an exercise, he accidentally fired his submachine gun and nearly killed the battalion commander. You can tell what he's like from his name. He's called Zalman Zulman, of all things. I've written a rhyme about him:

"Zalman Zulman's full of fun,
Always letting off his gun.
Zalman Zulman lost his grip,
Took an unexpected dip.
Zalman Zulman . . ."

"Just a minute. Does he play an instrument?"

"Who?"

"Zalman. The man you were talking about. What's the matter with your elbow?"

"What's that got to do with it?" Rami asked indignantly.

"With what?"

"With what we were talking about."

"You were telling me about someone called Zalman. I asked if he played an instrument. You haven't answered my question."

"But I don't see what . . ."

"You're very brown. It suits you."

"It's hardly surprising. We train all day in the sun. Of course we get brown. Listen: we went on a fifty-mile route march, with all the kit, gun, pack, spade, and all at the trot. Eight of the people in my squad . . ."

"Chilly, don't you think?"

". . . collapsed on the way. And we had to carry them on stretchers. I . . ."

"I'm cold. Couldn't you finish the story tomorrow? If you don't mind terribly."

"What's the matter?" Rami considered, and then asked thickly, "What's up? Is somebody waiting for you? Are you rushing off to . . . to keep an appointment?"

"Yes. I've got to take my father his dinner. He isn't well."

"What, again?" Rami asked absently. Noga explained that he had a pain in his chest and the doctor had ordered him to go to bed.

"Next week he's got to go and have an examination. That's all. Shall we meet here again tomorrow afternoon?"

Rami did not answer. He lit another cigarette and threw the lighted match away behind the bench. Noga said good night and started to go. Then she stopped, turned, and said:

"Don't smoke too much."

At that moment five steps separated them. Rami asked irritably why she should care whether he smoked a lot or a little. Noga ignored his question and said:

"You're very brown. It suits you. Good night."

Rami said nothing. He sat alone on the bench until the dancing started in the square, as it did every Friday night at a quarter past nine.

When it was over, shortly before midnight, he set off for his mother's room. He changed his course, however, because he met Dafna Isarov, who asked him if he was going home to bed already, and Rami thought he detected a sneer in her voice. So he turned off the path. His feet guided him toward the cow shed, where he had worked before he was called up. And as he walked he talked to himself.

This could never have happened to Yoash. It's happened to me, though. Women understand only one language, brute force. But, as mother said, I was always a delicate child. Hell. Now they're laughing. Everybody wants something bad to happen to someone else so as to make life more interesting. It's like that everywhere; it's like that on the kibbutz and it's even like that in the army. You're a child you're a child you're a child. You're like my little brother. Maybe being brown does suit me, but it hasn't got me anywhere. She didn't insult me for once. She didn't even call me a horse. What did she do to me tonight, how did she make fun of me? My Rami is a delicate, sensitive boy. I wish I could die. That'd show them. I can bend this sprinkler with my bare hands. That'll drive Theodor Herzl Goldring mad. I've got stronger hands than Yoash. If only he weren't dead, I'd show him. Where am I going? Walking around like some Jack looking for his Jill. Leaping on the mountains, skipping in the hills, as that filthy old lecher would say. People like that ought to be put down. Like Arabs. Punch him in the face, he raises his hands to protect himself, you hit him in the stomach and give him a kick for good measure. All over. Here we are at the cow shed. Hey, Titan, good bull. Are you awake? Bulls sleep standing up because they can't lie down because of the iron ring. If they come to slaughter you, Titan, don't let them. Don't give in. Show your mettle. Don't be a ghetto bull. Give them a *corrida*. We mustn't give in without a struggle. We must be strong and quick and light and violent like a jet fighter. Swoop and dart and turn and soar like a knife flashing through the sky like a fighter. A fighter is such a powerful thing. I could have been a pilot, but Mother.

Strange that the moon is shining. The moon does strange things. Changes things strangely. Changes the colors of things. Silver. My Rami is a delicate sensitive child Rami writes poems like Izo Zohar he loves nature hell he loves plants and animals hope they burn to death. Her father has a pain in his chest. It's because of old Berger. Dirty old man. Her father taught us a poem by Bialik once, called "The Slaughter," where it says that there is no justice in this world. It's true. It's a ghetto poem, but it's true. He's lived his life, he's got grown-up children, he's found his niche. Why did he steal her from me? What have I done to him? And she said I was brown and handsome. If I'm brown and handsome, and he's old and fat, then why.

When I die, she'll know. It'll shatter her. The moon colors everything white. Silver. Listen, Noga, listen. I've also got a pain in my chest, I'm also in pain, so why don't you. I make fun of Zalman Zulman, she makes fun of me, they all make fun of me. It shows there isn't any justice in the world, only slaughter, Titan, worse than anything the Devil could invent. That's from the same poem. The man who's being slaughtered starts thinking about justice. The man who's slaughtering him thinks only about violence. My mistake was not to use force on her. Why, Titan, why didn't I use force, do you know why? I'll tell you. Because my Rami is a delicate boy curse them he loves nature hope they burn he loves plants and animals filthy whores. That sounds like planes overhead. It's after midnight. I love these planes, roaring along without lights. There's going to be a big war. I'll die. Then they'll know.

The fish ponds. A light in Grisha's hut. A pressure lamp. I can hear Grisha's voice. In the boat. Shouting to his fishermen. He's been in three wars and he's come out alive.

Maybe Dafna, his daughter. Ridiculous. They'd laugh.
What's in this filthy shed? Barrels. Sacks of fish food. The
fishermen's supper. If they find me here. Grisha's belt. A pistol. It's a revolver. Fancy leaving a revolver in an empty
shed. They'll be coming back to eat soon. They'll laugh,
they'll laugh. They'll say I went for a walk to look for inspiration. I know how it works. It has a revolving drum with six
chambers. You put a bullet in each chamber. After each shot
the drum revolves and brings another bullet in line with the
barrel. That's how the revolver works. Now let's see how
Rami Rimon works. A trial. Without a judge. I'm the judge.
Now let's begin.

Rami takes a bullet out of the leather holster, a yellow
metal case containing a little brown metal projectile. First of
all, he puts the bullet in his mouth. A sharp, metallic taste.
Then he puts the bullet in one of the chambers. He spins the
drum without looking, because luck must be blind. He puts
the gun to his temple. The chances are five to one. He
squeezes the trigger. A dry thud. Rami inserts a second bullet. Spins the blind drum. Four to two. Gun to temple.
Squeezes. Dry thud. Maybe I'm being silly. We'll soon know,
Judge. I'm not trying to kill myself. It's only an experiment.
Up to five. A delicate sensitive child couldn't do this. A third
bullet. Blind spin. Cold damp hand. I've touched something
damp. If I can do this, I'm not a delicate sensitive child. Up
to five. Gun to temple. Squeeze the trigger. Dry thud. I'm
past halfway. Two more tries. Fourth bullet. Now the odds
are against me. Now comes the test. Watch carefully, Judge.
Spin. Slowly. The drum, slowly. Without looking. Slowly.
Temple. You're crazy. But you're no coward. Slowly squeeze.
It's cold here.

Now the fifth. Last one. Like an injection. Delicate sensitive child's trembling. Why? Nothing will happen because
nothing's happened so far, even though according to the odds
I should have died with the fourth bullet. Don't tremble, dear
little delicate child who cried all night with earache, don't
tremble, think of Grisha Isarov who's come out of three wars
alive. Yoash wouldn't have trembled, because he was Yoash.
Little ghetto boy, with a little cap and a gray coat and side
curls. I want to know how many I. Not to kill myself. Four.
That's enough. Madness to go on. No, we said five—five let it
be. Don't change your mind, coward, don't lie, you said five,
not four. Five let it be. Put the gun to your temple. Now

squeeze, horse, squeeze, you're a ghetto child, you're a little boy, you're my little brother, squeeze. Wait a moment. I'm allowed to think first. Suppose I die here. She'll know. She'll know I wasn't joking. But they'll say "broken heart" they'll say "unrequited love" they'll say "emotional crisis." Sticky, very sticky. Hell. Squeeze. You won't feel a thing. A bullet in the brain is instant death. No time for pain. And afterward? Like plunging through the sky. An invisible fighter. It doesn't hurt. Perhaps I've already pressed the trigger and died perhaps when you die nothing changes. Other people see a corpse blood bones and you carry on as usual. I can try again. If I press the trigger, it's a sign I'm still alive. Afterward everything will be black and warm. When you die it's warm even though the body gets cold. Warm and safe like under a blanket in winter. And quiet. Squeeze. You've got a chance. Like when we used to play dice when I was little and sometimes I wanted very badly to throw a six and I threw a six. Now I want very badly to press the trigger but my finger won't press. Trembling. Careful you don't press it accidentally. Everything is different when the moon shines yellow. Can hear Grisha cursing next week we're going to the firing range that'll be interesting I'll be top of the class I'm an excellent shot now count up to three and shoot. Eyes open. No. Eyes closed. No. One, two, th- no. Up to ten. One, two, three, four, five, six, seven, eight, nine, t-.

But Rami Rimon did not try his luck the fifth time. He put down the revolver and went out into the fields and wandered about till his feet guided him back to the cow shed. Grisha won't notice. And if he does, he'll have a shock. I forgot to check the most important thing. I didn't look inside the gun to see what would have happened if I'd pressed the fifth time. Better not to know. Some things are better left undone.

A new thought occurred to Rami. It soothed him like a gentle caress. Not all men are born to be heroes. Maybe I wasn't born to be a hero. But in every man there's something special, something that isn't in other men. In my nature, for instance, there's a certain sensitivity. A capacity to suffer and feel pain. Perhaps I was born to be an artist, or even a doctor. Some women go for doctors and others go for artists. Men aren't all cast in the same mold. It's true, I'm not Yoash. But Yoash wasn't me. I've got some things he didn't have. A painter, perhaps.

It'll be morning soon. Planes in the sky. Sad Zalman Zulman's full of fun, always letting off his gun. Zalman Zulman lost his grip, took an unexpected dip. Zalman Zulman, whore like me, looking for justice in the w.c. Zalman Zulman go to bed, time to rest your weary head.

I composed the poem. I can abolish it. It's an abolished poem.

(TRANSLATED BY NICHOLAS DE LANGE,
ASSISTED BY THE AUTHOR)

Lunch

(from *Count Me Out*)

by REBECCA RASS

The telephone rang. It was for her. Her ex-husband. He just heard she had come from abroad. Had five years already passed? They agreed to meet.

On the beach. A small Arab restaurant. The mosques of Jaffa behind. A young, dark-skinned barefoot boy for a waiter. Tahini salad. Strongly scented olive oil. Lots of garlic. Saltwater fish stuffed with fresh spices, grilled on charcoal. He was watching her, his back to the sea.

He had grown fat. A stripe of white hair. The same restless movements. The same deep voice. The same ironic smile. The same inquisitive eyes. The same guy, another edition. The memories, still rippling. Resurrection of long-forgotten images.

First love. The exquisite tension. The trembling heart. The reverberation of the flesh. The wild dark-red tulips on the rocky hills. The wild mushrooms in the musky forest. The poignant odor of sun-soaked soil wet with the first rain. Hand in hand in the shady eucalyptus grove.

The wind playing on the tall trees. The Mediterranean.

Yellow sand and naked bodies. Blazing sun burning fiery bodies. Souls on fire.

The wedding—in color prints and on slides. A long white wedding dress. A white lace veil. A white wreath. A golden loop for a ring. A deafening rock band. Glasses clinking: congratulations! A family photo. The camera freezes smiles and time. Mazel-tov.

The wedding ceremony under the canopy. The rabbi races through the text. What is it that he says and what is it to do with her? What are all doing here? Institutionalizing her love? Her intimacy made formal? She can step away and leave it all behind. Too late, she doesn't dare. The price of a coward: love, reduced in scope, made finite and called marriage, sealed with a golden ring shamelessly shining on her finger. Why is everybody so happy? She vows never to marry again.

Five years later. Another rabbi rushes through the text. What is it that he says? He unbinds her? What has that to do with her, anyway? Aren't love and separation a personal matter? She vows never to divorce again.

Zealously she keeps her pledges.

At the small restaurant. The roaring Mediterranean sea in the background. They clink glasses, she and her ex-husband. They smile amicably. They examine each other.

You haven't changed, he says. And what about me?

It was not him, yet he kept floating out of layers of past years. Behind him—surging waves and white foam, and five years of her life. Another world. An era from another century. A whole life. Very useful, very necessary, a life workshop. One graduates from school, college, and from marriage.

They smile in embarrassment. In silence. What do you say to a man with whom you lived for five years and haven't seen for another five? Nothing. Nothing to say. Close, familiar, yet strange. So far away, and no bridge in between. They look. They smile. They smile again. They watch. And they wonder. What has the time apart robbed them of, and what has it bestowed on them?

Now she watches him with open eyes, fully aware. Her soul does not surge with love or pain. Memories do not assail her judgment. Only a soft thrill and curiosity; looking back with wonder.

No, he says, he isn't really happy with himself. He looks at her: he misses flying to other spheres, the walks together in the reality of a different world. He misses the dream of first love, the innocence, the naiveté. The eucalyptus grove, the wind in the willows. And what about you, he asks.

Will she tell him, she wonders, that her real life started with the divorce? Just like modern novels, she thinks, and dips the white round Arab bread in the Tahini sauce. Nineteenth century novels ended with marriage, 20th century novels start with a divorce. Her life is divided in two: before and after the divorce. Something like before World War II and after World War II. She was surprised to find out that what the war did to the world, the end of her marriage did to her—it shattered her from top to bottom.

Like the devastated landscape of Europe, her soul was in ruins, wounded and bleeding. With everything inside dead, she groped her way back to life. She had to start the creation of her self all over again, be born in her own image.

Silence. Only the Mediterranean soars and foams. They watch each other motionless. Recollected images rise. Was it as it was? They weigh the memories, the plus and the minus, the bliss and the pain. The primal blue water in the background sings of eons, of past civilizations. It sings of eternity. For one short moment they hold hands again, running downhill together; then, embracing in tenderness and facing the sunrise, they promise each other love eternal.

The waiter brings a bottle of white burgundy. They toast each other, she and her ex-husband. Cheers, skoal! He places a warm, tanned hand—a hand looming from another world—on her own. He presses tightly. A spark lights his eyes. A wild thought: does he want to start it all again from the beginning?

And that is how it started, or rather ended: at midnight he came home, sat in the blue armchair, puffing circles of smoke around her. I fell in love, he said (just like that). I want a divorce. I've already investigated. It can be speedily arranged. In three months—and that was it. A nuclear explosion occurred somewhere in her mind, the earth opened up and she fell into its entrails.

From afar his voice reached her, dividing their property. The double bed for me, the clothes chest for you. The armchair for me, the couch for you. The blue rug for me, the red rug for you, the towels for me, the sheets for you. The wedding presents, the silver cutlery—three spoons for me, three for you. The vortex was raging, spinning around her. She let herself go.

She dips her pita bread in the Tahini salad, and with her fork picks out a slice of tomato soaked with olive oil and marjoram. She slowly sips her white burgundy.

The whole bottle of wine she had finished all by herself didn't help much. The apartment they were so proud of became a graveyard. The walls closed in on her. Everything around her, once so valued, was reduced in size, in value, in significance, in beauty. Once he had closed the door and left, his steps still echoing down the stairs, everything came awry. The ceiling lowered, the white walls darkened, the furniture crumbled. The mahogany table was only a lifeless pile of planks. The marriage certificate was only a paper bridge between separated hearts.

And this is how it went on: he left and closed the door. He came back and told her he could not live without her, and then left again. He loved her. He loved another. And left again. Alone, she roamed the underworld, visiting the dead. She became a snail. She started to crawl. Crawling, she inched her way through the intricate dark tunnels of the underworld, begging for her lost love, for the scent of eucalyptus at sunset and of daffodils in spring. She begged for the past that had evaporated, for a dream that had crashed, for a yester-world that had blown up. And when everything around her had tumbled and disintegrated, she still pleaded for time to stand still.

The Mediterranean in the background surges and froths. Arab children play in the sand. The waiter approaches, his arms full: now, says her ex-husband, a surprise. A big tray piled with different kinds of seafood lands on the middle of the table, joined by a chilled bottle of Israeli champagne. You see, he says with a smile, I've not forgotten. Your favorite food. Specially ordered. His eyes sparkle. They clink their glasses. Cheers again. At that moment the sunlight reaches their table. Blinded, she closes her eyes.

With her eyes closed she crawled through the pit of purgatory, at the edge of existence. The debris of the past adhered to her skin. Wherever she crawled, there it was, a cemetery clinging to her back. And again he came and again he left. Each time he closed the door and left, she was seized by an illogical terror that crippled her. Too weak to leave herself, too impotent to lock the door behind him and put an end to the torture, too helpless to make a decision, too crushed to

stand, devoid of all will of her own, she snailed on, at the
edge of extinction.

With glee they attack the plate of seafood. They pull off
the tails and heads of the small red shrimps, peel away the
shells and gobble up the soft white meat. Drops of lemon on
the oysters and then they suck them in; with a tiny fork they
pull the succulent mussels out of their nests. There is a taste
of sea in their mouths. He tells her about himself. His life.
His work. His loves. And what's happening with you? he
asks. They mention common friends.

At that moment in purgatory, it dawned on her that her infernal journey was not singular. Many make it, sooner or
later, this journey into purgatory, the underworld of the soul,
into the darkest cellars of oneself, an involuntary journey
from the conscious into the unconscious, to find meaning in
the meaningless, identity in the formless mass.

What are you thinking of? he asks. The sea glitters behind
him. Of travelling. Of journeys.

Yes, you've always loved to travel, he says and tells her
about his own travels, travels of a successful businessman.

She resumes the travel into herself, struggling in the dark
to find the road back to life. It was difficult. No road carved
through the devastated landscape of her soul, no paths cut
through the charcoal expanses of her mind. Groping her way
in the dark, she realized that she was tied by thousands of
cords, bound by endless knots that looped along the years
from her parents, family, society, school.

Whenever she thought that she'd made her own choice, followed her own path, it was clear to her now that she had
simply been led along a well-trodden path cut for her by others.

Then, one day, he came and solemnly declared that everything had come to an end. In a split second, life—detailed,
organized and planned for years ahead—dissolved. That moment the process of her liberation began but, reeling in pain,
she was too blind to notice. It was so difficult to be free and
take full responsibility over one's self, over one's life.

She was afraid to be alone, untied, unbound, to be loose.
To be free. Blinded, in pain she crawled on in the desert of
her soul, looking for a way out.

Hills of shells pile up between them. One after the other

they throw the shells at the sea. Some land on the beach, a few reach the edge of the water. The waiter brings in two Arab coffee-pots filled to the brim with aromatic Turkish coffee. He places a small plate of sweet honey cakes on the table. A late afternoon breeze drives away the heat of the day. She tastes the cakes. Too sweet.

She felt nausea coming up her belly. War waged inside her between what she was and what she wished to be, between the dependent crawling snail looking for a master, and herself as the master of herself. The deep, horrifying sensation of nausea did not leave her. Her inside, soul and flesh, strove to emerge through her mouth.

Then, unexpectedly, the desert winds dropped. Tranquility abided. Sweet exhaustion. Had she reached a land? A country? An independent state? Yes. Her own. But it was a virgin land. She had to build it all from the beginning. To create the borders, to invent a language, compose a constitution all her own, write her own ten commandments, decide on her personal geography. The restaurant is empty. The waiters stand idle, looking expressionless at the empty street. They are alone, a man and a woman. Apologetically they examine each other. With a sensation of failure. After all they failed each other, could not keep their promise of love. And when everything collapsed they fled, leaving all questions hanging in air.

A breeze blows up her skirt. His eyes follow the wind and land on her tanned thighs. Blushing, she covers them. He looks straight at her eyes and laughs into them. His eyes slide down her face, down her neck and stop for a moment by the edge of her open-necked dress, hesitating before sliding inside, in between her breasts, saying hello to old friends, weighing the memory against the reality.

Against her will, her breasts stretch themselves under her dress. I wasn't too good at it, was I? he says softly. While married, they never dared to speak about their intimate life. Then, unexpectedly he starts to talk, quietly, softly, from the depth of his heart, looking far into the sea, never at her. Of his despair he talks, of his pain. Of his failure to keep them both happy and their love intact. Of frustration that increased each day.

The waiter takes away the coffee-pots and the glasses. He brings in ice water, but her ex-husband, talking, does not notice. She examines him with new curiosity. For the first time she realizes that he has grown up.

Who is he now, anyway? Her eyes glide over his well-shaven cheeks, down his short beard, roaming freely on his hairy chest, discovering bunches of white hair. She looks for her old self curled against his chest. Her eyes undress him. He looks at her and stretches out his hand. In peace and harmony their hands clasp. Behind them, the waves rise and fall, surges of energy. She swam alone in that sea, rising and falling with the waves, searching for land. The awareness of her own passivity overwhelmed her. Why had she never challenged their failure? Rising up from the dead, she felt long subdued energy released inside her.

Sitting in the restaurant hand in hand, she feels an urge to challenge the past. Their failure. Hers. She feels the urge to bring their failed relations to triumph, the frustration of the past to satisfaction. Can she? Can they?

Without words, they read each other's mind. The sky is blue, the sea is blue and the sun colors a yellow path in between. Slowly they rise and pay the check. They enter his car. It's blue, too. Slowly they drive along the beach. North? he asks. North, she says.

To her surprise, the feeling of aloneness was a source of freedom and strength. It filled her with tremendous joy. She was ready to answer to the world inside her and the world outside her. A vast new land loomed ahead. And it was clear: she had to leave the old world and go.

The car is in perpetual motion. The motion makes their blood run fast. To their left, stretches the blue sea. The asphalt road stretches ahead. They sail into a different world, drive in a different dimension outside clocktime. Sea and water move along with them. They hardly talk, a unison of silence. Soon the sun will set. Three tall palm trees appear ahead. They drive off the highway along a dirt road that leads them between high cliffs. They park the car.

On the deck of the sailing ship, against the fiery background of the setting sun, she stood alone, waving goodbye to her parents, her country, her receding past. For the first time in her life she felt no fear, no doubt, no hesitation. A river of fire stretched from the ship's bow to the red ball of the setting sun. It was on this magic path that olden ships sailed to mythical lands in search of the secret of life eternal.

For the millionth time a daughter leaves her father's home in search of the golden fleece.

On the beach, only he and she, and the burning eye of the world to witness. She takes off her clothes, and faces him naked, laughing. He takes off his clothes, faces her with his tanned naked body. A river of fire stretches between them and the setting sun. Smiling, they let their eyes travel over each other. Is that the man with whom she was intimate? He stretches his hand to hold hers. She slides under his arm and runs to the edge of the water. Wild rocky beach, primal cliffs rise from the soft waves. Facing the sea, with her back to her ex-husband, she feels his eyes fasten on her nakedness, glide along her spine, on the hills of her buttocks, on the back of her thighs, invading her secrets. Soft tiny waves lick her feet. Electric waves shake in her groin. Wave after wave. In a minute she will be on fire. She plunges into the cool water. With her heart beating in the rhythm of the waves, on the deck of the ship, she swore to live by the size of her dreams, and not by the measure of their realization. She plunged headlong ahead, eager to exercise the life inside her. With a knapsack and a sleeping bag, she had set on her voyage. Paris. London. Dublin. Oslo. Stockholm. Copenhagen. Amsterdam. Berlin. New York. Mexico City. By bus. By train. By plane. By boat. Distances lost meaning. The world became a sprawling village. Borders dissolved. Languages. Cultures. The road circled and circulated, like the veins in her body, like the blood in her veins. Like the journey of the sun in the sky. In a world opposite to the one she was born into, she was a young woman moving with time. Freed from things, free to go on short notice, pack her sparse belongings and leave, go with the wind. Working at odd jobs, she never signed away her freedom, shunned all contracts. Surprisingly, she found out that life itself kept her floating. Like water itself, which holds up the swimmer, and drowns the non-swimmer.

Fast, she swims away from him. He follows, and catches up with her. She splashes water at his face. He does likewise. A moment of joy, of pleasure, of intimacy. The elements join forces to approximate fulfillment. The setting sun, the yellow sand, the cool water, the salty air. A man and a woman laughing in the cradle of the world. Out of the water she emerges, running along the warm beach. He follows her, trying to overtake her. When he almost does, she plunges again into the water, splashing at him. He escapes. She runs to catch him, and when she almost does, he suddenly turns around. She falls into his embracing arms.

All those years she had refused to be a victim. A victim to despair, to failure, to loneliness, to prowling fear, the common diseases of modern man. She had refused to be a victim to lack of means, to luxury, to pain. To age, to reality, to time. She had refused to serve, but strove to render the ordinary meaningful, the mundane—mysterious, the mortal—immortal and to add one single drop of magic to life. Through her dream, she had reached out to the meaning of reality.

For a long time they stand entangled, almost motionless, the water nibbles at their feet. They stream into one another and merge into one flesh. Their bodies forgive past humiliation, overcome once bitter pain. Then they set out to feast and triumph. The setting sun stretches itself on the water before them, leaving behind a red blazing trail that shines on them as they roll on the sand, in the shallow water.

Alone in the white spaces, a person alone in a living desert, panting desert, a primal beast. A woman—in mellowness, in fulfillment. All she had she would give, all that there was she would receive. And she did.

The past flows into the present, the pain into joy, hate into love, male into female, man into love, love into life.

For one eternal moment she is the goddess of the earth. The goddess of love, sending roots into the soil to fertilize the barren sands. For one eternal moment she is merged with the elements, with the earth and the stones and the sun and the wind. For one eternal moment she is the woman in all women.

The sun has set. Soft gray light embraces the white moon looming in the gray sky. There is peace. There is tenderness. There is mirth. There is soft silence.

It's already dark. The sea soars black and powerful. A soft breeze. Peace and harmony on earth. They dress languidly, and walk to the car. In silence, beyond words. He starts the car and puts on the lights. A stream of white light breaks into the night. They drive in silence, along streets of a different world. The moon rises and hangs up in the air, moving along with them. The motion of the car corresponds to the motion of her blood. The moonlight stretches out to her moving in the car a bridge of light.

City lights. City streets. City crowds throng the streets in the warm night. He stops the car on the street corner. It was here that he picked her up a few hours earlier. Their eyes meet for a moment. Their lunch is over. They shake warm hands. See you again. So long. See you again? She gets out and slams the door. The car lingers somewhat before a red light. Green. Here I stand, alone, in the intersection of city roads, with his blue car speeding out of my life into streets of another world. I turn and head for the sea at the end of the street. I breathe in the salty air. Standing there, leaning on the rusty railing, I feel the constant rhythm of the sea beating in my blood.

Facing the Forests

by ABRAHAM YEHOSHUA

Another winter lost in fog. As usual he did nothing; postponed appointments, left letters unwritten. Words weary him; his own, others' words. He drifts from one rented room to another, rootless, jobless. But for occasional tutoring of backward children he would starve to death. He is approaching thirty and a bald spot crowns his wilting head. His eyesight blurs; his dreams are dull. Unchanging they are, uneventful: a yellow waste where a few stunted trees may spring up in a moment of grace, and a naked woman.

Sometimes, at noon, returning from their offices, friends encounter him in the street: a grey moth in search of its first meal.

Solitude is what he needs.

He drops his arms to his sides in a gesture of despair, backs up against the nearest wall, crosses his legs and pleads in a whisper:

"But where? Go on, tell me, where?"

For, look, he is craving solitude.

They catch hold of him in the street, their eyes sparkling:

"Well, your lordship, we've found the solution to your lord-ship's problem at last." And he is quick to show an expectant eagerness, though cunning enough to leave means of retreat.

"What?"

The function of forest scout. Fire-watcher. Yes, it's something new. A dream of a job, a plum. Utter, profound solitude. There he will be able to scrape together whatever is falling apart.

Where did they get the idea?

From the papers, yes, from skimming the daily papers.

He is astonished, laughs. What's the idea? Forests? What forests? Since when do we have forests in this country? What do they mean?

But they refuse to smile. They are determined.

He glances at his watch, pretending haste. Will not a single spark light up in him then? For he, too, loathes himself, doesn't he?

And so when spring has set the windows ajar he shows up one morning at the Afforestation Department. A sunny office, a clerk, a typist, several typists. He enters, armed with impressive recommendations, heralded by telephone calls. The man in charge of forests, a worthy character edging his way to old age, is faintly amused (his position permits him as much). Much ado about nothing, about such a marginal job. Hence he is curious about the caller, considers rising to receive him even. The patch of wilderness atop the head of the candidate adds to his stature. The fellow inspires trust, surely, is surely meant for better things.

You certain this is what you want? The observation post is a grim place. Only primitive people can bear such solitude. What is it you wish to do there?

Well, he wishes to look at the forest, of course.

No, he has no family.

Yes, with glasses his vision is sound.

The old manager explains that, in accordance with a certain semi-official agreement, this work is reserved for social cases only and not for, how shall I put it, romantics, ha-ha, intellectuals in search of solitude. However, he is prepared, just this once, to make an exception and include an intellectual among the wretched assortment of his workers. Yes, he is himself getting sick of the social cases, the invalids, the cripples, the cranks. A fire breaks out, these fellows will do nothing till the fire brigade arrives but stand and stare panic-stricken at the flames. Whenever he is forced to send out one such unstable character he stays awake nights thinking what if in an obscure rage, against society or whatever, the fire-watcher should himself set the forest on fire. He feels certain that he, the man in front of him here, though occupied with affairs of the mind, will be sufficiently alive to his duty to abandon his books and fight the fire. Yes, it is a question of moral values.

Sorry, the manager has forgotten why it is this candidate wishes the job?

To look at the forest. To watch for fires.

A secretary is called in.

He is invited to sign a contract for six months: spring, summer (ah, summer is dangerous!), and half the autumn. Discipline, responsibility, vigilance, conditions of dismissal. A hush descends while he runs his eyes over the document. Manager and secretary are ready with pen, but he prefers to sign with his own. He signs several copies. First salary due on April the fifth. He inquires about the size of the forests, the height of trees. To tell the truth, he has never seen a real forest in this country yet. An occasional ancient grove, yes, but he hardly believes (ha-ha-ha) the authorities in charge of afforestation have anything to do with that. Yes, he keeps hearing over the radio about forests being planted to honor this, that, and the other personage. Though apparently one cannot actually see them yet. Trees grow slowly. He under-stands . . . this arid soil. . . . In other countries, now. . . .

At last he falters. He realizes, has realized from the start, that he has made a blunder, has sensed it from the laughter trembling in the secretary's eyes, from the shock coloring the face of the manager. The candidate has taken a careless step, trampled a tender spot.

What does he mean by small trees? He has obviously failed to use his eyes. Of course there are forests. Real forests. Jungles, no, but forests, yes indeed. If he will pardon the question: What does he know about what happens in this country, anyway? For even when he travels through it he won't bother to take his head out of his book. It's laughable, really, these flat allegations. He, the old man, has come across this kind of talk from young people, but the candidate is rather past that age. If he, the manager, had the time to spare, he could show maps. But soon he will see for himself.

There are forests in the hills of Judea, in Galilee, Samaria, elsewhere. Perhaps the candidate's eyesight is dim, after all. Perhaps he needs stronger spectacles. The manager would like to ask the candidate to take spare spectacles with him. The manager would rather not have any more trouble. Good-bye.

Where are they sending him?

A few days later he is back. This time he is received not by the manager, but by an underling. He is being sent to one of the larger forests. He won't be alone there, but with a laborer, an Arab. They feel certain he has no prejudices. Good-bye. Ah yes, departure is on Sunday.

Things happen fast. He severs connections and they come loose with surprising ease. He vacates his room and his land-lady is glad of it. He spends the last nights with one of his learned friends, who sets to work at once to prepare him a study schedule. While his zealous friend is busy in one room cramming books into a suitcase, the prospective fire-watcher fondles the beloved wife in another. He is pensive, his hands gentle, there is something of joy in his expectations of the morrow. What shall he study? His friends say: the Crusades. Yes, that would be just right for him. Everyone specializes.

But in the morning, when the Afforestation Department truck comes to fetch him out of his shattered sleep, he sud-denly imagines that all this has been set on foot just to get rid of him; and, shivering in the cold morning air, he consoles himself with the thought that this adventure will go the way of all others, be drowned in somnolence. He abandons him-self to the jolts and pitches of the truck. The laborers with their hoes and baskets sit huddled away from him in the back of the car. They sense that he belongs to another world. The bald patch, the glasses, are an indication.

Traveling half a day.

The truck leaves the highway, travels over long, alien dirt roads, among nameless new settlements. Laborers alight, oth-ers take their place. Everyone receives instructions from the driver, who is the one in command around here. We are go-ing south, are we? Wide country meeting a spring-blue sky. The ground is damp still; clods of earth drop off the truck's tires. It is late in the morning when he discovers the first trees scattered among rocks. Young slender pines, tiny, light green. "Then I was right," he tells himself with a smile. But farther

on the trees grow taller. Now the light bursts and splinters.
Long shadows steal aboard the truck, like stowaways. People
keep changing, and only the driver, the passenger, and his
suitcases stay put. The forests grow denser, no more bare
patches now. Pines, always, and only the one species, ob-
stinately, unvaryingly. He is tired, dusty, hungry, has long
ago lost all sense of direction. The sun is playing him tricks,
twisting around him. He does not see where he is going, only
what he is leaving behind. At three o'clock the truck is emptied of laborers and only he is left. For a long time the truck
climbs over a rugged track. He is cross, his mouth feels dry.
In despair he tries to pull a book out of one suitcase, but
then the truck stops. The driver gets off, bangs the door,
comes round to him and says:

"This is it. Your predecessor's already made off—yesterday. Your instructions are all up there. You at least can read,
for a change."

He hauls himself and his two suitcases down. An odd,
charming stone house stands on a hill. Pines of all sizes sur-
round it. He is at a high altitude here, though he cannot yet
see everything from where he is. Silence, a silence of trees.
The driver stretches his legs, looks around, breathes the air,
the light; then suddenly he nods good-bye and climbs back
into his cabin and switches the engine on.

He who must stay behind is seized with regret. Despair.
What now? Just a minute! He doesn't understand. He rushes
at the cab, beats his fist against the door, whispers furiously
at the surprised driver.

"But food. . . . What about food?"

It appears that the Arab takes care of everything.

Alone, he trudges uphill, a suitcase in each hand. Gradually the world comes into view. The front door stands open
and he enters a large room. Semi-darkness, objects on the
floor, food remnants, traces of a child. The despair mounts in
him. He lets go of the suitcases and climbs to the second
floor. The view! Five hills covered with a dense green
growth—pines. A silvery blue horizon with a distant sea. He
is instantly excited, on fire, forgetting everything. He is even
prepared to change his opinion of the Afforestation Department.

A telephone, binoculars, a sheet covered with instructions.
A large desk and an armchair beside it. He settles himself

into the chair and reads the instructions five times over, from beginning to end. Then he pulls out his pen and makes a few stylistic corrections. He glances fondly at the black instrument. He is in high spirits. He considers calling up one of his friends in town, saying something tender to one of his aging ladyloves. He might announce his safe arrival, describe the view perhaps. Never has he had a public telephone at his disposal. He lifts the receiver to his ear. An endless purring. He is not familiar with the procedure. He tries dialing.

In vain. The purr remains. At last he dials zero.

The Fire Brigade comes on with a startled, "What's happened?" Real alarm at the other side. (Where, where, confound it!) Before he has said a word, questions rain down on him. How large is the fire? What direction the wind? They are coming at once. He tries to put in a word, stutters, and already they are starting a car over there. Panic grips him. He jumps up, the receiver tight in his hand. With the last words in his power he explains everything. No. There is no fire. There is nothing. Only getting acquainted. He has just arrived. Wanted to get through to town. His name is so-and-so. That is all.

A hush at the other side. The voice changes. This must be the Chief now. Pleased to meet you, sir, we've taken down your name. Have you read all the instructions? Personal calls are quite out of the question. Anyway, you've only just arrived, haven't you? Or is there some urgent need? Your wife? Your children?

No, he has no family.

Well then, why the panic? Lonely? You'll get used to it. Please don't disturb again in the future. Good-bye.

He is tired, hungry. He has risen early, and he is unused to that. This high commanding view makes him dizzy. Needless to add—the silence. He picks up the binoculars, raises them to his eyes. The world leaps close, blurred. Pines lunge at him upright. He adjusts the forest, the hills, the sea horizon. He amuses himself a bit, then lets go of the binoculars and eases into the chair. He has a clear understanding of the job now. Just watching. His eyes grow heavy. He dozes, sleeps perhaps.

Suddenly he wakes—a red light is burning on his glasses. He is bewildered, scared, his senses heavy. The forest has caught fire and he has missed it. He jumps up, his heart beating wildly, grabs the telephone, the binoculars. But then it occurs to him that it is the sun, only the sun setting beyond the trees. He is facing west. Now he knows. He drops back into the chair. He imagines himself deserted in this place, forgotten. His glasses mist over and he takes them off, wipes them.

When dusk falls he hears steps.

An Arab and a little girl are approaching the house. Swiftly he rises to his feet. They notice him, look up and stop in their tracks—startled by the soft, scholarly-looking figure. He bows his head. They walk on but their steps are hesitant now. He goes down to them.

The Arab turns out to be old and dumb. His tongue was cut out during the war. By one of them or one of us? Does it matter? Who knows what the last words that stuck in his throat were? In the dark room, its windows ablaze with the last light, the fire-watcher shakes a heavy hand, bends to pat the child, who flinches, terrified.

The Arab puts on lights. The fire-watcher will sleep upstairs.

The first evening. The weak yellow light of the bulbs is depressing. For the time being he draws comfort only from the wide view, from the soft blue of the sea in the distance and the sun going into it. He sits cramped on his chair and watches the big forest entrusted to his eyes. He imagines fire may break out at any moment. The Arab carries up his supper. An odd taste, but he devours everything, leaves not a morsel. His eyes rove hungrily between the plate and the thick woods. He broods awhile about women, then removes his clothes, opens the suitcase that does not hold the books, takes out his things. It seems a long time since he left town. He wraps himself in blankets, lies facing the forest. What sort of sleep will come to one here? The Arab brings him a cup of coffee to help him stay awake. The fire-watcher would like to talk to him about something, about the view, about the poor lighting perhaps. He has words left in him still, from the city. But the Arab does not understand.

It is half-past nine—the beginning of night. He struggles against sleep. His eyes close and his conscience tortures him. The binoculars dangle from their strap around his neck, and from time to time he picks them up, lifts them to his eyes, glass clicking against glass. He stares to keep awake, finds himself in the forest, among pines, hunting for flames.

How long does it take for a forest to burn down? Perhaps

he will only look every hour, every two hours. Even if the forest should start to burn he would still manage to raise the alarm in time to save the rest. The Arab and his child are asleep, and he is up here, light-headed, between three walls and a void gaping to the sea. He must not roll over onto his other side. He nods, and his sleep is pervaded by the fear of fire, fire stealing upon him unawares. At midnight he transfers himself from bed to chair; it is safer this way. His spine aches, he is crying out for sleep, full of regret, alone against the dark empire swaying before him. Till at last the black hours of the first night pass, till out of the corner of his eye he sees the morning grow among the hills.

Only fatigue makes him stay on after the first night. The days and nights following move as on a screen, a mist lit once every twenty-four hours by the glow of the setting sun. It is not himself but a stranger who wanders those first days between the two stories of the house, the binoculars slung across his chest, chewing on the food left him by the unseen Arab. The heavy responsibility that has suddenly fallen upon his shoulders bewilders him. Hardest of all is the silence. Will he be able to open a book here? The view amazes and enchants him still and he cannot have enough of it. After ten days he can embrace all five hills in one brief glance. He has learned to sleep with his eyes open.

At last he opens the other suitcase, the one with the books. Are not the spring, the summer, and half the autumn still before him? The first day he devotes to sorting the books, spelling out titles, thumbing pages. One can't deny that there is some pleasure in handling the fat, fragrant volumes. The texts are in English, the quotations in Latin. Strange phrases from alien worlds. He worries a little. His subject, the Crusades. He has not gone into particulars yet. "Crusades," he whispers softly to himself and feels joy rising in him at the word, the sound. He feels certain there is some dark issue buried within the subject, that it will startle him, and that it will be just out of this drowsiness which envelops his mind that the matter will be revealed to him.

The following day is spent on pictures. Monks, cardinals; a few kings, thin knights; tiny, villainous Jews. Curious landscapes, maps. He studies them, compares, dozes. That night he is kept off his studies by a gnat. Next morning he opens the first book, reads the author's preface, his grateful acknowledgement. He reads other prefaces, various acknowledgements, publication data. He checks dates. At noon his attention is distracted by an imaginary flame flashing among the trees. He remains tense for hours, excited, searching with the binoculars, his hand on the telephone. At last, toward evening, he discovers that it is only the red dress of the Arab's little daughter who is skipping among the trees. The following day, when he is all set to decipher the first page, his father turns up suddenly with a suitcase in his hand.

"What's happened?" the father asks.

"Nothing. . . . Nothing's happened. . . ."

"But what made you become a forester then?"

"A bit of solitude. . . ."

"Solitude . . ." he marvels, "you want solitude?"

The father bends over the open book, removes his heavy glasses and peers closely at the text. "The Crusades," he murmurs. "Is that what you're engaged on?"

"Yes."

"Aren't I disturbing you in your work? I haven't come to disturb you. . . . I have a few days' leave. . . ."

"No, you're not disturbing me. . . ."

"Magnificent view."

"Yes, magnificent."

"You're thinner. . . ."

"Perhaps."

"Couldn't you study in the libraries?"

Silence. The father sniffs round the room like a little hedgehog. At noon he asks his son:

"Do you think it is lonely here? That you'll find solitude?"

"Yes, what's to disturb me?"

"I'm not going to disturb you."

"Of course not. . . . What makes you think that!"

"I'll go away soon."

"No, don't go. Please stay."

The father stays a week.

In the evening the father tries to become friendly with the Arab and his child. A few words of Arabic have stuck in his memory from the days of his youth, and he will seize any occasion to fill them with meaning. But his pronunciation is unintelligible to the Arab, who only nods his head dully.

They sit together, not speaking. The son cannot read a single line with the father there, even though the father keeps muttering, "Don't bother about me. I'll keep myself in the background." At night the father sleeps on the bed and the fire-watcher stretches himself out on the floor. Sometimes the father rises in the night to find his son awake. "Perhaps we could take turns," he says. "You go to sleep on the bed and I'll watch the forest."

In the daytime they change places—the son lies on the bed, the father sits at the desk.

During the last days of his visit the father occupies himself with the Arab. Questions bubble up in him. Who is the man? Where is he from? Who cut his tongue out? Why? Look, he has seen hatred in the man's eyes. Such a creature may set the forest on fire some day. Why not?

On his last day the father is given the binoculars to play with.

Suitcase in hand, back bent, he shakes his son's hand, tears in the eyes of the little father.

"I've been disturbing you, I know I have. . . ."

The son protests, mumbles about the oceans of time still before him—about half the spring, the whole long summer, half the distant autumn.

From his elevated seat he watches his father fumbling for the back of the truck. The driver is rude and impatient with him. When the truck moves off the father waves good-bye to the forest by mistake.

For a week he crawls from line to line over the difficult text. After every sentence he raises his head to look at the forest. He is still awaiting fire. The air grows hot. A haze shimmers above the sea horizon. When the Arab returns at dusk his garments are damp with sweat, the child's gestures tired.

He wonders whether it is still spring, or whether the summer has crept upon the world already. One can gather nothing from the forest, which shows no change. His hearing has grown acute, all his senses keener. The sound of trees whispers incessantly in his ears. His dreams are rich in trees. The women sprout leaves.

His text is difficult, the words distant. It has turned out to be a preface to the preface. Yet he does not skip a single passage. He translates every word, then rewrites the translation in rhyme.

No wonder that by Friday he can count but three pages read, out of thousands to go. "Played out," he whispers to himself and trails his fingertips over the desk. Perhaps he'll take a rest? Bring some order into the chaos of his room? He picks a page off the floor. What is this? The instruction sheet. Full of interest, he reads it once more, discovers a forgotten rule or one added by his own hand, perhaps.

"Let the fire-watcher go out from time to time for a short walk among the trees, in order to sharpen his senses."

His first steps in the forest are like a baby's. He circles the observation post, hugging its walls as though afraid to leave them. Yet the trees attract him. Little by little he ventures among the hills, deeper and deeper. If he should smell burning he will run back.

Here and there the sun appears through the foliage and a traveler among the trees is dappled with flickers of light. The pines stand erect, slim, serious; like a company of new recruits awaiting their commander. His body aches the ache of cramped limbs stretching; his legs are heavy. Suddenly he catches sight of the telephone line, a yellowish wire. Well, so this is his contact with the world. He starts tracing the wire, searching for its origin, is charmed by its pointless twists and loops between the trees. They must have let some joker unwind the drum over the hills.

Suddenly he hears voices. He wavers, stops, sees a little clearing in the wood. The Arab is seated on a pile of rocks, his hoe by his side. The child is talking to him excitedly, describing something with animated gestures. The fire-watcher tiptoes nearer. They are instantly aware of him and fall silent. The Arab jumps up, stands by his hoe as though hiding something. He faces them, wordless. He stands and stares, like a supervisor bothered by some obscure triviality. He smiles absently, his eyes stray, and slowly he withdraws with as much dignity as he can muster.

He has been wandering in the woods for over an hour now and is still making new discoveries. The names of donors, for example. Rocks bear copper plates, brilliantly burnished. He stoops, takes off his glasses, reads: Louis Schwartz of Chicago; the King of Burundi and his People. The names cling to him, like the falling pine needles that slip into his pocket. Name after name sticks to him as he walks, and by the time he reaches the observation post he can recite them all, a smile on his face.

Friday night.

His mind happens to be perfectly lucid at the moment.

Clear out on Sunday, he whispers suddenly, and starts humming a snatch of song, inaudibly at first, the sound humming inside him, but soon trilling and rising high to the darkening sky. Strings of light tear the sunset across and he shouts song at it, shrills recklessly, wanton with solitude. He starts one song, stops, plunges into another without change of key. His eyes fill with tears. He hears himself and falls silent.

The Arab and the girl emerge from the cover of the underwood and hurry to the house with bent heads.

He is utterly calm. He has begun counting the trees. Sunday the truck brings him his salary. He is amazed, gushes his thanks to the mocking driver. He takes the money and forgets his plan.

He returns to the books.

Summer. A change has come over him. The heat wells up in him, frightens him. A dry flow of desert wind may rouse the forest to suicide; hence, he redoubles his vigilance, presses the binoculars hard against his eyes, subjects the forest to a strict survey. How far has he come? Some twenty pages are behind him, thousands before. What does he remember? A few words, a bit of a theory, the atmosphere on the eve of the Crusades. He could have studied, could have concentrated, were it not for the gnats. Night after night he extinguishes the lights and sits in the darkness. The words have dropped away from him like husks.

Hikers start arriving in the forest. Lone hikers some of them, but mostly they come in groups. He follows them through the binoculars. Various interesting ages. They swarm over the forest, pour in among the trees, calling out to each other, laughing; then they cast off their rucksacks and unburden themselves of as many clothes as possible.

Water is what they want. Water!

He comes down to them, striking them with wonder. The bald head among green pines, the heavy glasses. Indeed, everything indicates an original character.

He stands by the water tap, firm, upright. Everyone begs permission to go upstairs for a look at the view. He consents, joyfully. They crowd into his little room, utter admiring exclamations. He smiles as though he had created it all. They are surprised by the sea. They had never imagined one could view the sea from here. Yet how soon they wish to go! One glance, a cry of admiration, and they grow restless, eager to be away.

Would they be interested in the names inscribed on the rocks?

They laugh.

The girls look at him kindly. No, he isn't handsome. But might he not become engraved on one of their hearts?

They light campfires.

They wish to cook their food, to warm themselves. A virtuous alarm strikes him. Tiny flames leap up, smoke blows about the treetops. A fire? Yes and no. He stays glued, through his binoculars, to the lively figures.

Toward evening he goes to explore. He wishes to sound a warning. Soundlessly he draws near the campfires, the figures wreathed in flames. He approaches them unnoticed, and they are startled to discover him beside them. The leader rises at once.

"Yes? What do you want?"

"The fire. . . . Be careful! One spark, and the forest may burn."

Laying their hands on their young hearts they give him their solemn promise to watch with all the eyes shining in a row before him. They will keep within bounds, of course they will, what does he think?

He draws aside. There, among the shadows, in the twilight of the fire, he lingers and lets his eyes rove. The girls, their bare creamy legs, slender toes. The flames crackle and sing, softly, gently. He clenches his fists in pain. If only he could warm his hands a little.

"Like to join us?" they ask politely. His vertical presence is faintly embarrassing.

No, thanks. He can't. He is busy. His studies. They have seen the books, haven't they? He withdraws with measured tread. But as soon as he has vanished from their view, he flings himself behind the trees, hides among the branches. He looks at the fire from afar, at the girls, till everything fades and blankets are spread for sleep. Giggles, shrieks. Before he can begin to think, it will be dawn. Silence is still best. At midnight he feels his way through the trees, back to the observation post. He sits in his place, waiting. One of the figures may be working its way in the darkness toward him. But no, nothing. They are tired, sleeping already.

And it is the same the next day, and all the days following.

From time to time he scribbles in his notebook. Stray thoughts, speculations, musings, outlines of assumptions. Not much. A sentence a day. He would like to gain a hold upon it all indirectly. Yet is doubtful whether he has gained a hold even upon the forest in front of his eyes. Look, here the Arab and the girl are disappearing among the trees, and he cannot find them. Toward evening they emerge from an unforeseen direction as though the forest had conceived them. He smiles at them both, but they recoil.

Ceremonies. A season of ceremonies. The forest turns ceremonial. The trees standing bowed, heavy with honor, take on meaning. White ribbons are strung to delimit new domains. Luxurious automobiles struggle over the rocky roads, a procession. Sometimes they are preceded by a motorcycle mounted by an excited policeman. Personages alight, shambling like black bears. Women flutter around them. Little by little they assemble, crush out cigarettes with their black shoes and fall silent—paying homage to the memory of themselves. A storm of obedient applause breaks out, a gleam of scissors, a flash of photographers, ribbons sag. A plaque is unveiled, a new truth is revealed to the world. A brief tour of the conquered wood, and then the distinguished gathering dissolves into its various vehicles and sallies forth.

Where has the light gone?

In the evening, when the fire-watcher comes down to the drooping ribbons, to the trees, he will find for example: "Donated by the Sackson Children in Honor of Daddy Sackson of Baltimore, a Fond Tribute to his Paternity. End-of-Summer Nineteen-Hundred-and. . . ."

Sometimes, observing from his height, the fire-watcher will notice one of the party darting troubled looks about him, raising his eyes at the trees as though searching for something. It takes many ceremonies before the fire-watcher understands that this is the manager in charge of Afforestation.

Once he goes down to him.

The manager is walking among his distinguished foreign party, is jesting with them in their language. The fire-watcher comes out of the trees. The distinguished party stops, startled. An uneasy silence falls over them.

"What do you want?" demands the manager masterfully.

The fire-watcher gives a weak smile.

"Don't you know me? I'm the watchman. . . . That is to say, the fire-watcher. Employee of yours. . . ."

"Ah!" fist beating against aged forehead, "I didn't recognize you, was alarmed, these tatters have changed your appearance so, this heavy beard. Well, young man, and how is the solitude?"

"Solitude?" he wonders.

The manager presents him to the distinguished party. "A scholar."

They smile, troubled, meet his hand with their fingertips, move on. They do not have complete faith in his cleanliness. The manager, on the other hand, looks at him affectionately. A thought crosses his mind and he stays behind a moment.

"Well, so there *are* forests." He grins with good-natured irony.

"Yes," admits the fire-watcher. "Forests, yes . . . but fires, no."

"Fires?" the manager wonders.

"Yes, fires. I spend whole days here sitting and wondering. Such a quiet summer."

"Well, why not? Actually, there hasn't been a fire here for several years now. To tell you the truth, I don't think there has ever been a fire in this forest."

"And I was under the impression. . . ."

"That what?"

"That fires broke out here every other day. By way of illustration, at least. This whole machinery waiting on the alert, is it all for nothing? The fire engines . . . telephone lines . . . the manpower. . . . For months my eyes have been strained with waiting."

"Waiting? Ha ha, what a joke!"

The manager wants to hurry along. But before he goes he would just like to have the fire-watcher's opinion of the Arab. The truck driver has got the idea into his head that the fellow is laying in a stock of kerosene. . . .

The watchman is stirred. "Kerosene?"

"Daresay it's some fancy of that malicious driver. This Arab is a placid kind of fellow, isn't he?"

"Wonderfully placid," agrees the fire-watcher eagerly.

"Because our forest is growing over, well, over a ruined village. . . ."

"A village?"

"A small village."

"A small village?"

"Yes, there used to be some sort of farmstead here. Arabs. But that is a thing of the past."

Of the past, certainly. What else?

Light springs up between his fingers. What date is today? There is no telling. He could lift the receiver and find out the date from the firemen bent over their fire engines, waiting in some unknown beyond, but he does not want to scare them yet.

He goes down to the tap and sprinkles a few drops of water over his beard. Then he climbs back to his room, snatches up the binoculars, and holds a pre-breakfast inspection. Excitement grips him. The forest filled with smoke? No, the binoculars are to blame. He wipes the lenses with a corner of his grimy shirt. The forest clears up at once. None of the trees has done any real growing overnight.

He goes down again. He picks up the dry loaf of bread and cuts himself a rough slice. He chews rapidly, his eyes roving over a torn strip of newspaper in which tomatoes are wrapped. He has no hunger for news, oh no, but he must keep his eyes in training lest they forget the shape of the printed letter. He returns to his observation post, his mouth struggling with an enormous half-rotten tomato. He sucks, swallows. Silence. He dozes a bit, wakes, looks for a long time at the treetops.

He remembers what he has read up to now perfectly well, forward and backward. The words wave and whirl within him. For the time being, therefore, for the past few weeks, that is, he has been devoting his zeal to one single sheet of paper. A picture? Rather, a map. A map of the area. He will display it on this wall here for the benefit of his successors. Look, he has signed his name already, signed it to begin with, lest he forget.

What is he drawing? Trees. But not only trees. Hills too, also a horizon. He is improving day by day. He might add birds as well; at least, say, those native to the area. What interests him in particular is the village buried beneath the trees. What was it the manager had said?—"A scholar." He strokes the beard and his hand lingers, disentangles a few hairs matted with filth. What time is it? Early still. He reads a line about the attitude of the Pope to the German Kaiser and falls asleep. He wakes with a start. He lights a cigarette, tosses the burning match out into the forest, but the match goes out in midair. He flings the cigarette butt among the trees, it drops on a stone and burns itself out.

He gets up, paces about restlessly. What time is it?

He goes in search of the Arab, to say good morning. He must impress his vigilance upon the man, lest he be murdered some morning between one doze and another. The fire-watcher strides rapidly between the pines. How light his foot-step has grown during the long summer months. His soundless appearance startles the two.

"Shalom," he says.

They reply.

The fire-watcher smiles to himself and hurries on as though he were extremely busy.

What does he find one fine day? Small tins filled with kerosene? Yes, hidden. Among the trees. How wonderful! The zeal with which someone has filled tin after tin and covered them up with the girl's old dress. He stoops over the treasure, the still liquid on whose face dead pine needles drift. His reflection floats back at him, together with the faint smell.

Blissfully he returns to the house, opens a can of meat and bolts its contents to the last sliver. He wipes his mouth and spits far out among the branch-filled air. He turns two pages of a book and reads the Cardinal's reply to a Jew's epistle. Funny, these twists and turns of the Latin. He falls asleep, wakes, wipes the dust off the silent telephone. To give him his due—he bestows meticulous care on the equipment that belongs to the Afforestation Department, whereas his own possessions are falling apart.

Wearily he chews his supper. The Arab and his daughter go to bed. Darkness. He turns over a few dark pages, swats a gnat, whistles. Night.

He does not fall asleep.

He is out there, he is counting trees, and at sixty-three the Arab is suddenly in front of him, breathing heavily, his face dull.

And what do you have to say, mister? From where have you sprung now?

The Arab spreads his arms in a gesture.

Yes, yes, he knows! The treasure is three trees ahead. Exactly.

The fire-watcher strides ahead and the Arab follows. Moonlight pours over the branches, makes them transparent. He leads the Arab to the exact place. There.

Here he kneels on the rustling earth. Who will give him back all the empty hours? He heaps up some brown needles, takes a match, lights it, and the match goes out at once. He takes another and cups his hands round it, strikes, and this too flares up and dies. The air is damp and traitorous. He rises. The Arab watches him, a gleam of lunatic hope in his eyes. The fire-watchers picks up a tin of the clear liquid, empties it over the heap of pine needles, tosses in a burning match and leaps up with the surging flame—singed, happy. Stunned, the Arab goes down on his knees. The fire-watcher spreads his palms over the flame and the Arab does likewise. Their bodies press in on the fire. He muses, his mind distracted. The fire shows signs of languishing, little by little it dies at his feet. They stomp out the last sparks meticulously. Thus far it was only a lesson. He rises wearily and leaves. The Arab slouches in his wake.

Who is sitting on the chair behind the book-laden desk? The child. Her eyes are wide open. The Arab has put her there to replace the roving fire-watcher. It's an idea.

Strange days follow. The needles seem to fall faster, the sun grows weaker, clouds come to stay and a new wind. The ceremonies are over. The donors have gone back to their countries, the hikers to their work, pupils to their study. His own books lie jumbled in a glow of dust. He is neglecting his duties, has left his chair, his desk, his faithful binoculars, and has begun roving endlessly about the forest, by day and by night; a broken twig in his hand, he slashes at the young tree trunks as he walks. Suddenly he slumps down, rests his head against a shining copper plaque, removes his glasses and peers through the foliage, searches the grey sky. Then he collects himself, jumps up to wander through the wood, among the thistles and rocks. He has spent a whole spring and a long summer, never once properly sleeping, and what wonder is it if these last days should be like a trance?

He has lost all hope of fire. Fire has no hold over this forest. He can therefore afford to stay among the trees, not facing them. In order to soothe his conscience he sits the girl in his chair. It has taken less than a minute to teach her the Hebrew word for "fire." How she has grown up during his stay here! Unexpectedly her limbs have ripened, her filth become a woman's smell. At first her old father had been forced to chain her to the chair, or she would have escaped. Yes, the old Arab has grown very attached to the fire-watcher, follows him wherever he goes. Ever since they hugged the little bonfire, the Arab, too, has grown languid. He has abandoned his hoe. The grass is turning yellow under his feet, the thistles multiply. The fire-watcher will be lying on the ground and see the dusky face thrusting at him through the branches. As a rule he ignores the Arab, continues lying with his eyes on the sky. But sometimes he calls him and the man comes and kneels by his side, his heavy eyes wild with terror and hope.

The fire-watcher talks to him therefore, quietly, reasonably. The Arab listens. Then the Arab explains something with hurried, confused gestures, squirming his severed tongue, tossing his head. He wishes to say that this was his house, that there used to be a village here, that they have hidden it all, buried it in the big forest.

The fire-watcher looks on at this. What is it that rouses such passion in the Arab? A dark affair, no doubt. Gradually he moves away, pretending not to understand. Was there really a village here? He sees nothing but trees.

More and more the Arab clings to him. They sit there, the three of them like a family, in the room on the second floor. The fire-watcher sprawling on the bed, the child chained to the chair, the Arab crouching on the floor. Together they wait for the fire. The forests are dark and strong, a slow-growing world. These are his last days. From time to time he gets up and throws one of the books back into the suitcase, startling the old Arab.

The nights are growing longer. Hot desert winds and raindrops mingle, soft shimmers of lightning over the sea. The last day is come. Tomorrow he will leave this place. He has discharged his duty faithfully. It isn't his fault that no fires have broken out. All the books are packed in the suitcase, scraps of paper litter the floor. The Arab has disappeared, has been missing since yesterday. The child is miserable. From time to time she raises her voice in a thin lament. The fire-watcher is growing worried. At noon the Arab turns up suddenly. The child runs toward him but he takes no notice of her. He turns to the fire-watcher instead, grabs him between two powerful hands and—feeble and soft that he is and suffering from a slight cold—impels him toward the edge of the observation post and explains whatever he can explain to him with no tongue. Perhaps he wishes to throw the fire-watcher down two stories and into the forest. His eyes are burning. But the fire-watcher is serene, unresponsive; he shades his eyes with his palm, shrugs his shoulders, gives a meaningless little smile. What else is left him?

He collects his clothes and bundles them into the other suitcase.

Toward evening the Arab disappears again. The child has gone to look for him and has come back empty-handed. The fire-watcher prepares supper and sets it before the child, but she cannot bring herself to eat. She scurries off once more into the forest to hunt for her father and returns in despair, by herself. Toward midnight she falls asleep at last. He undresses her and carries the shabby figure to the bed, covers it with the torn blanket. He lingers awhile. Then he returns to his observation post, sits on his chair, sleepy. Where will he be tomorrow? How about saying good-bye to the Fire Brigade? He picks up the receiver. Silence. The line is dead. Not a purr, not a gurgle. The sacred hush has invaded the wire as well.

He smiles contentedly. In the dark forest spread out before him the Arab is moving about like a silent dagger. He sits watching the world as one may watch a great play before the raising of the curtain. A little excitement, a little drowsing in one's seat. Midnight performance.

Then, suddenly—fire. Fire, unforeseen, leaping out of a corner. A long graceful flame. One tree is burning, a tree wrapped in prayer. For a long moment one tree is going through its hour of judgment and surrendering its spirit. He lifts the receiver. Yes, the line is dead. He is leaving here tomorrow.

The loneliness of a single flame in a big forest. He is beginning to worry whether the ground may not be too wet, the thistles too few, the show over after one flame. His eyes are closing. He rises and starts pacing nervously through the room. He starts counting the flames. The Arab is setting the forest on fire at its four corners, rushing through the trees like an evil spirit. The thoroughness with which he goes about his task amazes the fire-watcher. He goes down to look at the child. She is asleep. Back to the observation post—the forest is burning. He ought to run and raise the alarm, call for help.

But his movements are so tranquil, his limbs leaden. Downstairs again. He adjusts the blanket over the child, pushes a lock of hair out of her eyes, goes back up, and a blast of hot air blows in his face. A great light out there. Five hills ablaze. Flames surge as in a frenzy high over the trees, roar at the lighted sky. Pines split and crash. Wild excitement sweeps him, rapture. He is happy. The Arab is speaking to him out of the fire, saying everything, everything and at once.

Intense heat wells up from the leisurely burning forest. The fire is turning from vision to fact. He ought to take his two suitcases and disappear.

But he takes only the child.

At dawn, shivering and damp, he emerges from the cover of the rocks, polishes his glasses and lo, five bare black hills, wisps of smoke rising. The observation post juts out over the bare landscape. A great black demon grinning with white windows. For a moment it seems as though the forest had never burnt down but had simply pulled up its roots and gone off on a journey.

The air is chilly. He adjusts his rumpled clothes, does up the last surviving button, rubs his hands to warm them, then treads softly among the smoking embers.

He hears sounds of people everywhere. Utter destruction. Soot, a tangle of charred timber. Wherever he sets foot a thousand sparks fly. The commemorative plaques alone have survived. There they lie, lustrous in the sun: Louis Premington of New York; the King of Burundi and his People.

He enters the burnt building, climbs the singed stairs. Everything is still glowing hot. He arrives at his room. Shall we start with the books burnt to ashes? Or the contorted telephone? Or perhaps the binoculars fused to a lump? The map of the area has miraculously survived, is only blackened a bit at the edges. Gay fire kittens are still frolicking in the pillow and blankets. He turns his gaze to the five smoking hills, frowns. There, directly under him, at the foot of the building, he sees the manager of the forests, wrapped in an old windbreaker, his face blue with cold. How has this one sprung up here all of a sudden?

The manager throws his grey head back and sends up a look full of hatred. For a few seconds they stay thus, their eyes fixed on each other; at last the fire-watcher gives his employer a smile of recognition and slowly starts down. The manager approaches him with quick mad steps. He would tear him to pieces if he could. He is near collapse with fury and pain. In a choking voice he demands the whole story, at once.

But there is no story, is there? There just isn't anything to tell. All there is is: Suddenly the fire sprang up. I lifted the receiver—the line was dead. That's it. The child had to be saved.

The rest is obvious. Yes, the fire-watcher is sorry about the forest too. He has grown extremely attached to it during the spring, the summer, and half the autumn.

He feels that the manager would like to sink to the ground and beat his head against some rock. The fire-watcher is surprised. The forests are insured, aren't they? At least they ought to be, in his humble and practical opinion. And the fire won't be deducted from the budget of the manager's department, will it? Right now he would very much like to be told about other forest fires. He is willing to bet they were puny ones.

Soon he is surrounded by men in uniform. Though the fire has not been completely tracked down, they have unearthed some startling news.

It has been arson. Yes, arson. The smell of morning dew comes mingled with a smell of kerosene.

The manager is shattered. "Arson?" he turns to the fire-watcher.

The fire-watcher smiles gently.

The investigation is launched at once. First the firemen, who are supposed to write a report. They draw the fire-watcher aside, take out large sheets of paper, ball-points.

"What have you lost in the fire?" they inquire sympathetically.

"Oh, nothing of importance. Some clothes, a few books. Nothing. . . ."

By the time they are through it is far into the morning. The Arab and the child appear from nowhere, led by two policemen. Two sergeants improvise a kind of emergency interrogation cell among the rocks, place the fire-watcher on a stone and start cross-examining him. For hours they persist, and that surprises him—the plodding tenacity, the diligence, page upon written page. A veritable research is being compiled before his eyes. His glasses mist over with sweat. Inside the building they are conducting a simultaneous interrogation of the Arab. Only the questions are audible.

The forest manager dodges back and forth between the two interrogations, adding questions of his own, noting down replies. The interrogators have their subject with his back against the rock, they repeat the same questions over and over. A foul stench rises from the burnt forest, a huge carcass rotting away all around them. The interrogation gains momentum. What did he see? What did he hear? What did he do? It's insulting, this insistence on the plausible as though that were the point.

About noon his questioners change, two new ones appear and start the whole process over again. How humiliating to be interrogated thus, on scorched earth, on rocks, after a sleepless night. He spits, grows angry, loses his temper. He removes his glasses, starts contradicting himself. At three o'clock he breaks in their hands, is prepared to suggest the Arab as a possible clue.

This, of course, is what they have been waiting for. They had suspected the Arab all along, promptly handcuff him, and then all at once everything is rapidly wound up. The police drivers start their cars. The Arab is bundled into one of them. The child clings to him desperately. The fire-watcher walks over to the manager and boldly demands a solution for the child. The other makes no reply. His old eyes wander over the lost forest as though in parting. The fire-watcher repeats his demand in a loud voice. The manager steps nearer.

"What?" he mumbles in a feeble voice, his eyes watery. Suddenly he throws himself at the fire-watcher, attacks him with shriveled fists, hits out at him. With difficulty the policemen pull him back. To be sure, he blames only this one here. Yes, this one with the books, with the dim glasses.

Before he has time to say good-bye to the place, the fire-watcher is being borne away toward town. They dump him on one of the side streets. He enters the first restaurant he comes to and gorges himself. Afterward he paces the streets, bearded, dirty, sunburnt—a savage.

At night, in some shabby hotel room, he is free to have a proper sleep. Except that he will not fall asleep, will only go on drowsing. Green forests will spring up before his troubled eyes.

And so it will be all the days and nights after.

(TRANSLATED BY MIRIAM ARAD)

POETRY

YEHUDA AMICHAI

All the Generations Before Me

All the generations that preceded me contributed me
in small amounts, so that I would be erected here in
    Jerusalem
all at once, like a house of prayer or a charity institu-
    tion.
That commits one. My name is the name of my con-
    tributors.
That commits one.

I am getting to be the age my father was when he died.
My last will shows many superscriptions.
I must change my life and my death
daily, to fulfill all the predictions
concerning me. So they won't be lies.
That commits one.

I have passed my fortieth year.
There are posts they will not let me fill
because of that. Were I in Auschwitz,
they wouldn't put me to work.
They'd burn me right away.
That commits one.

(TRANSLATED BY ROBERT FRIEND)

The Sweet Breakdown of Abigail

We hit her with little blows
like an egg for peeling.

Desperate, perfume-blows
She hits back at the world.

With pointed gigglings she takes revenge
For all that sadness.

And with hasty fallings-in-love,
Like hiccups of emotion.

Terrorist of sweetness
She fills bombs
With despair and cinnamon, cloves and love-splinters.

At night when she tears her jewelry
Off herself
There's great danger she won't know the limit
And will go on tearing and slashing away
All of her life.

(TRANSLATED BY TED HUGHES)

Here

Here, under the kites that the kids fly
and those caught by last year's telephone wires, I stand
with the branches of my silent decisions
grown strong within me, and the small birds
of hesitation in my heart, and the great rocks of hesita-
    tion
before my feet, and my two eyes that are twins,
one of which is always busy and the other
in love. And my gray pants
and green sweater, and my face that absorbs
color and reflects color, and I don't know

what else I reflect and receive
and transmit and reject,
and how I've been an exchange mart for many things.
Export. Import. Frontier post. Customs barrier.
Watershed and graveyard. Meeting place. Departure
    point.

The wind comes through treetops and pauses
at every leaf; nevertheless, it passes
without stopping, and we
come and stay a while, and fall.

So much similarity in the world; like sisters:
thighs and hill slopes. A distant thought
like an act that grew here in flesh and hill;
like cypresses, dark events on the ridge.
The circle closes. I am its buckle.

Until I discovered that my hard forefathers
were soft inside, they were dead.
All the generations before me are circus acrobats,
standing on each other's shoulders.
Generally I'm at the bottom, with all of them,
a heavy weight, on my shoulders.
But sometimes I'm on top: one hand raised high
toward the Big Top. And the applause
in the arena below
is my reward, my blood.

(TRANSLATED BY RUTH NEVO)

RAQUEL CHALFI

Porcupine Fish

Apparently a fish like you and me.
But there is something nail-like about him.

Slowly he glides,
examining himself in that great mirror called water
and asking why,
why these nails planted in his flesh,

why this need for endless wariness
that sharpens him, keeps him from being one
with the blue enfolding softness.

And then
the waters breathe,
something moves,
something alien perhaps,
certainly malign.
His spines bristle.
He turns into something else—
a swollen ball,
a small mountain of fear—
all roar, if one could hear.
His mouth—small, tight, rectangular—
distorts into a smile.
And his eyes, tiny pools in a suddenly vast forehead,
whirl violent images in his brain.

This time, however,
it was nothing really.

And he subsides
into the rigid destiny
of his nail-like self.

(TRANSLATED BY ROBERT FRIEND)

I, the Barracuda

Not just a fish, but an official
legend of the sea.

Even the green morena, cruel beyond compare
in this green, dark, blue, far realm
is no match. For me sea-wrack bursts its pods
out of season, I ripen the deep-sea fruit,
like a sun.
Ripe darkness surrounds me. Almost bright.
All waiting to be gathered.
And the sea, to be caressed.
I devour the water like fire.

I am never afraid.
I have no weaknesses,
I know myself, and my neighbor.
I am very musical.

Take note.
Even the green morena is no match.
I am an intelligent creature.
I seek no prey because I'm hungry.
I thirst for battle
because of a pleasant tickling in my guts.

I have absolute pitch.

(TRANSLATED BY E. A. LEVENSTON)

DAVID AVIDAN

An Alien Comes to Town

It may be the screenplay that has delayed me,
the screenplay that will yet be bloodily written,
the screenplay that will snatch me out of my financial
mess, and provide me, at long last, with some glory.

The screenplay, then:

An alien person comes to town,
an alien person to an alien site.
That look in his eyes is a cautious one,
and his judo blackbelt is girded tight.
On an invisible subway-train
he shortly arrives in a locked-up room.
Pretty soon he starts signaling, then
the day of arrival is the day of doom.

A couple of telephones suddenly are
trying to yield a vague, faraway yawn.
Yet he keeps smoking his cigar,
reacting to all in the selfsame tone
as that of a previous alien who might
as well have come to an alien town,
where a raging rabble, alas damn right,
lynched him conjointly and one by one.
Now on his way to the terrace he starts,
holding a flamethrower of the best trade-mark.
The darkness around is his bodyguard,
for this is a proud and discerning dark.
Yet the rabble below is lit,
engaged in a hazy, banal sort of game.
And only a single flamethrower will spit
its deadly coldfire flame by flame.
A cold person comes to town,
a cold person to a cold site.
That look in his eyes is a precautious one,
and nobody'll lynch him, wrong or right.
From his terrace he will depart
when he'll feel like departing, with cheerful steps.
The darkness will still be his bodyguard,
when on his dagger he'll fall, self-stabbed.
At last the rabble, damn raging, damn right,
will slowly and gradually scatter away—
which may well convince our screenplaywright
to ignore that bitterly disastrous day,
reminding himself that an alien town
may yet become a familiar one,
provided that one will successfully get
out of her tenements, living or dead.

Is that what delayed me?

Go Out

Somebody, whose name I fail to recall, flew through
several highly advanced airports, just to
report to me, while hightripping thru marijuanita, some-
    thing

I keep telling myself: "out
of here, out out out of here. Look
at yourself in the mirror, man oh
man—the world is yours".
"But", I told him rather desperately, "but
that's just what I've been doing all these years".

Go Out in Your Maturity

Go out, by all means go out, but
not in your adolescence, not in your early
youth. Go out
like a ripe sourblooded tiger, contemplating
mother jungle with elastic skepticism, filing
each new obscurity as methodically as a
junior clerk, still flashing your memory on
sourer blood than this, never yet
tasted. Don't go
in your youth, in the autumn. Go
in the autumn of your youth. The world
is starving for pussycubs, wandering in their misfits,
    splashing
in extraheavy water. It tames them
into harmless purring tomsycats, lays them
on deep and dangerous carpets, in front of
electrovisual sets through which
they get acquainted with themselves for the first time,
    barely beneath
the very best of all cosmetics, by which they'll be fa-
    voured
unto death.

Half My Kingdom

Half my kingdom, said
the king, and had he

taken better care of his wording, as he did
of his sexualife, he would at least have
doubled that inevitable
reservation. Just half
my kingdom and no
more. This is
the monarchial maximum that we,
Xerxes and all his councillors, can
afford in such
problematic times as these. Otherwise
one might suddenly start hanging
bunches of families
in this messy city.

Terrible Granny
[An Affairy Tale]

Somewhere else I've pointed out that
the fairy-tale of Red Ridinghood is essentially
a story for adults, a definite case
of statutory rape. Yet
a further possibility I overlooked is the most terrible
of all. The wolf, mind you, the wolf
is in a diabolic fix. Let us assume, coldbloodedly but
not without full aesthetic awareness, that the wolf—
having bungled the role of grandmother—suddenly
became a grandmother himself, powerless
to pull himself out of the mess. Assume? It has
happened. "Come to me, come to me", venomously
   whispered
Grandma-wolf to Little Red Ridinghood, shutting
her decrepit old ears to the howling wolf-pack, capped
with white head-dresses, collapsing on snowy tundras,
   covered
with sugar-powder. "Come to me. Come to me. By my
   side, dearest,
you can stay a virgin forever".

Undeniably a horrific possibility, not to mention
the Lesbian innuendoes. Still, it isn't clear

for whom the danger is greater: for the wolf or for
marvellous, footloose Red Ridinghood who managed
to transmogrify the dirtiest mind yet not lose
one single berry of those she had picked
in the magic, predictable forest.

Just Wait and See

Let's talk this thing out like
one powerfield to another: "leave me
alone. Clear out,
will you? Wait for me
patiently and obediently
one whole generation".

(TRANSLATED BY THE AUTHOR)

T. CARMI

Landscapes

I

A white bird on a green river, two
then three,
One electric pole, two
three bushes.
More than that (roofs
and clouds and stalks of grass)
cannot be counted from a train,
which is why I am not mentioning them.
In fact, I think I'll simply note
just one bird,
possibly only its wings.

II

He was standing at the top of a tree
wearing blue overalls
sawing.

Suddenly his face tore open
his body twisted like a branch
    hands filled up with wind
and he fell.

I saw all this from a train window
after a meadow
before a team of horses.
I note only the falling.
I didn't hear the scream.

(TRANSLATED BY ANN ARIKHA)

The Snow God of Abu Tor

His eyes were knives.
His mouth—a red bracelet.
His nose—a carrot, of course.

We worshipped him all day.
We leaped in front of him shamelessly.
And at night, in the light of his pale creature,
we danced before his fulminating eyes,
his lips of carbuncle,
his bright flocks scattered over the earth.

O king of one night,
high and mighty ancient of a day.
O snow god!

We knew that your end is looming.
Before our battered eyes
you are turning to memory.
The bracelet goes back to the closet.
The carrot and the knives to the kitchen.
The child to the classroom.

And we, our mouths dry from praising,
stand in the sun-drenched yard
searching for white footprints.

Arrow

Against its will drawn back
and shot.
It cleaves the air
talking in the language
of hawk and gull.
At half way
it still remembers
the bow,
the hand that strung it.
From there it belongs
to nothing but its end
the round heart
where it will stick
quivering.

(TRANSLATED BY STEPHEN MITCHELL)

DAHLIA RAVIKOVITCH

The Dress
[*For Yitzhak Livini*]

You know, she said,
they've sewn you a dress
of fire.

Remember how Jason's wife
burned in her dress?
It's Medea, she said, Medea did her in.
You have to watch out, she said,
they've sewn you a dress that glows like an ember
and burns like coals.

Will you wear it? she said, don't wear it.
It's not the wind whistling,
it's the poison seeping in
You're not even a princess,
what will you do to Medea?
You must learn to know voices, she said,
it's not the wind whistling.

Do you remember, I said to her, when I was six?
They shampooed my hair and I went out into the street.
The smell of the shampoo followed me like a cloud.
Afterwards I was sick from the wind and the rain.
I didn't yet understand Greek tragedies,
but the smell of the perfume wafted
and I was very sick.
Today I understand that it's an unnatural perfume.

What will become of you, she said,
they've sewn you a burning dress.
They've sewn me a burning dress, I said, I know.
So why are you standing there, she said.
You should be careful.
Don't you know what a burning dress is?

I know, I said, but not how to be careful.
The smell of that perfume confuses me.
I said to her: No one has to agree with me.
I put no faith in Greek tragedies.

But the dress, she said, the dress burns with fire.
What are you saying, I screamed,
what are you saying?
I'm not wearing a dress at all.
It's me who's burning.

The Sound of Birds at Noon

This chirping
is certainly not malicious.
They sing without giving us a thought
and they are many
as the seed of Abraham.
They have their own life,
flight is a thing they take for granted.
Some of them are precious,
some are common,
but the wing is all grace.
Their heart is never heavy
even when they're pecking at worms.
Perhaps they're just lightheaded.
They were given the sky to rule
over day and night
and when they touch a branch
the branch too is theirs.
This chirping is completely free of malice.
Over the years, it even seems
to bear a note of compassion.

Pride

Even rocks break, I tell you,
and not from old age.
For years they lie on their backs
in the heat and the cold,
so many years
it almost seems peaceful.
They don't move from their place
and so the cracks are hidden.
A kind of pride.
Year after year passes over them

expectant, waiting.
The one who will shatter them later
has not yet come.
And so the moss grows,
the seaweeds are tossed about,
the sea pounces in, and returns.
And they, it seems, do not move.
Until a little seal comes
to rub against the rocks,
comes and goes away.
And suddenly the stone is wounded.
I told you, when rocks break
it comes as a surprise.
And all the more with people.

From Day to Night

Every day I get up again from sleep
as if it were my last awakening.
I don't know what awaits me—
from this one might say, perhaps,
that nothing awaits me.
This year's spring is like the one before.
The month of Iyar—I know what it is
but it doesn't matter to me.
I don't notice when day
passes into night—
just that the night is colder
and silence equal to them both.
In the morning, I hear the sound of birds.
Affection for them
eases me to sleep.
The one who is dear to me isn't here
and perhaps he isn't anywhere.
I go from day to day,
from day to night,
like a feather
that the bird doesn't feel
as it falls.

(TRANSLATED BY MARCIA FALK)

Distant Land

Tonight, in a sailing boat, I came back
From the isles of the sun, and their coral clusters.
There were girls with combs of gold
Left on the shore in the isles of the sun.

For four years of milk and honey
I roamed the shores on the isles of the sun.
The fruit stalls were heavily laden
And cherries glistened in the sun.

Oarsmen and boatmen from seventy lands
Sailed towards the isles of the sun.
Through four years by shining light
I kept counting ships of gold.

For four years, rounded like apples,
I kept stringing coral beads.
In the isles of the sun merchants and pedlars
Spread out sheets of crimson silk.

And the sea was unfathomable, deeper than any depth,
As I returned from the isles of the sun.
Heavy sundrops, with the weight of honey,
Dripped on the island before sunset.

(TRANSLATED BY A. C. JACOBS)[1]

DRAMA

The Remarkable Mr. Shabetai

by ERHRAIM KISHON

Characters:

EVE, A SOCIAL WORKER   MANAGER
SA'ADIA SHABETAI   MRS. SHABETAI

Moabara[1]—tin huts, neglected gardens, washing on lines

MANAGER (*Enters with Eve*): He must live somewhere around here. What number did you say, Miss?

EVE (*Young girl, white shirt, straw hat. Looks rather tired and hot; nervously fingers a brief case filled with papers and colored forms; tries hard to make the impression of an earnest, businesslike person, but succeeds only in emphasizing her youth and inexperience*): The name was Shabetai. (*Rummages among her papers, takes out one.*) Sa'adia Shabetai, Hut Number One Thirty-seven. His wife called at the office about two weeks ago.

MANAGER: What did she complain about?

EVE (*Consults paper*): About—about—about practically everything. Do you know the Shabetais?

MANAGER (*Nods his head as if to say "unfortunately"*): Yes, I know them. Quite a problem family.

EVE: Why?

MANAGER: Why? I'll tell you why—

[1] A transit camp made up of rickety tin huts into which new immigrants move for a few days and then stay for years. The government tries to keep *ma'abara* inmates happy.—Ed.

[263]

EVE: Just a moment! (*Takes out pad from brief case, readies pencil, then:*) Well?

MANAGER: Well, Sa'adia Shabetai is a sick man, blessed with a large family—

EVE (*Takes notes, mumbles*): Sick, large family—

MANAGER: He was three times in the hospital, but always escaped and came back here—

EVE (*Writes*): Three times, escaped—

MANAGER: But you'll see for yourself.

EVE (*Writes*): For yourself—

MANAGER (*Grins*): You took a course, Miss?

EVE (*Offended*): No. I graduated from the School for Social Workers.

MANAGER: Where?

EVE: In the States. On a scholarship. We learned there the most up-to-date psychological methods.

MANAGER: Very nice. And how are you doing here?

EVE (*Swallows hard*): Thank you. In fact I have not yet—

Mrs. Shabetai appears in opening of hut, looks at them with distrust. She is a scrawny and dejected creature, and again pregnant.

MANAGER: Were you ever sent to a *ma'abara?*

EVE: Only once.

MANAGER: When?

EVE (*Blushes*): Now.

MANAGER (*Suppresses a grin*): Very nice, Miss. I wish you the best of luck here. (*To Mrs. Shabetai.*) Are you Sa'adia Shabetai's wife?

Mrs. Shabetai merely stares.

MANAGER: She seems to be his wife. See you later, Miss. All the best. (*Exits.*)

EVE: See you later, I hope. (*Examines Mrs. Shabetai, who does likewise with Eve. Deep and protracted silence.*)

MRS. SHABETAI: Miss—

EVE: I'm Eve.

MRS. SHABETAI: You is the new social?

EVE: Yes, from now on I'll take care of your troubles. Are you Mrs. Shabetai?

MRS. SHABETAI: Who?

EVE: Are you Mrs. Shabetai?

MRS. SHABETAI: No, I'm his wife.

EVE: May I? (*Sits down on rickety bench in front of hut and takes out pad.*)

MRS. SHABETAI: Me no write, Miss.

EVE: My name is Eve.

MRS. SHABETAI: No bread, Miss. No work, seven children, Miss, *be'hyat Allah,* seven children and one here. (*Points to her belly.*) Ben-Gurion—[2]

EVE (*Very flushed, rummages in her brief case*): Mrs. Shabetai? Have you ever called at our office? (*Poises pencil.*)

MRS. SHABETAI: My man comes soon.

EVE: All right, I'll wait. (*Does not know what to do with herself. Writes something, erases it, reads a form.*)

MRS. SHABETAI: Miss—

EVE: Call me Eve!

MRS. SHABETAI: Here he is, Miss. My man. (*To her husband.*) Sa'adia, the new social is here.

Shabetai is a bearded Oriental Jew, of dignified and stately appearance, completely at ease.

EVE: Mr. Shabetai?

SHABETAI (*Points at bench*): Please. (*With brisk movement of the hand dismisses his wife, who disappears in hut.[3]*)

EVE (*Sits down*): Please, be seated. (*Shabetai ponderously lowers himself onto bench.*) Your wife told me that you don't work.

SHABETAI: No.

EVE: Have you a trade?

SHADETAI: I'm a shoemaker. But they don't want me.

EVE: Why?

SHABETAI: Don't know. They don't want me.

EVE: How long have you been a shoemaker?

SHABETAI: I haven't worked yet.

EVE: Never?

SHABETAI: Never.

EVE: So—so—what kind of shoemaker are you?

SHABETAI: I'm a shoemaker. But they don't want me.

EVE: Have you ever tried to find work as shoemaker?

SHABETAI: Not yet.

EVE (*Completely confused*): Why not?

---

[2] Oriental immigrants often mention Ben-Gurion for no apparent logical reason. This approximately corresponds to the Englishman's "Good Lord!" —E.K.

[3] It is common knowledge that in the Arab states women do not enjoy equal rights. Our modern laws aimed at correcting this evil keep running into the stubborn resistance of Oriental women. —E.K.

SHABETAI: I have a weak heart, Miss. I can do only light work.

EVE: Is shoemaking not light enough work?

SHABETAI: Not for me, because I have no practice.

EVE (*Scribbles on her pad*): And couldn't you get lighter work at the Labor Exchange?

SHABETAI: They won't give me. Perhaps you could give me work?

EVE: No. I don't handle such matters.

SHABETAI: You don't have to handle. Only give me a slip of paper.

EVE (*Flares up*): Just a moment, Mr. Shabetai! There seems to be a misunderstanding here! I did not come from the Labor Exchange!

SHABETAI: Only give me a slip of paper.[4]

EVE: I can't give you any slips of paper, Mr. Shabetai. I have no connection whatsoever with the Labor Exchange. My task is to help you with your personal and family problems. (*Paper, poised pencil.*) What in fact could we do for you, Mr. Shabetai?

SHABETAI: First of all, you could give me a slip of paper for the Labor Exchange.

EVE (*Loses her temper*): I won't give you any! (*Swallows hard.*) Mr. Shabetai! Please! Let's see your case history. (*Takes out card.*) How many children have you?

SHABETAI: Six. Shalom, Mordecai, Abdalla, Mazal, Habuba, Shimshon, and Uri.

EVE (*Writes down the names*): That's seven.

SHABETAI: Seven? All right, then seven. And Geola, too.

EVE: Who is Geola?

SHABETAI: She's an old woman living with us. She can't even move, only eats.

EVE: Is she a relation of yours?

SHABETAI: Don't know. She came with us. Must be a relation, otherwise she wouldn't live with us. But she can no longer move. She looks after the children.

EVE (*Shocked*): Very interesting, Mr. Shabetai—really a very—very—big family—children—

SHABETAI: You want to help, Miss?

EVE: Naturally. That's what I'm here for.

---

[4] A queer superstition, widely believed by common people, has it that a few lines jotted by the proper person on the back of a cigarette package can move mountains. This, by the way, is quite true. —E.K.

SHABETAI: Then you must give me a slip of paper.

EVE: You—! Let's first fill out your case card, Mr. Shabetai. Then we'll see what can be done. When did you marry?

SHABETAI: Who, me?

EVE: Yes.

SHABETAI: Before I came here.

EVE: How old were you then?

SHABETAI: Not old.

EVE: Still?

SHABETAI: Still. People marry young where I come from. (*Loses patience.*) Look, Miss. Just a slip of paper for the Labor Exchange, and that's all—only a slip of paper.

EVE (*Almost hysterically*): Mr. Shabetai! Didn't I tell you— Wait! Let's finish this first. Really, Mr. Shabetai— Were there many children in your family?

SHABETAI: Six.

EVE (*Writes*): Six.

SHABETAI: And one in my wife's belly.

EVE: Mr. Shabetai, I'm speaking about your parental family!

SHABETAI (*Opens wide eyes*): Parental family? Don't know them.

EVE: Did you have many brothers and sisters?

SHABETAI: Yes.

EVE: How many?

SHABETAI: That's not so simple, Miss. Many of them died.

EVE: Try to remember. It's important.

SHABETAI: That's important? That's important? I'll tell you what's important! A slip of paper is important!

EVE (*Completely at a loss what to do*): Mr. Shabetai, please!

MRS. SHABETAI (*Comes out of hut with a wooden tray, takes off towel from the clothesline, spreads it on the tray, puts on it a glass of tea which she serves to Eve*): Please, Miss.

EVE (*In a weak voice*): Call me Eve. (*Tastes tea, is unable to swallow it.*) Mr. Shabetai, how can I help you if you refuse to give me even the simplest information on your background?

SHABETAI: How?

EVE: Look, Mr. Shabetai. It is my task to probe into your social problems, which in fact stem from the lack of social security with which you are afflicted here.

SHABETAI: By whom?

Mrs. Shabetai listens to Eve's words with growing panic.

EVE: Let me explain. Let's say—let's say that in your child-hood you were bitten by a snake. (*Shabetai tries to in-terrupt her.*) All right, all right; I know you were not bitten, but let's pretend you were. Let's say that you were scared for a while, but later forgot the whole thing. But this event left a deep imprint on your tender, child's mind.

Mrs. Shabetai screams and runs into hut.

SHABETAI: What child?

EVE: You. You! When you were a child!

SHABETAI: Let's say.

EVE: All right. So what happens? After so-and-so-many years, you suddenly see a snake coiled round your bed-post—

SHABETAI: There are no snakes here, thank God. But there is also no work—

EVE: We are not speaking about work now!

SHABETAI: Miss! A slip of paper—

EVE (*Is on the verge of a nervous breakdown, but controls herself with difficulty and speaks slowly and patiently*): Mr. Shabetai, don't you see? Before I can help you, we must come to know each other, cooperate, become friends. I, for instance, when I came here, started by in-troducing myself, told you who I was, what I was, where I came from. Right, Mr. Shabetai?

SHABETAI: Right, Miss. What's your name?

EVE (*Flabbergasted*): My name? Eve!

SHABETAI: Are you married?

EVE: No—not yet—but, Mr. Shabetai—

SHABETAI: Hard work, what?

EVE (*Surprised*): Yes, rather hard. But it has its compensa-tions.

SHABETAI: 'pations?

EVE: Compensations.

SHABETAI: I see. (*Silence*) So you are a spinster. Any family?

EVE: Mother and father.

SHABETAI: Bless them. Rich?

EVE: No. Father is old—

SHABETAI: I know. He doesn't get work at the Labor Ex-change. Any brothers, sisters?

EVE: No.

SHABETAI: Poor girl.[5] You give the old ones any money?

---

[5] In the eyes of Oriental Jews, few children are a moral calamity. Many children, on the other hand, are an economic crisis. —E.K.

EVE: Of course.

SHABETAI: And how about your dowry?

EVE: That's not so important—

SHABETAI: All right. But you need a dress, yes? You need furniture, yes?

EVE: Yes.

SHABETAI: You see? Are you engaged?

EVE: I have a boy friend.

SHABETAI: And you have no money for the wedding.

EVE: We have no flat.

SHABETAI: That's bad. A boy and a girl need a house. Let's see. (*Ponders.*) There are some houses not far from here, in the village. The government will give you one.

EVE: Not to me. That's for new immigrants.

SHABETAI: Things can be arranged. Just go to your boss, Mrs. Weissferger,[6] and say to her, "Mrs. Weissferger! A girl has to marry, to marry she needs a house, so give me a house!" Mrs. Weissferger will give you a slip of paper—

EVE: No, she won't. She can't!

SHABETAI: She can, Miss Eve, she only says she can't. She gave such a slip of paper to my cousin. You only have to be patient, always go to her and say, "Mrs. Weissferger! Give me a slip of paper!" And in the end she will either give you that slip of paper, or ask for a transfer. Chin up! So you start all over again with the new boss. Never give up. You have a right to a house, you work a lot, do much good to others, they all come and tell you their troubles and Miss Eve wants to help, and all want money, but there is not enough money for all—

EVE: True—if you knew how right you are—

SHABETAI: I know! So what can you do? You help us only with words and that's very hard.

EVE: Very hard, Mr. Shabetai.

SHABETAI: How could Miss Eve give money, when she hasn't got any herself? What's your salary?

EVE: Not much.

SHABETAI: And a mother and a father and a wedding. You need a dress.

EVE: A dress? Ha! Just for the room I have to pay twenty-five pounds, I have to eat at a restaurant—

---

[6] The name of the lady in question was Weissberger, but Mr. Shabetai cannot be expected to pronounce such a barbaric name correctly. — E.K.

SHABETAI (*Shocked*): At a restaurant?

EVE (*Nods her head*): You bet! At least two pounds a day!

SHABETAI: Two pounds?!

EVE: Yes! And—

SHABETAI: Just a moment! (*Pulls out a piece of paper from his pocket, takes pencil from Eve.*) Go on.

EVE: And that's for just one meal!

SHABETAI (*Calculates*): Two pounds a day—that's—that's—

EVE: Fifty pounds a month!

SHABETAI: Fifty pounds! For just one meal a day!

EVE: Yes. (*With growing excitement.*) And what about dresses, and traveling, and the cinema—you would be surprised—

SHABETAI: Don't lose hope, Miss Eve. You are now in a difficult social position, but God will help, and everything will right itself. (*Silence. Then very solemnly.*) Miss Eve—let's say—when you were a child, did a snake bite you?

EVE (*Completely confused*): No.

SHABETAI: That's the reason for your 'cology.

EVE: My what?

SHABETAI: You know—what you told me. But chin up, Miss Eve. Our state is young, many people are as badly off as you. Every girl wants to marry, and there is no money. But patience. Everything will be all right. People are good, I am also here—

Bus horn in distance.

EVE (*Realizing the strange situation in which she is, jumps up shamefaced*): Excuse me, Mr. Shabetai. I must go now—the bus—(*Her case opens and the papers are scattered all over the place. Eve tries to gather them.*)

SHABETAI (*Helps her*): Never mind, never mind, Eve. Here is the case history. Don't lose it, it's very important—and don't worry, the Lord will help!

EVE: Thank you very much—really—I don't know—thank you, Mr. Shabetai—(*Exits running.*)

SHABETAI (*Shouts after her*): Good luck, Miss Eve! Come whenever you want to see me. We Jews must stick together. (*Slowly turns toward hut, mumbles.*) Such a social girl, tsk, tsk, tsk—poor social girl—

(TRANSLATED BY YAHANAN GOLDMAN)

PART IV

PERSIAN
LITERATURE

THE PERSIAN
BACKGROUND

In both Persian prose and Persian poetry, the truly modern turn was taken only in the year 1921. That was when S. M. Ali Jamalzadeh's first volume of anecdotal tales, *Once Upon a Time*, and Ali Esfendiary's first free-verse poems were published. The former carried a preface justifying the use of colloquial idiom and local color in depicting the everyday events of Persian life in the twentieth century. Esfendiary espoused a poetics that was no longer bound by the language, imagery, and meters prevalent in Persian verse for the previous thousand years. Quite legitimately, therefore, Jamalzadeh has been called the founder of modern Persian prose and Ali Esfendiary (better known by his pseudonym of Nima Yushij) the true begetter of the new poetry.

Both were products of an emerging middle class; but as Molière's *Bourgeois Gentleman* long ago implied, the proper language for that class was prose. It was not surprising, then, that prose, which had played a secondary role in the classical period of Persian literature, now became the dominant medium of literary expression. This development had been forecast in the year 1905, with the translation into Persian of the picaresque English novel *The Adventures of Hajji Baba of Isfahan*, written in 1824 by James J. Morier, an emissary to the Persian court. Iranophile English critics had questioned Morier's fairness as a satirist of the humbug in Persian high life, but Persian readers of the translation approved of its racy style and regarded its depiction of local lowlife as both charming and realistic. Its influence upon the development of a native naturalistic fiction has been enormous, visible even in Gholamhosein Saedi's "The Game Is Over."

But influence upon modern Persian fiction has not been only English, or only literary. What the Persian scholar Ehsan Yar Shater has listed as the forces shaping contemporary Iranian poetry can as well be said to have molded its fiction:

> . . . the political upheavals ushered in by the allied oc-
> cupation of Iran in 1941 . . . the spread of radical
> views and a fresh yearning for social and political re-
> structuring, clashes of conservative and leftist opinions,
> the subsequent polarization of political views, the
> growing conflict between Persian nationalistic and reli-
> gious allegiances, a conflict of a different nature between
> Persian nationalism and international Communism, and,
> finally, the utter defeat of the radical left.

To be sure, some of these ideological pressures were felt by writers before World War II, and under the former shah. Ali Dashti, a distinguished novelist and now a senator, was a prisoner of Reza Shah in his youth. Bozorg Alavi, co-founder of the communist Tudeh party, served a prison term in the thirties before choosing German exile in the fifties. Under the present monarch, however, thought control has been institutionalized. He has publicly stated that naturalism in writing is decadent and destructive, the product of diseased critical minds immersed in Western ideas. This places an enormous burden upon a writer: he may wish to tell the truth as he sees it, but he can appear to be defying the shah. The effect of direct and indirect censorship upon Persian artists can hardly be measured. Reza Baraheni, after a prison term imposed by the shah's secret police, SAVAK, is self-exiled in the United States. The poet Shamlu has also now chosen American residence. Gholamhosein Saedi, dramatist and short-story writer, was recently released after eleven months in the shah's prison, his health if not his spirit so diminished that he could neither write nor practice his profession of psychiatry. The choice facing writers, painters, and composers appears to be whether they will become puppets of the government or its victims.

It is not only foreign ideas, like naturalism, that present dangers to Persian writers; the native tradition is also fraught with difficulties. Sadeq Hedayat and his follower Bozorg Alavi are cases in point. Whatever the influences upon them of Marx and Freud, of Poe and Chekhov, of Dostoevsky and Rilke, they were both steeped in the lore of their native land. Hedayat wrote an important critical essay on Omar Khayyam and Alavi a history, in German, of Persian literature. One of the latter's short stories takes its title from the fourteenth-century Persian poet Hafiz, and another is infused with the theme of the father-son struggle depicted archetypically in Ferdowsi's epic of kings, *Shahnamah*. It is interesting that Reza Baraheni, one of Iran's foremost living writers, should link Ferdowsi and Hedayat, the two seminal figures in Iran's literary past and present. He writes:

> I see a very distinct line existing between *The Epic of Kings*, written by Ferdowsi a thousand years ago, and *The Blind Owl*, written by the first important Iranian novelist, Sadeq Hedayat, about forty years ago.

Baraheni goes on to an interesting generalization about the governing power of the Sohrab and Rustum theme in Persian literature:

> In most of the major stories of the past and present, the father of the family, the head of the tribe, the father of the society, the father of history, the king, in other words, the old man, wins, and the young men and women of the family and the society are defeated; they lose the battle without exception. The authority of the tradition of the fathers is with us all the time. In fact our history is the history of infanticide. And certainly if there is going to be a revolution, it will be the revolution of young men and women against the authority of the traditional fathers, the brutal fathers. But the structure of that tradition is still the most important characteristic of our contemporary literature, and in particular fiction.

Baraheni's own banned novel, *The Infernal Times of Agha-ye Ayyaz*, from which "The Dismemberment" is taken, is precisely on this theme. Echoing the past but arguing the future, it belongs with the best fiction of contemporary Iran: *Abu Khanom's Husband* by M. A. Afghani, *The Hidden Prince* by Hushang Golshiri, and *Tangsir* and *The Patient Stone* by Sadeq Chubak.[1]

More by indirection than by outright attack, Chubak focuses attention upon the poignant human problems of a changing society. This, too, is the theme of Massud Farzan's "The Plane Reservation," which passes no judgment upon the generational and cultural conflict it so delicately depicts. In

[1] It is reported that Chubak has also come to the United States to live.

Hushang Golshiri's "My China Doll," an ominous event, portending political oppression, is viewed through the eyes of a child deprived of her father's love.

The modern revolt against classical Persian poetry was somewhat retarded by a more persistent strength in the tradition. As late as 1953, a writer in the *Times Literary Supplement* could claim that in Persia "the classicists hold the field." The authority of world-renowned figures like Ferdowsi and Saadi, Attar and Rumi, Hafiz and Jami, and especially of Omar Khayyam, the darling of the West, was difficult to shake off. The classical tradition was extended unquestioningly into the present by Bahar (d. 1950); and by M. H. Shahryar, who employed the *ghazal* (lyric) of Hafiz in a modern manner. Indeed, the *ghazal* and the other standard forms—*qasida* (ode), *mathnawi* (couplet), and *rubaiyat* (quatrain)—still have their advocates against the intruder from the West, free verse. Even the mystical Sufi mode survives in the poetry of Sohrab Sepehri, who blends it with the quietism of Tao and Zen that are part of his acquired culture.

The argument about the New Poetry was only ostensibly about matters of form—meter, rhyme, metaphor; it had more to do with the substance of poetry and with its audience. Was poetry a form of social communication or of private expression? Was it to be addressed to a large public or, as in former times, to an elite? A. Bamdad, who writes under the pen name Shamlu, spoke for the social significance of poetry:

> The theme of yesterday's poet
> Was not of life.
> In the vivid sky of his imagination, he
> Would not converse with other than wine and mistress,
> Night and day drowned in dreams,
> Caught in the snare of the beloved's funny tresses;
> While another,
> With one hand feeling the wine-cup and the other a
>   lass's hair,
> Let loose intoxicated cries on God's earth!
>
> Poetry's theme
>   today
>   is a different matter . . .
> Poetry today is the weapon of the masses,

For poets themselves are branches from the forest of
masses,
Not jasmines and hyacinths of someone's hot-house.[2]

The tension between poetic tradition and the individual tal-
ent is best illustrated in the work of the remarkable woman
poet Forugh Farrokhzad. The very titles of her books reveal
the constraining effects of the tradition from which she re-
volted: *The Prisoner, The Wall, The Revolt, Another Birth.*
She was influenced not only by her compatriot Hafiz (like
whom she blends the sacred and the profane), but also by
Milton, Goethe, and Marx; and she feels free to quote from
both the Koran and the Bible. In her often whimsical defi-
ance of convention, she reminds one of Emily Dickinson, and
in her sometimes shattering and powerful imagery of Sylvia
Plath, whose work she knew.

The tendencies here cited do not exhaust the variety of
contemporary Persian poetry, in form or substance.[3] Like the
prose, it has been perhaps too self-conscious. In the opinion
of Massud Farzan, it has been a literature of ideas rather
than of experience, although the trend may now be reversing
itself.

It is generally believed that drama did not flourish in the
Islamic world because of the religious proscription against artistic representation of the human form. Yet the Persian
branch of Islam has produced a very powerful religious
drama, to which Matthew Arnold referred as the Persian Passion Play. These *tazia* or consolation pieces commemorate the
martyrdom of the Shia saints against their Sunni opponents.
They have not, however, begot any progeny and are themselves fast disappearing as public performances. Serious
drama has come to Iran mainly by way of translations of European works.

On the other hand, a long tradition of comic and satiric
theater, going back to origins in puppetry and court amuse-
ments called *tamasha,* was revived during the constitutional
struggle in the late nineteenth century and reasserted itself in

[2] Adapted from Manucher Aryanpur (*Books Abroad,* Spring 1972, p.
200).
[3] There is, for example, a lively Azerbaijani tradition in the north of
Iran, but since the poetry is written in a Turkish dialect, it has been
omitted from this book.

the wake of Reza Shah's abdication in 1941. With the resurgence of the monarchy after 1953, however, censorship curtailed much of this activity except in the bland versions performed in the *chai-khanehs* (tea houses). The development of radio and television drama has been under strict government control, but nevertheless a good deal of artistry and more than a hint of Western absurdity have surfaced in plays and playlets of recent years.

Allegorical and psychological effects are the forte of Iran's foremost playwright, Gholamhossein Saedi, who, now living under virtual house arrest in Tehran, wrote under the pen name Murad. His play *The Cow* became a motion picture and won a high place a few years ago at the Venice Film Festival. *The Crows* is an early play that suggests the influence of Pirandello and carries its own Iranian kind of political message—trust no one, not even characters in a play. The future of the dramatic genre, as perhaps of all Iranian literature, will depend upon the degree of independence granted to literary artists. Free-thinking Iranians may have to develop their art in diaspora.

FICTION

◆

The Lead Soldier

by BOZORG ALAVI

For the last four or five years, at least four times a day, I have been riding the buses on the Maidan-e Sepah/Shahpur route. And the strange thing is that I have come to understand more in these buses than I have ever learned in the course of eight years in elementary and two in intermediate school. But perhaps it's not so strange, after all, for I was fundamentally a dull and diffident child. Whenever I failed to understand something two or three times in succession and asked our teacher about it (God pardon him!), he would say: "Some folk never understand." But on these buses one important fact has come within my grasp. Sometimes, under the weight of the passengers' resentment at further delay, they would, while still not full,[1] have to go nearly as far as the Hasanabad intersection. In such a case the driver's mate would of course keep a sharp lookout for any passenger who might want to board. And if he didn't happen to notice one, the driver would say: "Where are your wits, man? Come on, sling that 10 shahis' worth aboard!" or "Pick up that 10 shahis' worth from the roadside!" Anyway, this talk of 10 shahis was much repeated, "10-shahis" of course meaning "a passenger." For the driver, everybody whatsoever was worth 10 shahis,[2] whereas such a person might sometimes be, for example, Haji Ali Agha Chubchi, who possessed more than 100,000 tomans; or the head of the Livestock Control, who had paid 800 tomans goodwill for his job and, apart from two or three thousand tomans' profit, had a salary of 400 tomans a month. Likewise in my own case, though on payday I possess nearly 700 times 10 shahis, my value for him was still the same 10 shahis; and on the day before payday, when, after paying for a ticket, my pocket was as clean as a believer's heart, it made no difference in my value to him.

One day, in one of these buses, a slatternly little female was sitting. She had placed a lead soldier on the window ledge, and from time to time she would pick it up and stick it in her mouth, finally putting it back in its place. Every time the toy fell over from the vibration of the bus, she would lift it up again and put it in her mouth. I watched her behavior for a time; then, when I looked behind me, I saw F. sitting there, and he greeted me politely. (I had come to know him in the course of a journey to southern Iran.) Later, as I got off the bus, I recalled that this acquaintance of mine himself made this type of lead soldier and sold them to the stores. A while passed, and I did not see F. again. At that time I was working for the Opium Control, and they posted me to Fasa, where I fell sick. I returned to Tehran and was unemployed for some time. On my return—nearly two years later—I went to see F. The reason for this was that one of the Finance officials in Fasa knew him and had sent him, through me, a quantity of opium.

[1] Such buses, or communal taxis, wait for a full load at the starting point.
[2] 10 shakis is the equivalent of an American penny; a toman is worth about fifteen cents. —Ed.

There seemed something strange to me about my friend.
His workroom, which had formerly been full of pots, sheets
of lead, charcoal, pans and bellows—yet all in good order—
appeared today in utter confusion. He prepared the brazier,[3]
and we spread a rug and sat together in the porch. The talk
turned on the woman in the bus. Then he related his own
story to me, at first almost unwillingly, and then—as he saw
that I had no ulterior motive—with quickening pace. But it
was all without order, most of it in such a form that I could
not get the hang of it at all. In the event, he didn't even relate
the last part of it himself, and I gathered, this way and that,
that he had got into trouble. But, to the end, I never properly
understood the real cause of his madness.

"First I must recall my whole story to my own mind, and
then tell it to you. What story, though? I myself don't know
where to begin. From the day I was born? From the day I was
able to distinguish my left hand from my right? Or shall I begin with my family life? What sort of man my father was?
How much I loved my mother? No, I don't have the stomach
for that. . . ."

Opium smokers have a special way of speaking. They will
start a sentence, then stick a piece of opium on the pipe; and
until the opium is finished, the sentence doesn't get finished
either. The listener needs to be patient and not be put off by
the sizzling of the opium. But what makes the talk of these
opium addicts agreeable is the sweet, soft sound of their
voices.

"Do you remember by any chance in what hellhole it was
we became acquainted? It was on the road south. I don't
know, it might have been Kazerun. When I parted from
you—yes, it must be five years ago now—I went to Bushire. I
went there intending to stay a month, on a special job, but in
fact stayed for a year. They even fired me from the Department, after ordering me back to Tehran, because I wouldn't
go and stayed on. . . . Your patience is running out. You
want to know what's my connection with that woman you
saw in the bus that day with that toy in her hand. All in good
time! You must understand that from the very first, from the
time I left my father's home, I could never get beyond all this
junk you see around you. There were days when I ate neither

---

[3] To give a feeble warmth, but also to prepare his opium.

lunch nor supper, for if I had anything I sold it and spent the proceeds on opium. This life of mine, though, is all my father's fault. Or maybe not? Otherwise, why didn't I become a man, eh? You don't like me because I smoke opium, and you're right. But you don't realize that I too am disgusted with myself. You've no idea. Here, look at my hands or my shirt collar. It could easily be two weeks now since I splashed any water on my face. Just suppose . . . But what could happen now? I wasn't always an opium-smoker, I wasn't always like this, I wasn't made like this.

"When I was in Bushire I used not to smoke opium. Then I started. About that time, my mother had just died. Whenever I think of it my body starts to tremble. She did love me. Even when I was 16, until my mother placed her hand in mine sleep wouldn't come to me. These are not things everyone can understand. In Bushire. . . . yes, in Bushire I lived in the house of my boss at the office (the poor devil's in jail now on a charge of opium smuggling). It came about like this: I had something of a voice, having learned to recite the Koran with my father; and that head of department was a man of 'discriminating taste': every evening he would gather all the 'boys' together, *aragh*[4] and wine were set out, and our party was under way. You must realize, however, that until that time I had never drunk *aragh*, or—I tell you the truth and may I be flayed if not!—been guilty of any other stupidity. No 'gang' counted me among its members at this time. Apart from the fact that I was a preacher's child, I was a morose type, not given to letting myself go. My greatest pleasure in life was to sit beside my mother, take her soft hands in mine, and offer her comfort. . . . One night they gave me too much *aragh*, and I passed out. About that night I don't recall a thing. In the morning I saw Kowkab sitting in the room. She had brought a bowl and pitcher, and was trying to sponge the carpet on which I had vomited the night before. Her face was uncovered, and I could see her clearly. She had red lips, her hair had fallen like a curtain over her forehead, her face was round and plump. Later I learned that the boss had brought this Kowkab from Shiraz as a wet nurse, and she had been hired by them for a year. Now, because she was a good maidservant, they wanted to keep her on, although her year was up. All this, she related to me her-

---

[4] *aragh*: Anglicized as "arrack"; as used in Iran, often a general term for strong liquor of any kind.

self: 'O.K. I was hired for a year. I put up with all their little ways. But now I don't want to stay any longer. The master's fine, indeed none of them has any real faults, and I love the child. But to put it plainly, I want to go to Shiraz, I want to go and get married. I want to join my former husband. His military service is up now. He divorced me once, but I can be his wife again. I'm going. I'm not theirs to buy.' And she meant what she said. I forgot to say that when Kowkab was confiding in me I replied: 'You're right. If I were in the master's place, I'd help you on your way.' Yes, she meant what she said. One evening when I went home, I saw Kowkab was in my room. She had come so that *I* could send her to Shiraz. This was the point at which my adventures with this Kowkab really started. . . ."

The rings of opium smoke, first whitish and then a sort of blue, gave his remarks a philosophical setting.

"Every time this woman entered my life she turned everything topsy-turvy. If you imagine there was the slightest desire or passion between us, it wasn't so; I liked her, I even loved her, but as a man loves his mother. There was no bond between us. The torments I have suffered in life, the calamities that have befallen me—directly or indirectly—through Kowkab: they were all my inevitable and predetermined fate. I was condemned to this life. The very first day I entered life, my growing up in that house, under the control of that father, in the lap of that mother—all these things led me to choose such a course in life as I did. It all had its causes. Poor wretch, I was but a plaything. Oh if only, instead of saying 'I want' I could say 'They made me want.' "

Successive and interminable fits of coughing interrupted his words. After a few minutes he began again.

"I've got off the point. One night Kowkab was in my room. She had come with the intention of setting off in the morning. It was agreed that in the morning I would get her a bus[5] and set her on her way to Shiraz. I only had the one room. I had bought a *gelim*[6] and laid it out there, but half the room had no floor covering. Kowkab opened her bundle, spread it on the floor and went to sleep. Early next morning I went to see about the bus and fixed everything up.

"When I returned home at noon I saw Kowkab was miss-

---

[5] Really a hired car, serving as a small bus. Cf. note 1.
[6] *gelim*: carpet without pile, serving several purposes.

ing. I had arranged with the garage proprietor that the passenger would set out in the late afternoon. I waited for her
for a while, idling my time away instead of going back to the
office. About sunset I noticed Kowkab was back, in a bad
temper. 'I've been looking for you since morning. Last night,
when I was getting all my stuff together in a hurry, I forgot
something. If I don't find it, something terrible's bound to
happen to me on the road.' For answer, I pulled my boots on
and went off to work. That night I came home late, and
found Kowkab sitting by her bundle and turning her stuff
over. I asked her: 'What have you lost, then?' for I saw she
was sobbing. 'A toy.' 'What sort of toy?' 'A lead soldier.' Surprised, I said: 'A lead soldier costs 10 shahis. It's not worth
all this weeping and groaning.' But she seemed not to understand my words: '10 shahis? It was worth my life itself. . . .'

"This lead soldier Kowkab had got from her master's child.
One day she was taking the child for a walk, and she bought
this soldier in a variety store. But because it cut the child's
hand, the mistress wouldn't let her give it to him to play with
any more. This was why Kowkab had become annoyed with
her and didn't want to stay on any longer. From then on she
had always kept the toy soldier with her, and now she was
grieving over it and taking its loss as a bad omen.

"After she had lived with me for some days she said to
me: 'You know, I'm all upset. I don't want to go to Shiraz
any more. I feel my husband's fed up with me now, and
won't take me on again. If you like, I'll be your servant here;
otherwise, I'll go somewhere else. I must at least stay in this
town until I find that lead soldier, or I'll die of grief.'

"Kowkab stayed, and didn't die. She stayed for a month,
and made my life hell. At night I went onto the roof,[7] while
Kowkab slept in the room. In the morning she would make
my tea; she would wash my linen and cook my lunch; and
sometimes we would eat together. The way she looked after
me, I could fancy she was my mother, a fancy that kept me
happy. In the evening we would sit together. A month passed
in this way. At the end of that time I was summoned to
Tehran, and I told Kowkab I had to go, but would take her
with me if she wished. 'No. I'm going to stay here. I must
find that soldier or I'll die.' Then she thought a bit: 'When

[7] Traditionally, the flat roofs of Middle Eastern houses were used for
sleeping in the warmer weather.

are you going to Tehran?' 'I'm starting Saturday.' She stood
up to go and prepare supper, and said: 'I'll find myself a
place by Saturday.' 'All right,' I said, 'till Saturday.' But on
Saturday I didn't start, nor on the next Saturday. Even on the
third Saturday I was still there. A message came from
Tehran, asking why I hadn't given notice of my departure. I
tore it up. From the fourth week onward my salary was cut
off. During the space of these four weeks Kowkab too had
done nothing about finding herself a place. One evening I
asked her: 'This lead soldier you had, what was it like? Perhaps I can buy you one exactly like it.'

" 'Don't trouble yourself needlessly. I've been all over this
town, and there's not a lead soldier like the one I had to be
found anywhere. But see here, you toss and turn a lot at
night. Last night I came to your bedside. Why do you make
such a fuss about your mother?'

"She was right. I remember I was dreaming that an officer,
with a naked sword, was attacking my mother, while my father stood by and didn't utter a word. But the real reason was
that in those days I used to drink a lot of *aragh*.

"Next day I went with Kowkab to buy a lead soldier. To
no avail. Everywhere we went Kowkab would say: 'No, none
of these is the right one.' Then it occurred to me that I myself could make the soldier for her just as Kowkab wanted it.
I made wooden molds and bought lead. But you've seen them
yourself and know all about them. . . . Anyway, the lead
soldier would never turn out the way Kowkab wanted it.
(But it didn't matter, for I was selling the soldiers, and living
on the proceeds, just as I do now.) What was the use? That
original soldier would never turn out right, not in a whole
year of trying. We continued to pass our days in this way,
while at night we talked together. Sometimes Kowkab would
speak of her husband, who at that time was in the
Army. . . ."

At this point I interrupted F. because I couldn't make head
or tail of the matter. After all, a man doesn't give himself all
that trouble for the sake of a maidservant. But I sensed that
this episode had left a great mark on him and affected him
sorely. I guessed he was refraining from revealing an important point, so I asked him: "But didn't you love her, despite
the fact that you yourself said earlier there was no bond between you?" My friend didn't answer me, but went on with
his story:

"After four months it finally dawned on me that possibly such a lead soldier as Kowkab was talking about simply didn't exist. Accordingly, one morning when I got up, instead of pouring lead soldiers I began to carve and make a mold. I was trying to make an impressive figure of a man, but this mold wouldn't come out as I wanted. Its face wouldn't turn out properly the way I had in mind. I wanted to make it impressive, but it came out unintentionally in the likeness of my father. . . . What torment and affliction I suffered, trying to get this mold right! But never mind. It's all right for you: nobody can understand. You were just asking whether I loved her. What does that mean? I've suffered worse calamities than this. The pleasure which is natural to you is a torment to me. I was condemned not to be able to love. There are a thousand torments and tortures in the world, but nobody has been able to conceive of an affliction whereby there may be people who simply cannot love. Misfortune? 'Misfortune' is no name for a pain like mine. I don't believe in things of the spirit. Ugh! I can't stand it. . . . This soldier was eventually finished, but at the price of my own life. Now, after a year, I've realized that Kowkab was right: this wasn't the sort of lead soldier she meant. Anyway, I made one and put it in her bundle. I even did the same thing several nights in succession. . . . It all came to an end. The first stage of my life was over. One morning, when I got up, I saw she was missing."

He himself never related the rest of his story to me. That day, his coughing didn't give him the chance; but the real reason was that he didn't like my last question. Next day, when I went to see him he wasn't in the mood, and later— however much I pressed—he remained withdrawn. But this lack of compliance on his part only made me more curious and eager. I speculated that he might have committed a crime, and had been about to confess on the spur of the moment to gain peace of mind. Accordingly, I began to frequent his place more and more. One day I asked him where Kowkab was now, but he answered he didn't know. "Do you think she's still alive?" "For me, at any rate, she's dead." "Don't you want to see her again?" He didn't reply, so I asked him another question: "How long is it since you have seen her?" "If you want me to be at peace, don't ask me such things. For me, Kowkab is dead, just as my mother is dead."

No further word came from him. His house was in Esma'il Bazzaz Avenue. I struck up an acquaintance with the place and the neighbors, but from the inquiries I made about him I picked up nothing. The grocer at the street corner said: "We never see him, and scarcely anyone visits his house. Sometimes a woman comes, but she leaves immediately. No one has ever spent the night at his place." The servant from next door said he had seen him one evening in the Ferdows Park, but that was all. Eventually, I heard from the local *mirab*,[8] who happened to be standing there, that on most nights he would wander round those streets near the Agha Cemetery and the Maidan-e Paghapogh, returning home toward morning. I thought this woman would be Kowkab, but it came out later that it was his sister, Amin-Agha. He himself, however, was wandering around late at night looking for Kowkab. One day, in his porch, I came face to face with Amin-Agha. She had never married; and around thirty or so she had "got religion," made a trip to Karbala[9] and then become a female preacher. Now she had moved up in the world and was teaching Koran in girls' schools. Inevitably, we exchanged a few words about him.

Amin-Agha had a thin, narrow face, with a boil scar on her lip which made her really ill-favored. As I have said, she was still unmarried. She was forever turning her prayer beads and reciting ritual formulas. I wanted to find out whether she had any information about her brother's life in Bushire or not. Slightly raising her veil, so that I could covertly glimpse her boil scar, she said: "I ask God's pardon! If my father (God forgive me!) only knows what blasphemies are coming from my mouth, he must be trembling in his grave. Especially my father, who never liked that child anyway—unlike my mama, who loved him dearly. I remember from earliest childhood, while I was the eldest daughter, she was ready to throw all five of us into the grave; but not a hair of that one's head must be hurt. He wasn't even the baby of the family. God have mercy on my little sister Begom-Agha (who gave up her life to You), she was the baby. She married, but they didn't like each other, and she fell sick and

---

[8] *mirab*: water controller; traditionally (before the introduction of piped water) he regulated the flow of water from the mountains as it passed along the streets and into domestic cisterns. He needed to be a trusted local figure, and much of his work was done at night.
[9] The great Shi'ite shrine in Iraq.

died. But my mama's love for this other child was beyond words. They would have died for each other. They were like lovers. Again and again, my mother would say to him gently: 'You are my Joseph.'[10] That's the way of it, that's the way it was. You want the truth of it? That lad got the way he was out of grief over the death of my mama; from that time on he lost all self-control. There was nothing of this before he went to Bushire (when my mother gave up her life to You). The real reason for his traveling to Bushire was that my papa married again, and my brother couldn't stand to see this creature in the house after the death of his mother. You know how it is. My papa, on his side, couldn't stand the sight of his son.

"We were sitting around the *korsi*,[11] and the boy's foot was tapping it and shaking the lamp. If you only knew all the things he used to do. There was trouble over pens and school-books, trouble over coming home late, trouble over supper, over lunch. Now that mother of his was dead. (What affliction my mama suffered on account of those two! It's enough to break any Moslem's heart.) Finally, one day father and son really had a row—one of those rows where they said whatever was on the tip of their tongue. He declared that if my father, instead of taking all these 'common-law wives,' had spent a little on my mother, she wouldn't have died. But what do you think my father said then? (May I be struck dumb, may I be dumbstruck! I'll swear on seven Korans, I would never accuse anyone.) He said: 'You've laid hands on my wife!' But it was a lie, a lie made up by that slit-eyed slut—may God make her heart and liver bleed on a corpse washer's slab! That was the moment my brother said he wouldn't stay in the house any longer."

Then I asked: "I don't suppose you have any information about his life in Bushire? And what about after he came back from there?" "I do indeed. He himself told me quite a few things about Shiraz too, but all muddled up. Anyway, I never properly got the hang of it. (God, dear Lord, take away the brood of all these women I know only too well, from off the face of the earth!) Yes, when he came back from Bushire, he

[10] Joseph is the classic figure of manly beauty in "popular" Islamic literature, and the Potiphar's wife (Zolaikhā) episode is a standard love theme.
[11] *korsi:* a low table, with a brazier beneath, and blankets draped over; sitting around it in winter was an intimate family occasion.

brought this sickness with him." "What sickness?" "You don't know? I'm talking about this insanity of his.

"When he first came back from Bushire he lived at my place. Every morning when I got up, I'd see he'd rummaged through all my stuff, and even thrown it out. Even my prayer mat (which Heaven itself would never touch) had been treated in the same way. The first day, I thought we must have had burglars, but then I noticed nothing was missing. Moreover, it was a daily occurrence. One night I kept watch, and saw it was him. As I went to bed every night, he would get up and proceed to go through my bundles. I asked him what he thought he was doing, but he paid no attention to what I was saying. We were all at sixes and sevens. When I would ask him about it next morning, he would have absolutely no idea what I was talking about. I realized this was an incurable sickness he'd been afflicted with. He seemed to be searching for something. And he's still the same. At nights, up he jumps, and anything like a bundle, he'll open it up. But the worst part is these lice, which are all over his body: his head and face are covered with them. I asked Haji Mirza Reza, the local leech, about them, and he said he'll go blind from it eventually. God knows, I'm troubled enough about it, but what can a poor creature like me do? . . . ."

Isn't moonlight beautiful? Of course, because all the romantic, lyrical visions of poets and writers = scattered curls + the bank of a stream + moonlight. This of course ignores the fact that moonlight, under varying conditions, may be good or bad. But moonlight + women whose price is 10 shahis + muledrivers who come to town and go back to their villages with the clap = misery and misfortune. This moonlight which I have seen is like the white layer of dirt they throw on the unmade roads to the south of the city; while these creatures in black veils, who hug the walls of the side streets in the cold, are like caked blood on a wound. I am following one of them now. Usually, when I go near one of them, they say: "Come into the alley." And when I do, they say: "First give me 10 shahis!"[12]

I'm on the trail of Kowkab. Like it or not, my friend's fate has made a deep impression on me. His blotchy forehead, his

[12] See the beginning of the story. In the same passage is a reference to the trifling bus fare, which coincides with the prostitutes' rates (and also with the price of the lead soldier).

bleary eyes, and he dying from opium. Only this woman can
save him. Then I think to myself: Suppose he does die, what
effect will it have on the order of the universe? A logical and
valid idea in itself. But . . . perhaps Kowkab too, in her way,
is a more useful member of society—more useful, anyway,
than Mr. Chubchi.

Kowkab spends the evenings in the streets around the Ferdows Park. From the Tamaddon (= Civilization!) Cinema to
the Maidan-e Shah and the Bus Depot—that's her beat, her
zone of influence. Suppose I see her, what can she do? Perhaps persuade him to become a man once more. Such a disgusting life, after all, can't go on. For some while now, I and
Amin-Agha have been running his life for him. The old maid
has arranged positively to bring Kowkab to see me tonight.

"I don't care how much you press me, I won't go to see
that rusty little pimp again. What trouble and bitterness I
have suffered through him! You've no idea. I've given my all
for him. I nearly killed myself for him, and may God treat
him likewise! You may say to yourselves that I'm a terribly
stony-hearted creature, but I call God and my father's spirit
to witness that it's not so. Let me tell you the whole story.

"I got to know him in Bushire. I was a good girl in those
days. I was his maidservant, and kept everything in order for
him. I did absolutely everything for him. One evening he said
to me: 'Kowkab, I love you very much. You're like my
mother: your eyes are like hers, so let's see what your
mouth's like, and your nose.' At that time I was pure and
good and innocent; no one outside the family circle had seen
so much as the tip of my fingernail. I was not at all prepared
for immoral goings-on, and I certainly had no idea what he
could want from me. One evening I said to him naively: 'I'm
ready to become your temporary wife.[13] Let's go to the
preacher tomorrow and fix it up. If you think I'm suitable
and want me, I've no objection.' At this he burst out laughing
like a madman. Seeing how it was, I said no more."

Kowkab was sitting at the *korsi* in my room, furtively
drinking *aragh* and smoking, and telling me all she'd been
through. She had a wrinkled face, but fresh, with pockmarks
visible on it. Her locks hung down like the hairs of a soft
broom over her face. All in all, you certainly couldn't call

[13] In accordance with traditional practice, particularly in Iran, but
now officially disapproved.

Kowkab pretty, and she had all sorts of other faults as well. Suddenly I remembered those lead soldiers and asked: "OK. What was this business with the lead soldier?"

"Good grief! He told you about that too, eh? He's really crazy, that one. By my father's soul, I swear that what I say is no lie. It was a sort of amulet I had bought myself. Well, not really an amulet. But, anyway, you want the truth. In those days I loved my Cossack soldier-husband very much, and I had bought it in memory of him. When it was lost, I was very upset. But it wasn't all that big a to-do. It was all a trick on what's-his-name's part to keep me there in a strange place. One night I got up. I saw he'd made one of those soldiers we used to make together at that time—but this one was neither one thing nor the other, without proper form or shape, naked like an apparition in the desert, I can't bring myself to say the rest—and he'd placed it in my bundle. You want the truth, don't you? I was scared, and in the morning I fled and came to Shiraz. I couldn't find my husband there, and went in search of him. People said he'd married again, so here was another calamity. What bitterness I suffered there! Never mind. But just think: a woman alone, in a city, with no one, what's she supposed to do? I had no skills, and I was young. Wherever I tried to work as a servant, the lady didn't like it. If the household had no lady, I didn't get a moment's peace from the master. Eventually a truck driver took me in for a while, and then brought me to Tehran. After that I got into this line of business. One day I was walking around in the National Park, and *he* saw me there. He'd smartened himself up a bit. As soon as he spotted me, he came after me and took me off to his place. No matter what I did, he wouldn't let me out of the house again. How can I explain it all to you now? He kept telling me I was like his mother, and that he loved me like her. I would say to him: 'All right, if you want me, treat me right. Either marry me or take me as a temporary wife. We can't go on this way.' To this he would reply: 'No. You're my mother: a man can't marry his mother.' "

I interrupted her: "If he really wanted you, though, why didn't he take you in marriage?"

"How can I explain it to you so that you will understand? He just wasn't a man. He would fly at me like a madman, slobbering all over my head and face till I struck him. Then he would hit me and swear at me, and tear out my hair. One day he hit me so hard with a stick that I fainted. I fled from his house, but wherever I went he would chase after me and beat me. Again and again he would find me and take me back to his place. Then I would escape again. For a whole year my wretched life went on like this."At this point she was overcome by tears again.

"During all this time I never went with anyone else. I'm telling you the truth, really I am. You know, I'm not afraid of anyone, not even Heaven itself. But, just think, they won't let me into the cafés, and I can't stand on the Lalehzar or the Avenue Istanbul. My place is in the streets near the Agha Cemetery. On the other hand, I'm my own boss, and I've got nothing anyone can take from me. I was ready to offer myself even to drivers' mates, but who will have anything to do with me? Home, life, husband, children, parents, money—I don't own a thing. But at least I'm not afraid, not even of Heaven. Press me all you like, I still won't go to that little runt's place. But if I do go, and he tries to touch me, I'll give him what for. This time I'll kill him, I tell you. What have I to be afraid of? I don't suppose you know what happened the last night?

"It was last winter. In the evening I went to my room to lie down, when I saw he'd set fire to the quilt and the furniture, and then poured water on them to put the fire out. He must have come when I wasn't there, turned my bundle inside out, and completely smashed the *korsi*. So the fire in the brazier shot onto the quilt, and the whole room nearly went up in flames. That's why he went and poured water over everything. So, poor devil, I now had nowhere to sleep. I was trembling like a leaf. I tried everything to get him to let me into his room, not that anybody would want to pal up with him! Finally, and in the end, a gentleman from the yard next door took my hand and led me into his own room. You can't blame me. I had nowhere to go. Next morning, when *he* realized what had happened, he wanted to kill the poor landlady. He started shouting: 'You've betrayed my mother, I'll kill you!' So, fearing that things might get really bad, I fled, and never went back there again. You can cut me up in little pieces, I'll never go there again."

I didn't cut Kowkab into little pieces, but gave her a little money. Moreover, the *aragh* had had its effect, and the poor creature had no place to go. So I took her hand and led her to my friend's house. When she had gone into the room, I stood for a while in the corridor. But there was no commotion, so I turned round and left.

Next day the weather was extremely cold, and snow covered the whole city. When I left the office I went looking for my friend in Esma'il Bazzaz Avenue. The house door was locked, and an official wax seal had been placed upon it. For a while I walked along the road. Eventually I came to the Maidan-e Shah, where I got on a bus to go home. In the bus people were talking about a man having strangled a woman the night before. Near Dardar Street a man was standing, holding a suitcase and scratching the back of his neck. The bus driver's mate hadn't noticed this potential passenger, so the driver stopped the bus and said to him: "Come on, get that 10 shahis' worth off the road!" The man scratching his neck put his hand in his pocket as though looking for some money. As he came to board the bus, his case hit the step, the lid opened, and a large quantity of lead soldiers poured out onto the snow. The driver wouldn't wait any longer, and started the bus moving. The man who had been scratching his neck gathered up the soldiers, picked up his case, and shouted "Stop!"; but the driver paid no attention. Only his mate called out: "Get lost, you pimp! I suppose you think it's fun to give other people trouble?"

(TRANSLATED BY G. M. WICKENS)

The Dismemberment

(from *The Infernal Times of Agha-ye Ayyaz*)

by REZA BARAHENI

He commanded, "Bring the saw up here."
    Ascending the ladder, I was in a position to see the withered, fleshless, dust- and blood-smeared limbs of that one.

I gazed at them, afraid, my mouth parched and dry, my
breath strangled in my throat, the saw, large and gleaming
white, savage saw with teeth, long and sharp, rude and merciless, held in one hand, my other hand grasping the rungs of
the ladder, one by one—staring at him, appalled, from behind—that one, who was breathing heavily and mumbling
something which I couldn't hear. And as I moved up, rung
by rung, my eyes were fixed on neither earth nor sky, but
first on his feet, then the calves of his legs, then his burnt-out
thighs—that one, the man whose name I am afraid to let pass
my lips, although I admire it—and, of course he had a tattered loincloth, there, red and gray, blood-soaked, around his
waist, a narrow waist, the hair around his waist sticky with
blood as if they had wanted to pluck out each hair with their
dagger-like, dreadful, sharp nails, but had instead picked at
the flesh underneath, leaving the hair standing in place on a
surface of torn and ravaged flesh.

"The saw!" he commanded.

"Bringing it," I said.

"Faster," he said, "bring it faster!"

"Bringing it faster!" I said.

And I moved faster—as if I were able to!—and closed my
eyes so as not to see—as if I were able to!—as if it were possible to become blind!—there before my eyes loomed the
bloodied spike, whose gleaming point had passed through his
body and protruded from his back—his back, him, that one
whose name I did so like—point passing through his body
and out his back through the timber of the rack to which he
was fastened. Now I opened my eyes and looked at the spike
with my eyes open and it was the same I had seen with my
eyes closed.

"The saw!" he shouted.

And I said, "Bringing it," and took another step upward
and raised my right hand and stretched the handle of the
saw, the handle on Mahmoud's end, out to Mahmoud, and
Mahmoud, from the other side of the man, from the side
where his face—and the face of that one whose name made
me afraid because I liked it so—could be seen, took the saw
by its long, white, vertical handle.

And he said, "Up, come higher up so that we can begin."

And I moved another rung higher up, stopping right next to
his head; his sweat-soaked, burning, fiery profile seemed . . .
in an aura of light? . . . No, but red and vast and even god-

like. His thick beard seemed to grow out of his face in my direction.

"Measure the arm!" shouted Mahmoud, his end of the saw in hand, and I changed the handle of my end of the saw to my left hand and raised my right hand and bent forward a bit and placed my little finger on the pulsating wrist of him—that one whom I liked so because I was afraid of him—and spread my comparatively rude fingers up his forearm, the fingers of the right hand along his naked forearm below the elbow, touching his inflamed body, sensing his humid, torrential fever to the capillary depths of me.

Then the cries, I heard the wailing, the rhythmical, howling voices of the assembled host of my countrymen, crying out in chorus, "His right hand first! His right hand first! His right hand first!"

And, these words having been repeated several times, like a ritual tribal chant, Mahmoud shouted, "Begin!" and with a harmonious, rhythmical motion we began, Mahmoud pulling the saw as I released it, I pulling the saw as Mahmoud released it and the saw slipping and slicing through the flesh with the grating sound of a potter's wheel in a Ghaznein or Rey or Baghdad bazaar. What with Mahmoud pulling mightily upon the saw when I released it and myself pulling mightily upon the saw when Mahmoud released it, the arm was soon severed, two hands-breadth lengths from the wrist, just above the elbow, and Mahmoud shouted, "Bring the oil! Oil!" And from the foot of the ladder they handed me the bucket full of boiling, steaming, fiery hot oil, and I handed it to Mahmoud, and he managed with agility to hold it and to twist the severed stump of the arm into the oil and keep it there until the blood coagulated.

And then I heard his loud voice, like a spear—his voice, that one whom I liked because I feared him so—shouting something like *"Annal haq!"*[1] or perhaps that very phrase "Annal haq!" And the people, the calamity-stricken dogs, wailed an answer in chorus: "Now his left hand! Now his left hand! Now his left hand!" And we fell to our work, but cutting through the left arm was harder than cutting through the right arm had been; this one thing I couldn't understand: why should cutting through one arm be more difficult than cutting through the other? Isn't it so, after all, that a man's

---

[1] Literally, "I am the Truth"; metaphorically, "I am God."

two arms are equal in strength or in weakness, equally thick and muscular or spindly and stringy and weak? I had descended the ladder. Mahmoud had done the same. The warmodored blood of the one-armed man had spilled onto my knees and the apron of my winding sheet which had soaked it up drop by drop. I had descended the ladder, and then Mahmoud moved his ladder to the other side and I did the same, moved my ladder to the other side, and although there were still chopped-ground pieces of flesh and bone on the saw, the saw still seeming to vibrate with that awful grating sound, I felt no shame at holding it in my hand—it was our intention, our aim to kill any and all shame in ourselves; and we had killed shame in ourselves, because shame for Mahmoud was a worthless commodity—the sweat of shame must never befoul the countenance of man. Saw in hand, after changing the place of my ladder, I felt more at ease and ascended the ladder rung by rung. Mahmoud did the same. I was more nimble this time; I was a better murderer; I was more of a murderer. Mahmoud had once told me, "A man gets used to it." And I had been able to get used to it, this being the first time I had ever dismembered anyone. Mahmoud had said, "A man gets used to it," and then had told me how he himself, at the very beginning, had been ill-at-ease at the prospect of taking up a sword or spear or even a small dagger in his hand but how later he had been able to attack a man who had angered him with a small cheese knife: the man had leveled accusations at Mahmoud's ancestry, and Mahmoud had flung the knife straight at him, and the knife had struck the man directly in the right shoulder, in such a way that it deprived the howling wretch of the use of his arm. After that, it had been mere child's play to attack another man, this one thick-boned, thick-bodied, larger than himself—attacking from behind, of course, and laying him out with a single blow—and Mahmoud's confrères had dragged the corpse to the river and given it a kick and a push with their heavy-booted feet, after allowing the blood to drain out through the gashes, a kick and a push and a toss into the river like a sack full of old bones and bloodless meat; after that Mahmoud had become famous for his courage and his valor by strangling two men with his bare hands—killing another man by a fierce kick to the ribs—killing one of his own brothers by night, they said, and blinding one of his own sons by day. He had also slain many in war, and when they took prisoners and brought the captured commandants, lately converted into eunuches, before him or when they brought the young soldiers before him, some with nails extracted, tongues sliced out, fingers, ears or noses sliced off, Mahmoud would stand them all beside the river as target dummies for his sword practice; he had tested his speed at decapitation by sword and was found capable of knocking the heads off twenty castrated captains in the wink of an eye; Mahmoud was capable of noting with complete composure the place between the thighs of those captives whose manliness they had torn out by the roots—Mahmoud had the habit of noting this and suddenly erupting with a laughter so deep and wild and lusty and joyful, so full of relish that the newly castrated victims felt themselves strong and sound as ever—for a moment, of course, only for a moment—because they heard the laughter and the next moment a spasm in their throats, a turbulence in their bowels, eyeballs darting to and fro in alarm, skulls swelling with a brain-rattling raging convulsion that forced the eyeballs to protrude from their sockets looking like rotten, trampled peaches: Mahmoud appeared on the back of his tall, narrow-bodied, immaculately trimmed white horse, and, first bending down to kiss his horse's neck, he took his sword from our elder servant and galloped away, and there was an end to the convulsions and spasms, an end to the turbulence in the bowels and eyeballs protruding from their sockets—the sword swinging horizontally sliced through unresistant soft as cheese necks and sliced and severed and hacked, and Mahmoud flung his sword into the sand with the skill and artistry only he among men could aspire to, the elder servant being responsible for gathering in these swords. And when Mahmoud came back, dismounted, and washed his hands and face, cleansing himself for prayer with fresh spring water, then all men of this land stood in emulation of their leader at prayer.

"What are you wasting time for? Begin!" he said, and I began, but I don't know why cutting through his left arm was harder than cutting through his right—I mean, the left arm was literally more difficult to cut through! Was I not more at ease this time? Nimbler? More of a murderer? Why was his left arm so difficult to cut through? I looked to Mahmoud and saw that it hadn't surprised him at all; in sensing my confusion, he said, "It's always like this—the resistance increases—but the resistance of this stubborn head of a braying ass will lessen!" Starting in again, we cut only through the skin—thin, sickly arm resisting like a bar of iron—Mahmoud, enraged, removed his left hand from the handle of the saw and grabbed him by the beard, growling, "If you resist, I'll cut your head off!" and receiving no answer, as he—that one whom I did so like—had seemed to sink into himself after having once cried out and seemed to have no intention of ever saying anything again, shouted, "You there! Bring me an axe! A Tashkent blade!" Before long they gave him one from below, and he gave it to me and said, "Go a step higher, give the axe a good powerful swing and cut the cursed thing off at the shoulder! No more need for measuring!" And I did what he told me, and never had I done anything that he had not told me: went a step higher, raised the axe above my head and the crowd and Mahmoud, and swung the blade in a wide arc from east to west. "Whap!" It came down and the arm, instead of hanging from the left side of his body, was now hanging from the left side of the rack. Then they gave the oil to Mahmoud from below, and Mahmoud took the oil to the severed stump and plunged the stump, like the head of an animal, into the oil and with this action arose a scream, a strong and loud and mythic cry: *"Annal haq!"* or something like *"Annal haq!"*—and then the people, yelping and howling dogs, crying in chorus: "And now his feet! And now his feet! And now his feet!" And we, upon hearing their cry, we—who had gone so far as to place the responsibility for the affairs of the people in their very own hands and had said, "We will provide the backdrop. You will be encouraged and rewarded for effort. You will be moved to great works. You will but speak and we will act upon your word"—upon hearing the cry "And now his feet!" descended our ladders calmly and obediently, the axe in my hand and the bucket of burning oil in Mahmoud's hand—the hand of my Agha, my master . . . my God. We descended to treat those feet—his feet, the feet of that one whom I did like awfully well because I feared him and did not know why I feared and liked him—to the pummeling they deserved.

As we descended everything was quiet. The people were waiting, after all their clamor—the bearded lambs, weak, mustachioed little lambs to be bought and sold on the bazaar, young and old, ugly and handsome, were waiting, still far from any real comprehension of blood. But I could hear the warm call of blood, the sound of the beating pulse in the severed stump of his arm pounding to my ears, and the smell of blood, that warm odor of blood, first to strike the nose at birth, I again tasted and perceived; it went warmly and pleasantly to work in the fibers of my brain, and I sensed that my eyes had become red, sunset red, that beautiful shade of red, blood red.

Having descended, we found that they had placed two stools on either side of the man bound to the rack, the man from whose stumps blood was still dripping onto the ground. Mahmoud wanted wine. They brought it. I wanted water. They brought it. We both wet our lips, he with wine, I with water. Mahmoud looked at me, and I bowed my head. He looked at me out of the corners of his eyes. Whenever he grew heated, whenever he drank wine and grew heated, whenever he became amorous, he would look at me out of the corners of his eyes, and the corners of his two eyes would shine like lamps. And now here, right in front of the people standing around us but at some distance from us, Mahmoud laughed with his eyes, looking at me as a lover does, as a man full of lust does. I was ready to kiss his hands, his powerful hands, I was willing, not just from habit, but from love, to kiss his powerful hands. Whenever he glanced at me from the corners of his eyes gleaming like two lamps, I returned his glance only for a moment, a fast fleeting moment, and like the swift motion sound of Mahmoud's sword through the air, a look with the speed of a sword slicing the air, in this fleeting look everything was exchanged between Mahmoud and me—memories of our alliance exchanged with each other—I became subdued and gentle—Mahmoud seemed to swell to a magnificence, the magnificence of an eagle, and I, gentle and subdued as the amorous female dove—he became hot and sharp and large and powerful—I became deep and delicate and soft and felt the scraping of his rough, tumultuous fingers over my body—I sensed that I must kiss the sand of the Oxus shore once again, must wash my mouth with the sand of the shore, fill my mouth with the sand of the shore, must claw at the sand of the shore of the Oxus and stuff the soft, delicate, humid sand into my mouth, a lover of that asphyxiation, that dying, that burial in the sand. Mahmoud looked at me out of the corners of his eyes. He circled the man bound to the rack, the tall man bound to the rack, and the rack itself. The people were more intent upon watching the man with no arms than watching me and Mahmoud. Af-

ter their chorus of clamor, they were watching the man and
enjoying themselves. Mahmoud looked at me. His eyes had
become like flames. The wine had already found its way to
his eyes. He had already set the bucket of oil down. His
hands were still spattered with blood. Like myself, he wore a
winding sheet. This custom I do not understand. If I put on a
winding sheet, that's one thing, but why Mahmoud? A winding sheet is not fitting for him; a man who gives the orders
shouldn't wear a winding sheet. He came over, a full head
taller than I. He placed his long, powerful, red, warm,
blood-covered hands on my neck. He bent down to me, moving his head closer to mine; he pulled me to him, pressed me
to him, turned his head away from me, and I raised my head.
How pure I still was, how gentle and kind and womanish and
even childish! I raised my head and looked at him, my eyelids half-closed, he pressed his lips to mine, gently at first,
then passionately and cruelly, and my knees trembled, then
my shoulders, then the space between them, then my knees
again and the back muscles of my upper arms—I trembled,
trembled, trembled, my fingers growing longer and more delicate, transformed into long, narrow filaments, dark and passionate, and relieved of my inhibitions, I put my arms around
his neck and lifted my heels from off the sand, kissing him
with my whole mouth, with full lips, as if through this kiss I
could attach my chest and belly and crotch to his body and
hold them there and die in his mouth . . . And then the
cursed howling of the people arose once more: "And now his
feet! And now his feet! And now his feet!" Mahmoud pit-
ilessly dropped me at the peak, wrenched his lips from mine,
his hands from my body, and just like that, moved away
from me, and like a bud blossoming for him suspended in
midair, I broke on my branch, withered and fell, the choral
clamor of the howl-composing dogs having subsided, to hear
his voice, the voice which had just now enclosed me in the
fortress of its love, saying, "Begin!" And fallen from the sky
unsatisfied, I moved toward the feet of the man bound to the
rack. Blood-befouled oil still dripped from his severed left
arm. His two arms hung toward the earth, hung from the rack,
severed from the trunk, and shiny white bone could be seen
protruding from the midst of the torn, worthless heap of flesh,
the coagulated blood, the veins, connected and disconnected,
of each arm. Already flies and mosquitoes were settling on the
carcasses. Of what possible use are arms that have been sep-

arated from the body? Arms which will never again be able to perform the orders of their owner? The fingers dead and clutched stiffly together? What possible task can they perform? . . . Mahmoud said, "What is it? What are you looking up there for?" I turned with an unwitting laugh, raising my head to look up there again, and, indeed, such a spectacle was quite something to behold—the sight of that creature up there was quite something to behold. That man hanging up there—was he able to turn his head back and see to his left? If he could turn his head and see his arms now, what would he really think of them? I wasn't immersed in my own thoughts about him—I was immersed in his thoughts, sensed myself swimming about in his mind and turning slowly to his severed arms. Rather, I *was* he and was turning toward my *own* arms—my head not unlike the face of a clock, clock face hanging from the sky, and now the clock-hands of my mind gearing me for the movement toward my arms—swimming deep to the inside of his mind, my mind, looking at my arms, more like two decapitated children than like arms cut off, popping out in blisters. I wanted to, at that moment, pick up something and drive the flies and mosquitoes away from the stumps of my arms, but I had no hands. Then it happened that I raised my own, intact arms and jumped and waved in the direction of my arms which were his arms, and suddenly a swarm of flies and mosquitoes arose from the severed stump, and then, as if nothing had happened, I descended into my own thoughts about my arms: what had I felt when they were cutting them off? Of what particular nature was my agony? Difficult to tell, but when I was able to recall the sound of the grating of the saw or the falling of the axe and to hear it, I raised my right hand, unwittingly, and took firmly ahold of my left arm where it had been cut off by the axe—as if trying to reaffirm the existence of my own hands and arms. Mahmoud said, "Are you all right? What is it with you? Why have you turned so pale?" "Nothing," I said, "the weather's too hot." He sent them to bring water, and when they brought it, he said, "Wash your hands and face." On Mahmoud's order I washed my hands and face as if I were performing some kind of sacred ritual. At Mahmoud's orders I had become handsomer, my hair growing longer and shinier, giving off a subtle perfume, my heart becoming pure and naive. And at Mahmoud's orders I would frequently sense a sacred aura of radiance about my head and often times around my buttocks, such a soft, languorous feeling when this radiance wound itself down into the cleft of my buttocks and the space between my thighs and concentrated there. And I would feel that Mahmoud must be with me; his warm and lustful breath, regular and rhythmical, condensing on the back of my neck, must, in its rising and falling rhythm, invade me and drive me to completion—must rule me and drive me forward—and I must strain and struggle, clawing at the pillow or mat or stones or sand and cram myself full of Mahmoud—always waiting for the dagger at my back—Mahmoud the dagger at my back—if he were to abandon me, I would die, no longer to have those sweet and feverish moments of ecstasy, the hot breath of Mahmoud full of fire and violence, his caressing murmurs.

He said, "It's taking a long time," and I said, "Yes," and he said, "It's getting late," and I said, "Yes," and he said, "When you're feeling a little better, we'll begin," and I said, "I'm better," and he said, "Well, let's begin then," and I said, "Begun!" And we moved toward the small gleaming saws. And surely this part of our work wasn't terribly difficult, because cutting off feet, on the whole, is easy work. It's not unlike beheading a chicken. . . . In my own mind I had practiced the action of cutting off a foot scores of times and Mahmoud had cut off scores of feet. We both had the necessary skill and were able to maintain our coolness through an extreme of concentration on the job at hand, although we knew that the man they had hung up there, before being stretched and hung on the rack, had run so much that his legs were streaming with blood. Directly preceding his run they had placed a helmet on his head, one of those helmets which cover the entire head and face and neck, on which nothing can make a dent, and then, with full ceremony, as if they were dressing a young bride in her wedding gown, they had dressed him in flimsy armor of polished tin During those several moments neither he nor they had spoken a word. And then the man who had dressed him in the armor and the man who had placed the helmet on his head stood aside, and the people, these very dog-wailing people, this howling chorus, standing a stone's throw away from him, had shouted: "Run! Run! Run!" And he had started to run and the whole city of men had begun to pursue him over the sand with rough, hard, small stones which had been gathered from the riverbed over the last three or four days. When they had commenced throwing, he, with all the power left in his body, had run in darkness and terror and infinite loneliness, and the people with all the force in their bodies ran after him, chasing him under the sun, and stoned him, pelted him with stones so relentlessly that the iron hook of his helmet nearly opened, which would have resulted in the helmet falling off his head, leaving him bareheaded to face the stones and to be crushed and maimed by them. Finally, from an excess of fatigue and thirst, an excess of terror and despair, he had fallen, his two eyes staring wildly out of the two small holes in the helmet, looking frantically through these two small holes, moving in terror from side to side, seeing nothing but the sand and sensing the demons, pelting him with stones, and when he had fallen several comparatively large stones had struck his tin armor and helmet and the clang of stone striking his helmet exploding through his brain and buzzing in his ears, deafening them—trapped in an utterly dark world, trapped in his tin armor and the dark enclosure of his helmet. The guards had come and eventually ordered the stoning to stop and the people, who always yielded to the strength and power of the guards and, in truth, were incapable of anything but obedience, had stopped throwing stones at him. Then the sweating guards and their thick-necked hefty son of a bitch squadron leaders had divested him of helmet and armor and carefully, almost respectfully, laid them to the side of the sand, and then one of the guards had emptied two buckets of water over him and he had regained consciousness, and the guards had permitted him to rest a bit, and when he was able to raise his head just a bit off the ground, they had clasped him under the armpits and dragged him slowly to the rack. On two sides of the rack were fastened sheets of cloth on which were written the sentence of the man: to be stoned, to be nailed upon the rack, to be dismembered, the tenor of the words indicating that they had wanted to make the condemned man understand: "Because you have eyes, we will pluck your two eyes out." This was a sacred tribal ritual, although the tribe itself understood nothing of it, but in that limbo state of theirs between animal and human they needed some stimulus, to overthrow the monotony and custom of their ordinary lives and absorb their imaginations in the eternal quest for excitement and stimulation and more excitement and more stimulation like a fireworks display going on forever, colorful and enervating, carrying them soaring to the very zenith of emotion, impelling them to sudden and momentary and collective action. And Mahmoud and I had been able to introduce into their daily routine something harsh and swift, harsh and swift and fraught with vision, that would totally shatter their subjectivity and free them from their looseness and their torpor, preparing at the same time something beautiful and wondrous, a kind of nourishment for their subconscious, trusting that the more violent and intense and emotional it was, the faster it would sink into their imaginations, that any event of a fierce and deeply affecting nature would, regardless of how terrible, how hellish, by forced penetration of all the crevices and orifices of their unconscious, transform them completely to the depths of their being in such a way that they would come to sense the Mahmoudi will—the Mahmoudi will which changes and affects everything in such a way that they would be compelled to accept Mahmoud's way, and, through him, my way—wanting Mahmoud and, through Mahmoud, wanting me as well. And I want it this way, for I believe, and this belief constitutes a sizable portion of my instincts and emotions, that all the crevices and orifices of mankind and history, and contemporary mankind in particular, must come to be crammed full of Mahmoud; for I believe that contemporary mankind has (and this applies to the past as well) no being apart from Mahmoud. If it were otherwise, there would be no reason for me to sit on this side and Mahmoud on that, cutting off the feet of the man bound to the rack. No action is practical for Mahmoud without prior knowledge and calculation; he understands everything well; his genius is in his meticulously precise comprehension of the need for action followed by direct or indirect action. Dismemberment, for example, was a singularly fixed and definite action—Mahmoud had perceived that the action should be performed, the man dismembered, but he had also designated a special procedure for the action, and I well knew that he privately insisted on this order and for this reason it had been so set up that he sever the left foot and I the right. Of course, it really made no difference, right or left—a foot is a foot—what difference if a man severs the left or severs the right? But I always agree with Mahmoud and grant that he has the power to see the truth, and he liked to begin everything from the left side; it is the people's custom, he said, to believe in the superiority of the right side, and in order that they might not think of

him as boasting of his superiority, he liked to begin everything from the left side. For this reason, Mahmoud and I had
agreed that I would always start from the right and he from
the left. Subconsciously he had perceived that to the left, perhaps, will go the victory, so he started from the left and gave
the right to others, believing that the illusion of superiority
should belong to the others, the essential victory, meaning the
victory of pretensions to belonging to the left, should be his.
Mahmoud was not a deceiver of the people, but a man who
transformed their consciousness, transfigured their souls and
looks and actions and words, and even revolutionized their
instincts and approaches to life. All his people, even his own
guards, disliked something in him, but when he turned his
face upon them and stood before them and looked straight
into their eyes, they immediately stood alert and attentive,
ready at a single glance or gesture of his hands or a simple
direction of his tongue to realize his wishes; there was great
force in even the movement of Mahmoud's finger. One day
Mahmoud, without any cause, except perhaps to intimidate
the others, had shouted at one of his officers, a man who had
boasted of being braver than himself in the taking of a
fortress, "Go off somewhere and die!" and the brave officer
had immediately unsheathed his dagger and slit his own jugu-
lar vein, falling at Mahmoud's feet. Another time he had ordered a poet, who had wanted me for a night in private
conference, to eat a chunk of fresh, steaming cow dung in his
presence, and later, in Kashmir, had ordered him to milk the
goats and herd the cows. I have never forgotten the delicate
hands of that poet, fondling my neck and under my ear
lobes. I don't imagine that he will have forgotten my ear
lobes after all that, or that Mahmoud will have forgotten his
transgression. The day will no doubt come to pass when he
will shout: "Hold the head of this cursed poet under hot
water until he ceases to breathe!" I alone know this man
Mahmoud; now that the two of us have made our ablutions
for the performance of this sacred tribal ritual, now more
than ever before, I know Mahmoud. He had given himself to
the ritual of dismemberment with all the rigor of a Hindu ascetic, and, in truth, the dismemberment bore no little resem-
blance to a sacred ritual in which a man meditates upon the
achievement of an ascetic discipline and absolute resignation.
The act itself was a pious prayer-chant rising from the saw
teeth points, from the meeting of intractable saw ledge and

bone. Mahmoud respected the tribal, national rites. He could cut through the feet of a man in such a way that you would swear he was kneeling in devotion on a prayer rug, that he had been transformed into dust and ashes of the ground. In essence, whatever takes place before one's eyes, one must take delight in the disciplined harmony of an event ruled by a perfect order. Mahmoud had created the harmony and rhythm of this prayer which arose from the gleaming, grating teeth of the saw, and the radiant aura of this harmony settled upon the teeth of the people and stimulated their mouths to water, their hearts to pound, and the metamorphosed heart, twisted, diverted from its initial direction, lost its original beat and began to beat with another purpose; poor hearts that have given themselves up to be transformed and diverted eternally, accepting everything easily—everything, of course, by which Mahmoud, through his own actions or those of his guards, had sought to conquer them. The heart stretched out of shape, expanded, or contracted into a round ball, or took a variety of other forms. They had interfered with the ordered rhythm and harmony of the natural human heart, the heart belonging to the earth, to the earth and the mud and the water, to the uprush and flow of things; they had imposed upon it another order, which brought itself another rhythm, another harmony, designed for the realization of other ends, and had done this in such a way that the heart had been converted into an automatic device, the key to the initial and continued beating of which lay concealed in the seal-ring of Mahmoud and his guards. The people and their hearts were in need of guidance, a discipline other than nature; if not, would they have surrendered their own natural order of things? They needed some discipline beyond the bestial. Mahmoud had revealed this discipline, this new order of things. It originated from his thoughts, soaring, with magnificent slogans and concise catch-phrases, like eagles' wings spread into the hearts of the people seeking something to replace their hearts' natural order. This new order had changed the hue of things earthly and heavenly, had penetrated and taken root in all the subjective and objective states of the tribe. The heart beat, and with every beat, cried out: "Mahmoud!" Didn't my own heart—didn't my own heart cry out, "Mahmoud! Mahmoud!" Didn't my arms and the sharp, red button ends of my joyous young pectorals, didn't my smooth, ivory flanks, my curved eyelids, and the black curls at my temples, from which the initial sweat of my passion always flowed, rolling deliciously down my cheek between my ear and lip, didn't my whole being shriek, "Mahmoud! Mahmoud!"? Was not the name of Mahmoud written on the satin white joints of my knees, on my ankles, on the roselike knuckles of my hands? Did I not coo the name "Mahmoud . . . Mahmoud . . ." in the agonies of my passion? When I awoke at morning, was it not the name of Mahmoud I heard echoing from every wall and door? Hadn't I seen the manly face of Mahmoud on all the banners which fifty modern, hired painters had depicted with the perfumed odor of their colors? Hadn't a thousand poets described, in words of frankincense and balsam perfumes, soothing, agreeable rhythms woven into their texture, from every syllable of which rang the noblest and loftiest of sentiments, his thick, powerful, taut and muscular arms for me to see, his discerning eagle eyes, his chest covered with kinky capillary flowers of hair, for me to see and arise in worship of Mahmoud? Hadn't these poets placed him, in admiration of his radiance and beneficence, upon the backs of golden horses for me to see? Hadn't all this display been set before my eyes that I might trust in his magnificence and genius and power forever? Had they not conveyed him in and out of the objective and subjective gates of my consciousness, strewing the way with heaps of slaughtered enemies, that I might see this earthly God being transformed into a heavenly one? And, when all is said and done, had not he, this Mahmoud, descended from that godly sky to grace us here below—had he not embraced me and drowned me in himself that I might revere him—I revered him because he had seized me in his embrace—he was mixed in with my very being, his name constantly buzzing in my head like the chant of prayer beads, calling me to his side. And I, his devoted one, took so much ecstasy in the universe of his tumultuous hands that if they had cut off my head in that state, I would have been unaware. And this God who had descended from the sky, who had been with me so often, was now seated, wearing a winding sheet, across from me, who was also wearing a winding sheet, and was allowing me to participate in a holy, religious ritual, a grand, tribal historical ritual. He had descended from the sky to sit across from me, and he said, "Cut, my flower, cut, for it's getting late," and the grating sound of the saw to which ears had become accustomed, the ears of the people as well as our own, arose. Before doing

anything, of course, we had felt for and found that little
bulge on the foot. And while searching for it, we had looked
at each other—we must have been proud of all this—I had
lifted my head to look into the eyes of Mahmoud only in order to find the small bulge, and Mahmoud had looked at me
amorously as if wanting to reward me by helping me find the
bulge immediately, and I, under the burning sun, had felt in
his caressing glance of favor and violent delicacy that I was
being bathed in cool water, in a fresh spring in the middle of
the forest, and his look was so mesmerizing that I could hear
the simple, soft and lyrical sound of my own muscles moving
in the water and could see myself there, even when the grate
of the saw was most deafening, submerged in his loving be-
nevolence.

The grating of the saws, the saws of dismemberment,
spread through space, through the silence of space. We had
bound the legs of the condemned man so tightly that even the
worst of tortures could not have caused them to jerk. The
legs were black and blue and blood-covered, and while cutting through, I looked only at the foot, thinking of this small
and delicate foot, this worthless portion of mine to be severed
from the leg, from cities and fields and villages it must have
passed, in what water and on what mornings it must have
been washed, in the caressing hands of what woman it must
have been fondled —this sort of feeling came easily to me—
and the sound of the saw winding through space, calling the
foot to witness—the foot like a slender column, old and left
over from ancient times, the veins like the faded, illegible
characters of an inscription, the inside of the bone exactly
like the slightly varicolored circles of a black carrot, only
thicker, firmer and more visible. The saw cut through and the
foot was becoming severed from the leg, soaked in blood, the
blood sinking into the sand, the black blood, and the end of
the leg like a dirty pole-end pouring out blood, black blood. I
looked at Mahmoud, who had settled to the ground on his
firm and powerful knees and was finishing up the work. He
was never afraid of blood, and had accustomed us to not
being afraid of blood. He was capable of making his ablutions in blood and standing before the people in prayer, capable, following the slaughter of the populace of a small town,
of delivering an oration on the greatness of God, capable of
freeing twenty of the tribe's thinkers from his prisons only to
catch and kill them all later in one place saying that they had

been standing under a wall when it fell. But he was a person who, whatever he wanted, others wanted as well: If he wanted blood, the people wanted blood, too; if he wanted water, the people wanted water, too; and if he wanted nothing, the people, too, wanted nothing. Of course it would hardly ever occur that Mahmoud would want nothing for himself. He might possibly at times want nothing for the people, and they accepted this, as well—-the totality of this nothing put at their disposal by Mahmoud. But it would hardly ever occur to him to want only nothing for himself. In addition, over his years of inexperience and experience, over the years of this great historical experience, he had realized that the people cannot be kept waiting; the people must be kept busy; they must be engaged in some kind of violent and intense activity. He believed that the people, all of the people, were childish and must have their toys and games in the form of murders, martyrdoms, religious trinkets, celebrations, periods of mourning, wars—not, of course, real, all-out wars— hunger and famine, drought and thirst, depravity, rot, cholera, and plague. And the people must always be patient. They must attend to the great words, words great and sonorous; the men and women who speak these words must learn how to be proud, must learn how to absorb the words of these men and women into their consciousness and take pride in themselves and Mahmoud throughout history and throughout the world. I pondered on this and contented myself with my worthless portion of the dismemberment. I sawed through to the flesh on the underside. And then we separated the feet from the legs and threw them into a bucket and took the two small buckets of hot oil which they had brought over to the pole-like, severed stumps of his legs and held the ends of the stumps in the oil. Mahmoud arose. But this time no such thunderous voice as before issued from the fellow nailed to the rack by four nails. Rather, I heard him whispering, "My feet, my children. My feet, my children." And in truth, from just whose throat had it come? And why was this pleading voice so familiar? The sound was like the caressing voice of a woman in the ears of the man bound to the rack. Had ever a woman praised her feet in such a way? It seemed then as if a woman had stretched herself out upon his body, caressing the feet, her feet at his head, her head at his feet, moaning, "My feet, my children." And now he, somewhere in his mind, from some corner of his mind, from some corner of his dismembered, metamorphosed memory, could clearly hear that caressing, feminine voice and repeated, "My feet, my children," and we had thrown his feet, like two freshly smothered infants, into a bucket, and Mahmoud, ignoring the whispering man, said, "Tiring work; it would seem that cutting off feet is more difficult than cutting off arms," and I said, "That's true," realizing that I had been mistaken in this, and listened to the agonized whispers of the man bound to the rack, asking myself why this pleading voice was so familiar. And the people? For them it was impossible to see the feet. In addition, when we had severed the arms of the man bound to the rack, the people, each arm having come loose and each stump having been held in oil, had heard the thunderous cry of *"Annal haq!"* and become excited and had shouted, and their shouts in full powered unison and harmony had reached everyone and everything in this world which has ears and mind. The *"Annal haq"* cry of the man had incited them against him, and their howling cries had refreshed and stimulated us. In truth between us and the people a question and answer of a very particular nature had formed. But we had answered first and had let them ask the question, and then we had given another answer and given them permission to ask another question, and they had imagined that in this succession of questions and answers they were asking us first and then we were answering. We knew all too well that the opposite of this was true. We had set the answer before them in the form of an objectively perceived event, a murder, a suicide, a slaughter, a dismemberment, a lunacy. This was a questioning and answering in which they were obliged to participate but never had before. Our answer to their question, the question they had not asked, had provided a backdrop of fact; they were not to question that fact, rather, that fact having been established, go beyond to question on the basis of that fact, and we, at some later stage, answer them, an answer in the form of a violent act, a lunacy, a stripping naked, another brilliant gamble. And they became contented; even in the depths of their unconscious they were unable to perceive that this scale of weights and measures was missing a pan, that there was only one side to this scale, that being the side on which Mahmoud and I were sitting, the two of us, with sobriety and dignity, at the maximum of love and at one in each other's arms. But now we had accustomed them to a routine, the

man saying *"Annal haq"* with the severing of each hand, and
for this reason, when the man bound to the rack after the
severing of his feet, instead of crying *"Annal haq,"* had contented himself with saying and repeating, "My feet, my children," and the people were unable to hear this beautiful,
lyrical utterance, in that harmonious epical world of theirs,
and find a place for it, and a kind of murmur, an ignorant
muttering of anger had arisen. They didn't want to merely
watch, but wanted, and to a degree saw themselves condemned, to hear the voice of the victim. Of course, they, like
all true born artists who approach the world through intuition
and direct sensual relation to it, had become aware of the
technical, artistic and subconscious problem of the eyes and
ears as the two doors, the two large doors of man's imaginative vision. These two doors admit the basic nourishment and
primary materials to the mind; they strike a match, and the
imaginative faculty, like a storeroom full of cotton, suddenly
bursts into flame, and this conflagration of a hundred flames,
large and small, in the form of words, flows onto the tongue
and changes into shouting, those wailing shouts speaking of
their thirst for imagination and adventure. The one thing the
people never counted in all this was the torture endured by
their eyes and ears. The imaginative faculty threw them forward in such a way that they acted as if they hadn't perceived that they had been stripped naked under the influence
of the movement of the wind or the collision of the air
against their bodies; and because this time the storeroom of
their stimulation seeking imagination had not burst into
flame, instead of changing to a chorus of howlers, they had
mumbled and whispered among themselves, and the whispering grew into grumbling and the grumbling into an uproar,
indicating that they were not satisfied. This, of course, was
the opposite of what Mahmoud had foreseen. He detested
these whisper-mumbling grumblings of the people, and perhaps he was right, because he believed that rebellion of the
people develops from this very thing. Mahmoud did not wish
the people to have differences among themselves; they must
be united. If they were dissatisfied, they should have let Mahmoud hear of it. If they were satisfied, they should have let
Mahmoud hear of it, as one, and in the official manner. They
never opposed Mahmoud. Really, the thought of opposition
to Mahmoud never occurred to them. They hovered in space
neither hating nor loving Mahmoud, but their hatred was not

of the kind which terminates in rebellion. Thus, it was necessary for them to declare that they were satisfied, to ask for more; they wanted something more exciting from Mahmoud, so why didn't they shout and demand it of him? Mahmoud had the power to decide at once and to act at once and thus, when addressing me in a manly but gentle voice he said, "Sweet one, get those feet and bring them here," I understood immediately how he intended to answer the insatiable eagerness for spectacle. I went to the bucket and got the feet; they were warm and slippery and soft, and it seemed that they had become pieces of boneless, lean, red meat. I brought the feet to Mahmoud. He took them and looked at them and gave a laugh, and this in such a way that it seemed as if he were standing there looking at a pair of nice, clean, shiny shoes. He shouted, "Bring me two short spears!" and they brought them immediately. Holding the feet at the heel, he stuck them, one by one, on the ends of the spears and pressed on them to secure them, and then he said to me, "Go stand on that side," and he crossed over to the left side of the man bound to the rack and stopped opposite me and said, "Hoist the spear aloft, sweet one." And he hoisted his spear, too, and the spears, on their ends the feet of the man bound to the rack, took a position on either side of the head of the man bound to the rack, the right foot in my keeping and the left in Mahmoud's, because of Mahmoud's leftist affectations, and then I heard the weak and beautiful and lyrical voice of the man bound to the rack saying, "My feet, my children," and then the wailing voice of the people, the howling of the dogs in chorus crying, "And now his tongue! And now his tongue! And now his tongue!" And when this had been repeated a number of times in full chorus, we lowered the spears. We took the feet off the ends of the spears and threw them into the bucket, and without keeping them waiting, proceeded to answer the hearty shouts of the people: we requested a long and sharp pair of scissors, and when they brought them we requested a ladder, and when they had brought the ladders, two ladders, one for Mahmoud and one for me, we ascended them to tear out the roots of his speech, of the implement of speech. . . .

. . . Mahmoud, who had reached the top of the ladder, called down, "What are you standing there looking so dumbstruck for, on the second rung of the ladder? Up, boy, up, come higher!" So I moved on up, reaching the top of the ladder on the left side of the man's face, and then, working together, we cut out his tongue. With no trembling of our hands, no error in our work; and in cutting out his tongue, what else did we cut out? By cutting out his tongue we forced him to accept strangulation as his fate. We converted the tongue into a memory in his mind and himself into a captive of the tongueless ruins of his memory. We taught him to keep our tyranny imprisoned in his mind; by cutting out his tongue we made him his own prisoner, keeper of his own prison and prisoner of himself. We bound him within silent walls, unknown walls, timeless walls, tongueless walls. We forced him not to think, and if he should think not to speak, because he no longer had a tongue; the tongue that moved freely in his mouth, pushing words out through his lips and teeth, words concrete, sane, emotional and intellectual, had been cut out by the roots, and the slippery, blood-covered tongue, blood fresh and brightly colored, was held in Mahmoud's hand, and Mahmoud tossed it into a tub which had been placed beside the buckets. Words ceased to exist, and he forgot letters and sounds and words and speech: the joyous, lyrical *s*'s, the *sh*'s of shimmering celebration, the *p*'s of steely power, the blazing *b*'s, the pain-diminishing *d*'s he forgot, *p*'s spitting upon the *f*'s foundering in misery, the *ch* of birds chirping the names of swallow and chickadee in flight, the sacred *m*'s of mind and meaning, the fascinating infatuation of the *n*'s, the tall aspen trees of towering *a*'s.[2] . . . he forgot all connections, swallowing them deep into his mind, affixing deaf and dumb locks to them, hiding them away in the tongueless cells of silence. His tongue had been stilled, tossed into a bucket of coagulating blood like the corpse of a headless kitten. The artful workings of the tongue in the limited space of the mouth had ceased, plunged into absolute silence—the tongue which had once begun to form words, imitating sounds and voices one by one: birds, mothers, fathers, the flow of water, the fluttering of the leaves—the tongue which later had overflowed itself with words of affection, had adopted the nimbleness and agility and liveliness of a new-flying bird, had started out in childhood pronouncing the words of book after book, at first slowly, with difficulty and curiosity, then easily, artfully and with agility, every word penetrating the mind like a ray of the sun and setting it aflame, awakening feelings

[2] The Persian aleph (or A) is a long, thin vertical stroke.—Ed.

latent and primitive, original and creative, which built bridges
from word to word, the tongue pushing itself forward and
side to side articulating the mind, performing mellifluently,
had proceeded from lane to lane: had said to a woman, "I
love you,"—had called a mother "Mother,"—had called a father "Father,"—had greeted a little boy affectionately with a
"Hi there,"—had shown a little girl a dove, calling it "Dove,"
and the little girl had imitated, saying "Dove, dove." The
tongue, like a conquering but unconquered spirit, had violated the limits of the mouth, and on the public roads before
small assemblages the mouth had opened and the golden
tongue had burst forth with the word "Freedom!" and had
moved onto the crossroads to proclaim "Freedom!" and had
violated, yes violated, the narrow circumference of the
crossroads to bellow "Freedom!" in the public squares, and
the throat, that wondrously natural loudspeaker, had project-
ed it with a hitherto unequaled magnificence. Yes, he, the man
whom we had imprisoned, stoned, and then dismembered,
had stood at the crossroads of history and had shouted:
"Freedom!" And we, with a simple pair of scissors, had
driven him back into the dungeon of his memory. We had
thrown open a cleft in his mind and had buried his tongue in
the small grave of that cleft. Mahmoud and I had cut out his
tongue and had thrown it into the middle of a tub full of his
coagulating throat's blood. And now his mouth was full of
blood, and Mahmoud shouted, "Swallow it!" and he couldn't
because his mouth was full of blood and Mahmoud shouted
for the last time, "Swallow it!" And giving me a piece of
cloth, he said, "Wipe the blood off his mouth," and he
couldn't swallow and the foaming blood flowed from his
mouth and I wiped the vomited blood away from around
his mouth with my cloth, and while I was doing this, he
who was nailed up there opened his eyes suddenly, and
I, who was standing there, looked into them. My face was
reflected in his eyes, but from behind that reflection of
my face, his eyes looked at me; his two eyes like prisoners
looking outside through holes in the prison wall, peered at me
from their deep-set sockets. He had taken on a sort of bizarre, unaccountable actuality. I couldn't tell whether his look
was one of rage or hatred or of surrender—he simply looked
at me—I couldn't tell whether supplication or helplessness or
rebellion lay concealed there—he simply looked—I couldn't
tell whether his look was directed at me or at something else,

whether he cared anything for me or not, whether he knew anything or not—he simply looked. No movement in his eyes—he simply looked—how real these eyes had become! The eye sockets were like two hollowed-out stones into which had been set two bloodshot emeralds, and the bushy eyebrows seemed to have been woven into the two sides of his forehead out of reddish-brown hair and drops of blood and sweat, but nothing could equal the lucid, eternal actuality of his eyes. Mahmoud, who had already descended the ladder, called, "Shut his eyes," and I raised my blood-soaked hands and shut them, and the look of those eyes simply staring at me was no longer upon me. I wiped around his mouth and beard with my cloth, descending the ladder when I finished. Mahmoud said, "I knew the tongue would finish him off," and I said, "Yes." And then Mahmoud called for a spear in the same manner that he always called for everything, and as soon as they had brought one, he took the spear and impaled the tongue which lay in the coagulating blood, and he lifted it on the point of the spear, and he raised it on high, in accordance with national custom, holding it there and shouting, "He is dead! Here is his tongue!" And the people commenced cheering and shouting and in the turmoil they pushed aside the guards and rushed forward and surrounded the three of us, Mahmoud and me and the dead man bound to the rack, and looked at me first, laughing, and then at Mahmoud, laughing, and then at the image of the man on the rack, laughing as if to burst their bellies, laughing uncontrollably, as if to burst their bellies and endanger civil health and well-being, and then trumpets sounded from the four corners of the desert, and the initial rites of the festival were performed. And as soon as the rites had begun, the people, astonished, watching the corpse, backed slowly away. Faced with this great historical victory they were capable of only laughter which froze into awe. In the long run it was imperative for them to face this historical moment, and now was set before them something great, something which would settle into the depths of their consciousness and transform them with a nauseating and crippling power, something which, like a sharp spike, would impale and split the fiber of their souls, striking home, obliterating them. At first they had exploded into one extreme, the extreme of collective, full bodied laughter, and since it was the laughter of intoxication, for one intense moment of excitement their lips and teeth and eyes and bellies had burst into motion; their hearts' blood had come to a boil, streaming into their eyes, their ears, their cheeks, and they, their nostrils dilating with the convulsion of laughter, were frozen in place. And they, as if a large hand had grabbed them, who seemed to be asleep, by the shoulders and shaken them and awakened them, they came to themselves with those same lips and open mouths and red eyes and laughter-convulsed faces, or it is possible, of course, that they had not come to themselves at all, rather that a large hand had swooped down from the sky or shot up out of the earth to wipe the collective laughter off their faces, and they had set foot into the hemisphere of another extreme, the extreme of awe. They had surged forward laughing, and the laughter had expanded and encompassed them all, had violated the limits of their lips and mouths and reduced even the air, the free air to laughter, and suddenly, that invisible hand, be it earthly or heavenly, had, with one swipe, mopped the laughter from their convulsed faces. A hand had swept back the waves of laughter and nothing remained but awe. If the first extreme had exploded its way to the outer world, the second extreme had sobbed its way convulsively and terrifyingly to the inner world—a sobbing that no one would ever hear—a sobbing that even the weeper himself would never hear. In between these two extremes, in a limbo between the hell of laughter and the hell of awe (Paradise never!) they had tried to comprehend something of their destiny, and therefore, with the rhythmical coordination of an army which withdraws cunningly to catch the enemy later in ambush, they had moved back, awe-stricken and conquered, as if trying during their withdrawal to hang onto something, something beyond the meanings of commonplace concepts such as life and death, murder and martyrdom, something beyond these routine individual concepts, in which might be revealed the effect of their universal destiny on the course of history, time and the future, something that might invest their convulsive laughter and their mute awe with a significance, not simple but profound, albeit lucid and illuminating. Had they been able to hang onto something at that moment? Surely they had done their best, surely they had made every effort to escape being transformed in their perplexity and their awe; surely they had tried to deliver themselves . . . from what? . . . they were still in the dark as to what they were trying to deliver themselves from, still in the dark as to what course of action to take should they be delivered. And into the hands of what force were they to deliver themselves as an alternative to this force which impelled them to jump from one totally positive extreme to one totally negative. No matter how hard they tried, they were unable to find anything meaningful in this limbo between two extremes, between two hells; their vain efforts reached a climax, rather an anticlimax in their withdrawal. And when Mahmoud's voice was heard shouting "Bring a charcharkheh!"[3] they awoke, emerged from that sleep state at an extreme of rhythmical awe. They looked around themselves; they looked at each other; they even rubbed their eyes and stretched, and, no longer awed, wondered why and of what they had stood in awe. They looked at each other and tried to speak to each other but were unable. They had only a mutual awareness of their situation in common, an awareness originating from the imperceptible ties that bound them together. They could not tell under the spell of what magic, what opiate they had been, but as they looked at each other, it came back to them where they were, what they had done, what they should do and with whom they should do it. Mahmoud and I came back to them, as well, and especially Mahmoud who again shouted: "Bring a charcharkheh!" And they really snapped to it and withdrew behind the lines that had been designated for them. The guards again returned and took up their posts, facing them, their backs to us. A smile of self-esteem could be seen on their faces; pride sat upon their chests like the coruscating insect of a medal. They stood behind the designated lines, as if destiny, not Mahmoud, had drawn them, full of pride, indefatigable, contented and as unswerving in their devotion as faithful dogs, dogs, who remain, even after long days of starvation, faithful to their merciless masters. When Mahmoud shouted, "Bring a charcharkheh!" they displayed a mood of expectation, a curiosity as to how this "charcharkheh" would be used: Do the wheels of such a thing move? What person or persons would it carry? And, over what roads would this strange thing, the "charcharkheh," pass? Things excited them more than human beings, and upon hearing the word "charcharkheh" their mouths fell open in amazement, as if they had been stimulated sexually. I could even sense this stimulation swelling up beneath their clothing. Of course, at first

---

[3] A four-wheeled chariot.—Ed.

they were ashamed, only daring to sneak looks at one another, but then, when Mahmoud shouted again, "Bring a
charcharkheh!" and repeated it several times, they got over
their shame and laughed a bit and turned to look at the men
beside them and behind them. They did this simultaneously,
with an artful harmony of action. Then it was that their
smiles appeared and they began shifting their weight from
one foot to another, and they were plunged into a state of
still hesitant lustfulness, and in that state, their hands seemed
to hang from the atmosphere, which had absorbed their
bodies and arms and shoulders, and a voluptuous lethargy
possessed them, under the spell of which they were unable to
think what to do with themselves, their hands, the swelling
beneath their clothing. A sensation like the burning flame of
a lantern had begun to play across their buttocks, and this
flame, set in motion, had begun to oscillate from one buttock
to the other, and they were unable to deal with this oscillat-
ing sensation which had combined pleasurably, rhythmically,
in harmony with the swelling under their clothing. The backs
of their thighs grew taut, and the hairs on their thighs stood
on end like tiny sharp spears pointing toward the body center
of their lust, and they were unable to deal with the sensation
of these hairs standing on end. In this state of expectancy, every moment of which seemed like a century, they were unable to think of what to do with their hands, the backs, the
fronts, the sides of their bodies, until Mahmoud shouted once
more: "I said bring a charcharkheh!" And upon once again
hearing the shout, especially the word "charcharkheh," they
grew bolder and raised their hands and seized at the clothing
of others, in front of them and behind them, according to
their sexual and spiritual proclivities. And each of them, having one on the back or front of another, used his other
hand, feverish with excitement, to loosen and throw aside his
own garments. The word "charcharkheh" had driven them to
such a frenzy of excitement that they had turned to fire itself
and desired consummate penetration of another or of themselves by another, and, in fact, the more skilled ones had already been able to bend over for another or to bend over in
front of another, or to kneel before another or to push another to his knees before them, to facilitate the penetration of
themselves or others who wished to be penetrated. At first
they did this in separate columns of two, naturally in ram-
pant disorder at this stage, but as soon as the two or three or

four in each column were able to get their hands on each other, bestowing their bounty on the ones before them and drinking deep of the bounty of those behind, and when each of the men in each column commenced to puff and pant in a soft, lustful, sensuous way; driven to and fro with each breath, when the movement of one column fell into rhythm with the movement of another column and eventually the movements of all the clusters fell into rhythm with the movements of each other, establishing the inevitable harmony of action, if you had watched from afar, you would have seen that all of the people, that is to say, all of the men, were locked to each other, and, panting and thirsting and fever-stricken, were undulating to and fro in perfect harmony with their hearts' beat; if you had looked from afar, you would have seen that the people had understood "the middle road of moderation in all things" and had plunged themselves into the middle of each other's roads, their chins pressed to the spine in the small of each other's backs, pumping forward and backward. And all of them having been absorbed into the pervading harmony of action, these columns of men, these magnificent men of history, these men who could change human destiny, these rugged, gigantic men, started to whisper something, a murmur at first, of course, gradually becoming a distinct voice, the voice of each one blending with the rhythmic movements of legs and thighs and buttocks, into a single melodious, truly resplendent cry—a single, united cry, distinct and lustful and virile arose to the sky devastating the four corners of the world. They shouted, "Charcharkheh! Charcharkheh! Charcharkheh!" And then the heads of the long columns of men locked together moved together and formed the columns into a circle, the man at the fore of each column joining himself to the aft of the next and the circles stretching in length as those with no one before them sought and found and penetrated those with no one behind.

The joining of fore to aft of the columns took little more than a moment, forming, as a result, a long spiraling, snake-twisted column, opening and stretching out to include the other columns, to join itself to the men with no one behind them, like a gigantic loop, a snake-twisted, masculine and impotent column growing longer and longer by the moment. At first there had been two points, one before and one behind, and a straight line had joined these two points, and then another line had formed through the attraction of two

other points to each other, then other lines had formed between other points, then a single straight column and beside it
other straight columns, and then the columns had twisted and
straightened and in this movement had formed curves like
small circles and the other columns had penetrated them
from behind and then other columns penetrated other
columns, and this coiling snake had been formed, and now its
loop was opened from the end and moved toward the west,
all moving in a single column toward the west, each of them
wallowing and steaming intensely in the depths of another,
their hands clasped about the bellies of those ahead and sensing the hands of those behind clasped about their own bellies,
the chins of those in front pressed to the back of still another,
in a single column, wallowing and steaming in the depths of
each other. Then this straight line stretched itself from east to
west, and the thousand-headed snake opened its coil and extended its whole length from east to west, and Mahmoud
shouted once more, "Charcharkheh! Charcharkheh!" and
they, gasping and thirsting and fever-stricken, shouted back
"Charcharkhch!" and repeated "Charcharkheh! Charcharkheh! Charcharkheh!" The thousand-headed snake had now
become a long dragon, striving with its head to bite its own
tail. Still shouting "Charcharkheh! Charcharkheh!" moving
from side to side and shouting from the head of the column
to the tail, wallowing and steaming inside each other, they
moved clenched together so tightly, so rhythmically and har-
moniously from fore and aft, that the circle about to form in
the next few moments was pulled tighter as if they were par-
ticipating in some kind of religious ritual, a religious ritual in
which one must forget himself and take part in a group effort, in this form of course, by means of universal copulation,
the depths of one be hacked out and he, by extraordinary effort, hack out the depths of another that the religious ritual
might be performed at the peak, at the climax of pleasure,
pain and torture. The sweaty odor of bodies, the odor of nav-
els adhering to the flesh of the back, of buttocks held fast to
the groin, of hands clasped around waists, the sensual odor of
the tight, wet and sticky inner depths, of phalluses thrust into
these depths, had arisen, and this religious ritual, the ritual of
virile religion, was set in the midst of these funky body perfumes, and the dragon slouched forward and tried to bite its
own tail, taking the form of a circle—no—an interwinding
cord of flesh, pulling back at the tail end, lurching forward at

the head. And finally the head reached the tail, and before the eyes of all the people of this land, that is to say of all the men locked together, the head connected with the tail, and then the shouting of the voices reached its climax, the panting and puffing quickened, the odors thickened and the cry of "Charcharkheh! Charcharkheh! Charcharkheh!" split the sky . . . Mustachioed men, bearded men, these great historical men, the men of this great sexual resurrection, the men of this gigantic circle of lust, were climaxing and coming inside one another, and this upon simply hearing the word "Charcharkheh," which they were supposed to have brought but had not brought yet. There was also another possibility: perhaps it wasn't the charcharkheh that had excited them. Perhaps it was the execution, the execution which had taken several hours, which had moved them to behave in this manner. Perhaps it was the odor of blood, blood dripping from the severed stumps of arms and legs soaking our winding sheets, that had driven the people, already thirsting for the blood of the man bound to the rack, to this frenzied orgy of universal copulation. Perhaps the sight of that blind and tongueless figure, that armless, legless carcass hanging above all of them in the middle of this circle of desert (who looked disheveled, sweaty, like a man in the midst of copulation with a woman), had moved them to drown themselves in each other.

I think Mahmoud had a lot to do with this. Having finished off the man on the rack, he now wished to bring the mass hysteria of the people to a resounding climax. The people could never have foreseen this; they could not have known that they would suddenly, at the height of their passionate display, be seized unawares and driven their better instincts overcome, to take part in an action of which the imagination of man can hardly conceive. At the climax of this event, Mahmoud had given them a great gift, a gift consisting of only a single word; but this word had a double significance for them. Mahmoud had shouted, "Charcharkheh," and the people had seen in that word the crystallization of all their desires and had been exalted; they had caught this great gift of Mahmoud, this emotion-packed word, and pressed it to their breasts and been driven wild by it. They had been excited by an object, nay, not even the object itself but the sound, the sound of the name of that object, and this had been a major factor in transforming their minds. Although they had ultimately directed their assault upon flesh, arms, legs and orifices of flesh, it had been, after all, this beautiful sound of "Charcharkheh" that had raised them to this fever pitch of excitement; and it had been this object and the very name of this object which had given them the courage to perform. I really wanted, while they were boiling and wallowing in each other and shouting "Charcharkheh," to be there in the middle of them—no—to be in their minds that I might understand what form this "Charcharkheh" had taken in their minds that they had been able to associate "Charcharkheh" with copulation. Of course, I knew that people were excited by luxuries—a pretty pen, a delicate pencil, a crown, a few medals, a hand with fingers covered by expensive varicolored jewels, a henna-dyed beard, a thick mustache excited them. Such luxuries, not even of the body and therefore able to excite anyone, excited these people. I had often seen the people stare in amazement and wonder as Mahmoud mounted his "Charcharkheh" and rode it from street to street all the way to the palace. Of course they were watching Mahmoud, but they had never seen Mahmoud in the street without his "Charcharkheh" and they imagined this "Charcharkheh" to be bound up with some kind of secret and that this secret related Mahmoud and the "Charcharkheh" to each other and invested them with the power to excite and stimulate the people. When the people saw Mahmoud's "Charcharkheh" in the streets, moving swiftly along, their pubic hair began to tingle and a bulge swelled beneath their clothing. At first they were gentle and soft, but they soon became rough and dangerous and laid hands on themselves underneath their clothing. Summer, winter, spring or fall—it made no difference to them. As Mahmoud went by mounted upon the "Charcharkheh" they became excited and beat themselves off, and before they could finish, Mahmoud and his "Charcharkheh" passed from their street on to his palace, one of the many palaces he had in the city itself or on the outskirts of the city, and they retained only a kind of dizzy, lustful torpor, a heavy sleepiness issuing from the blood vessels around the eyelids, a kind of dreamy languor and lethargy, and stumbled off to their huts with the image of a crumpled "Charcharkheh," a "Charcharkheh" deflated and dissolved and deteriorated, an image of the "Charcharkheh" like fat heated on the fire, melting and dripping onto the ground. They found something religious in this ritual, something which drew them inward from the margins and sides of the square, drew them to the center, and changed them into martyrs and heroes, into murderers and victims, even into religious objects like windows of a mosque, coffins of wood, into a ceremonial chant. And this religious ritual burgeoned in their depths, in their bowels, in their groins, from their dirt-crusted knees and filthy ankles and stinking toes, a fiery spark burgeoning within them from the tips of their toes, driving their senses and emotions, their fervor and frenzy upward with the speed of nervous impulse to the heart and from there, with that same speed and pervasiveness of nervous impulse, to the brain, and then these people, standing there in the closely packed crowd with their erect phalluses were transformed into actors in a great religious mystery of hysteria. And when they raised their arms and beat their breasts mercilessly and tore out their hair and pummelled their own heads, and when they lashed roughly at their own backs with chains and the blood streamed from the torn flesh and crushed bones of their backs, and when they jabbed at their own heads with daggers, their right hands clasped in the hands of the men in front of them, and split the flesh open to the skull, and when after the performance of all these pious actions, actions ominous and sensuous and fraught with evil, they began to moan and weep, wallowing in each other, anointing each other with their own blood and sweat, at that moment someone should have been there to perceive and depict and portray the magnificence of this hysteria, in which the national genius was expressed to the full—no—not only a single perception, a single portrait—rather a perception, a portrait of the event from every possible angle—someone who would hold this portrait before the eyes of history, so that history, great and holy and ancient history which had led them to this, would deign to give them a smile of support and patronage, a smile which should resemble the foam appearing on the lips of a mad man, dripping from the lips of an epileptic at the height of a seizure. They had brought the "Charcharkheh—Charcharkheh—Charcharkheh," and Mahmoud was writing this history, this very history. Mahmoud was able to write history. At this very moment he was writing it. The people had never seen the "Charcharkheh" come to a standstill before their eyes. They had always seen the "Charcharkheh" moving, Mahmoud mounted upon it. But they had never seen the "Charcharkheh" come to a standstill before their very eyes. The "Charcharkheh"

was strongly built. It had four large iron wheels. Its knotted
wood of walnut gleamed. The nails holding it together shone
like burning stars. Two tall horses, which were known to be
the gift of one of the Arab Emirs to Mahmoud, one white
and one black, were harnessed to the "Charcharkheh." A
wood pole separated the two horses from each other; the two
horses seemed like two statuesque generals, fully ripe and
perfect. The word "Charcharkheh" was still sensual to the
spectators and now they saw to their utmost astonishment
that the "Charcharkheh" had materialized, the abstraction of
the word became the actuality of the object itself, for now
not the word but the "Charcharkheh" itself stood before
them. The astonished people were mesmerized by the beauty,
by the symmetry and latent force of the horses and the
"Charcharkheh." Mahmoud looked neither at the horses nor
at the "Charcharkheh." He watched the people, and the people watched the horses and the "Charcharkheh." And I stood
there watching Mahmoud and the people and the horses and
the "Charcharkheh." Mahmoud always gave his permission to
the people to look at pretty things, and this "Charcharkheh,"
this symmetrical beauty, built by Mahmoud's craftsmen, was
indeed a pretty thing, and Mahmoud always permitted the
people to look at pretty things. According to Mahmoud, one
must bedazzle the people, and the people must live bedazzled
and open their lips bedazzled and speak bedazzled. Mahmoud
somehow always kept them in that state of suspense, that
concentrated state of bedazzlement, that state of consternation. Should they become demystified, turn their backs on
Mahmoud, evacuate the cities, pick a direction and leave?
Mahmoud watched the people, trying to see what actions
would ensue, those moments of burgeoning lust, the ceremony of universal copulation having come to an end. Frantic
with joy at seeing the "Charcharkheh" and the horses, the
people laughed, rubbed their hands together, emitting squeaking sounds, puckering their lips at the horses and making
smooching sounds, as if they were all standing at the side of
a huge vessel on the seashore waiting for a lovely woman to
alight from the ship so that they might, all together from up
close, witness the advent of her beauty. And it so happened
that the voice of Mahmoud, my master, was heard at that
very moment. He took his eyes from the people and spinning
victoriously around shouted, "Load it on!" and the guards
got down to work, and their skill and their knowhow was in-

deed surprising. One of them who was sitting on the "Charcharkheh" and holding the reins of both horses in his hands, drove the "Charcharkheh," that huge symmetrical framework, gradually backward, bringing the rear of the "Charcharkheh" to a place right in front of the man bound to the rack. He did this in such a way that the horses might not chance to see the dismembered man on the rack. Mahmoud knew very well that if the sideways glance of one of the horses should chance to fall upon one of the blood-smeared arms, if they should chance to see but once a leg of the dismembered man or his metamorphosed face, they would bolt in such an extreme of panic that they would never again be coerced to return to men or the city or the harness of the "Charcharkheh."

The people, standing in curved lines in that vast desert of sun and earth, eyeing me and Mahmoud and the horses and the dismembered man from not too far away, showed by emitting slight sounds that they had the indefatigable desire to be drowned in wonder and awe. The sun was high above—the earth vast—the horses beautiful—the "Charcharkheh" rhythmical—the man bound to the rack luminous and exciting and tragic: What more could they want? They were set on a plane face to face with nature as well as art, with life and the living as well as with death and the dead, with beauty as well as with tragedy. All of the elements of their bedazzled state had a geometric harmony, which even at the height of artificiality had not lost its natural essence and seemed so apropos, so symmetrical, so glorious and exciting that no one could have any doubt of the grandeur of a power that could create such harmony. Not only were the fingerprints of Mahmoud on the arms of the dismembered man, on his severed legs, on his blood-soaked tongue pulled out by the roots, but his shadow was imprinted on the sun and the very air which carried the sunlight to the earth, on the very light of day which caused the grains of sand to glitter like the stars. The fingerprints of Mahmoud were imprinted upon everything everywhere, and they stood in awe of his all-conquering, all-corrupting, beautiful and exalted magnificence.

Having witnessed a ritual which was both primitive and civilized, they were savoring the rich taste of a feeling of holiness, and this feeling of holiness reached its climax when, at the order of Mahmoud and with my help, the tall guards uprooted the two posts on either side of the man bound to the rack from where they had been driven into the ground and several of them who were the strongest lifted the rack with such perfect rhythm, care and power that the dead man on the rack was not joggled even slightly, raising it slowly from several sides onto their shoulders and carrying it slowly and setting it down on the "Charcharkheh." Then arose the voice of the people, and wild screams arose in unison, in harmony changing now into a panther-like chorus. Devoid of meaning, they were something savage, a drawn-out single-toned shriek. It expressed agony, but not agony alone, and it expressed pleasure, but not pleasure alone; it expressed a combination of both. It was a shriek, savage and ominous and fiery, genuine and rich, an instinctive shriek but devoid of meaning.

When they had heard the word "Charcharkheh" from the tongue of Mahmoud, they had plunged into an orgy of universal copulation, but now that the man bound to the rack and the huge figure of his body could be seen looming above them the shrieks they emitted plunged them into utter savagery. They forgot their identities; they forgot their own history; they were forgetting their own culture, the virile erection of a phallus in the pages of history; and the only things that they saw and could see were the blood-dripping mouth, the tightly closed eyes, the severed stumps of arms, the severed stumps of legs which grew larger moment by moment, invading their whole mind and soul, and they, in agony combined with pleasure, were emitting such a brutal and savage shriek that no word in the lexicon of human tongues could suffice to define it. And this shriek reminded me of a shriek I had uttered at one of the stages of the many stages of my metamorphosis in the course of my history, and this shriek should have reminded me of that shriek, for although that shriek had been the shriek of an individual, it had always stood implanted in my mind like a long spear, always erect, a fiery blood-red flame. This spear of shriek I had never forgotten. I had uttered this shriek when metamorphosed from subject into object, and behold now the shriek of my nation, the shriek which they utter in their metamorphosis from subject into object! My nation, my passive nation, penetrated by all actions, subjugated by all the verbs, all the verbs like spears, which, once erected, must penetrate and subjugate. For this very reason, I, whose curls had been trimmed at the hands of Mahmoud,[4] who was a specimen of this great family of mankind, meaning this passive nation of mine, must speak of my remembrances of my own shriek during the metamorphosis from subject to object in order to explain the meaning behind the shriek of my passive nation. Because what has happened to me as an individual, in bedrooms, on the rocks and on the sands, has happened to my nation collectively. Everything that has happened to me individually, in my body, in my heart, in my brains and in my depths, in the everywhere of my roots and sinews, my skin and flesh and bones and cartilage, yes cartilage, has happened as well to these cartilage people of my nation. My nation, my passive nation, trapped in this cartilage state; in the course of history my people have not become flesh as flesh that they might decay and under the dynamic sway of time and flood and invasion and devastation pass away, nor have they stood erect in correlation to the word "bone," in the form of bone as bone, to fall violently upon the jagged lines of history and smash them to pieces. My nation, my passive nation, from my point of view, as I, I whose curls were trimmed at the hands of Mahmoud, see it, is a shrieking cartilage. I am part and parcel of you, and when you flip through my pages you flip through your own. When Mahmoud trimmed my curls, he laid his hands upon your curls as well. I am a page of history, and every page of history is but a reiteration of the trimming of my curls, for the cypress to be beautiful must be trimmed.

—(TRANSLATED BY CARTER BRYANT)

---

[4] It is recounted in many Persian works that one night Soltan Mahmoud became drunk and, moved by his favorite slave's beautiful hair, wanted to make love to him right in front of all his guests. An adviser pointed out that the king should be careful not to commit such a sin in public. Mahmoud had Ayyaz' hair cut with a knife, but next day he was full of regret and anger. A poet, sent to pacify him, composed a quatrain, the famous line of which reads: "The cypress to be beautiful must be trimmed."

The Plane Reservation

by MASSUD FARZAN

We lived on 23 Sadness Street. But it was a narrow street—
cars couldn't enter—so I asked the cabdriver to drop me on
the corner of Sadness and Pomegranate Blossoms. I paid the
fare we had settled at the airport, plus a generous tip. The
driver asked for more, speaking slowly and with funny gestures. I said no, and why do you speak like that, I am not a
foreigner; I am just a Persian like yourself. He became embarrassed and I paid him a little more. He then helped me
carry the heavy suitcase as far as 23 Sadness Street.

I knocked the horseshoe knocker that dangled in the afternoon breeze. An old woman opened the door a crack, peeped
and immediately ran back into the house. "Khanom, my
baksheesh! Mr. Morad come!" I recognized the voice of the
old laundress and remembered how I used to eavesdrop her
conversations with herself. I passed the dark vestibule,
knocked my head on the transom overhead and figured out
how much taller I must have gotten since I had last passed
under it. The little brick-covered yard, surrounded by four
big walls, had been watered for coolness. In front of the yard
stood the two little flowerbeds with flowers of many colors
and with assorted vegetables. In the middle there was the
little pond. A goldfish hung from the water surface, eating
bubbles.

My mother rushed through the sitting room window to the
yard, her prayer chador safety-pinned under her chin. "My
son! Thanks Allah!" She opened her arms. My head down, I
saw her shoulders shake. I stood wordless, without tears of
happiness. I did not feel happy.

"Have you lost some weight, Morad? You look so different. Come through the window. That's all right, you needn't take off your shoes."

The living room was covered with thick native rugs, from wall to wall. There was no furniture except for a chair in a corner. Against the wall facing the yard and the flowerbeds there were two cushions. In the middle of the room my mother's prayer-spread lay open on the floor.

"You aren't through with your prayer, Mom. Go ahead and finish it first."

"I am going to. But first let me fix you a glass of quince sharbat, it is good for the heart. Why did you sit on the floor? We have put the chair for you."

"I don't need to sit on the chair, Mom. It feels so good to spread my legs on these thick rugs."

"Drink your sharbat, it is good for the heart."

"All right. You go ahead and finish your prayer now."

She stood before her prayer-spread, facing Mecca, and began to move her lips. I noticed that she was saying her prayer slowly and deliberately and that her chador reached the floor, covering her entire feet. I remembered that she didn't used to wear her chador so long. Nor was her rosary so big. Mother must be getting old.

Outside, a man was selling ice. And in a distance a voice called out: THIS EVENING! IT WILL HAPPEN THIS EVENING AT EIGHT!

I sipped the quince sharbat and watched the yard. The flowerbeds were certainly my father's work; carefully cultivated and yet going wild and wayward. So many things in that ten by fifteen feet. Vivid green spotted with flowers red and yellow, pink and blue. Red roses surrounded by lettuce. Little violets at the foot of delpheniums. Petunias everywhere.

Four walls, thick and tall, surrounded the yard, keeping out whatever rays there were left of the setting sun.

A little clay-roofed closet huddled back in the corner, on the other side of the flowerbeds. It was the toilet. It had no stool, no toilet seat. You merely squatted over a funnel-shaped pit, dark and deep. You could keep the door open, if you wished, watching the flowers, the rooftops, and the sky. Nobody to see you except maybe a couple of sparrows or a lone pigeon. I remembered how my father used to sit there, sometimes for half an hour or more. My mother would then go to wash her hands in the pond and call out, "Aren't you going to come out of that toilet?" Or, "Do you know you have been sitting in there for forty minutes?" My father wouldn't say anything. I knew that he didn't want to come out. He liked very much to think or meditate without being disturbed. My mother would make snide remarks whenever she caught him in deep reflection. "Inventing again, eh?" she would say and disturb his thoughts.

My father was an inventor. He had invented many things, although none of them had worked out. With each invention, he thought that he would make lots of money. He never told anybody what he would do once he got rich. But I knew what he would do. He would buy a house with a bigger yard, perhaps a garden, with a big pond; have a lot of goldfish; cultivate a great variety of flowers and vegetables. He would go on pilgrimage to Mecca and give to the poor. He would elicit respect from those he didn't like. He would cease to worry about his future in this world and beyond. But with each invention something would go wrong at the last moment, and he would abandon it only to start inventing something else. That would make my mother bolder and warier. She thought that whenever my father was silent and staring into the blank, he was conceiving a new invention. So she was always on the watch for those moments.

One day my father had come home with a big box under his arms. He had bought a radio. We all rejoiced. Every evening we sat on the rugs and listened. My father seemed to listen more attentively than everyone else. But it did not take long before my mother discovered what he was really doing. I think what gave him away was the faraway look in his eyes and the faint motionless smile on his face. My mother called him a sneak, a hopeless dreamer and other names. My father looked quite embarrassed. From then on he used to spend more time in the toilet at the corner of the yard.

That was many years ago. My mother was getting old; my father must be getting older. Maybe now they understood their common lot and forgave each other's foibles.

Once again the voice outside called out: IT WILL HAPPEN THIS EVENING AT EIGHT!

My mother finished her prayer. She carefully folded the prayer-spread and put it away on the shelf by the radio. "Tell me what you'd like to eat and I'll cook it for you. You really look so dark and thin."

I didn't know what to answer. "Am I? Maybe that's because I am now taller than I was when I left."

"As a boy you were so good looking," she went on. "We were all thinking you would come back from America fat and white."

Suddenly it occurred to me that she was blaming me.

"Look at that picture of your brother over your head. See the belly, *mashallah?* Isn't that something? He's married, that's right. Maybe that is the reason. Which reminds me, you haven't gotten married, have you?"

"No, Mom, not yet. As a matter of fact, I may get married here."

"Good, I tell everybody that you are my wisest son. Is that why you came back?"

"Well, not really. To be frank, Mom, I came back in order to see what I can do for, I mean to have a close look at you and Pop and make sure that you are happy together. Now tell me, how are you getting along? How is Pop?"

"Don't worry about him. The bad vessel is seldom broken, as the saying goes."

THIS EVENING. . . .

My mother turned to the door. "He's not inventing anymore, if that's what you mean, but he's taken something else."

I listened.

"He's now buying lottery tickets *every* week. He also writes poetry. He thinks that—"

Just then the door opened and my father came in, holding a full grocery bag under his chin and a melon in the curve of his arm. The melon rolled on the floor; we salaamed and embraced.

"You've kept yourself pretty well," I lied. "You look good, Pop."

"Do I really?" He smiled diffidently and watched my mother from the corner of his eye. "How do you find our little house? I mean next to American houses. Modest, eh?"

"I never saw flowerbeds like this anywhere," I said. My father smiled with mild contentment. "You should've seen it last month, Morad, we had roses as big as sunflowers." He walked to the window and gently threw the melon into the pond to get cool there.

THIS EVENING AT EIGHT! The voice was now very close, loud and clear.

"What does that mean?" I asked.

My father's face lit up. My mother looked at him reproachfully. "He's selling lottery tickets," he finally said. "The draw is this evening at eight." He stole a look at the clock on the radio.

My mother went out to the kitchen. I thought it was time to ask him if he was happy in his job and at home, whether he got along well with Mom. But just then he took his ashtray and cushion and sat beside me. "There is something I wanted to tell you," he began in a low, confidential tone, "I hope you won't mind it. What I wanted to say, Morad, you see, maybe you've forgotten all this time you were abroad, but in this country people look at your appearance and judge you accordingly; as the poet said: Feel the skin of a melon/Before thou purchaseth one. You see, if you were fat and white, if you had a nice double chin and a potbelly, then there wouldn't be any problem and I wouldn't take up your time telling you all this. I mean people would then think that you're rich; you would be respected wherever you went in the country. But unfortunately you and I are the wiry type and rather dark. It would be a blasphemy to complain about it. Allah must have wanted it to be that way and we just can't do anything about it. But there is something we *can* do."

He leaned over and whispered, "Buy yourself a nice new suit and change your necktie. What is that you're wearing? As the poet said: What is in my weary heart/That while I'm quiet, it's in turmoil? Maybe that is not the appropriate poem; there is a better one in Sa'di's *Rose Garden*. I can't remember it now, but it doesn't matter. What I am trying to tell you, Morad, I'm really ashamed to mention it, but the barber on the corner of Pomegranate Street wears a better tie than yours. I always watch him closely when he cuts my hair, he wears genuine Silka tie, I am not lying to you. And his shoes are always polished. I myself can't afford to be very well dressed, but at least I can have a crease in my trousers. I can afford to have a shoeshine once in a while. I'll be darned if I can tell when it was last you got a shoeshine."

His face was quite somber. Apparently he wasn't any more pleased with his returning son than my mother was. Why did they keep asking me to go back? What made them believe that I would return someone other than I was, fatter and whiter than I was, as young as I was ten years ago? One thing was clear—they were disillusioned at the one who had returned. But I didn't resent that at all. If only I could make sure that they got along together, that they were a bit happier than I remembered them to be.

My father put half a cigarette in a cigarette holder. "That's all I wanted to say, Morad. But I am not a narrow-minded old man; you'll of course do whatever you choose. As the poet has said: I advise whatever methinks fit/You either profit by it or resent it."

Just then my mother came, hugging the big copper tray of supper. "What were you whispering to each other?" she asked.

"I was just telling Morad how he would look like a real gentleman if he had his shoes shined."

She said she agreed with him on that. I fetched the melon from the pond.

After supper my mother went to the kitchen to do the dishes. My father took a pencil and a piece of paper. He then turned on the radio. "I have a little lottery ticket. Who knows, Morad, maybe you've brought good luck to our house tonight."

At eight o'clock the radio chimed eight times, followed by a minute of silence. Then the announcer said that the draw procedures were being broadcast live from the Horizon Hall. My father took out his ticket and put it upside down on the floor beside his cigarette case and abacus. He then began to jot down the winning numbers on the sheet of paper.

My mother finished the dishes while the draw was still going on. She came in with a small tray of green beans and sat down to string them. I noticed that she was watching my father from the corner of her eye.

Having written all the winning numbers, my father turned over the ticket and began to check its number against the winning numbers. He started with the top prize and went down. His hand hovered over each number for a second before going to the next. The pencil trembled a little. My mother held a bean and forgot to string it. My eyes raced from him to her and back to him.

Suddenly my father threw the pencil up in the air. "Ten tumans! won ten tumans!" Immediately I made a mental calculation: one dollar and twenty-five cents. My mother was now bending over the tray, stringing rapidly; she didn't want father to see the broad smile that had spread all over her face.

I found myself outside in the yard. The night had fallen. I

had to think. I sat over the deep pit. I left the door open. There was a full moon and the crickets sang. I sat there for several minutes, my chin propped in my hand. I wanted to sit more, but I thought that they might wonder where I was and get worried. I went back to the living room. My father was now sitting beside my mother, helping her string the beans; I dropped a bulb into my Agfa and snapped a picture. They smiled. I hurried back to the yard. The goldfish was motionless at the bottom of the pond. The night smelled of petunias. I sat over the pit again. I thought, what a marvelous picture that will be. Stringing beans together in peace and harmony!

In the morning I would get my shoes shined. I would also buy a few fish for the pond and make a plane reservation.

My China Doll

by HUSHANG GOLSHIRI

Mama says he'll come back. I know he won't come back. If he were going to come back, Mama wouldn't cry. Would she? I wish you could see. No. I wish I couldn't see. Now, you be Mama. So what if your hair is brown. Look, Mama was sitting like this. Pull your feet up. Put your hands on your forehead. But you can't. Her shoulders were shaking, like this. The newspaper was in front of her, on the floor. I can't cry like Mama. Daddy surely could. Uncle Nasser can too, if he wants to. That's why grownups are grownups; they can say, "Don't cry, Maryam." Or, I don't know, they can say, "Why did you take the matches, girl?"

OK, so I took them. I don't want to light any fires. Do I? Daddy is good; he never says "Don't!" But then why did he say, "Don't let me see my Maryam cry"? I want to, but I know I can't. That is, if I could cry like Mama cries, for Daddy, I would. But I can't. Do dolls cry too? I know *you* can't; not like Mama, like Grandmother, like Uncle Nasser. If you can, then why didn't you cry when that brat Mehri broke my doll? I mean my china doll. Grandmother said, "Don't cry, Maryam; I'll give her to the china-mender to glue her back together."

I said, "Then what?"

She said, "Then she'll be like before."

I said, "I don't want it, I don't want it! She'll be just like our big teapot!"

Daddy said, "If my little girl doesn't cry, Daddy will buy her a new one, a big one."

He didn't buy it. Daddy's good. If he comes back, I won't tell him, "Go buy it." I won't even cry. Remember how Grandmother cried? I told you about that. In her black dress; she fell on Grandfather's grave and cried. I cried, too. Daddy didn't cry. Maybe he did, like dolls do; like you, whose tears nobody can see, whose voice doesn't come out. I can't. I cried so much you can't imagine. Because I knew Grandfather would never stretch out his stick again; he used to say, "Little Maryam, how many spans long is my cane?"

I'd say, "Seven."

He'd say, "No, five."

"Seven."

He'd say, "Ten and a half and one of your little fingers."

"No, seven."

He'd say, "Measure it yourself."

I'd measure it. He thought I didn't know that when my hand reached the top of the stick, he'd grab my wrist and sit me down on his knees. And that's just what I wanted. I'd put my hand in his vest pocket and bring out his watch. Grandfather would open it and put it next to my ear. I'd say, "How old are your hands, Grandfather?"

He'd say, "Well, pretty old."

His hands, the backs of his hands, were funny. Like his face. He'd say, "It's *their* fault, baby."

He meant the hands of the watch, that red one that went around all the time, faster than the others. Where is his watch now? Did they bury it with Grandfather? *You* don't know. What are you, Shorty? You're just a little short person. Always coming and going. Hah, go that way, come this way; but don't go and come so much so I get dizzy, huh? Daddy was over there. I didn't recognize him. Shorty, you stand here, just come and go all the time. Mama took my hand. She said, "What do you want the matches for anyway, girl?"

I said, "I don't know."

But now I know. I'll put them side by side. One, two . . . like this. Mama and me are on this side of the matchsticks, Daddy on the other, on the other side of them. Shorty, you come in the middle. Now us, the ones who are on this side, we have to yell all the time. The people on the other side of the matchsticks have to yell all the time, too. Daddy yelled, "How's my Maryam? Send a kiss for Daddy?"

Now you, Shorty, come over here, in front of me, here. So Daddy can't see I'm sending him a kiss. Daddy said . . . I don't remember what he said. Mama took my hand, like this. Daddy said, "My little girl mustn't cry, OK? Daddy's all right."

Daddy didn't look like Daddy at all. Like Shorty, who doesn't look like Daddy at all. If that brat Mehri hadn't broken my china doll, I'd put it on that side now, in Daddy's place, beside those others on that side, beside Daddy. Mama said, "Don't you say, 'Where's my doll,' see?"

I said, "Mama, where's Daddy?"

She said, "He's over there, dear. Behind that man. He's coming over. Don't forget, now."

It wasn't Daddy; he looked funny. I knew that Daddy was Daddy from his smile. Then Daddy said, "My Maryam should send me a kiss."

I told you. Afterward he didn't talk to me any more. He talked to Mama. Now the china doll must say, "Esmat, don't let me see you lose face in front of them."

Then he must yell and talk and point to Shorty all the time. And you say, "What's going to happen, what will become of you?"

Then Daddy said, "What? What will happen? Well, that's clear enough. They're not doing charity work here. Anyway, whatever happens, you mustn't let the child worry."

He meant me. I don't know what Mama said then. She shouted. Everybody shouted. There was so much noise, everybody yelled so much . . . It was like when that brat Hassan blows his trumpet. No matter how much Grandmother shouts, nobody understands who's saying what. Now he must say, "Esmat, dry your tears. I don't want them to see you crying."

And he must point to Shorty again. I didn't see Mama cry.
I said, "Mama, pick me up."

Mama said . . . I don't know. I don't remember. I wasn't
tired. I wanted to see, if Mama cried, should I cry too.
Mama dried her eyes, like this. Now you, Shorty, stand facing us, me and Mama and everybody who's on this side.
Open your arms, like this. Now say, "Ladies, please, time's
up, please go now."

Now turn around and tell Daddy and the others. Tell
them, tell them something so they all leave, so Daddy leaves
too. Daddy had gotten thin. But he laughed, like when he
used to pick me up and tickle me under the arms, like this. I
can't laugh now. Uncle Nasser pulled that brat Mehri's ear
and said, "Girl, what are you doing with Maryam's dolls,
anyway?"

He did the right thing. If my china doll were here, if
Mehri hadn't broken it, it'd turn around now and wave. I
have to wave too, like this. And then cry. Daddy wanted to
come. He couldn't. Shorty, you go over there and stop
Daddy. Mama said, "Didn't Daddy tell you not to cry?"

I wanted not to. I always listen to what Daddy says. If he
comes back, even if he pulls my ear like Uncle Nasser, I
won't cry. And I'll never hit Daddy. He used to say, "Hit
me."

I'd box his ears. And he'd laugh. He'd say, "Hit me hard."

I'd hit him, one on this side, one on that side, like this.
Shorty, you've fallen over. Daddy didn't fall. Get up, there.
I'll hit you gently, with my finger; I'll hit Daddy this way, if
he comes. Maybe it'd hurt him, too. Grandmother always
used to say, "Oh, God, what's going to happen to my son, if
what they say is true?"

I said, "What do they say?"

Mama said, "Grandmother, in front of Maryam?"

Mama's bad. Not always; just when she doesn't let Grandmother talk, talk about Daddy; she's bad, when she says
loudly: Grandmother!

She says it too when Grandmother cries. But once she
burst into tears herself, in front of me, she burst into tears.
When Uncle Nasser came . . . Shorty, you be Uncle Nasser.
Come here. When you come into the house, you have to
stand right there. Come, take this paper in your hand too, it's
the newspaper. Mama said, "Since you insist, open the door
yourself."

Now, Shorty, as soon as he sees Mama, he must hang his head, like this.

Now hit yourself, hard. You—you can't! Look, you have to hit both your hands hard on your head and sit down on the ground, like me, no, like Mama. Sit down and say, "What misfortune has come upon me, brother?"

Shorty, give her the newspaper.

Mama kept turning over the newspaper. Mama's hands trembled. She said, "Where is it, then?"

Uncle Nasser ran into Grandmother's room. Now, you read. I don't know what. Say something, like when they talk on the radio, or like on Uncle Nasser's television; they sit like this and talk all the time. Mama says, "They're reading from something; look how they keep lowering their eyes."

It's not clear. Maybe so. Mama doesn't tell lies. Didn't she say, "Your father has gone to Abadan to buy it for you; you know it can't be found here"?

Uncle Nasser said, "I'll buy it for her myself."

I said, "I don't want it."

Of course, I do want it. If Daddy buys it; if he comes back. He won't come back. Otherwise why did Mama cry? She was reading and crying. Sometimes they smile, too, when they read the newspaper. Like this. I can't smile now, like them. Mama can't, either. Uncle Nasser came over to me and patted my head, my hair. You, Shorty . . . No, I don't want you to pat me on the head. Uncle Nasser patted me in a funny way. I didn't like it. I didn't want him to mess up my hair, like that lady. The one who . . . OK, don't get mad, Shorty, now you're that man. Your desk is here, a big, big desk. On the desk—I don't know—there's everything. Me and Mama and Grandmother went in. Uncle Nasser didn't come. He said, "You go, I'll wait for you here, in that ice cream store."

I said, "I'll go with Uncle Nasser."

I didn't want an ice cream. Daddy said, "Don't say it, don't ever say it."

Mama said, "You've got to come with us. Understand? Remember to say to the man, 'I want my Daddy.' "

Uncle Nasser said, "Yes, sweetie. When you come back I'll buy you two ice creams."

I said, "I want them now."

Mama said, "Maryam!"

You say it too, loud: "Maryam!" Grab my wrist and pull.

Then knock on the door, a big door; now a head . . . Come on, Shorty, look through my fingers, at Mama, look at me too. Now, like Mama, you have to say some things so I understand; you and me and Grandmother have come to see Daddy. Go on, say it. When the door opened we went in. That man said . . . I don't know. He was very tall. He was taller than Mommy. He was fat, too. Grandmother said, "Oh, my poor son!"

She said it softly. Now, Shorty, you're that man, you're tall and very very big, you have a mustache too. Smile and say, "Wait in that room."

Then a lady came. She was pretty, like my own china doll. No, that's Daddy; because she isn't here, she's Daddy. That lady is there for sure. She was like those ladies that talk on television, no, those who read from the newspaper and smile. Mama cried. The day that . . . I mean all day. I told you. The lady came and said, "Ladies, you must excuse me."

Then she said some other things. First she put her hand into Grandmother's blouse. Grandmother said, "Really, Miss, I . . ."

Mama said, "Grandmother."

She said it softly. But her face was like the times when she says it out loud, like when she wants to scold me. She doesn't do it any more. I wish she would. Even if she grabbed my hands and slapped them I wouldn't cry. Even when I picked up one of Daddy's books she didn't scold me. She just took it and put it back. You say, "Maryam dear, you mustn't bother Daddy's things."

I wanted to say, "But Daddy isn't coming back." I didn't. I thought, If I don't say it, surely he'll come back. If I put my hands on his books, if I tear up just one of them, he'll appear. He used to grab my ears. He wouldn't pull them much. Just a little. He'd say, "One day Daddy'll cut off his little girl's ears and hand them to her."

Even if I was bad, or wanted to go out with him, he'd say, "Now it's really time for Daddy to come and grab those two ears and look into his Maryam's eyes."

One day when he looked, however much he wanted to look in a bad way, he couldn't. Uncle Nasser can. Now now. He grabbed Mehri's ear and pulled it. Daddy couldn't. Then we both laughed. We really laughed. See, I pulled Daddy's ears too. Daddy's ears were small. When he'd sit down I could grab his ears and look into his eyes. That lady sat down in front of me, like this. She said, "May I, little lady?"

Grandmother said, "Why her?"

Mama said again, "Grandmother, didn't you hear what the lady said?"

Then the lady put her hand in my hair. Mama had braided my hair. She'd gathered it on top of my head. You can't imagine how pretty I was. That's why I kissed the lady. Then she put her hand . . . Look, now I'm that lady. So, if I put my hand under your skirt, do you like it? She did it with Mama, too. And with Grandmother. Grandmother said, "God forbid!"

Mama didn't say, "Grandmother!" She should have. The lady said, "Little lady, you're very pretty. Do you go to school?"

Mama said, "No; she'll go next year."

What business is it of hers? I'll put my books in my bag. I'll tie a red ribbon, like Uncle Nasser's Mehri's ribbon, in a bow and put it on my head; Mama will do it. I can count to fifty. Daddy taught me. One, two, three, four . . . No, I can't now. Daddy used to say, "My daughter's going to be an artist. My daughter will sit there at her table and draw so Daddy can do his work."

Then he'd sit at his desk and read. No matter how many times I said, "Daddy!" he wouldn't hear. Then, when I'd yell "Daddy! Daddy!" he'd take off his glasses. He'd say, "What is it, honey?"

I'd say, "Look, Daddy, see what I drew."

He'd say, "Give it to Daddy to see."

Grandmother would say, "If you draw my picture just once I'll fix your Daddy."

She thought she could. Daddy would laugh. He'd look and laugh. He'd show it to Uncle Nasser. It's easy. Look, like this: this is Grandmother's stomach. Now. Here, this is her head, these are her eyes. Her mouth has to be very big; she's scolding me. Daddy used to say, "So where's her nose?"

I'd say, "Her mouth is so big you can't see it."

Like this picture where she doesn't have any. OK, now, Shorty, you're sitting at your desk. This is Mama. Wait, let me draw Grandmother's hand. My hand was in Grandmother's. Now you, Shorty, get up from behind your desk, come over here, smile. Say hello to Grandmother and Mama. Then bend over and grab my cheek. Like this. It didn't hurt.

But anyway, now I don't like it. Shorty, talk, ask me, "What's your name?"

And Grandmother, with her big mouth, has to say, "It's Maryam; she's your servant."

Then a man brought tea. He didn't bring me any. I don't want any. Now Grandmother has to say some things that I don't understand. Say them; but talk about Daddy. Say, "Sir, whatever they are, they're young. They've read some things. . . ."

She meant Daddy. Mama's face looked funny. Shorty, you're not supposed to see. Stand facing Grandmother; you should have some tea in your hand. Say, "Well, that's their responsibility. Whenever they come and . . ."

I don't know. He talked like the newspaper. I think he wanted Daddy to go, to sit down like this, to look at his newspaper under his lids and talk like that.

Now you talk, talk like Mama, talk about Daddy, things that even Grandmother doesn't understand. Now Shorty has to say, "All right. Go tomorrow. You should take the child, too, if he agrees."

Grandmother hit me with this part of her hand. I knew why she was hitting me. I hung my head. Grandmother hit me; she hit me hard. I looked at her. She made a funny face. Only her nose could be seen. Now I have to say to Shorty, "Sir, I want my Daddy."

Shorty has to say, "You're going to see him, sweetie. But remember to say, 'Daddy, when are you coming home?' "

Mama said, "What if he won't consent?"

Shorty, you're supposed not to understand that Mama means Daddy. Now say, "Well, make her consent; say it several times so that she learns."

Mama didn't say any more. Grandmother said, "She means my son."

Shorty has to say . . . No, first he has to put his hands behind him and go over to his table, then say, "Well, then, I don't know."

Now, Shorty, we're going, me and Mama and Grandmother. Come here. Bend over and say quietly, "You didn't say what your name was, pretty girl."

Then say, "Tomorrow, for sure, go and see Daddy."

Daddy wasn't there. Daddy didn't come. Now I have to say, "Mama, why didn't he come?"

She said, "I don't know. I guess Daddy doesn't like Mama."

"Why, Mama?"

You say, "Daddy's good, dear."

"No, he's bad, he doesn't like Mama."

I said so to Mama. Mama didn't say any more. She just wiped her eyes. Grandmother didn't come. She couldn't. She just lay in her bed and moaned. Grandmother's leg hurt. Uncle Nasser will come and sit beside her and talk to her. He won't bring that brat Mehri. When I go over to Grandmother they don't talk any more. Now Shorty has to say . . . No, don't say it. I'll say for Uncle Nasser, "It's tomorrow, Mother."

Grandmother has to say, "I wish I could see him. I'm afraid of dying without seeing my son."

Mama said, "Don't talk like that, Grandmother."

She said, "I know I won't see him."

Mama saw me and didn't cry any more. She wasn't crying for Grandmother. It was for Daddy.

Uncle Nasser said, "They won't let anybody in, but it's possible to see him. I and my sister-in-law will go."

Mama said, "Brother!"

She said it loud. Uncle Nasser said, "Hey, you brat, are you here?"

I said, "I'm coming too."

Now Mama has to say, "Maryam?"

If she hadn't said anything, they would have taken me. They didn't take me. Uncle Nasser said, "If you're a good girl I'll buy you a big doll."

Daddy wouldn't have said, "If you're a good girl." He'd say, "What do you want it to be like?"

I'd say, "Like that one; I want just that one."

Daddy said, "If they mend it it'll be ugly."

Grandmother has to say, "Did you see him?"

Uncle Nasser said, "Only for a minute. He was all right."

I said, "Did he have hair on his head?"

He said, "Yes, dear. And he told me, 'Uncle Nasser must cut off Maryam's ears and hand them to her.' "

I said, "He doesn't say that. He doesn't say that now."

When Daddy'd say it, I'd grab my ears and run away. Daddy would laugh and come after me. Now, Grandmother must say, "Why didn't they let you in?"

Uncle Nasser said, "It was surrounded, they didn't let anyone in."

I said, "What does sounded mean?"

Uncle Nasser didn't say. So what. I know; for sure, twenty, no, fifty people like Shorty were there. You stand over there, Shorty. Another here. Lots more. The china doll has to stand in the middle, if she were here. Mehri knocked her down out of spite, I know it was out of spite. Uncle Nasser said, "Tomorrow they'll certainly write it in the papers."

Mama said, "I don't think so."

Grandmother said, "If only I had good legs, if only I were able."

Grandmother can't stand up any more. I wish she could. Uncle Nasser and Mama hold her up. Like a china doll whose legs have fallen off. Her head was broken. In three pieces. Daddy said, "Take her and throw her in the garbage can."

I said, "Isn't she dead, Daddy?"

He said, "Dolls don't die, baby; they break."

I said, "No, they die. Dolls die too, like Grandfather."

I buried her myself. In the garden. I made a little hole for her, I wrapped her in my little white handkerchief, then I buried her. I poured water on her, too. Then I picked a few flowers and scattered their petals over her. If Grandfather had been there he wouldn't have let me pick them. That man sat down beside Grandfather's grave. He said things out of a book that I didn't understand. He read quickly and shook his head. We don't have any roses. When Grandfather was here we did. Grandfather would say, "Then the sister went, she picked up his bones and washed them with rosewater and buried them under the rose tree; then he turned into a nightingale, and flew away. The nightingale went and sat . . ." I don't feel like telling you now. Grandmother doesn't feel like it either. Uncle Nasser said, "Don't cry, Mother. He'll stay a few years; then he'll come back."

Mama said, "How many years?"

You say, "How many years?" Then run to the other room. I wanted to cry, too. I didn't. Daddy said, "Don't cry." Daddy said, "Don't let my Maryam ask for her father—ask *them*." He said that the same day he didn't look like Daddy, he looked like the china doll, like when that brat Mehri broke her. His face looked funny. Mama had collapsed on the bed. Uncle Nasser said something that Mama said. You say it.

No, don't say it. Mama said something bad. Mama is very bad, sometimes she's bad, when she talks to spite Uncle Nasser, when she talks about Daddy. Daddy was very big. He'd pick me up and put me on his shoulders. He'd say, "My Maryam has to stand on Daddy's hands."

Like this. He'd say, "She has to close her eyes."

I was up there, near the light. Mama said so. I told you. Uncle Nasser saw me. If he hadn't seen me he wouldn't have said, "What do you want here, child?"

Then they didn't talk any more. If they talked, if they talked about Daddy in front of me, Daddy surely would have come back. Shorty didn't let him. Did you hit him with these hands, huh? Daddy got like my china doll. He was broken. You are bad. I'll tear off your legs. I'll tear off your arms. I'll tear off your head, too. I won't bury you, either, like I buried the china doll, under the rose tree. I'll throw you in the garbage can. I won't cry for you, either. But I can't not cry.

(TRANSLATED BY JULIE S. MEISAMI)

The Stray Dog

by SADEQ HEDAYAT

A few small stores; a bakery, a butcher's stall, a grocery, two tea houses, and a barber shop contributed to the basic requisites of the primitive way of life that made up Varamin Square.

The merciless sun had nearly grilled and half-broiled the traffic circle and its inhabitants, who anxiously waited for the first evening breeze and the shades of night.

The people, the stores, the trees and the beasts were exhausted. A sultry heat weighed heavily overhead and a soft dust wavered in the azure blue sky.

The traffic of cars thickened the dust. On one side of the Square was an old sycamore whose innards had rotted away but which had spread its misshapen rheumatic branches with a strange persistence. Beneath the shade of its dust-laden leaves on a wide spacious platform, two street urchins with loud cries hawked their wares of rice-pudding and pumpkin seeds. A dense, muddy stream pushed its way through the gutter in front of the tea house. The only building that attracted the eye was the well-known tower of Varamin with its cracked cylindrical body and its conical top. The sparrows had built their nests in the crevices made by the fallen bricks. Silent, they slumbered in the intense heat. Only the whimpering of a dog broke the silence.

This was a Scottish setter with sooty muzzle and black spots on its legs as if splashed by muddy water. He had drooping ears, a pointed tail, and a dirty coat, but two intelligent human-like eyes shone in his shaggy snout. In the depth of his eyes a human spirit was discernible. In his benighted life something eternal undulated in his eyes and had a message that could not be conveyed, for it had been trapped just behind his pupils—it was neither the glimmer nor the color, some other unbelievable thing, like what you might see in the eyes of a wounded gazelle. Not only was there a similarity between his eyes and the eyes of a man but a sameness and equality. A pair of greenish-blue eyes filled with pain and hopeful waiting discernible only in the visage of a lost and wayward dog.

But no one saw or heeded his painful beseeching looks! The errand boy of the bakery beat him when he found him in front of the shop. The butcher's apprentice threw stones at him if he saw him near his stall.

If he took refuge in the shade of a car, the driver was sure to entertain him with a rough kick of his spiked boots, and when one and all tired of victimizing him, it was the turn of the urchin who sold rice pudding to take special pleasure in torturing him.

At each cry of pain that escaped the dog, the rice-pudding vendor boy threw another stone, which invariably hit with devilish accuracy and brought out his noisy laughter with cries of "You untouchable cur!" It seemed that the others were his accomplices, for they encouraged the boy in an underhanded, sly way and burst into laughter.

One and all, all of them beat him to please their Almighty God. To them it was natural to torture the dirty untouchable dog which their religion had set a curse upon. At last the rice-pudding boy chastised him so much that the animal was forced to run away through the narrow alley leading to the tower.

He pulled himself with difficulty on an empty stomach and took refuge in a *jube*.[1] Once there he laid his head on his pasterns, put out his tongue, and in a state verging on wakefulness and dreaming, watched the green fields that waved in the wind. He was tired out and his nerves ached.

In the damp air of the *jube* a certain unnameable feeling of well-being pervaded his whole body. Diverse smells of the dead and the living things resuscitated in his muzzle a confusion of faraway memories.

Whenever he fixed his eyes on the green fields, his instinctive urges were roused, reviving old memories in his brain.

But this time, the feeling was so strong that it seemed as if an unknown voice urged him to movement; to jump and frolic. He felt a great urge to run and jump about in these green fields.

This feeling was hereditary, for all his ancestors had been bred in the open spaces of the Scottish meadows and green forests.

But now his whole being was so sore that he could not move. A painful feeling mixed with weakness and lethargy pervaded him. A whole file of forgotten and lost sensations were excited.

Formerly he had different checks and different requirements. He had bound himself to the beck and call of his Master; to drive out strange persons and dogs from his Master's premises; to play with his Master's child. He knew how to behave with the known and the authorized people and how to treat strangers; to eat on time; and when to expect fondling.

But now all these checks were removed. Now his whole life had narrowed to the permanent quest for food, which he got by rummaging fearfully in garbage piles; to being beaten throughout the day; and howls and whimpering had become his sole means of defense.

Once upon a time he had been brave, fearless, clean and full of life, but now he had become a yellow timid scapegoat. He had become a bag of nerves: if he heard a voice, or

---

[1] *jube*: an open channel for water in the streets of Iranian cities.

something near him moved, he would nearly jump out of his skin and shiver.

He even dreaded his own voice. He had got used to dirt and refuse. His body itched, and he did not have the guts to hunt out the lice, or enough self-respect to lick himself clean. He felt that he had become a part of the garbage. Something in him had died, had burnt out.

Two winters had passed since he landed in this out-of-the-way hell of a place, and all this time he had not eaten a full meal, nor slept a happy comfortable sleep. His passions and feelings were strangled. None had pampered him. No one had looked into his eyes. Although the people here resembled his Master in appearance, his Master's feelings and character were a world apart from these people. It was as if the people he knew before were nearer to his world. They seemed to understand his pains and feelings better, and they backed him up.

Of the smells that reached his nostrils and made him light-headed, there was the smell of the rice pudding coming from the pot set in front of the street boy. The white liquid so much resembled his mother's milk that it brought back memories of puppyhood.

Suddenly he went numb, remembering when he was a tiny thing sucking that warm invigorating liquid from his mother's breasts while his mother licked him clean with her strong tongue. The strong smell that came from his mother's bosom and from his pup-brother, the poignant and the heavy smell of his mother and her milk, revived in his nostrils. When he was fully satisfied, his body used to become warm and relaxed; a liquid warmth would run through his veins and arteries. His head would feel heavy and drop from his mother's breasts and a deep slumber would follow, filled with sensual feelings for the nearness of that fount of life; so close and so full of abundance.

His pup-brother's downy body, his mother's bark, all these were treasured in his mind. He remembered his old wooden kennel, the games he used to play with his pup-brother in that small garden. He would bite the tips of his brother's ears and they would both fall, get up again, and run. Then he found a new playmate. This was his Master's son. At the end of the garden he ran after him and barked and bit his clothes.

He could never forget his Master's caresses nor the lumps

of sugar the Master used to feed him with his own hands, never; but he loved his Master's son even more, for he was his playmate and never beat him.

Then after some time he lost all traces of his mother and pup-brother. There remained only his Master, the Master's son, the Master's wife and their old servant. How well he recognized their individual scents and their footsteps from a distance!

When lunch or dinner was served he would walk round the table smelling different dishes of food, and sometimes his Master's wife would throw him a choice morsel despite the strong protests of her husband. Then the old servant would come and would call him "Pat, Pat" and pile his food in a special dish which lay near his wooden kennel.

Pat's troubles started when his rut came on, for his Master would not let him out of the house to run after bitches. As fate would have it, one day in the fall, his Master, with two other people whom Pat knew well and who often came to their house, got into a car and called Pat and made him sit next to them in the car. Pat had been in cars with his Master before, but this time he was in heat and was beset with a strong, disturbing urge.

After a few hours of driving they got off at this same square. His Master with the other two men made their way through this same street that passes by the tower, but suddenly the scent of a bitch, the traces of her scent, turned him mad. He sniffed and followed the scent and at last through a *jube* entered a garden.

Near evening twice he heard his Master calling him, "Pat, Pat!" Was it really his Master's voice or an echo of it? He could not be sure, for he did not want it to be. His Master's voice always had a strange effect on him: it was a reminder of what he knew were his duties. But a Power over and above other forces had made him oblivious to all but the bitch. He was deaf to all external sounds. He felt an intense sensation, and the bitch's scent was so strong, heavy, and poignant that he felt light-headed.

His nerves, muscles, and senses were no longer at his command. In the face of the new and unique experience, he was powerless, but his delectation was short-lived. The owner of the garden and his men assailed him with clubs and spade handles and routed him through the water channel.

Once out, Pat, confused and tired but light and relieved, jolted himself into reality and began to look for the Master.

In some back alleys he could smell thin traces of his Master's scent, which he inspected elaborately, leaving his own scent at regular intervals.

He even explored the ruins outside the village. Then he came back, for he was sure that his Master had returned to the square. But there in the traffic circle his Master's thin scent got lost in other scents.

Was it possible that his Master had gone and left him there? He felt a sensational anxiety mixed with fear.

How could he live without his Master, without his god? His Master was a god to him. He was sure his Master would come and seek him out.

Panicked, he ran down several roads. It was useless.

Night came and Pat, tired out and disappointed, returned to the square. There was no trace of his Master.

He rounded the village a few more times and at last went to the *jube* which led to the bitch, but they had obstructed the way with heavy stones.

He set to digging the ground with gusto to open a hole to the garden, but it was impossible.

When he saw that it was hopeless, he napped there.

In the middle of the night the sound of his own wailing in his dreams woke him up. In a panic, he was soon on his feet, went through several alleys, sniffed the walls, and strayed here and there.

He felt starved, and when he returned to the square, the smell of various foods reached his nostrils—the smell of the left-over meat, the fresh bread and yoghurt. All of the odors had commingled.

He must beg food from these people who looked like his Master, and if he was lucky enough to have no rival to drive him out, perhaps one of these creatures who held food in his possession would take care of him.

Cautiously and with much foreboding he went towards a bakery which had just opened.

The strong smell of baked dough pervaded the air. Someone who held some bread under his arm called to him "Come . . . Come . . ."

How strange this voice seemed to his ears. The stranger threw him a piece of the warm bread. After a little hesitation Pat ate the bread and shook his tail for him.

The stranger put his bread on the shop's platform, and then timidly and with much caution, caressed Pat's head, and using his two hands opened his collar. How relieved he felt!

It was as if all the responsibilities, checks and duties were lifted off his neck. But when again he shook his tail and neared the owner of the bakery shop, a heavy shoe shot into his groin, and whimpering he ran away.

The owner religiously dipped his hands in the gutter water three times to wash off the ill effects of having touched the unclean dog.

Pat recognized his neck band which still hung in front of the shop.

Since that day, save kicks, stones and a good taste of the club, Pat had not received anything from these people.

It was as if they were all his sworn enemies and took pleasure in tormenting him.

Pat felt that he had entered into a new world which was not his and contained no one who cared a whit about his sentiments and idiosyncrasies.

The first few days were passed with much difficulty but by and by he adjusted. In addition to this, he had found a place at the bend of the alley on the right-hand side where people emptied refuse cans and where he could find tasty morsels in the garbage, such as bones, fat, skin, fish heads and many other foods that he could not recognize.

The rest of the day he spent in front of the bakery and the butcher's stall.

His eyes were fixed on the hands of the butcher, but he received more beatings than delicious bits. Altogether he had made peace with his new mode of life.

Of his past life there remained only a hodge-podge of ambiguous and erased traces and only some distant scents. When he had it hard, he found a sort of refuge and solace in this lost paradise and automatically gave himself up to the memories of those bygone days.

But the thing that tortured him more than anything was his craving to be fondled.

He was like a child who had been constantly used roughly and been constantly abused but retained his tender feelings. Especially now in his new pain-ridden life, more than ever before he felt the need for kindness and attention.

His eyes begged for such treatment and he was prepared to

give his life to the first person who was kind to him or caressed his head.

He was in dire need to show his sincerity to someone, to sacrifice his life for that someone.

He longed to show his adoration and fidelity, but no one cared two straws for him. The eyes he looked into had nothing in them save enmity and evil designs. Any movement he made to attract the attention of these people only increased their rage and anger.

When Pat was having his forty winks inside the *jube,* he moaned, and this wakened him up several times, as if he were beset by nightmares.

He felt a great hunger; there was the smell of grilled mutton meat in the air. A cruel hunger tortured his insides, so much so that he forgot his weakness and other pains, with difficulty got to his feet, and wearily set out towards the traffic circle.

Now at this time one of those noisy cars, followed by a whirlwind of dust, drove into Varamin Square.

A man got out, went to Pat and stroked his head. He was not his Master. Pat was not deceived, for he knew his Master's scent very well.

But why did he pat him? Pat shook his tail and threw the man a suspicious look.

Wasn't he being deceived? But no, for he no longer had a collar round his neck so that he would pat him for it.

The man turned and again caressed him. Pat followed the man. His surprise increased as the man entered a room that Pat knew very well, from where the smell of food always emanated.

The man sat on a bench near the wall. They brought him fresh bread, yoghurt, eggs and other foods.

The man dipped bits and pieces of bread in yoghurt and threw them in front of him.

At first Pat gulped these in a hurry, then ate them at his leisure.

At the same time his soulful emerald eyes, beautiful and full of supplication and gratitude, were fixed on the face of the man and all the while he shook his tail.

Was he dreaming or was he awake? Unbelievably, he had eaten his fill without having his meal interrupted by severe punishment.

Was it possible that he had found a new Master? Despite the heat, the man got up, went towards the alley leading to the tower.

Once there, he hesitated, then crossed several labyrinthine winding alleys.

Pat followed him. The man went to the ruins that had some walls. His Master had also gone there.

Perhaps these men were also after picking up the scent of females of their own species. Pat waited for him in the shade of a wall.

After a while, through another route, they returned to the Square.

There again the man patted him, and after taking a short walk round the circle, went and sat in one of the cars that Pat knew.

Pat did not dare to climb in; he sat near the car and looked at the man.

Suddenly the car started in a burst of dust and Pat without any hesitation began to run after it.

No, he had learned his lesson, he did not want to lose his benefactor again. Notwithstanding the pain he felt throughout his body, his tongue was out and he ran in leaps and bounds after the car.

The car had left the village and was crossing a desert.

Two or three times Pat overtook the car but again lagged behind.

Despair made him summon all his power and burst into sudden leaps, but the car was faster. He could not reach the car and the running greatly weakened him.

He felt a great weakness at the pit of his stomach and all at once sensed that his limbs no longer obeyed his commands and could not make the slightest movement.

All his efforts were pointless. He didn't know why he had run or where he was going.

He could neither go ahead nor back. He stopped, short of breath, his tongue hanging out.

His eyes had darkened. With bent head and with much labor, he pulled himself out of the middle of the road and went and laid his belly on wet and hot sand near a ditch on the edge of a field.

By means of his instinct that had never lied to him, he felt that he would never be able to move from that place.

His thoughts and feelings had become obscure and obliterated.

He felt an intense pain in his belly and a sick light glowed in his eyes.

In the throes of his convulsions, little by little his paws and legs lost their senses.

A cold sweat descended on him. This was a pleasant and tender coolness.

Near evening three hungry crows were flying over Pat's head, for they had picked up Pat's scent from afar.

One of them approached cautiously and sat near him and looked carefully; when it discovered that Pat was not yet dead, it flew away. These three crows had come to take out his greenish-blue eyes.

(TRANSLATED BY SIAVOSH DANESH
AND EDITED BY LEO HAMALIAN)

The Game Is Over

by GHOLAMHOSEIN SAEDI

Hasani himself told me. He said, "Let's go over to my place tonight." I'd never been to their place, nor had he to mine; that is, I'd always been too afraid of what my father would do to ask him over, and he, he too, feared his father. But that night being unlike other nights, I couldn't get out of it; Hasani was mad at me, he imagined I no longer liked him, I wasn't his friend—so I went; it was the first time I had set foot in his place. We always ran into each other outdoors; mornings I would go by his little shanty and would whistle loud like a bulbul, with a pretty bulbul's[1] whistle that he himself had taught me. And so, it was as if I had whistled,

---

[1] *bulbul*: nightingale.

"Come on, Hasani, it's time to get going." Hasani would pick up a can and come out. Instead of saying Hi, we would box with each other a bit, with firm, respectable punches that hurt. So had we arranged—whenever we would see each other, whenever we would part, we would box. Unless we were angry with one another, or we had cheated each other. Next we would set out and pass among all the little hovels and plunge into Body Washer's Hollow, where city garbage trucks dumped refuse, and we would delve into the trash; one day I would gather some tin and Hasani a little glass, and another day Hasani would gather some tin and I a little glass. Now and then we would come up with something better, an empty vegetable oil can, a baby's bottle, a broken doll, an odd useless shoe, a perfectly good sugar bowl with a handle missing, or a plastic pitcher. Once I found a golden talisman bearing a Koranic verse such as would be hung around a baby's neck, and Hasani had once found an unopened package of imported cigarettes. Whenever we became tired, we would go to the side of the hollow where the big terrace was which ended at Hajj Timur's Kiln, that no longer operated and was in ruins, that was abandoned to God's care.

Along the terrace itself, here and there and every few steps, there would be big wells, not just two or three, but well after well. Once it came to me to count them by twos; after we passed fifty we got tired of it and quit. Whenever we came up to the wells we would play diverting games; we would lie down and crawl forward until our chests were over the wells, and we would make strange sounds. The sounds would wind around the well and re-emerge. Each well had its special quality and would answer in a certain way. Mostly we would just laugh into the well, and instead of laughter, the sound of crying would echo from within. Then fear would seize us, we would laugh some more, louder, and the sound of crying would become yet stronger. Hasani and I were generally alone; other children would hardly ever come into the hollow—their mamas wouldn't let them, fearing they would fall into a well or that some other catastrophe would happen to them. But Hasani and I, as we had grown, and as we had always come home with a full sack, our mamas no longer interfered, and never said a word about it.

That day in the afternoon, the afternoon before the very night, I went to Hasani's place. He came out looking very blue. His brow was furrowed, it was clear from his eyes that he had cried a lot; he wasn't up for anything, his heart wasn't in it. When we went out to the hollow, he just went around absently, dug his stick into the garbage, and swore at his papa a bit. I knew what had happened. His father had come home furious from work at noon, he had argued with his boss and been fired; and when he came home, he had jumped Hasani, and had beaten him as if there were no tomorrow.

We had heard Hasani's cries, and my ma had cursed Hasani's papa, saying, "Why on earth are you kicking around an innocent child?" I saw the marks of the belt on his shoulders, and a place under one eye that had swollen and turned black and blue. Every night when Hasani's father came home, still dressed, face and hands unwashed, he would start beating up on Hasani; he would beat him until it was time to eat, with blows of the fist and with kicks, with a club, with a rope, with a belt. He cursed Hasani and beat him until he cried bloody murder, so that his screams were heard all over.

The neighbors would go running up and would free him with pleas of "May we be struck dead if you don't let him go!" Hasani's father would beat him every night, but my papa would beat Ahmad and me only once or twice a week when he was out of sorts or his business dealings had gone badly. He would beat me until it was time for dinner. My ma would begin to weep and would cry out, "You bastard, why are you killing my children, why are you maiming them?" My father would turn on her and begin beating her, and she would cry, "Children, get out! Out, children!" By the time we had gotten out, my father would have calmed down and, sitting down quietly in a corner, chewing his mustache, would say, "Call the children and let's guzzle down something."

But Hasani's father didn't molest the other children; he would beat only Hasani, and his ma would never say get out! He would trap Hasani amidst blows and kicks, he would clasp his head and pound it against the wall. This day was the first that he had unleashed his spleen on Hasani at noontime. Hasani was quite morose and so I tried to cheer him up. I said, "Let's go on up." We left the hollow and arrived at the terrace of the wells, to sit alongside one of them. No matter what I tried, he remained mute and sullen. Finally I stretched out along the well's edge and stuck my head in, making the sounds of a cow, a pup, laughing, crying, doing whatever I knew. But, would you believe it, Hasani just sat there frowning gloomily, rhythmically striking his toe with his stick. Finally with my bulbul's whistle I said, "Hasani, what's with you?"

Hasani didn't answer. I called again, "Hasani, oh Hasani." He turned and muttered, "What?" I said, "Why all this grumpiness?"

"I don't need a reason."

"By God, stop your frowning. What are you frowning for?"

"I didn't make myself start frowning, how can I quit?"

I stood up and said, "Come on, get up, get up and let's do something so you'll cheer up."

Hasani, who was striking his toe with his stick, grumped, "Like what?"

I thought a bit and didn't come up with anything to bring him around. I said, "Let's go to the road and watch the cars."

"What for?"

"We'll go like the other day and count the hearses, we'll see how many go by in an hour."

"However many go by, go by. What's the point?"

"You want to go on top of Hajj Timur's Kiln and throw rocks?"

He said listlessly, "I don't feel like it. If you want, go by yourself and throw rocks."

I sat down on a hill of garbage. No way was he going to listen to what I was saying. I said, "Better yet, get up, let's go to the square, there's lots to see."

"What's there to see?"

"We'll look at movie posters, then we'll go behind the stone cutter's square, and watch Sagdast the Dervish do magic tricks."

"By the time we get to the square it'll be night."

"We'll go by bus."

"With what money?"

"I have twelve rials."

"Keep it for yourself."

"Let's go eat something. OK?"

He replied angrily, "There's no reason to eat anything."

I had come to the end of my wits. I went on gazing here and there around me, and my eyes fell on Shokrai's garden. I said, "Hey, Hasani, do you want to go steal walnuts?"

"Yeah, since I haven't been beaten enough today, let's go get caught by the gardener."

A while passed; neither of us said anything. Two men appeared from behind the ovens, stood watching us for a while, and then headed for the garden and jumped over the wall. The sounds of shouts and then of several men's laughter arose from within.

I said to Hasani, "Now, why are you angry with me?"

"I'm not angry with you."

We fell silent again. Hasani went on striking his toe with his stick. I said, "Cut that out. Are you going nuts?"

"All right. It doesn't hurt."

"Now you say something to do."

"I don't have anything to say."

I shouted angrily, "You're getting pretty sickening. Get up, let's go."

We both rose and set out. As we were passing between the wells I said, "Hasani."

"What?"

"Out with it, whatever you want, whatever you have in mind, I'm up for it."

"I want to beat the crap out of that punk father of mine."

"Fine. Well, go beat the crap out of him."

"I can't do it alone."

"It's obvious that you can't."

He stopped suddenly and asked, "Are you willing to go with me and give him what's coming to him?"

I thought a bit. Hasani's father was the enemy of children, one couldn't so much as look at him, he never answered anyone's hellos, he just went by glaring. My father would say that this bastard's crazy, a bit cracked, unsound of mind, you might say. Now how was I to go jump him? And if I didn't do it, Hasani would get annoyed and angry with me. I didn't want Hasani mad at me. I was reflecting on this when Hasani said, "Don't you want to help me?"

"Why not? I want to, I want to a lot."

"Then why don't you answer me?"

"So how are we to jump him?"

"You come to our place tonight. We each hide in a corner. When he comes after me, we suddenly attack and grab his legs and knock him down and wipe him out."

"And then what?"

"And then nothing. Just that he'll know what it feels like to be beaten. I'll be satisfied."

"OK."

So it was that we went to his place—not yet at night, but just at sunset when the sky was gray. Hasani's father hadn't shown up yet. Hasani's mother told us to go bring water for them. We went to the tap, got the water, and were waiting there, shifting from foot to foot, when Hasani's father appeared in the distance, bent over and with a bag over his shoulder. Hasani said, "The son of a bitch is coming."

We hurried off, took a short cut, and came up to his shanty. Hasani's ma was sitting outside cooking tomatoes over the lantern. Hasani's little brother was resting with his mama's arm around him, and was bawling. We went into the yard and, setting the pitcher of water by the window, went in. Their room was dark. Hasani's mother called from outside, "Hey, Hasani, light the lamp."

Hasani lit the lamp. His little sister had fallen asleep in a corner of the room. I hissed, "What do we do now?"

"Nothing. Sit there by the door and let things be."

I sat waiting. Hasani sat down at the other side of the room. No sign of the man yet.

Hasani said, "Don't forget just to grab his leg."

"What will you do?"

"First I'll jab him in the jaw, then I'll jump him and pound him into the ground."

Fear enveloped me. I didn't know how things would come out. I was waiting in this state when we heard his father outside roar and commence shouting, "You filthy slut, I hadn't come, what were you cooking dinner for?"

Hasani's mother answered, "What the hell am I to do, you always want to wolf something down about nightfall."

Hasani's father shouted, "Are you and your whelps eating too, you slut?"

Hasani's mother cried out, "Help, people! Help! Would to God that you get crippled and your legs be broken at the roots."

Hasani said, "You hear?"

"Hear what?"

"He's kicking my ma. The crazy pig!"

The yells of Hasani's father were heard again: "What's this son of a bitch doing hanging around here?"

"So where's he supposed to hang around?"

"How should I know, somewhere else, some other corner."

He came in the yard and set his bag and things beside the door. He began coughing, convulsing with cough after cough, spitting up phlegm. He cursed a while under his breath; he picked up the water jug, rinsed out his mouth, swallowed several gulps, and advanced towards the room. He took off his shoes. My heart had stopped. As his father entered the room, Hasani was the image of a frightened cat, half-crouching and inching back. His father gnashed his teeth and snarled a low snarl. Hasani, pinned against the wall, said, "What are you going to do?" His father smirked, "Nothing. With you, you snotty brat, what can one do?" Suddenly he became aware of me. He looked me over head to foot and fingered his mustache. I, terrified, began drawing back, still sitting. He sneered, "Light of my eyes, what's that fat baboon doing here?"

"He's my friend, Abdul Agha's son."

"Well then, what's he doing in my house?"

"I told him to come."

"You mean the wretches don't have a hovel of their own to crawl into?"

"Sure they have a house, a much nicer one too."

"So how did he wind up here?"

He turned to me and yelled, "Get up, beat it, go crawl into your own hovel."

As I rose fearfully he shrieked, "Yallah! Get hopping."

Said Hasani from the back of the room, "He's not going. He stays here."

Hasani's father turned and with clenched fists headed for Hasani, arms extended at either side, snarling, "You fruit of adultery, you've become so brazen you're standing as tall as your father?"

Hasani's little sister awoke with a start and ran panic-stricken and crying from the room. Hasani's father was advancing, raising his fists, when suddenly Hasani shouted, "Come on!" I charged in. As Hasani's father swung his fists down, Hasani leaped aside. The fists struck the wall. I threw myself forward and seized his leg. Hasani slipped out of his father's grasp and caught the other leg. We both jerked and Hasani's father fell shouting upon us. First a fist connected with my head and then another with Hasani's. The third and fourth struck our heads at the same time. The two of us struggled and freed ourselves from under the older man. Hasani, cursing under his breath, planted a firm kick in his father's flank and we both flew through the door. The sound of the man's yells boomed out, saying repeatedly, "Now I'm really going to get you pimps. You weren't enough so you're going for your cutthroat to do me in?"

He ran after us. Hasani's ma stood by the lantern wailing, not knowing what to do. We went by her and flew like the wind along a bypath toward the hollow. We heard the voice of Hasani's father shouting, "Catch them! Catch them!"

He ran for several paces behind us and then stood cursing and wailing. It had grown dark—no one followed us and no one felt like catching us. We vaulted into the hollow, panting, took each other's hands and waited to see if Hasani's father or anyone else would appear to seize us. I told Hasani, "Better we get out of the hollow."

"Yeah. Or you'll see the son of a bitch coming along with a club in his hand. Then we'll have had it."

We climbed out of the hollow and sat down on a small rise. As we caught our breath, I said to Hasani, "We did a good job of getting away from him."

"It's a shame we couldn't really work him over."

"When do you want to go back home?"

"Go home, like hell! God, he's just waiting for me to go back so he can get his hands on me and put me on the rack."

"So what do you want to do?"

"Nothing."

"Where will you spend the night?"

"Nowhere. I've got nowhere to go."

"Come over to our place."

"Right, fall into your pa's clutches. All of those bastards are cut from the same cloth; there's not a shred of mercy in them."

"If you don't go back tonight, what will you do tomorrow? What will you do day after tomorrow? Finally you'll have to go back."

"I'm not so sure. One of these days you'll look and see that I've up and gone somewhere else."

"Like where?"

"Wherever."

"To do what?"

"How should I know what I'll wind up doing? I'll become an apprentice, I'll run errands, I'll be a porter."

"You're little. No one will hire you."

"Why not!"

"Because you don't know how to do anything."

"So I don't know a trade, I can wash and sweep in front of stores."

"After all, you'd have to be bigger for them to accept you."

"I could still collect trash and sell it."

"Nights, where will you sleep?"

"In the ruins."

"It's no good. A day, two days, OK, finally you'll die of hunger or something will happen to you."

"Never! I won't die. I'll go and beg and stay alive."

"Right. So keep on dreaming."

"So what should I do?"

"I don't know what you should do, it seems better to me that you go back home."

We both fell silent. The moon had come out and most everywhere was lit up, except for the dark circles of the wells which nothing could light up. Lanterns could be seen here and there among the shanties. Hasani looked them over and said, "There's no going back home now, he'd peel the skin off my head."

We again fell silent and listened to the crickets. Hasani suddenly jumped up and said, "Listen, I've got a plan. You get up now and run like hell to the houses and start crying and carrying on and yelling and start an uproar and say Hasani's fallen in a well."

I jumped up with my heart leaping to my throat, and I cried, "You mean you want to throw yourself into a well?"

"You think I'm such a jackass that I'd throw myself into a well? You just say I've fallen, and then you'll see my pa pass out cold, then you'll see him get his."

"And then?"

"And then nothing. I'll go and settle down somewhere."

"Then they'll go search the wells."

"They can't search all the wells. What if they look at one or two? Finally they'll get tired and guess that I've died. Then they'll get together and cry for me, and read out of the Koran. My ma and pa will beat their heads and say nice things about me."

"Hasani, this isn't a good thing to do."

"Why isn't it?"

"If your father should waste away or your ma die out of grief, what will you do?"

"You're imagining things, it's not like that at all. I know

them better. They won't waste away and they won't die out of grief. When at last they've made mincemeat of themselves and beaten their heads and chests you come quietly and let me know, I'll go running home. When they see I'm alive and haven't fallen in the well, you don't know how happy they'll be. I think my pa will make peace and not beat me any more."

"After all . . ."

"After all what?"

"After all I'm afraid of your father. I'm afraid after I say this thing he'll get me and kill me."

"What do you have to do with my father? When you get to the houses, start crying out and beating on your head and say 'Hasani's fallen in the well! Hasani's fallen in the well!' "

"Then I'll have to cry. What if I can't?"

Hasani looked me up and down and said, "What a jackass you are! In the dark who will know whether you're crying or not?"

"OK. Then what will you do?"

"I'll go sit in some cranny of the kiln."

"And when you die of hunger?"

He asked with a note of surprise, "You mean you won't bring me water and bread? Huh? You really won't come?"

"Of course I'll come."

"Fine, so get going."

I was starting to go when Hasani spoke again. I said, "What is it?"

"Don't forget I'm hungry. Bring me some bread and water in the morning."

"OK, I'll come for certain."

I circled the kiln and went between the wells and plunged into the hollow. Some dogs were gathered there; they fled when they saw me. My throat was clogged with dust, so I drank a little water at the tap. I remembered that I had to run harder and to yell bloody murder. At once I was as if uprooted. I sped screaming toward the shanties. A crowd was gathered around our place. I didn't know what was up. You would think, to hear me, Hasani had really and truly fallen into the well; I started to raise a ruckus and to wail. The crowd milled forward. I saw my father and Hasani's father, who it seemed bounded at me in unison. I wailed with a tear-choked voice, "Hasani, Hasani!" Hasani's father, standing there with a club in his hand, asked, "What happened to Hasani? Huh? What happened?"

"He fell, he fell, he fell!"

And I started crying in earnest, tears pouring down my face. Hasani's pa shouted, "Where did he fall, tell me, where did Hasani fall?" I yelled, "In the well, he fell in the well!" For a moment all were silent, and then a strange murmuring arose. A jumble of voices near and far shouted, "Hasani's fallen in the well, Hasani's fallen in the well!"

People lost their heads and didn't know what to do. Those who were in their houses poured out. Some brought lanterns, and all set out running for the upper part of the hollow. I was stretched out on the ground and wailing when my papa bent over me and took my hand to pull me to my feet, saying, "Get up, come on, let's see, which well did he fall into?" We went running after the others. We hadn't yet crossed the road when several men surrounded me, running right along with my papa and me, asking repeatedly, "Which well, which one did he fall in?"

We passed the hollow and reached the terrace of the wells. The moon had risen farther and the circles of the wells had become darker, more abysmal. Everyone was standing around; Hasani's father swayed like a willow. He seized my arms and shook me, saying, "Which one? Which one?"

Before I could answer, he threw himself onto the trash heap and began wailing loudly. Two or three men approached him. Abbas Charkhi kept trying to comfort him, saying, "Don't worry a bit, we'll have him out of there in no time, nothing's the matter, don't cry, take it easy, for we'll find him soon."

By the time Hasani's father had settled down, a chorus of murmurs had arisen. The women arrived weeping, Hasani's mother in front of them all, pounding her head and clawing at her face, moaning from the bottom of her heart, "My Hasani, my Hasani, my Hasani!"

She said other things that couldn't be understood. Abbas Charkhi came nearer and said to me, "Listen, child. Tell us which one he has fallen into."

"I don't know."

Hasani's father rushed me shouting, "Bastard! Say what really happened to my child!" Agha Ghader restrained him and told him, "Get hold of yourself. Let him say what happened." I swallowed my sobs and said, "Hasani's father had caught us and was going to beat us up."

Hasani's father broke in, "Just tell us where he fell!"

My papa told me, "Hurry up and tell us!"

Abbas Charkhi said, "Let him have his say, man. How did it happen?"

"We got out and came here. Hasani was way in front of me, we were both running. Hasani was afraid his pa would catch up and grab us, he ran faster than me. I turned around and looked behind me and saw he wasn't coming, nobody was coming. I yelled, 'Wait, Hasani!' but he didn't wait. Just then all of a sudden he screamed and fell."

Hasani's father shouted, "Where did he fall!"

"I thought the earth had swallowed him up. I called and called, but he didn't answer. However much I looked I couldn't find him."

"Which one did he fall in!"

Abbas Charkhi said threateningly, "How should he know which one he fell in? Let's go find him ourselves."

Then he turned to the men and said, "Get moving, come forward, be careful!"

As they set out they fell silent. No one cried, no one shouted. Only Hasani's mother slowly moaned as the other women kept telling her, "Be calm, sister, don't fuss, they'll find him now and get him out."

A number kept going "Shhh." You'd think Hasani was sleeping and likely to awaken. They passed alongside several wells, then Hasani's father lowed like a cow, "Hasani, Hasani." He was so enraged and nasty that if Hasani had, say, actually fallen in a well and could come out, he would have seized him and subjected him to more blows and kicks. Abbas Charkhi said, "Calm down a bit. Cool down and let us go about our work."

Someone said from out of the darkness, "We must have rope and lanterns. We can't go into wells empty-handed."

Several went running to the houses, and a couple of lanterns were brought up. Abbas Charkhi took one of the lanterns and, stretching out by one of the wells, held it over the opening. Everyone had formed a circle around the well. Abbas, his head in the well, said in a muffled voice, "I don't think he's fallen in this one."

And so they went to the next well. This time it was Mosayyeb who stretched out flat and, holding the lantern over the well, said with an elastic voice like a peddlar's, "Where are you, child, where are you?"

There was no answer; they went on to the third well. Then to the fourth well. Then to the fifth well. Then to the sixth. Then they split into two groups, into four groups. Then extra lanterns were brought, seven or eight lanterns and a lot of rope. Several began knotting the ropes. The more they went on with no sign of Hasani, the more angry they grew, and the more argumentative. After a while everyone was called to one well, that is, Abbas Charkhi called everyone, and everyone hastily swarmed to it. Abbas Agha said agitatedly, "I think he's here, I heard something, it's as if someone is crying in there." All fell silent. Several stretched out and stuck their heads in the well, listened and said, "Yeah. This is it."

Hasani's papa started raising Cain: "Hurry, hurry, get my boy out of there, get my boy out!"

Mosayyeb said, "Who will go down?"

Ghader said, "The well is old, it might cave in."

Hasani's father said, "By God, it won't fall in. Go on in, go in and get him out."

Everyone looked at one another. Abbas Charkhi said, "No one's man enough? I'll go myself. Pass the rope and let's see."

Abbas' wife cried out from among the women, "Not you, not you, you can't, you don't know how!"

Abbas shouted angrily, "What's it to you, bitch? Shut up. I can't let the boy die in there!"

His wife shoved everyone aside, ran up, and clung to Abbas Agha, saying, "Don't go in, don't go in, by God, don't go in!"

Abbas gave his wife a firm slap and said, "Get lost, you're being impossible."

Then he shouted with firmness, "Rope!" They brought rope and tied it around Abbas' waist. Then they tested the knots one by one. Abbas Agha said, "Be careful. Don't let go of me on the way down!"

Several said, "Don't worry. We'll be careful."

Abbas made ready; he grabbed one of the lanterns, doubled over and looked down the well, then handed the lantern to someone and said "Bismillah" loudly. Everyone prayed then. Hasani's father raised his hands to the sky and said, "O Most Merciful of the merciful, O Grandfather of Hosein the Oppressed, O Grandfather of Fatemeh the Pure, O Grandfather of Khadijeh the Magnificent, bring up my child alive, bring Hasani back alive!"

Abbas was hanging in the well with his elbows resting on the rim and was saying, "Watch that rope closely; when I jerk on it pull me up." His wife behind us started crying; my ma comforted her. Then Abbas descended. The rope was held by five or six of the men, who clutched it tightly and released it handspan by handspan. They muttered things to each other. Hasani's pa was walking around in circles, saying things like, "O God! O God!" I had completely forgotten that Hasani was at the kiln; in the bottom of my heart I was saying, "Oh, if only Hasani were in there and Abbas Agha wouldn't come out empty-handed, and everything would be OK!" After a while my pa, who was holding the rope with the others, said, "Haul it up, haul it up, haul it up."

Rahmat said, "What for?"

"The rope is shaking, are you blind or something?"

All fell silent, and they started drawing up the rope. Hasani's father was peering over the heads of the others and waiting for Abbas Agha to appear. Then Abbas' two hands grasped the rim of the well, he drew his elbows up to the rim, hauled himself over it, and flung himself across the ground. Ghader asked, "Wasn't he in there? Wasn't he in there?" Hasani's pa started with a wail to cry and groan. Abbas Agha rolled over and sat up, saying, "I was suffocating."

Ghader said, "That's all?"

"All there was in there was the carcass of a fat dog."

Mosayyeb said, "You're sure?"

"Imbecile, I couldn't tell Hasani from a dead dog?"

He got up and removed the rope from his waist. Everyone came together again and went to another well, then to a third, then to a fourth. They divided again, redivided, and would kneel over each well, calling Hasani. At that point I ran off and headed for the houses, slipping through the shadows and byways so that none would see me. I drank some water from the tap and then passed behind the tin wall. I crept into our own place. No one was there. I scooped up a loaf of flatbread and a handleless pitcher. I scurried out, and, reaching the tap again, collected some water. I passed the hollow, turned at the roadside, and reached Hajj Timur's Kiln at the same recess Hasani was staying in. I peeped in and softly called him. He didn't answer. I called him again; he didn't answer. I called him loudly; there was nothing. I was afraid. Then I said to myself, "God forbid he mistake me for someone else," and I started whistling—the whistle of a bulbul saying, "Come on, Hasani, it's time to get going." At once the sound of Hasani's whistle came from above my head. He was stretched out on the platform and was watching me. I said, "Hey, Hasani!"

"Come up carefully."

I handed him the pitcher, grasped the bricks of the wall, and climbed. We both crawled slowly forward and sat by the base of the kiln's chimney. I said, "Hadn't we decided that you would wait down there?"

"I climbed up to see what was going on."

"You know what would happen if they saw you?"

"No way. No one will see me."

He began to laugh.

"What are you laughing for?"

"I'm laughing at my old man, at all of them. Look at them, how should they know?"

He pointed to the terrace of the wells. A number with lanterns in hand were going this way and that around the wells. Others were as if nailed to one well, and weren't moving.

"We've done something very bad, Hasani."

"Why?"

"Your father's killing himself, you don't know the state he's in."

"Don't worry, he won't kill himself. What's my mother doing?"

"She's beating her head and chest. She keeps crying."

"Let her."

"You don't know how it is. Abbas Agha went down a well, and instead of finding you, he found a fat dog's body down there."

"He's found his father's body."

We both laughed. I took out the bread and we split it. I wasn't thirsty, but Hasani gulped down some water. I said, "Now shouldn't we go down to them?"

"For what?"

"To get the thing over with; they can't go through all those wells one by one."

"It's much too soon. Let them try."

"Some of them might fall in a well and die."

"Don't worry. They all have dogs' lives and nothing'll happen to them."

"This is an awful thing we've done."

He turned and looked me up and down, and said, "Isn't it an awful thing they do always coming and going and beating us before we eat?"

"For God's sake cut it out, Hasani. Come on, let's go back."

"I can't go."

"After all, why not?"

"I'll go back and what will I say?"

"Say you'd gone to Shokrai's garden to eat walnuts."

"Then they'd find out you were lying."

"I'll say, how should I know where you'd gone, I thought you'd fallen in the well."

"No, the cat will be out of the bag, and it'll all be up for us."

"By God, let it be. Come on."

"I'm not coming. I can't come."

"Then I'll go and say Hasani hasn't fallen in a well, that you're staying at Hajj Timur's Kiln."

He turned, looked at me angrily, and said, "Fine. Go and tell. From then on we'll have nothing to do with each other, you'll see me when you see the back of your ear."

"Then when do you want to go back to your house?"

"The day of mourning, when they read the Koran for me. All of a sudden I'll come in. That will feel so great!"

"Don't talk garbage. What'll be so great about it?"

"It's so obvious. When everyone is beating their heads and chests, I'll just quietly saunter up, walk in real nonchalantly and say 'Salaam.' First everyone will be scared, they'll cringe, the women'll scream, the children will run away thinking I've come back from the other world. Then when they see, no, it's just me, I'm alive, I see, I laugh, I move my hands and feet, they'll all be happy, they'll leap in the air, they'll fall on the ground, they'll keep hugging me and kissing my face. You don't think that's going to be fun? Really?"

I again fastened my eyes upon the people going around the wells with their lanterns. Now and then I would hear the shouting of the men or the women. I said, "So I guess I'll be going back."

"Go on, but don't let on to them where I am."

I crawled down from the recess on all fours, looked around, and jumped to the ground. I passed by the roadside, fell into the hollow, and climbed out again. Everyone had formed a circle around one well. I too went running up to it. I saw my mother pounding on her head and wailing. The men had a rope hanging down the well. I squeezed through and reached the rim. I saw Abbas Agha saying to the other men, "Haul up, haul up."

Ghader asked, "What for?"

"Are you blind or something, can't you see it's shaking?"

All fell silent and started hauling on the rope. Hasani's father behind me was rhythmically beating on his chest and saying, "O Great Khadijeh! O Prophet Mostafa! O Stranger of Strangers! O Lord of the Martyrs!"

Then I saw my papa with his elbows on the rim of the well drawing himself up. He was black from head to foot and was gasping. Abbas Agha said, "Lie down, stretch out and catch your breath." Several men clasped my father under the arms and stretched him out alongside the well.

Come morning, no one went to work, all returned exhausted to their shanties. They hadn't found Hasani. Abbas Charkhi said, "It's no use, no one can inspect all the wells."

They had just been around the deeper wells which opened to one another and through which sewage passed. In their black depths weird things had been seen. Usta Habib had run across some creature, about the size of a cow, having four tails and with a dead man's head between its teeth, going this way and that. The Sayyed had encountered a bunch of naked people covered with wool clinging to the sides of the well; when they saw him they leaped into the sewage and disappeared. Mir Jalal had seen with his own eyes huge, black wings that flew around by themselves. They said weird sounds had come forth from the very depths, sounds of cats wailing, and the raucous laughter of women unseen. Several had even heard cymbals and trumpets, such as are played during the mourning ceremonies on the Day of Ashura, and they had heard wailing and crying behind them.

Abbas Agha said that it was no use, the jig was up, there was no way to find Hasani. So then they returned home tired and sleepy, and collapsed. All but Hasani's father, who kept on wandering about, around the shanties, jerking his head right to left, forward to back, pounding his hands together and saying, "Did you see what happened? Did you see how my child has gone away? How death has taken him?"

Hasani's father no longer wailed and cried. Instead he began getting hung up on pointless things, the roofs of the houses, the dark openings of tombs, covered barrels ranged along the walls, stains on the gunny sacks hung in front of the houses. Now and then he would stop and bend over to pick some indifferent thing up off the ground, like a scrap of tin, or a broken glass cup, or a worn-out shoe, and would fiddle with it, only to throw it away and go after something else, muttering, "Now they're eating him, it's all over, my Hasani is finished."

I circled around him several times; it was always the same, he wouldn't see me, or he would see me and not care. After a few minutes of this, I remembered that Hasani would be hungry and waiting for me. I went to our place. All were asleep. My pa had flopped over so that his muddy feet stuck out. I snitched a loaf of bread and a fistful of sugar that was near at hand. I went out again. Everything was sullen and gloomy. I saw Hasani's father standing behind a house scraping his fingernail across something on the wall. The sun had risen and lit everything up. When I came up to the tap I drank some water. No one was around. I plunged into the hollow, and beyond the upper margin, I reached Hajj Timur's kiln, and went toward the recess, knowing Hasani was there. Hasani was sleeping. When I called him he awoke violently, frightened, shouting, "Who is it? Who is it?"

"Don't worry. It's just me."

He rose and sat up. His appearance had changed, his eyes were sunken, his hands shook. I said, "What's new with you? Anything happened?"

"I dreamed that I fell in a well and whatever I tried I couldn't get out."

"It's your own fault, you wanted to keep up this game. Your pa has cracked up and lost his mind."

He said nothing but drew himself outside. We both sat in the sun. I handed him the bread and handful of lump sugar. He hadn't finished his water. He picked up the pitcher, gulped some down, and splashed some over his face. As he came to he asked, "How have things gone?"

"They're sure now you've died."

"What did you do?"

"I didn't do anything. I didn't say anything."

"Now what do they want to do?"

"They haven't decided on anything."

"Aren't they going to read the Koran for me?"

"I don't know, I haven't heard anything."

"I think they'll do it this afternoon."

"Where do you get that?"

"Do you remember when Bibi's grandson died? They read the Koran the day after."

"If it's like that, this is your big day all right."

"Yeah, God let it be today. I can't put up with any more of this."

"God willing this will be the day."

"You won't forget to come tell me?"

"No, why should I forget? But get yourself ready for a real beating."

"No way. I'll just make them happy."

"Go on thinking that. You'll see."

"Want to bet?"

"What's the bet?"

"If they get sore about like why am I alive and didn't die and they rush me and beat me up, you win, and if they're glad, I win and you'll get a real beating from me."

"Great—I've gone through all this for you and in return you want to beat me up?"

He laughed and said, "I'm kidding, I'll buy you an ice cream."

"OK. You're on."

He tore off a piece of bread and stuffed it in his mouth. He asked, "Now what do we do?"

"Nothing. You go stay in this cranny, and I go to the houses to see what happens."

"If the reading is tonight, you'll let me know?"

"Sure."

The reading, Hasani's reading, was that afternoon, in front of the houses. Abbas Agha had nailed a piece of black cloth on the end of a stick and had speared the stick into the ground at the head of the square. All were sitting outside, the women on one side and the men on the other. People from other places had been informed and were coming in bands. From Yusof Shah Hollow, from the tenements of Sarpich, the kilns of Shamsabad, the hovels of Shotor Khun and Molla Ahmad Hollow. They were all strangers, with many-colored clothing. As they entered the square, the women ran up to Hasani's mother, who was sitting with her gashed and bloody face in front of their house, without tears, striking her head and sometimes pounding her chest. As the women came before her they would begin to cry, lashing out at their own faces and saying, "Dear sister, dear sister, what has befallen you, what has befallen you?"

Hasani's father was sitting in front of our place, not exactly sitting, but sprawled on the ground, staring ahead senseless. Whoever came and understood who the dead boy's father was came forward and proffered a greeting. Not hearing a reply, he would turn aside to seat himself. Abbas Agha, who was standing, bellowed, "Fatihah!"

The men recited the Fatihah, the Opening of the Koran. Usta Habib went about the assemblage with a pitcher giving water to the thirsty. Two old men who had come from the Ghoriba Hollow with a pouch of tobacco were rapidly rolling cigarettes in newsprint and setting them in a tray. Bibi's eldest son Ramazan was passing the tray among the people. All smoked and drank, aside from Hasani's pa, who did neither, and who would often run his tongue over his lips, and would sometimes spit on the ground.

An hour had passed when a number appeared hastening from the road. Everyone turned and looked. Abbas Agha shouted, "The Gypsies of the Black Tents from Elders' Hollow are coming. Let's go meet them."

Several set out. The Gypsies, puffing heavily, came forward running, many holding banners. In front of everyone were several old men in worn-out clothing who, distraught, beat their breasts. Amidst them was a thin *akhond*[1] with a long neck and a small turban. The women came behind, all of them barefoot and dusty. As they reached the little square, the sounds of prayers arose. The men and women separated, the women running shrieking toward Hasani's ma, the old man greeting his pa, he not answering. Then the *akhond* went off to sit on the steps of our place. Esmail Agha shouted, "Make prayers! Make them loud!"

All offered prayers. The *akhond* said in a hoarse, nasal voice, "Be seated, all be seated, all be seated, be seated so that we may weep and recite the doleful story of Ghasem son of Hasan, how he found martyrdom at Karbala, in remembrance of this other unfortunate youth." He first read a strange prayer and then started into reciting the story. Crying and wailing arose spontaneously. Everyone cried, the men cried, the women cried, their children cried, even I cried. Only Hasani's father did not cry but kept wandering from

---

[1] *akhond*: clergyman.

here to there running his tongue over his parched lips. The crying grew louder and louder, the Gypsies rose and bared their chests, the *akhond* rose and bared his chest, saying with a loud voice, "Now to rejoice the Lord of the Martyrs and the dear unfortunate one, we will beat our breasts."

He began reciting songs of mourning. The Gypsies began beating their breasts. The other men stood and bared their breasts and began beating them. The shrieks of the women swelled in volume as they stood arm in arm, wailing. Suddenly I remembered now is the time. Now I must go tell Hasani.

No one was paying any attention to me, no one was paying any attention to anyone at all but himself. I slipped away quietly, first I backed away, then I turned and sped off. I wiped away my tears. As I reached the tap, I drank some water, then I plunged into the Body Washer's Hollow and climbed out. No one was around. I started running. Streaking like the wind I circled the rings of the wells and went on. My heart was full of dread, sweat was pouring down my face as I reached Hajj Timur's Kiln, circled, and popped up in front of Hasani's niche. Hasani was stretched out on the platform. When he saw me he stood up, strode out, and said,

"What's happening?"

"They're mourning you."

"What are they doing?"

"People have come from everywhere and are beating their chests for you."

He stared at me for a moment and said, "What were you crying for?"

"For you."

"What a jackass you are! You knew I was alive and hadn't died."

"It's all the fault of the *akhond* that the Gypsies brought along. He made everybody cry."

He clapped his hands together in delight and said, "So it's time, right?"

"All right, I think it's time."

"Now we'll see who wins the bet."

"May God have you win."

He laughed and said, "Run, we're off!"

At once he was as if torn from the spot. And I after him. We both charged ahead, but Hasani, like the wind, was flying; he ran so fast no one could catch up with him. Several times I shouted, "Hasani! Hasani!"

He answered, "Hoo! Hoo!"

When suddenly, I don't know at all what happened, how could I say what happened, Hasani struck his foot against a heap of rubbish and—just so—fell, he fell right into a well. I thought—I mean I didn't think Hasani had fallen in a well—I thought that the earth had swallowed him. I ran up. There was no Hasani, Hasani had fallen in a well. In a huge well, bigger than all the rest of them. My tongue became tied in knots. I wanted to shout "Hasani!" but I couldn't, I had no voice, my mouth wouldn't open. No matter how much I tried, I couldn't say "Hasani!" I sat on the hill of garbage and clutched my shoulders. I couldn't catch my breath. Three times I pounded my head on the garbage and then I got up, not of myself—it seemed something picked me up and set me on my two feet. I started to run again. Faster than ever, faster than Hasani had run. I wished I had leaped and fallen in a well. Suddenly I found myself running down the road. As I reached the tap, I caught my breath, my tongue came untied, and I said softly, "Hasani! Hasani! Hasani!"

As I entered the square, the breast beating had come to an end, and all were silently sitting facing each other. Ramazan was passing out cigarettes among the men and Usta Habib was going here and there carrying the pitcher of water. I shrieked, "Hasani! Hasani! Hasani!" I pounded my head hard with my fists and rolled on the ground. All rose and swarmed over me. Abbas Agha, who was the first to reach me, took my hands so I wouldn't beat on myself and asked me, "What happened? What happened?"

I shouted, "Hasani, Hasani fell in the well!"

I rolled over and bit the ground. A murmuring and then a clamor arose. Everyone wanted to calm me down, they kept saying, "OK, OK, may God have mercy on him, don't hit yourself any more, be calm." I shouted, "Just now he fell, just now, this very minute he fell, Hasani fell in the well." My pa pushed the others back and came forward saying, "Shut up, child. Don't make things more painful for his father and mother."

"He fell, he fell in the well before my eyes."

"I said shut your mouth, be silent, you little jackass."

He picked me up and gave me a hard slap on the ear. Esmail Agha pulled my father back and roared, "Don't hit him, you son of a bitch, can't you see he's out of his head and his senses are deranged?" He took me in his arms then and said, "Calm down, calm down."

Usta Habib put a glass of water into the hand of Esmail Agha, and Esmail Agha poured it over my face. However much I struggled to get free from the arms of Esmail Agha it was no use. Several helped him keep me from fleeing. I was wailing loudly, "Hasani fell, he fell in the well! Hasani! Hasani!" when Esmail Agha clapped a large hand over my mouth, and everyone dragged me into our own house. As I was dragged past Hasani's father, I looked at him and pointed at the wells with my hand. He didn't look at me, he wasn't aware of me, he just went on staring ahead. As we entered my house, Esmail Agha said, "Be still, child, everyone knows Hasani was your friend, you liked each other a great deal, now what can one do, this was the will of fate."

I yelled, "He fell just now, he fell just now!"

I tried to break away and get out but they didn't allow it. My pa said, "What do we do with him? Huh? What do we do with him?" Esmail Agha said, "He's gone crazy. It's best we bind his hands and feet." So then they bound my hands and feet. I started to wail. My father said, "What do we do about his wailing?" Esmail Agha said, "We'll gag him." They gagged me and tossed me into a corner. My father rubbed his hands together and said over and over, "What will I do, my God, my God, if he stays this way, what the hell am I to do!"

Esmail Agha said, "Don't worry, right now we'll go ask the *akhond* of the Gypsies to write out a talisman for him, then he'll improve."

Usta Habib said, "If he doesn't get better we'll take him to the shrine at Shah Abdul Azim." My father moaned a long-drawn-out moan, and began walking in circles, saying, "O Imam of the Age, O Imam of the Age, O Imam of the Age!" Esmail Agha said, "Better we leave him alone, perhaps he'll come around." They left the house and fastened the door. The sounds of the gathering's prayers arose again and the hoarse, nasal voice of the *akhond* of the Gypsies read the eulogy.

(TRANSLATED BY ROBERT A. CAMPBELL)

POETRY

FORUGH FARROKHZAD

God's Revolt

Were I God, I'd call one night upon the Angels
    To drop the sun's disc in the furnace of the dark.
In wrath, I'd tell the keepers of this world's garden
    To strip the months' yellow leaves from the branches of the
      nights.

All in the night, behind the veils of my own Majesty's audi-
      ence-hall,
    My raging anger's fist would overset the world;
My tired hands, after millennia of silence,
    Would rain down mountains into oceans' open mouths.

The feet of thousands of feverish stars, I would unshackle,
    I'd cast fire's blood into the quiet veins of forests;
I'd tear smoke's veils, so that in the roaring of the wind
    Fire's daughter could dance, drunk, in forests' embrace.

Into the charmer's reed I'd blow a nightly wind,
    So that rivers from their beds would rise like thirsty ser-
      pents,
And—tired of a lifetime's sliding over bosoms dank—
    Would sink into the dark morass' heart of night's own sky.

I'd tell the winds to calm, so that upon the bank of feverish
      night
    Skiffs might be launched, tipsy with the perfume of red
      roses.
I'd open up the graves, and vagrant spirits in their thousands
    Would hide once more within the bodies' fortress.

Were I God, I'd call one night upon the Angels

To boil Kowsar[1] water within Hellfire's furnace,
And—burning torch in hand—to drive the flocks of ab-
stinents
Out of the green, polluted pastures of Paradise,

Tired of divine restraint, all in the night at Satan's pillow,
Down error's steep slope I'd once again seek refuge;
With all the glory of the golden crown of Lordship, I would
choose
The dark and pain-stained pleasure of a sin's embrace.

(TRANSLATED BY G. M. WICKENS)

O Realm Bejewelled

I came out a winner
Got myself registered
Dressed up in an ID Card with a name
I'm numbered, therefore I am
Long live 678 stamped at Precinct 5 Tehran resident

Now all my worries are over
At the loving breast of my motherland
Glorious history trickling warmly down
Crooning culture and civilization
Rattlerattle goes its law
Oooo
My worries are all over now

Ecstatic with joy
I stride to my window and fervidly, six hundred seventy-
eight times, gulp lungfuls of air, shitdusted
and treated with essence of piss and garbage
And at the bottom of six hundred seventy-eight IOU's
and on the heads of six hundred seventy-eight jobforms I
sign *Forugh Farrokhzad*

[1] A river of the Muslim Paradise.

What bliss to live
in this land of poetry, roses and bulbul birds
especially since they've taken note, after so many years,
    that one actually exists
What do I see here
with my first registered glimpse through the blinds but
    six hundred seventy-eight poets
every one of them with the mug of some exotic bum
scounging in the dump for rhymes and meters, the
    phonies

And at the noise of my first registered steps
six hundred seventy-eight mystical bulbuls flit
    from their slimy swamp
transmogrifying themselves into six hundred seventy-
    eight old crows flapping lazily
off the edge of the day

And my first registered inhalation
comes soaked with the scent of six hundred seventy-eight
    neoprine roses
distilled at the giant PLASCO factory

Yes what bliss living
in the town Sheik Abou Ben Boffo the junkie fiddler
    was born in
and Sheik Hearthrob Tambourine, that son of a son of
    a drum
My city of superstar legs and hips and boobs and slick
    pix on the covers of *ART*
incubator of that school of thought whose founders de-
    clare *What the hell you want me to do about it*
nursery of intellectual Olympics *Ye-Ye*
where Media Central is broadcasting turned-on prodigies
blowing their own kazoos on our portable TV's

And as for our Persian intelligentsia
whenever they put in an appearance at senior citizen
    classes
their chests are bedecked with six hundred seventy-eight
    electric kebab griddles
left wrists and right wrists braceleted with six hundred
    seventy-eight Timex watches, and they know
in their hearts the empty pocket makes you weak,
    and not the empty head

I came out a winner oh my yes came out a winner
Now by way of celebrating
I place six hundred seventy-eight votive candles at my
    dressing table mirror and proudly light them (charge
    it to my account)

And hop on my windowsill to offer for your consider-
    ation some words concerning
pardon the expression, please, the authorized goals of
    life

And to thunderous applause I raise my pick
to break ground for the lofty tower of my life
just where the hair parts on top of my head

I live oh my yes like the abandoned Zend River,
    which lived once too
snatching my share of whatever we the living have
    sole rights to
Beginning tomorrow I'll stroll
through our town's alleys where national blessings
    abound,
among shady groves of carefree telephone poles
I will scrawl six hundred seventy-eight times, yes
    proudly, on the walls of the public johns

THIS SONG I SANG FOR JACKASSES HEEHAWS

Beginning tomorrow, like a bold patriot
I'll cherish in heart and mind
some of the noble ideal we pursue
each Wednesday afternoon
so avidly so anxiously
one share in that hundred-dollar lottery of whims
good for furniture, curtains and a fridge
or redeemable for six hundred seventy-eight naturalized
    votes
which I can donate tomorrow night to six hundred sev-
    enty-eight sons of the fatherland

Beginning tomorrow, after a few snorts
at a bag of pure first-rate shit
in the back room of Xachik's shop

and three glasses of ersatz Pepsi
and intoning some Hallelujahs and woofwoofs and
    miaows
I'll be ready to enroll in the ranks of academe among
    the surplus ordures of the intellectual élite
and disciples of the Oompah Oompahpah School
and the manuscript of my Great Persian Novel
will go to the bankrupt press
some time in the Tabriz Solar Year One Thousand
    Six Hundred Seventy & Eight
its plot outline on both sides of six hundred
    seventy-eight packets of
Genuine Special OSHNU cigarettes

Beginning tomorrow, with utter confidence
I can invite myself to six hundred seventy-eight sessions
    of a certified velvet-upholstered association
at the Congress for Collecting and Guaranteeing the Fu-
    ture
or the Senate of Grateful Praise
because I've read *every* issue of the *JOURNAL OF
    ART & SCIENCE* and all the numbers of
    ETIQUETTE & SUCKING
and learned 'How to Write'

So, here I am front and center with the chorus of con-
    structive citizens
advanced through our awe-inspiring science skills
to the breakthrough point for synthesizing clouds
thanks to our discovery of the neon billboard
where else but in the R & D Institutes of our fried
    chicken stands
Here am I front and center with the chorus of construc-
    tive clients
who, lacking bread, have substituted for it
an empty horizon
bordered on the North by the refreshing greenery of Ar-
    row Piazza
on the South by our venerable Execution Square
and reaching, via the overpopulated wards, all the way
    to Artillery Plaza
and, safe beneath its bright Canopy of Security
all the livelong day six hundred seventy-eight plump
    plaster swans

accompanied   by   six   hundred   and   seventy-eight
    amoretti—
cherubs concocted of mud and sand, by the way—are
    busily propagandizing our projects for stability, and
    silence

(TRANSLATED BY JASCHA KESSLER WITH AMIN BANANI)

Earthly Verses

Then
the sun grew cold
and blessing left the lands

The grass in the plains dried up
The fishes in the seas dried up
And the earth
no longer accepted its dead

Night, in all the pale windows,
constantly swelled and overflowed
like a doubtful notion
and the roads gave up
their prolongation, into darkness

No one thought of love any more
No one thought of conquest any more
No one
thought of anything any more

In the caves of loneliness
futility was born
The blood smelled of bhang and opium
Pregnant women
gave birth to headless infants
and the cradles, out of shame,
took refuge in the graves

What black and bitter days!
Bread had triumphed over
the wondrous strength of prophecy
The prophets, hungry and impoverished,

fled from the promised lands of God
and the lost lambs
no longer heard the shepherd crying "Hey",
in the consternation of the plains

In the eyes of the mirrors, it seemed
that movements, colors, images
were reflected upside down
Over the heads of base buffoons
and the shameless faces of prostitutes
burned a holy, brilliant halo
like a blazing parasol

The swamps of alcohol,
with their acrid, poisoned fumes,
drew towards their depths
the motionless mass of the enlightened
And in old cupboards
sly, destructive mice
chewed the gilded pages of books

The sun had died
The sun had died, and Tomorrow
had, in the children's minds,
a vague, lost meaning
They formed
the strangeness of this old word
in their copybooks
with a large, black spot

The people
The fallen group of people,
discouraged, crushed, dazed,
travelled from one exile to another
under the ill-omened burden of their bodies
and the painful desire for murder
swelled in their hands

Sometimes a spark, an insignificant spark,
suddenly shattered from within
this silent, lifeless group
They attacked each other
Men tore each other's throats
with knives,
and slept

with immature girls
in a bed of blood

They drowned in their own terror
The fearful sense of sinfulness
had paralyzed
their blind, dull souls

Always, at the hanging ceremonies,
when the rope's
pressure forced from their sockets
the convulsive eyes of the condemned,
they withdrew into themselves
and their old, tired nerves were taut
with a voluptuous image

But always, on the edges of the squares,
you would see these small murderers
standing,
staring, bewildered,
at the constant flowing of the fountains

Perhaps,
behind the crushed eyes, in the depths of stagnation,
something half alive, distressed,
still remained
which, in its dying struggle, sought
to believe in the purity of the waters' sound

Perhaps; but what an endless emptiness
The sun had died
and no one knew
that the name of that sorrowful dove
which had fled from their hearts, is Faith

Oh, prisoner's voice,
will the complaint of your despair never,
from any side of this hated night,
find a tunnel to the light?
Oh, prisoner's voice,
last voice of all.

Another Birth

All my existence is a dark verse
which will take you within itself, repeating,
to the dawn of eternal burstings and growings.
In this verse I sighed to you . . . Ah,
in this verse
I grafted you to tree and water and fire.

*   *   *

Perhaps life
is a street which, every day, a woman with a basket
    crosses.
Perhaps life
is a rope with which a man hangs himself from a
    branch.
Perhaps life is a child coming home from school.

Perhaps life is the lighting of a cigarette, in the slack
    space between two embraces,
or the giddy progress of a passerby
who tips his hat
and, with a meaningless smile, says to another passerby,
    "Good Morning."

Perhaps life is that closed-off moment
when my look destroys itself in the pupil of your eyes:
and in this is a sensation
which I will mix with the perception of the moon and
    the reception of darkness.

In a room the size of one loneliness,
my heart
which is the size of one love
looks at the simple pretexts of its happiness:
at the lovely fading of the flowers in the base,
the sapling you planted in the garden of our house,
and the song of the canaries
which sing—the size of one window.

Ah . . .
This is my lot.
This is my lot.
My lot
is a sky which the dropping of a curtain takes from me.
My lot is to go down an abandoned stairway
and join with something in decay and exile.
My lot is a sad walk in the garden of memories,
and dying in the sadness of a voice which says to me,
"I love
your hands."

I will plant my hands in the garden.
I will sprout—I know, I know, I know.
And in the furrows of my inky fingers, swallows
will lay eggs.

In my two ears I hang earrings
of twin red cherries
and stick dahlia petals to my fingernails.
There is a street where
the boys who were in love with me, still
with the same ruffled hair, thin necks and bony legs,
think of the innocent smiles of a girl whom, one night,
the wind carried away.

There is a street which my heart
has stolen from the places of my childhood.

The journey of a mass in the line of time
making pregnant with a mass the dry line of time
a mass of conscious image
which returns from feasting with a mirror.

And thus it is
that someone dies
and someone remains.

*   *   *

No fisherman will find a pearl in the vile stream which
    flows into a ditch.

I know a small, sad fairy
who lives in an ocean
and softly, softly, plays

her heart in a wooden pipe:
a small, sad fairy
who dies at night from a kiss
and at dawn, with a kiss, will be born into the world.

(TRANSLATED BY JULIE S. MEISAMI)

Window

one window for seeing
one window for hearing
one window that as a tubular body of a well
reaches at its depth into the heart of the earth
and opens to the vastness of this blue-colored recurrent
    kindness
one window that fills the little hands of loneliness
with the nocturnal gift
of the fragrance of the generous stars.
And thence, it is possible
to invite the sun to the desolation of the little geraniums
one window is enough for me.

I come from the realm of dolls
from beneath the shadow of paper trees
in the garden of an illustrated book
from the dry seasons of the barren experiences of friend-
    ship and love
in the dirt-alleys of innocence
from the years of the growth of the pale letters of the al-
    phabet
behind the desks of the tubercular schools
from the moment that the children could
spell "stone" on the black-board
and the startled starlings flew off the aged tree.

I come from within the roots of the carnivorous plants
and my brain still
overflows with the cry of horror of the butterfly
that they had crucified
in a notebook with a pin

When my faith hung from the frail rope of justice
and throughout the town

they tore to pieces the heart of my lights
when they blind-folded the childish eyes of my love
with the dark kerchief of laws
and from the anxious temples of my dreams
sprang out fountains of blood
when my life amounted to nothing, any longer
nothing except the tic toc of the clock on the wall
I understood that madly I must, must, must
love.

One window is enough for me
one window into the moment of consciousness and
    observation and silence
Now the walnut plant
has grown tall enough to explain the meaning of the
    wall
for its younger leaves
Ask the mirror
the name of your saviour
the earth that trembles beneath your feet
is it not more alone than you?
The prophets delivered the message of destruction
to our century
Are these continuous explosions
and poisoned clouds
the echoes of holy verses?
Oh friend, oh brother, oh blood-kin
When you reach the moon
record the history of the massacre of the flowers.

The dreams, always
fall from the height of their naivete and they die
I would smell the fragrance of a four-leaf clover
that has grown upon the grave of old concepts.
The woman that was buried in the shroud of her expec-
    tations and her chastity
was she my youth?
Will I again ascend the steps of my curiosity
to greet the good God who walks upon the roof top?

I feel that the time has passed
I feel that "the moment" of my portion is of the pages
    of history
I feel that the table is a false distance between my hair
    and

the hands of this sad stranger.

Speak a word to me
The person that bestows upon you the kindness of a liv-
    ing body
Would want from you what else but the perception of
    the sense of existence?

Speak a word to me
I, in the shelter of my window,
have communication with the sun.

(TRANSLATED BY ARDAVAN DAVARAN)

Friday

Silent Friday
deserted Friday
Friday of back streets, old miseries
Friday's languorous, languishing thoughts
Friday's spasms of yawns and stretching
futile Friday
sacrificed Friday

the house vacant
dismal house
house shuttered against the coming of the young
gloomed house vainly recalling the sun
house of desolations, doubting, divinings
curtains house, books house, closets and pictures house

*   *   *

O how my life passed, calmly proud
a strange and foreign stream
flowing through the heart of these mute, deserted Fri-
    days
the heart of these vacant, desolating houses
O how my life passed calmly proud . . .

(TRANSLATED BY JASCHA KESSLER WITH AMIN BANANI)

SOHRAB SEPEHRI

from

The Sound of Water's Footsteps

I am from Kashan . . .
I am a Moslem
my Mecca is a red rose
my prayer-spread the stream, my holy clay the light
my prayer-rug the field
I do ablutions to the rhythm of the rain upon the win-
    dowpane
In my prayer runs the moon, runs the light
the particles of my prayer have turned translucent
I answer to the prayer call of the wind's muezzin[1]
upon the minaret of the cypress tree
I say my prayer in the mosque of grass
and follow the sitting and rising of the wave.

My kaaba is by the water
beneath the acacia trees, and moves
like a breeze from orchard to orchard
from city to city
the Sacred Stone of my kaaba
    is the garden's light.

Our garden was on the other side of knowledge, in the
    shade
a place where the feeling interlaced with grass
the convergence point of glance, the cage, and the look-
    ing-glass
our garden was, perhaps, an arc from the green circle of
    happiness
the hard fruits I chewed, in dreams, were God's.
Those days the water I drank had no philosophy
the berries I picked had no knowledge

---

[1] *muezzin*: A Moslem cantor who calls the faithful to prayer. —Ed.

as soon as a pomegranate cracked
it became the stand of desire's fountain
when a bird sang, the joy of my listening trembled
whenever loneliness pressed its face against the window-
    pane
light came and put its arm around my shoulder
love came and told jokes—
what was life but a raining of new years
a pine full of starlings
light and joy standing in line
taking free rides to the pond full of music.

Then slowly the child tiptoed on the street of dragonflies
    and faded out of sight
I packed my belongings and left the city of carefree
my heart heavy with the nostalgia of dragonflies
I went to the world's party
to grief
to the garden of gnosis
to the patio of knowledge
I walked by the staircase of religion
and went as far as the street of doubt
as far as the cool air of desirelessness
as far as the rainy night of love
as far as the Woman
as far as pleasure's lamp
I heard the wingbeats of loneliness
and I saw many things
I saw a child who smelled the moonlight
I saw a cage without a door
where light fluttered its wings
a ladder upon which love climbed
to heaven's rooftop
a woman who rubbed the sunbeam in a mortar
at noon they had bread on their table, fresh basil leaves,
    a tray of dews, a bright bowl of ease

I saw many things upon the earth:
I saw a beggar who went from door to door
singing the larks' song
I saw a poet who addressed the lily of the valley as
    "lady" . . .
I saw a train carrying light
I saw a train carrying politics (and going so empty)

I saw a train carrying morning-glory seeds and canary
    songs
and a plane, through its window
a thousand feet high, one could see the earth:
one could see the hoopoe's crest
the butterfly's beauty-spots
the passage of a fly across the alley of loneliness
the luminous wish of a sparrow descending from a pine
the coming-of-age of the sun
and the bright embrace of the doll with the dawn.

Stairs that led to lust
stairs that led to the cellar of alcohol,
to the ordained putrefaction of the rose
to the perception of the arithmetic of life
stairs that led to the rooftop of illumination
stairs that led to the platform of the apocalypse.
. . .

I hear the sound of gardens breathing
the sound of the darkness raining from a leaf
the light clearing its throat behind the tree
the sneeze of water from every crack of the rock
the whisper of the swallow from spring's rooftop
the sound, so pure, of the window of silence
the sound, so light, of love shedding skin
the density of longing gathered in the wing
the bursting of the soul's resistance.
I hear the footsteps of desire
and the ordained sound from the passageways of blood
the throbbing of the wild pigeon's early dawn
the heartbeats of Friday night
the flow of the carnation on the mind
the sound of the rain on love's wet eyelids
the song of pomegranate orchards
the smash of the glass of happiness at night
the ripping of beauty's paper
the comings and goings of the wind in the wandering ex-
    ile's bowl.

I am near the beginning of earth
I take the pulse of flowers
I am acquainted with water's wet fate, trees' green
    course

my soul flows to the direction that is new
my soul is so young
it coughs with joy
my soul is a loafer
it counts raindrops, the brick tiles
sometimes, like a stream pebble, my soul is washed clean
    and shines
I haven't seen two pine trees hate each other
I haven't seen a poplar sell its shadow
the elm tree gives its branch to the crow at no charge
wherever there is a leaf I rejoice
the field-poppy has bathed me in the verve of life.
I don't know
why they say: a horse is a noble beast
a dove is pretty
and nobody keeps a hawk
why is a clover in bloom lesser than a red tulip . . .

Maybe our mission is not to fathom the "secret" of the
    rose
our mission is to swim in the essence of the rose
to wash our hands, before dinner, in the ecstasy of a leaf
to be born at dawn with the sun
to give wings to rapture, to let the passions take flight
to recognize the sky between the two syllables of "being"
to unburden the sparrow from the load of knowledge
to take back the name from the cloud,
the pine, the gnat, the summer
to climb to the altitude of love upon the wet feet of the
    rain
to open the door to man, to light, the plant, the moth
Maybe our mission is
to pause between the morning glory and Century
and run to the call of Truth.

(TRANSLATED BY MASSUD FARZAN)

AHMAD SHAMLU

Toward the Horizon

One day we will find our pigeons once more,
and kindness will take the hand of beauty

A day when the smallest song is a kiss,
and every man
a brother
to every other man

A day when they
no longer close the doors of their houses; when
locks

        are a myth

and hearts

        enough for life

A day when the meaning of every speech

        is loving,

so that you need not follow every speech
to catch the last word

A day when the rhythm of each word

        is life,

so that I no longer have to search for rhymes
for the sake of the last poem

A day when every lip

        is a song

so that the smallest song
may be a kiss

A day when you will come,

                                    come forever,

and kindness
will be one
with beauty

A day when, once more,
                we scatter grain

                                    for our pigeons

I am waiting for that day
even if it is a day
when I
no longer am

Hamlet

To be
or not to be
is not the question:
it is a temptation

The poisoned wine in the cup; and
the sword dipped in poison

                            in the hand of the enemy—

Everything
                clear and calculated

                    in advance,

and the curtain
                will fall

                        at the appointed moment.

Did my father sleep in the garden of Gethsemane,
that my role is the legacy of his deceiving trust,

and the bed of his deceit

my uncle's pleasure-ground!

(All of this

I suddenly understood

with a glance,

by chance,

at the audience.)

If trust had not,
                 like another Satan

in another Gethsemane,

lulled to sleep with ignorance

this other Cain—
God!
God!

What a deception—but, what a deception!
When he who sits beyond the dull curtain of darkness,
    watching,
knows the whole catastrophe,
and recognizes beforehand,
                 word for word,

my song of grief.

Beyond the dull curtain of darkness,
                 eyes,

the audience of my pain,

have spent coins of gold and silver
to obtain pleasure
from the design of weeping freely
in the confusion of voices and the breathing of him
                 who, seeming to pretend,

in truth
         contemplates hesitation.

Why should I ask their help, who finally
will call me and my uncle
         to bow before them, equally,

however much my suffering has been proclaimed to
   them?

                              when

Claudius
                is no longer an uncle's name

but a general concept
and the curtain . . .
at the appointed time . . .

With all this,
                         from the time that the truth,

like a wandering, restless spirit, was revealed to me,
and the stench of the world
                     assaulted my nostrils

like the smoke of a torch on false stages:
Question?—no, it is a temptation:
To be
or
not to be.

Threnody

On the leaden background of the dawn
the rider
           is standing still

the wind dishevels
                     the long mane of his horse.

God O God
the riders shouldn't stand still
at a time when warning is given.

                    &

By the burnt-down shed
the girl
           is standing still

her thin skirt

moving in the wind.

God O God
the girls shouldn't stand still
when the men
tired and despairing
                    are growing old.

Elegy for Forough

Looking for you
I weep at the doorway of the mountain
at the threshold of the sea and grass
Looking for you
I weep at the path of the winds
at the crossroad of seasons
in the broken rectangle of a window that sets the
                                        sky

in an old frame
Waiting for your picture
how long
            how long
one will turn the pages of this empty notebook?

                    *   *   *

To accept the course of the wind
and love
who is the sister of death.
Eternity
            shared its secret

                    with you. . . .

                    *   *   *

Your name is a dawn passing across the sky's brow
—Hallowed be your name!—
and we are still
turning around the day and night
tomorrow and tomorrow.

DRAMA

The Crows

by GOWHAR MURAD

(*A play in one act*)

Characters
HADI, an actor
BEHRUZ, a playwright
NAHID, Behruz' wife
TWO GARDENERS

A summer day in the country, a garden in full bloom. Behruz, the owner of the garden, and his city friend Hadi are strolling along a path while Nahid trails behind holding a child.

HADI: Yes, I know . . . but it's not that serious . . . You shouldn't pay any attention.
BEHRUZ: But you can't imagine how much I have suffered from all the jokes and snickers. I've told myself a thousand times that it was a mistake to publish "Memory of Atiq's Promise." You don't know what a flood of criticism and sarcasm ensued from every corner. In my letter to you I barely touched on it. A week after the publication I couldn't even step outside the house. After fully blasting the play, the paper went on to say, "Sir"—meaning me—"this kind of work isn't going to put bread on your table. Forget about your pride, stop fooling around and wasting ink and paper . . . if for no other reason than for the sake of your wife and child." And on top of that, they added a few inane verses satirizing the play. And then there was the letter from a high school teacher. After criticizing the play, he added sarcastically, "I know you will become the Molière of Iran." One of the week-

lies, I can't remember which one, said, "With the publication of this play, a Shakespeare in prose has risen on the horizon. We are dispatching our photographer forthwith to get an image of this newborn phenomenon from all angles." Goddammit! That's enough to tear a man apart.

HADI: No . . . No . . . Don't be silly. You can't take what everybody says seriously. When I first started in the theater, I never saw anything but cynical looks on people's faces. Now, I'm so used to things that even the applause doesn't mean anything. Do you see my point?

BEHRUZ: You may be right. It probably isn't worth the bother. But it is so discouraging. . . .

HADI (*Leaning against a tree*): When I'm on stage, I forget everything else. Honest to God. I see no one. I pay attention to nothing but what the playwright has written. When you write you have to forget everything else too.

BEHRUZ: By the way, what do you think of *The Crows*, the play I read to you yesterday? Did you really like it? Honestly.

HADI: It was tremendous . . . I swear. Would you believe I have memorized every line already? I read it more than five or six times last night and memorized all of it. If you wouldn't mind, when I get back to the city I'll have it staged at my own expense.

BEHRUZ (*Laughs*): I wonder where Nahid got to? Nahid, Nahid!

HADI: She's picking flowers. . . . Hey! Do you want to play out the last scene of *The Crows*?

BEHRUZ: Sure, but I'll . . .

HADI: OK . . . I'll be the First Murderer and you be the Second.

NAHID (*Comes over; the child laughs when it sees its father*): What's going on?

BEHRUZ: We want to play-act a little. We're going to do the last scene of *The Crows*.

NAHID: Good. I'm glad to see you two are up to your old tricks again.

HADI: Is there anything wrong, Nahid?

NAHID: No . . . I'm just going back to pick more flowers. (*She goes off some distance.*)

BEHRUZ: Let's begin.

HADI: OK . . . Let's see, I'm the First Murderer.

FIRST MURDERER (*Hadi glares at his friend and looks angry and upset*): You know, it was all your fault. Goddam bastard! You're the one who dragged me into this and made a criminal out of me.

SECOND MURDERER: Me! Me! You were a two-bit punk from the beginning. I guess you'd like to forget what you did to that poor slob in the park that day.

FIRST MURDERER: Shut your mouth, you . . . I swear I'm going to carve out your heart and that ugly mug of yours one day.

SECOND MURDERER: Sure, that's what I get for not turning you over to the cops.

FIRST MURDERER: Cops, is it? Cops! Squealing bastard.

SECOND MURDERER: Yeah, the cops. If it weren't for the fact that I'd be ashamed to be connected with the likes of you . . .

FIRST MURDERER: Ashamed of me? You! That's a laugh.

SECOND MURDERER: Stop shouting. Keep it down. Do you want everybody to hear you?

FIRST MURDERER (*Taking a deep breath*): Listen . . . Didn't you make me go with you to that woman's place and get me drunk? You made sure I had a couple of bottles . . . you don't remember? And you promised me all kinds of things. Didn't you then hand me the knife and show me how to use it? Didn't you clap your hand over his mouth when I stuck the knife in his gut? Didn't you? It wasn't my fault . . . I was drunk. You had it all planned. You scheming skunk, you filthy—

SECOND MURDERER: That's a lie. A lie. Sure, I was with you. I was passing by, I heard a scream and saw you run out the gate, knife in hand. I don't even know you!

FIRST MURDERER (*Rolling his eyes in disbelief, he takes a butcher knife out of his inside coat pocket*): So you don't know me?

SECOND MURDERER: You'd better be careful or I'll choke you right now.

FIRST MURDERER: I'll be careful . . . you, you—(*He rushes at the Second Murderer, raises his knife, and plunges it into his stomach.*) Choke me, will you! (*He stabs again.*)

The Second Murderer screams and falls. Nahid rushes over and sees her husband lying in a pool of blood. She runs, screaming "Murder, Murder!"

FIRST MURDERER: Come on, choke me. . . . You tricked me.
You got me drunk. This is what you deserve, goddam
bastard. Didn't you know that your soul is not yours?
Do you know me now?
*Hearing Nahid scream, two gardeners rush up with
shovels in their hands.*

(TRANSLATED AND ADAPTED BY EDEN NABY)

PART V

TURKISH LITERATURE

THE TURKISH BACKGROUND

The native traditions that fed contemporary Turkish literature were threefold: the classical or Divan poetry of the Ottomans, modeled on Arab and Persian forms and intended for a court elite; a religious literature connected with the *tekkes* or cells of practicing mystics; and an oral folk tradition, nationalistic and democratic in its impulse, that antedated the first two.

The republic of Kemal Ataturk, by at once ridding the country of both the caliphate and the sultanate in the 1920s, paved the way for the ascendency of the folk tradition. A leading Turkish scholar describes it as a tradition of social criticism kept alive among the people even during the time when Divan court literature under the Ottoman Sultanate was dominant. "While the palace poets subserved," says Talat Halman, the Turkish critic and translator, "most of those outside of the cultural hierarchy subverted." This "Turkish" culture as opposed to the "Ottoman" saw no quarrel with a return of poetry—under the new government—to its native syllabic meters and away from the quantitative meters of Arabo-Persian verse that had shaped the Divan tradition. It had no quarrel, either, with the attempt to purify the Turkish language of its foreign borrowings, for which it had never had any need. (In 1920, 75 percent of the written vocabulary was borrowed mainly from Persian and Arabic; in 1970, only 20 percent was borrowed.) If the native folk tradition was not equally ready to accept the anticlerical bias of the new government, and if it could not easily give up the Arabic for the Latin alphabet, it nevertheless felt closer to the new republic than to the old social order that had assigned it a demeaning status.

This revived tradition, anti-Establishment in spirit, could thrive as long as the young Turks and the Republic were themselves engaged in reform. The new nationalist spirit was harmonious with a folk pride that went back to pre-Ottoman and pre-Islamic times. Moreover, the Divan literature had been deliberately escapist while the folk tradition was naturally realistic. And when Ataturk urged a poet to write with a purpose, it seemed as if social commitment in literature had received an official sanction.

Today's reforms, however, often become tomorrow's oppressions, and writers who had opposed the old Ottoman tyranny in the name of justice under the new republic later had to oppose that same republic in the name of a newer and more liberal ideology. The problem of loyalities became complicated as fresh ideologies from the West left their impact on the Turkish mind and imagination: liberal democracy with universal suffrage, egalitarian communism, and other forms of rule. As Halman puts it, Turkish literature became both an agent and a mirror of these changes.

The nineteenth-century dominance of French literature has been shared, in the present century, by British and American influences, particularly since World War II. (In the past thirty years, according to Halman, 1,500 American titles alone have been translated into Turkish—remarkable in a nation in which 60 percent of the population is still illiterate.) But from the West came not only the winds of ideological change—whether toward the left or the right—but also the concept of the writer as an autonomous agent who has the right to produce a literature of no social significance whatsoever. These antithetical forces give to contemporary Turkish literature a steady pendular movement between populist and elitist poles. In the opinion of Kemal Karpat, the art for art's sake school has as little chance of prevailing in Turkey today as had the old Divan literature a generation ago, since both turn away from social reality. The larger thrust of contemporary literature has certainly been in the direction of social realism inspired by a desire to amend. Yet the counter influence has not wholly died out. Recently there has been a renewed interest in the traditional *ghazal* form, the chief vehicle of Divan poetry. This, side by side with contemporary treatments of such current themes as the assassinations of Kennedy and King, the war in Vietnam, and the struggles in Algiers and Cyprus!

The outstanding figure in Turkish poetry of the twentieth century has undoubtedly been Nazim Hikmet Ran (1920–1963), who transmitted into Turkish literature both the free-verse style of the Soviet poet Mayakovsky and the revolutionary doctrines of the Marxist thinkers. Jailed in the reaction that followed the Kemalist reforms, Hikmet was freed in 1950 and exiled himself to the Soviet Union, where he died a martyr to the leftist—and occasionally unpopular—causes he had espoused. (For instance, he was the only major Turkish writer to speak out against the Armenian massacres in 1915 and 1922.) Although his books were banned in Turkey from the late 1930s to the late 1940s and again from 1951 until his death, there has been a vast revival of his work. A recent New York review, *Nightclub Cantata*, included his verses set to music by the composer Elizabeth Swados. Despite its strong invective against social injustice, national humiliation at imperialist hands, and indifference to suffering, Hikmet's poetry is frequently lyrical, sensual, tender, and romantic.

The fate of Turkish poetry after Nazim Hikmet passed into the hands of a talented trio—Melih Anday, Oktay Rifat, and Orhan Kanik—who during the 1940s set out "to liberate poetry from its restrictions" of vocabulary, meter, and metaphor. But this movement was not destined to endure. A decade and a half later, Rifat and Anday were moving in the opposite direction, toward a poetry abstract and introverted. This new poetry prided itself on its lack of semantic meaning. "Poetry tells or explains nothing because beauty explains nothing," said Rifat in a burst of confusion. Another poet, Ilhan Berk, asserted the escapist credo that "Art is for invention's sake." This turn from the public "we" to the private "I" is not uncommon when writers begin to feel a sense of alienation from the social norm. It was left to Fazil Husnu Daglarca, the most important poet of Turkey in the period after the Second World War, to bring about a kind of synthesis of these polar trends. Having himself been brought up on charges by the public prosecutor, though subsequently acquitted, Daglarca marked out a path of social engagement without the sacrifice of artistic integrity, all in a variety of poetic forms but with special skill in the short epigrammatic stanza. His vast body of verse, whose themes range from metaphysics to social problems, from the stark life of the Anatolian plateau to the Vietnam War, is best sampled by the English reader in a bilingual volume entitled *Fazil Husnu Daglarca: Selected Poems* (1969).

Criticism of societal forms has perhaps been even stronger

in contemporary Turkish fiction than in the poetry, and many of the major novelists and short-story writers have run afoul of the government for their political views. Both Aziz Nesin, a satirist who attacked bureaucratic bumbling and depicted the crimes of a capitalist society, and Orhan Kemal, who, according to Talat Halman, more successfully than any other Turkish author captured the suffering of the working class in the major cities, have been in jail. The works of Sabahattin Ali, a short-story writer of leftist leanings who was killed at the Bulgarian border trying to escape, were forbidden in his native land. Even Yashar Kemal, the leading writer of fiction today and a man proud of his radicalism, has not been able to get his most famous novel accepted for filming because of censorship.

The impulse to criticize society received its greatest impetus from a book of nonfiction by Mahmut Makal, the youthful product of a government institution specifically set up to educate village boys. This book was the epoch-making *Our Village,* which in 1950 revealed the deprivations under which the peasants lived, the ignorance of the local clerical teachers, and the abuse of women. Here is a characteristic passage:

> In the eyes of the villager, women are pratically of no value whatever. Only at the time of their marriage do they excite a little interest in their persons. On the other hand, the woman is completely dependent on the man. She dare not do anything against his orders. The man will lie on his bed and order her about: "Wife, do this, or do that." Not for her to suggest: "Husband, let's do it this way." The extent of a woman's respect for her husband is the measure of her character and integrity. The man can strike her, curse her, beat her up, make her weep, cause her pain, and she may not say a word. She can't. She tries not to do the things which her husband has forbidden; but very often, after having been thrashed by him for no cause whatever, on the most ridiculous pretext, the woman is quite nonplussed what to do.

The village had been dealt with by earlier writers, but they were not villagers themselves. Rather they were urbanites who looked with bemused detachment—or genuine pity— upon an existence they had not experienced directly. Mahmut

Makal's book, though it was questioned as unfair and un-representative, turned the attention of village writers such as Yashar Kemal to materials that were close at hand and yet had a wide-ranging appeal, both to Turkish urbanites and to readers in other lands. Out of this concern with rural life, there emerged a genre called the "village novel," which reached its apogee with the work of Kemal: *Memed, My Hawk*, translated by Edouard Roditi in 1961, *Iron Earth, Copper Sky*, translated by his wife Thilda Kemal in 1974, and the novella contained in this volume.

The pre-eminence of the "committed" writers of fiction has been challenged, but not successfully so far, by a more cosmopolitan school who are concerned mainly with avant-garde techniques of narration learned from Joyce and other Westerners given to experiment. Oktay Akbal has carved a place for himself in the school known as "the Turkish nouvelle vague," whose principal themes are "dehumanization, moral disintegration, absurdity, lack of heroism, ennui, futility, hypocrisy," in the words of Talat Halman. Sait Faik has gained both a popular and a critical reputation with his tender studies of the inner lives of the denizens of his beloved Istanbul. Aziz Nesin, the satirist previously mentioned, has by now published more than sixty books.

Aldous Huxley has said somewhere that Englishmen did not know how the Englishman should behave until Falstaff was created. Something similar might be said of the typical Turk and the traditional drama of Turkey, the *Karagöz* or shadow play. This genre was brought to Turkey in the sixteenth century from Egypt, whence it had come from the Far East via India. The stock characters—the boastful, lowbrow Karagöz and the pretentious highbrow Hacivat—were a suitable paradigm of the class conflicts of Turkish life under Ottoman rule. This fact, plus the simple and raucous plots, and Karagöz' uninterrupted powers of critical comment, enabled the shadow plays to delight both the young and the old and to subject social, political, and religious institutions to satirical bloodletting. An analogous theater of unknown origin, the Orta Oyunu (sometimes called the Turkish *commedia dell' arte*), employed human actors instead of puppets, but like the *Karagöz*, relied upon broad humor. These two traditions have barely survived into the modern era, but their absurd and nonrealistic elements have to some extent been embodied in the drama that has grown up under Western influence.

The contemporary theater in Turkey emerged during the nineteenth century, first with successful translations of Molière into the Turkish vernacular, then with adaptations of Western forms to native themes and situations. Under Ataturk, state theaters were founded and these received encouragement from the political reforms of 1960. Supplementing original plays by such early modern writers as Namik Kemal and Abdulhak Hamit Tarhan, the prose fiction of the leading writers has been adapted to the stage in treatments both tragic and comic. Among the problems the plays deal with are the oppressed state of women, sex, and marriage, and religious, psychological, and philosophical conflicts. There have been plays about the artist's alienation from bourgeois society; and such universal myths as those of Medea and Gilgamesh have been dramatized, the characters drawn from Turkish life and history. An audience familiar with the nonillusionistic character of the *Karagöz* and Orta Oyunu has had no trouble accepting the sophisticated "alienation" technique of the theater of Bertolt Brecht. Yet the fact remains that in modern Turkey no playwright, native or foreign, has enjoyed as wide a fame as Shakespeare in translation. Perhaps in no other non-English-speaking country outside of the mainstream of Western culture has Shakespeare been as dominant a force in the theater as in twentieth-century Turkey. One of the pleasures of visiting Istanbul is sitting on a grassy knoll overlooking the castle of Rumelihisar while Shakespeare is performed at dusk against the thrilling backdrop of the Bosporus.

What the future holds for Turkish drama cannot be readily predicted from the present state of the art. That future will undoubtedly be determined, as elsewhere in the Middle East, by the degree to which literary artists in general can acquire the freedom of expression so vital to a living theater. The comedy-fantasy here offered—*In Ambush* by Cahit Atay— since its first production in 1962 has enjoyed wide popular appeal, both in the major cities of Turkey (Istanbul and Ankara) and in the smaller communities. Its translator sees beneath its comic surface a veiled attack, by an "alliance of the underprivileged and the intellectual classes," upon the exploitive feudal landowner. In this respect, Atay is performing the same double service of entertainment and social therapy that the native Turkish theater rendered for hundreds of years.

FICTION

---◆---

Mademoiselle Mathilda

by OKTAY AKBAL

I guess I had first laid eyes on Mademoiselle Mathilda in one of those narrow gloomy streets. She must have been quite young then—a Greek girl, seventeen or eighteen years old, a ball of fire. I had probably caught a glimpse of her at an apartment window or in front of a door or behind the counter of a shooting gallery as I passed through the maze of those streets with my school bag on my back. Plunging deep into my memory, I recall all the perilous houses and alleyways. The school administration declared the streets at the bottom of the slope "off limits to students," but of course none of us paid any attention. For one thing, that place was a shortcut: Instead of climbing the steep slope buffeted by winter winds and snow, we could breeze through the street of strange lonesome people and shady houses that both frightened us and appealed to our childish curiosity. I remember vividly how the alleys drifted in heavy languid sleep in the morning. The heads of a few unsleeping women would lean out of the windows. Doors would be closed slowly, sluggishly. No sooner than we came out of school late in the afternoon we would be confronted with the "naked truth." Plump "girls," half-naked, stood at doorways, kept kidding around, sometimes joked with passersby, while a bunch of men and soldiers stared at them with wild and lustful eyes. A phonograph record blared—"Come on, drink up." We never even noticed this palpable and disgusting vulgarity. We looked at the "girls" with affection. A few among them would flirt with us jokingly. Some would quickly strip off their slips to bare their flesh to us. But most of them looked at us with pity in their eyes. The streets in that district looked alike. Rows of ice-cream men and bagel-sellers set the borders of the street of dangerous houses. Sometimes the vendors wouldn't let us go through. Cursing like anything, they chased us away. Now, in the midst of these scattered memories, I have a vague recollection of running into that blond Greek girl quite often near the shady streets. She had such warmth. She fluttered like a feather. Wasn't she the girl I saw going down the avenue with the steps, arm in arm with either a swarthy young man or a pot-bellied out-of-towner? Mademoiselle Mathilda had a place in the farrago of my childhood recollections. Sure enough. But how and where? I used to wrack my brains, but always failed to find out.

The minute I saw Mademoiselle Mathilda at the cafe owned by Herr Schmidt, a German Jew, I knew she was no stranger to me. She still had blond hair, but this was a sallow, dead color. There was lipstick on her lips, but blood was gone from them. Her face had nearly vanished under blotches of powder. Her legs were like a pair of sticks. Yet, she seemed to bring to me from a bygone age some memories with that voice of hers, with her glimpses. Could it be that she too remembered me? Or maybe she was accustomed to smiling at everyone. She came to the cafe every evening to play bezique. She spoke French, sometimes English. She always showed up alone, as darkness descended. Sitting in the armchair by the window, she chatted with the retired consul, and played either bezique or chess with him. The *pension* where she lived was nearby. She stayed there until the evening. Probably slept or at least remained in bed. She must have been working in a bar or in one of those dancing salons which are so small you can hardly take two steps. But in which one? Actually not one of us wondered about this. Because, to tell the truth, Mademoiselle Mathilda was scarcely a woman any more. How did she manage to stand on those legs which were like thin sticks? How was it that they didn't break right in the middle? Even the most unabashed womanizer among us saw Mademoiselle Mathilda as something other than woman despite all her make-up and lipstick, all her coquettish ways and flirtatious smiles. I can't say anything for others, but I used to look forward to Mathilda's appearance at the cafe. From the time I first laid eyes on her, I was convinced that we were old acquaintances and there was a bond between us, a deep link. Sometimes she would not show up for days. Madam Schmidt would say: "She's sick." They seemed to be close friends, but Madame didn't know much

about Mademoiselle Mathilda's past either. Supposedly she
came from Italy ten years ago. She was with a Turkish
businessman. A few years later, the story goes, he dropped
her. So she started singing at bars. One day, she was stricken
with an illness, confined to bed for many months, and lost
her beauty. She was a woman of many affairs and adventures. Knew countless men. They say she used to be extremely beautiful. Once, an official at the Italian Consulate
fell in love with her and squandered his last penny on her
. . . All these were lies. I knew the truth. I knew it as if I
had witnessed it with my own eyes. She had never even
seen Italy or Greece. She was born and raised in Istanbul,
one of the people of my childhood. But could I convince anyone? Would anyone believe what I say? What could I say to
whom?

It was during the visit of an American fleet to Istanbul.
Again, Mathilda wasn't around. She didn't show up at the
cafe in the evening or at night. Madame said these were big-
money days for Mathilda. In spite of all the commotion in
the avenue, our cafe was quiet. We had been playing cards
for hours on end. A few people went for dinner. No one was
left in the cafe except two friends and Madame Schmidt. The
street was filled with people who overflowed into the avenue.
A vapid big-city crowd. With all those U.S. sailors, you could
hardly walk or go anywhere. I guess the thing to do is to sit
by the dusty window which has a view of the junction and to
watch the night, the night people, and the interior of the
apartment building across the street. . . . The American
tunes on the radio were presumably being broadcast in honor
of our guests. A *Johnny*[1] or two, all boozed up, ambled
along in front of the window and waved to us. There was a
woman at a window across the street. She was half-naked.
Did she exhibit herself to us or the passersby? All three of us
were deep in thought. Not gone. Just absorbed in that moment. We weren't beating our brains or forcing our imagination. We were resting within that moment. All of a sudden,
the door was flung open, and Mathilda stormed in. She was
full of joyful laughter. She had with her an American sailor,
a tall youth with sharp features. They were both drunk. She
came over to us. She said in French: "Je vous présente mon
fiancé . . . C'est Jerry . . ." He was just a lad with barely any

[1] Slang term for man.

hair on his face. He couldn't have been a day older than nine-
teen. He looked around stupidly, then sank into a chair. But
when he heard the catchy American tune on the radio, he
couldn't restrain himself: He rose to his feet and began to
jump and thump. . . . A few minutes later, he collapsed into
an armchair and dozed off. Tonight Mathilda was more terri-
fying than ever. She had never seemed uglier to us. Her lipstick was smeared all over her mouth. The peroxide of her
hair was gone. She looked frightfully frail. She was all eyes
now. And such deep traces of her good old days were etched
in those dark blue eyes. She kept telling us—Jerry asked her
to go to America with him. There they'll get married. He has
a ranch near Dallas. His mother and his sister. A ranch house.
A small town, like the ones in films. Drugstores, which are
half pharmacy, half ice-cream parlor. Picnics. Couples getting
married in a tiny church. Newlyweds going on their honey-
moon in small cars. These were the dreams that Mathilda, the
Greek belle of my childhood, could never part with. She had
kept that dream world alive ever since those early years.
Jerry was fast asleep. She shook him: "Jerry, honey!" she
said in English. The lad with the sharp features opened his
eyes. Mathilda helped him get up, took him by the arm. They
went out. None of us said a word. We kept imagining that
now they must be clambering up the stairs to a stinking room
on the third or fourth floor. What sort of room was that, we
wondered, what sort of bed? What color? What sort of photo-
graphs lined the mirror before which Mathilda combed her
hair, put her lipstick on, and plucked her eyebrows? Assorted
poses of Mathilda, the Greek belle at age seventeen, already
famous in the entertainment district, in the year 1935. . . . At
midnight, walking on a desolate bridge, a solitary stroller, I
could visualize those faded photos. There, Mathilda on the
beach. Mathilda at a dance. With her mother. With her first
lover. Mathilda in her school uniform. Walking in a street.
There, at the window of the house in the red-light district.
Mathilda watching the schoolchildren going by that house
with their knapsacks on their backs. . . .

Suddenly I felt I had turned into a boy. I was thirteen
again. We were playing soccer, and the ball went into the
back street. I jumped over the wall and ran along the road
that led into the forbidden streets. I stood before a small
wooden house. A girl at the window smiled at me all of a
sudden. Her hair was flying in the wind. She pointed to

where the ball had rolled. I had already forgotten all about
the ball. Stunned, I kept staring at her. Those eyes and her
hair held me captive. They would never loosen their grip over
my mind for the rest of my life. The unintelligible lyrics of a
song in Greek echoed through the wind. I paid no attention
to the soccer ball, and just didn't hear the shouts of my
friends in the school yard. The bell announcing the end of
the recess didn't ring in my ears. Just then, in the house, a
woman's hoarse voice rose all the way to the girl at the window: "Maaaathildaaaa!"

(TRANSLATED BY TALAT S. HALMAN)

The Mirror at the Beach

by SAIT FAIK

A man who was later declared insane broke the mirror at the
beach. Some said that he had gotten angry at this glasslike
mirror, which, with its quicksilver peeling off, made one look
green. No, others said, he used to sell mirrors at one time. He
imported them from Italy, went bankrupt, got a bee in his
bonnet; sad now whenever he sees a mirror, he can't help
breaking it. The mirror at the beach and I are the only ones
who know the truth of the matter.

"Then you are the person who broke it," you'll say, "and
now you're playing a part." All right. I am the one. It has
been decided that I am mad, a pretty harmless madman who
takes revenge on mirrors. No, no, this is false. Here is the
truth.

There is no reason for my breaking the mirror. No reason
at all. I can't even say I got bored and broke it to amuse myself. It made handsome people ugly—nonsense! A mirror that
makes handsome people seem ugly reflects their souls. One
cannot hang such a mirror at the beach.

"Or did you start seeing the ugly parts of people, seeing
them reversed, just as writing seems reversed when held up to

a mirror?" If you say such a thing, I will state that I dislike philosophy and that I am disgusted by the philosophy of genius.

No, the mirror was O.K. It didn't play such tricks. I don't care when it was invented or by what fool, but it's handy in combing your hair, looking for black marks on your face, making sure that everything is all right after you have wiped your nose, or for saying, "Gracious! my eyes aren't bad at all. And look at that line that turns down at my mouth. Damn it! It gives meaning to my face. Women don't appreciate men and that's all there is to it."

All sorts of conversations with oneself can be prolonged by the help of a mirror. We have a young girl looking in it, a man thinking in it, and someone in love with himself kissing in it. We have old people seeing death in it, the coffin and the shroud, and consumptives seeing the light of the awful fever in their eyes. You can be friends with a mirror or just the opposite. Now you can, if you want, throw the blame of breaking a mirror onto philosophy, literature, psychology, medicine, or neurology. But my breaking of the mirror at the beach has no reason whatsoever. I'll tell you about my day. I know it's ridiculous to search for reasons there, but still:

A little boy was playing under the olive tree. I approached him. He handed me the green olives fearfully.

"Are these yours?" he asked.

"Of course," I said.

"I didn't throw stones," he said, "they fell by themselves."

"What are they?" I asked.

"Bitter things."

His blue eyes with their red lashes flashed on and off like lighthouses.

"Do you know what they are?" I asked.

"No," he said.

"Don't you know what olives are?"

"Of course I know."

"Well, these are olives."

"The ones we eat at breakfast?"

"Do you eat olives at breakfast?"

"Of course."

"Who's your father?"

"I don't have one."

Bluish-white eyelids came down with their golden light on his blue eyes.

"My father died," he said, pouting with his thick lips.

"Where did he die?"

"In the war."

"What war?"

"The War of Independence."[1]

My friend, my soul, my beloved, my son, dearest part of me, I thought.

"You may play with the olives," I said aloud, "but don't throw stones."

"Are the olives yours?"

"No, they belong to no one."

"May I take them home?"

"They are wrinkled, wormy, no good."

"Then I'll play with them," he said.

"O. K., but don't try to eat them; they are all bitter."

"Are good olives bitter, too?"

"Yes."

"Then how do they get sweet?"

"I don't know much about that myself."

"Who does know?"

"Why?"

"I would take some for breakfast."

"Do you have a mother?"

"Sure."

"What does she do?"

"She washes clothes."

"What will you be when you grow up?"

"Me?" he asked. He raised his eyes to mine. We both looked into the blue. "I'll be a bootblack."

"Why a bootblack?"

"What d'ya want me to be?"

"Be a doctor," I said.

"I won't," he said.

"Why not?"

"I said I won't."

"But why?"

"I don't like doctors."

"Oh no," I said, "is that possible?"

"Of course I don't like them. Mother got sick. He came to our house and we had to break our money-box. He took all the quarters and only the nickels were left. And those went for the prescriptions, and they were hardly enough."

[1] The war of 1920 against the Allies.

"But your mother got well?"

"Yeah, but our money was gone. I didn't eat for two days."

"O. K.," I said, "be a teacher."

"I don't go to school."

"Why?"

"The teacher beats me."

"Why is that?"

"I am naughty, that's why."

"You shouldn't behave badly," I said.

"I don't know what behaving badly is."

"Doing what the teacher says not to do."

"You can't tell. One day a friend of mine called me the washerwoman's bastard. And so I beat him. And the teacher beat me. After that they always called me the washerwoman's bastard. But I didn't beat no one because that was being naughty. A few days later I took my friend's pencil. He had two. They beat me and said I was a thief. But I didn't have no pencil, so I took it. But they said *that's* being very naughty. I won't take anybody's pencil again, I said. I took a notebook. This time they not only beat me but they kicked me out."

"You've behaved very badly."

"Sure I have. I don't want to be a good man."

"What *do* you want to be?"

"Didn't I say a bootblack? My brother Ahmet is a bootblack, too."

"Do you like your brother?"

"Sure I do. My mother likes him too. Some nights he stays with us and gives us money. If we're hungry he bring us bread."

"Isn't he your real brother?"

"How do you mean, my *real* brother?"

"Why, simply your *real* brother. Isn't he your father's son?"

"Course he ain't."

"Whose son is he?"

"Don't know."

"How old is he?"

"Older than me."

"How old are you?"

"Nine."

"He?"

"Older."

"How much?"

"As old as you."

"Oh, I see. Now, what'll you do when you're a bootblack?"

"I'll shine shoes."

"Then?"

"I'll earn money."

"Then?"

"I'll smoke."

"And then?"

"Oh, go to hell!"

"Now that's not a good expression. I'll box your ears."

"If I tell my mother?"

"Give her my greetings, too."

A round-faced woman, rather like a Tartar, with a scarf over her head was coming towards us. The boy ran to her.

"Look, Mom, olives," he said.

The woman: "Throw them away."

The child considered for a moment. He walked towards me. Before the woman could say, "What the hell are you doing?" he threw the olives at my face. I laughed.

"Never mind," I said to her, "he is only a child."

"He kept talking to me for hours," the boy said.

The woman answered, "The gentleman likes you, so he talks with you. Don't be so wild."

"But I don't like him. I said I wanted to be a bootblack like Ahmet. He says I'm gonna be a doc."

"How nice of him!"

"Let *him* be a doc! Didn't you say, 'God damn those fellows, nothing will satisfy them'?"

"Did I? Didn't I say, 'May God never make you need them'?"

"Yes, you did."

The woman turned to me.

"Isn't it so, sir? May God never make you need neither a doc nor a judge."

"You're right," I said.

The boy got wilder. He tugged at his mother's skirts. He looked at me with enmity.

"I'm going to be a bootblack, aren't I?"

The woman: "What else *can* you be?"

The boy: "What was my father, Mom?"

The woman: "A bootblack."

The boy to me: "See, my father was a bootblack, too."

"Is that so?" I asked the woman.

"Yes," she said.

"What war did he die in?" I asked.

The woman: "He didn't die in the war."

The boy: "Didn't you tell me so?"

"O course I didn't. Who did?"

"Ahmet."

"God damn Ahmet!"

"But he brings us bread."

"Shut up. Get going!"

The boy had gathered new olives. The woman said, "Throw those bitter things away."

And the boy threw them at my face again. This time, his mother gave him a hard slap on the face and he ran towards the ruins. There, from beside a fallen mosque wall:

"Why don't you take the fellow to your cellar?" he shouted.

His mother shouted back, "Shameless pig!" and ran for him, not forgetting to wink at me. I followed her as if enchanted. We entered through an opening in some gunny-sacking used as a door. Then we turned the handle of a door of the kind seen in public baths. Inside there was a dirty human smell, like that of a lavatory. On the table covered with linoleum were two tomatoes and a cucumber.

"Shall we buy some raki?" the woman asked.

"No," I said, fearing to lose the lust that was crushing my innards.

"Ain't got no money, eh?"

"I have," I said, "but I don't want to drink in the heat of the day."

She fixed her eyes upon mine and tapped my purse pocket with her hand. I took out a two-and-a-half note. She didn't like it. I found a second one with some difficulty.

"I haven't got another cent," I said.

She laughed and, putting her arms about my neck, sat on my lap. The little boy was perched on a pile of stones in a corner of the hut. He stuck out his head and looked at us with his blue eyes.

"The boy?" I said.

"Never mind," the woman said. "He is used to it."

The boy stared at me with fixed eyes for maybe half an

hour. Every now and then he threw olives at us which he somehow had put into his pocket.

Suddenly he took his head between his hands and began screaming like an animal.

"Throw him a few pennies or he won't shut up," said the woman in a whistle-like voice.

First I threw nickels. No use. Another nickel and then a quarter. There was silence for five minutes. Then the hut rang with a shrill cry. He imitated the whistle of a train, his eyes on mine.

"Just let Ahmet come and you'll see," he said.

I threw him another quarter.

"If you don't give me another one—"

He didn't finish his sentence, for his mother got up and slapped him so hard on the face that it would have felled *me* to the ground.

"Now give him a quarter," she told me.

The boy's little black hand was held out. He took the coin; he turned his back to us. Now he lay like a dog, his ears pricked to our voices.

When I came out into the melting noon light, I had a throbbing at my temples. I instantly ran to the beach.

Did I go to the beach to cleanse myself, to throw something off, to be comfortable? No, but as soon as I came out of the hut, I was sweating (especially my head) like a pitcher which is taken from a well to the heat outside. I passed my fingers through my hair and felt a moisture being sucked up by the ends of my fingernails, or so I thought. I had the feeling that if I looked at my hand I would realize that this moisture was not sweat, that blood was oozing through my skin.

The feeling made me run to the beach. I thought I saw nothing until I went in the sea. However, when the coolness covered my body, I remembered seeing a green blade of grass, a ruin, a child, some smoke, a railroad, a dog. Then I saw the eyes of the woman's boy fixed on my back. How the bastard stared at one! The water was good, but this was of no importance. It only made me see that what I thought was blood was sweat after all. If it had been the former the water would have gotten red. That was the only good the water did to me. My temples were still throbbing and I was still perspiring in the coolness of the sea. Still that lavatory smell, that cool, very cool air of the cellar, that boy with hands black and cracked like barley-bread and with blue eyes fixed on us hovered constantly somewhere between my brain and my eye in the form of smoke that could, if I wanted it to, be transformed into a soul.

Now you think you have found the reason for the breaking of the mirror. You tell me I saw myself in it clearly, with all the dirtiness, the ugliness, and vulgarity. I say absolutely no! You smile, because you see humanity in all its ugliness, with all man's miseries. . . . No, by God, no!

Then you'll say, "You're downright cracked." But why should you? To stoop and pick up a stone unconsciously, pick it up as though you were going to make it skip four or five times on the smooth sea surface, and then to break the dirty mirror at the beach, thinking of nothing, with no purpose, not even accidentally. Why not?

The people ran. I ran. They couldn't catch me. After a long time I returned and lay face downward under a tree overlooking the beach. All of them had gathered about the owner's hut. Half an hour had elapsed and still they were talking about me. They stayed for another hour, talking, laughing, giving opinions. Then a policeman came. They told him. He listened and looked as if he were speaking his mind.

I found the road to the wharf too long, myself too tired. I waited for the night under the tree. A yellow moon rose. Voices, laughter, and songs began to come from the casinos. Then I put my hand to my hair and it was in a mess. I took out a comb and combed it. I lit a cigarette. I placed a waltz tune on my lips and put my hands in my trouser pockets. I passed along the beach, whistling, like everybody else, pretending to be a happy man, as though I were not the one who had broken the mirror.

(TRANSLATED BY SPIRO K. KOSTOF)

Baby Born in the Field

by ORHAN KEMAL

In the cotton field which stretched as far as the eye could see, farm hands, fifteen or twenty in a row, worked steadily at the weeds around the seedlings.

The temperature soared to a hundred and forty-nine in the sun. No bird flew in the shimmering, dust-gray sky. The sun seemed to sway. The peasants, soaked with sweat, pushed and pulled their hoes in a steady rhythm. The sharp edges of the hoes chopped the parched soil with a "thrush, thrush, thrush" sound. The song the farm hands sang in unison to the measured beat of their hoes was swallowed up in the sun's scorching heat:

> Into what is left back they sow millet
> They sow it they reap it and they wrap it
> My darling sent me pear and pomegranate

Ferho Uzeyir wiped the sweat off his swollen hands on his baggy black trousers and turned his bloodshot eyes on his wife swinging her hoe beside him. He spoke in Kurdish, "Wha? Whatsa matter?"

Gulizar was a broad-shouldered husky woman. Her dried-up face, glittering with sweat, was contorted with deep lines and grimaces of intense pain.

She did not answer. Angered, Ferho Uzeyir jabbed his elbow into her side: "What's up with you, woman?"

Gulizar gave her husband a weary glance. Her eyes had sunk with fright into their sockets. Her hoe suddenly slipped from her hands to the ground. Pressing her huge belly with her hands, she bent over, then fell to her knees on the red earth everywhere cracked by the blistering sun.

The foreman, who stood under his big black umbrella, called out: "Gulizar! Is that it? Quit workin'! G'on, quit!"

She was writhing with pain. She stuck her shriveled yet strong fingers deep into a crack of the soil, squeezing them tensely. With an almost superhuman effort, she struggled to control herself. Pitch black blotches fluttered before her eyes. Suddenly she groaned, "Uggghhh!" It was a shame—a disgrace—for a woman in labor to be heard by strange men. Ferho Uzeyir cursed and swung a mighty kick into his wife's side.

The woman crouched meekly on the ground. She knew her husband would never forgive her for this. As she struggled to rise on hands pressed against the hot earth, the foreman repeated: "Gulizar! Quit, sister, quit! G'on now, quit!"

Her pains suddenly stopped, but she felt they would come back—this time more sharply. She headed for the ditch, the farm's boundary, about a thousand feet away.

Ferho Uzeyir growled after his wife, then called to his nine-year-old daughter standing barefoot beside the foreman: "Take y' mom's place!"

The girl knew this was coming. She picked up the hoe that was as tall as she and whose handle was still covered with the sweat of her mother's hands, and fell into line.

All this was a common affair. The hoeing continued to the beat of the song sung in unison.

The sun fell full on the ditch with its slabs of dung. Green lizards glided over the red earth. Gulizar stood erect in the ditch, looked all around her, listening intently through the scorching heat. There was no one in sight. The radiant void, echoing a shrike's shrieks, stretched endlessly.

She emptied the pockets of her baggy black pants, put a few items she had gathered when she knew her time was due: two long pieces of thread wrapped around a bit of pasteboard, a rusty razor blade, several pieces of cloth in different colors, rags, salt and a dried-up lemon. She had found these in the farm's garbage can. She would squeeze the lemon into the baby's eyes and rub the baby with salt.

She stripped below the waist, and folded the baggy pants under a big piece of rock, spread the rags on the ground, unraveled the thread and cut the lemon in two. About to kneel, she heard something move behind her. She covered herself below the waist, turned around. It was a huge dog! She picked up a stone and flung it. Frightened, the dog fled, but did not disappear. It waited, sniffing the air with its wet nose.

Gulizar was worried. What if she delivered the baby right now and fainted—the dog might tear her child to pieces! She remembered Ferice, the Kurdish girl. Ferice too had given birth in a ditch like this and, after placing the baby beside her, had fainted. When she came to, she had looked around—the baby was gone. She had searched high and low . . . At last, far away beneath a shrub, she had found her baby being torn to pieces by a huge dog!

Gulizar took another look at the dog, studying it closely. The dog stared back at her—it had a strange look . . .

"Saffron," she said. "That look of yours ain't no good, Saffron." She wondered how she might call her daughter who was about a thousand feet away. "G'on, beat it. You goddam dirty dog!"

Reluctantly, the dog backed away about thirty feet, stopped, sat on its haunches and, with a blue gleam in its eyes, waited.

At that moment Gulizar felt another pang, the sharpest yet. Groaning, she fell to her naked knees, resting her body on her hands gripping the ground. The vein on her neck, thick as a finger, throbbed. Now came pain after pain, each sharper than the one before. Suddenly a gush of warm blood . . . Her face took on a terrified expression. The whole world collapsed before her eyes.

"Ferho, man," the foreman said. "Go take a look at that dame . . . She may die or somethin'."

Ferho Uzeyir glanced in the direction of the ditch where his wife was in labor, shook his head, cursed and went on working. Anger at his wife swelled inside. Cold sweat poured from his forehead, trickling through his thick bushy eyebrows.

"Look here, son," the foreman repeated. "Go see what's what with that dame. You never can tell!"

Ferho Uzeyir threw his hoe aside and walked over. He would give her a kick and another kick . . . He just couldn't get over the way that good-for-nothing woman had made a monkey of him.

He stopped by the ditch, stared down. Gulizar had fallen on the ground sideways. In the midst of blood-stained rags, the baby—purple all over—was twitching and a huge dog was pulling at it.

He jumped into the ditch. The dog leaped away, licking its blood-covered mouth. Ferho Uzeyir brushed away the green-winged flies gathered on his baby's face. The infant, its eyes closed, kept making motions. Ferho opened the pieces of cloth. The baby was a boy!

A boy!

Ferho changed instantly. He lifted his head to the sky. A smile filled his harsh face. He picked the baby and the bloody rags from the ground.

"My son!" he shouted.

He was nearly insane with joy. After four girls—a boy!

Gulizar, sensing the presence of her man beside her, opened her eyes and, in spite of her condition, tried to get up.

"Good for you!" Ferho Uzeyir said. "Good for you, woman!"

He dashed out of the ditch with his boy in his arms. The foreman saw him coming across the cracked red soil. "There, there . . ." he said. "That's Ferho comin' this way!"

Hoeing stopped. The farm hands, leaning on their hoes, stared. Ferho came up panting, out of breath, shouting: "My son! I got me a son!"

He pressed his baby, still purple all over inside the blood-drenched rags, to his bosom.

"Hey, careful, man," the foreman said. "Take care, man! Quit pressin' like that—you gonna choke 'im . . . Now get down to the farm-house. Tell the cook I sent you. Tell 'im he oughta give you some oil and molasses. Let's make her drink some. G'on!"

Ferho Uzeyir no longer felt tired, the heat no longer bothered him. Now he was as young as a twenty-year-old boy, as light as a bird.

He headed for the farm's mud-baked huts whose thatched roofs loomed ahead.

(TRANSLATED BY TALAT S. HALMAN)

A Dirty Story

by YASHAR KEMAL

The three of them were sitting on the damp earth, their backs against the dung-daubed brush-wall and their knees drawn up to their chests, when another man walked up and crouched beside them.

'Have you heard?' said one of them excitedly. 'Broken-Nose Jabbar's done it again! You know Jabbar, the fellow who brings all those women from the mountain villages and sells them in the plain? Well, this time he's come down with a couple of real beauties. The lads of Misdik have got together and bought one of them on the spot, and now they're having fun and making her dance and all that . . . It's unbelievable! Where does the fellow find so many women? How does he get them to come with him? He's the devil's own son, he is . . .'

'Well, that's how he makes a living,' commented one of the men. 'Ever since I can remember, this Jabbar's been peddling women for the villagers of the Chukurova plain. Allah provides for all and sundry . . .'

'He's still got the other one,' said the newcomer, 'and he's ready to give her away for a hundred liras.'

'He'll find a customer soon enough,' put in another man whose head was hunched between his shoulders. 'A good woman's worth more than a team of oxen, at least, in the Chukurova plain she is. You can always put her to the plough and, come summer, she'll bind and carry the sheaves, hoe, do anything. What's a hundred liras? Why, a woman brings in that much in one single summer. In the fields, at home, in bed. There's nothing like a woman. What's a hundred liras?'

Just then, Hollow Osman came up mumbling to himself

and flopped down beside them without a word of greeting. He was a tall, broad-shouldered man with a rather shapeless pot-bellied body. His lips drooped foolishly and his eyes had an odd squint-like gaze.

'Hey, Osman,' the man who had been talking addressed him. 'Broken-Nose Jabbar's got a woman for sale again. Only a hundred liras. Tell Mistress Huru to buy her for you and have done with living alone and sleeping in barns like a dog.'

Osman shrugged his shoulders doubtfully.

'Look here, man,' pursued the other, 'this is a chance in a million. What's a hundred liras? You've been slaving for that Huru since you dropped out of your mother's womb and she's never paid you a lira. She owes you this. And anyway she'll get back her money's worth in just one summer. A woman's good for everything, in the house, in the fields, in bed . . .'

Osman rose abruptly.

'I'll ask the Mistress,' he said. 'How should I know? . . .'

A couple of days later, a short, broad-hipped girl with blue beads strung into her plaited hair was seen at the door of Huru's barn in which Hollow Osman always slept. She was staring out with huge wondering eyes.

A month passed. Two months . . . And passers-by grew familiar with the sight of the strange wide-eyed girl at the barn door.

One day, a small dark boy with a face the size of a hand was seen pelting through the village. He rushed up to his mother where she sat on the threshold of her hut gossiping with Seedy Doneh.

'Mother,' he screeched, 'I've seen them! It's the truth, I swear it is. Uncle Osman's wife with . . . May my eyes drop out right here if I'm telling a lie."

Seedy Doneh turned to him sharply.

'What?' she cried. 'Say it again. What's that about Fadik?'

'She was with the Agha's son. I saw them with my own eyes. He went into the barn with her. They couldn't see me where I was hiding. Then he took off his boots, you know the shiny yellow boots he wears . . . And then they lay down and . . . Let my two eyes drop out if . . .'

'I knew it!' crowed Seedy Doneh. 'I knew it would turn out this way.'

'Hollow Osman never had any manhood in him anyway,'

said the child's mother. 'Always under that viper-tongued Huru's petticoats . . .'

'Didn't I tell you, Ansha, the very first day she came here that this would happen?' said Doneh. 'I said this girl's ready to play around. Pretending she was too bashful to speak to anyone. Ah, still waters run deep . . .'

She rose quickly and hurried off to spread the news.

'Have you heard? Just as I foretold . . . Still waters . . . The Agha's son . . . Fadik . . .'

In a trice all the neighbouring women had crowded at Ansha's door, trying to squeeze the last drop of information out of the child.

'Come on, tell us,' urged one of the women for perhaps the hundredth time. 'How did you see them?'

'Let my two eyes drop out right here if I'm lying,' the child repeated again and again with unabated excitement. 'The Agha's son came in, and then they lay down, both of them, and did things . . . I was watching through a chink in the wall. Uncle Osman's wife, you know, was crying. I can't do it, she was saying, and she was sobbing away all the time. Then the Agha's son pulled off those shiny yellow boots of his . . . Then I ran right here to tell Mother.'

The news spread through the village like wildfire. People could talk about nothing else. Seedy Doneh, for one, seemed to have made it her job to leave no man or woman uninformed. As she scoured the village for new listeners, she chanced upon Osman himself.

'Haven't you heard what's come upon you?' she said, drawing him aside behind the wall of a hut. 'You're disgraced, you jackass. The Agha's son has got his fingers up your wife's skirt. Try and clear your good name now if you can!'

Osman did not seem to understand.

'I don't know . . .' he murmured, shrugging his shoulders. 'I'll have to ask the Mistress. What would the Agha's son want with my wife?'

Doneh was incensed.

'What would he want with her, blockhead?' she screamed. 'Damn you, your wife's become a whore, that's what! She's turned your home into a brothel. Anyone can come in and have her.' She flounced off still screaming. 'I spit on you! I spit on your manhood . . .'

Osman was upset.

'What are you shouting for, woman?' he called after her. 'People will think something's wrong. I have to ask the Mistress. She knows everything. How should I know?'

He started walking home, his long arms dangling at his sides as though they had been hitched to his shoulders as an afterthought, his fingers sticking out wide apart as was his habit. This time he was waylaid by their next-door neighbour, Zeynep, who planted herself before him and tackled him at the top of her voice.

'Ah Osman! You'd be better off dead! Why don't you go and bury yourself? The whole village knows about it. Your wife . . . The Agha's son . . . Ah Osman, how could you have brought such a woman into your home? Where's your honour now? Disgraced . . . Ah Osman!'

He stared at her in bewilderment.

'How should I know?' he stammered, his huge hands opening out like pitchforks. 'The Mistress knows all about such things. I'll go and ask her.'

Zeynep turned her back on him in exasperation, her large skirt ballooning about her legs.

'Go bury yourself, Osman! I hope I see you dead after this.'

A group of children were playing tipcat near by. Suddenly one of them broke into a chant.

'Go bury yourself, Osman . . . See you dead, Osman . . .'

The other children joined in mechanically without interrupting their game.

Osman stared at them and turned away.

'How should I know?' he muttered. 'I must go to the Mistress.'

He found Huru sitting at her spinning-wheel. Fadik was there too, squatting near the hearth and listlessly chewing mastic-gum.

'Mistress,' said Osman, 'have you heard what Seedy Doneh's saying? She's saying I'm disgraced . . .'

Huru stepped on the pedal forcefully and brought the wheel to a stop.

'What's that?' she said. 'What about Seedy Doneh?'

'I don't know . . . She said Fadik . . .'

'Look here,' said Huru, 'you mustn't believe those lying bitches. You've got a good wife. Where would you find such a woman?'

'I don't know. Go bury yourself, they said. The children too . . .'

'Shut up,' cried Huru, annoyed. 'People always gossip about a beautiful woman. They go looking for the mote in their neighbour's eye without seeing the beam in their own. They'd better hold their peace because I've got a tongue in my head too . . .'

Osman smiled with relief.

'How could I know?' he said.

Down in the villages of the Chukurova plain, a sure sign of oncoming spring is when the women are seen with their heads on one another's lap, picking the lice out of one another's hair. So it was, on one of the first warm days of the year. A balmy sun shone caressingly down on the fields and village, and not a leaf stirred. A group of women were sitting before their huts on the dusty ground, busy with the lice and wagging their tongues for all they were worth. An acrid odour of sweat hung about the group. Seedy Doneh was rummaging in the hair of a large woman who was stretched full length on the ground. She decided that she had been silent long enough.

'No,' she declared suddenly, 'it's not as you say, sister! He didn't force her or any such thing. She simply fell for him the minute she saw those shiny yellow boots. If you're going to believe Huru! . . . She's got to deny it, of course.'

'That Huru was born with a silver spoon in her mouth,' said white-haired, toothless old Zala, wiping her blood-stained fingers on her ragged skirt. 'Hollow Osman's been slaving for her like twenty men ever since she took him in, a kid the size of your hand! And all for a mere pittance of food. And now there's the woman too. Tell me, what's there left for Huru to do?'

'Ah,' sighed another woman, 'fortune has smiled on Huru, she has indeed! She's got two people serving her now.'

'And both for nothing,' old Zala reminded her.

'What it amounts to,' said Seedy Doneh spitefully, 'is that Huru used to have one wife and now she's got two. Osman was always a woman, and as for Fadik she's a real woman. He-he!'

'That she is, a real woman!' the others agreed.

'Huru says the Agha's son took her by force,' pursued Doneh. 'All right, but what about the others? What about those lining up at her door all through the night, eh? She never says no to any one of them, does she? She takes in everyone, young and old.'

'The Lady Bountiful, that's what she is,' said Elif. 'And do you know something? Now that Fadik's here, the young men are leaving Omarja's yellow bitch in peace . . .'

'They've got somewhere better to go!' cackled the others.

Omarja's dumpy wife jumped up from where she was sitting on the edge of the group.

'Now look here, Elif!' she cried. 'What's all this about our yellow dog? Stop blackening people's characters, will you?'

'Well, it's no lie, is it?' Doneh challenged her. 'When was that bitch ever at your door where she should be all night? No, instead, there she came trotting up a-mornings with a rope dangling from her neck!'

'Don't go slandering our dog,' protested Omarja's wife. 'Why, if Omarja hears this, he'll kill the poor creature. Upon my word he will!'

'Go on!' said Doneh derisively. 'Don't you come telling me that Omarja doesn't know his yellow bitch is the paramour of all the village youths! What about that time when Stumpy Veli caught some of them down by the river, all taking it in turns over her? Is there anyone in this village who didn't hear of that? It's no use trying to whitewash your bitch to us!'

Omarja's wife was alarmed.

'Don't, sister,' she pleaded. 'Omarja'll shoot the dog, that's sure . . .'

'Well, I'm not to blame for that, sister,' retorted Doneh tartly. 'Anyway, the bitch'll be all right now that Fadik's around. And so will Kurdish Velo's donkey . . .'

Kurdish Velo's wife began to fidget nervously.

'Not our fault,' she blurted out in her broken Turkish. 'We lock our donkey in, but they come and break the door! Velo furious. Velo say people round here savage. He say, with an animal deadly sin! He say he kill someone. Then he complain to the Headman. Velo going sell this donkey.'

'You know what I think?' interposed Seedy Doneh. 'They're going to make it hot for her in this village. Yes, they'll do what they did to Esheh.'

'Poor Esheh,' sighed old Zala. 'What a woman she was before her man got thrown into prison! She would never have come to that, but she had no one to protect her. May they rot in hell, those that forced her into it! But she is dead and gone, poor thing.'

'Eh!' said Doneh. 'How could she be otherwise after the youths of five villages had done with her?' She straightened up. 'Look here, sister,' she said to the woman whose head was on her lap, 'I couldn't get through your lice in days! They say the Government's invented some medicine for lice which they call Dee-Dee. Ah, if only we had a spoonful of that . . . Do you know, women, that Huru keeps watch over Fadik at night? She tells the youths when to come in and then drives them out with a stick. Ha-ha, and she wants us to believe in Fadik's virtue . . .'

'That's because it suits her. Where will she find people who'll work for nothing like those two?'

'Well, the lads are well provided for this year,' snickered Doneh. 'Who knows but that Huru may hop in and help Fadik out!'

Just then, Huru loomed up from behind a hut. She was a large woman with a sharp chin and a wrinkled face. Her greying hair was always carefully dyed with henna.

'Whores!' she shouted at the top of her voice, as she bore down upon them with arms akimbo. 'City trollops! You get hold of a poor fellow's wife and let your tongues go wagging away. Tell me, are you any better than she? What do you want of this harmless mountain girl?' She pounced on Doneh who cringed back. 'As for you, you filthy shitty-assed bitch, you'll shut your mouth or I'll start telling the truth about you and that husband of yours who pretends he's a man. You know me, don't you?'

Doneh blenched.

'Me, sister?' she stammered. 'Me? I never . . . Other people's good name . . .'

The women were dispersing hastily. Only Kurdish Velo's wife, unaware of what was going on, continued picking lice out of her companion's hair.

'Velo says in our country women like this burnt alive. He says there no virtue in this Chukurova. No honour . . .'

The eastern sky had only just begun to pale as, with a great hullabaloo and calls and cries, the women and children drove the cattle out to pasture. Before their houses, red-aproned matrons were busy at the churns beating yoghurt. The damp air smelled of spring.

Osman had long ago yoked the oxen and was waiting at Huru's door.

She appeared in the doorway.

'Osman, my lion,' she said, 'you're not to come back until you've ploughed through the whole field. The girl Aysheh will look after your food and get you some bedding. Mind you do the sowing properly, my child. Husneh's hard pressed this year. And there's your wife to feed too now . . .'

Husneh was Huru's only child, whom in a moment of aberration she had given in marriage to Ali Efendi, a low-salaried tax-collector. All the product of her land, everything Huru had, was for this daughter.

Osman did not move or say a word. He stood there in the half light, a large black shadow near the yoked oxen whose tails were flapping their legs in slow rhythm.

Huru stepped up to him.

'What's the matter with you, Osman, my child,' she said anxiously. 'Is anything wrong?'

'Mistress,' whispered Osman, 'it's what Seedy Doneh's saying. And Zeynep too . . . That my house . . . I don't know . . .'

Huru flared up.

'Shut up, you spineless dolt,' she cried. 'Don't you come babbling to me about the filthy inventions of those city trollops. I paid that broken-nosed thief a hundred good banknotes for the girl, didn't I? Did I ask you for as much as a lira? You listen to me. You can find fault with pure gold, but not with Fadik. Don't let me hear such nonsense from you again!'

Osman hesitated.

'I don't know . . .' he murmured, as he turned at last and drove the oxen off before him.

It was mid-morning. A bright sun glowed over the sparkling fields.

Osman was struggling with the lean, emaciated oxen, which after ploughing through only one acre had stretched themselves on the ground and simply refused to budge. Flushed and breathless, he let himself drop on to a mound and took his head in his hands. After a while, he rose and tried pulling the animals up by the tail.

'Accursed beasts,' he muttered. 'The Mistress says Husneh's in need this year. Get up this minute, accursed beasts!'

He pushed and heaved, but to no avail. Suddenly in a burst of fury, he flung himself on the black ox, dug his teeth into its nose and shook it with all his might. Then he straightened up and looked about him sheepishly.

'If anyone saw me . . .' He swore as he spat out blood. 'What can I do? Husneh's in need and there's Fadik to feed too. And now these heathen beasts . . . I don't know.'

It was in this state of perplexity that Stumpy Veli found him when he strolled over from a neighbouring field.

'So the team's collapsed, eh?' he commented. 'Well, it was to be expected. Look at how their ribs are sticking out. You won't be able to get anything out of them.'

'I don't know,' muttered Osman faintly. 'Husneh's in a bad way and I got married . . .'

'And a fine mess that's landed you in,' burst out Veli angrily. 'You'd have been better off dead!'

'I don't know,' said Osman. 'The Mistress paid a hundred liras for her . . .'

Stumpy Veli took hold of his arm and made him sit down.

'Look, Osman,' he said, 'the villagers told me to talk to you. They say you're giving the village a bad name. Ever since the Agha's son took up with your wife, all the other youths have followed suit and your house is just like a brothel now. The villagers say you've got to repudiate her. If you don't, they'll drive you both out. The honour of the whole village is at stake, and you know honour doesn't grow on trees . . .'

Osman, his head hanging down, was as still as a statue. A stray ant had caught his eye.

What's this ant doing around here at this time of day, he wondered to himself. Where can its nest be?

Veli nudged him sharply.

'Damn you, man!' he cried. 'Think what'll happen if the police get wind of this. She hasn't got any papers. Why, if the gendarmes once lay their hands on her, you know how it'll be. They'll play around with her for months, poor creature.'

Osman started as though an electric current had been sent through his large frame.

'I haven't got any papers either,' he whispered.

Veli drew nearer. Their shoulders touched. Osman's were trembling fitfully.

'Papers are the business of the Government,' Veli said. 'You and me, we can't understand such things. If we did, then what would we need a Government for? Now, listen to me. If the gendarmes get hold of her, we'll be the laughing-stock of villages for miles around. We'll never be able to hold up our heads again in the Chukurova. You mustn't trifle with the honour of the whole village. Get rid of her before she drags you into more trouble.'

'But where will I be without her?' protested Osman. 'I'll die, that's all. Who'll do my washing? Who'll cook bulgur pi-laff for me? I'll starve to death if I have to eat gruel again every day. I just can't do without her.'

'The villagers will buy you another woman,' said Veli. 'We'll collect the money among us. A better woman, an honourable one, and beautiful too . . . I'll go up into the mountain villages and pick one for you myself. Just you pack this one off quickly . . .'

'I don't know,' said Osman. 'It's the Mistress knows about these things.'

Veli was exasperated.

'Damn the Mistress!' he shouted. 'It's up to you, you idiot!'

Then he softened. He tried persuasion again. He talked and talked. He talked himself hoarse, but Osman sat there immovable as a rock, his mouth clamped tight. Finally Veli spat in his face and stalked off.

It was well on in the afternoon when it occurred to Osman to unyoke the team. He had not stirred since Veli's departure. As for the oxen, they had just lain there placidly chewing the cud. He managed to get them to their feet and let them wander about the field, while he walked back to the village. He made straight for the Agha's house and waited in the yard, not speaking to anyone, until he saw the Agha's son riding in, the bridle of his horse lathered with sweat.

The Agha's son was taken aback. He dismounted quickly, but Osman waylaid him.

'Listen,' he pleaded, 'you're the son of our all-powerful Agha. What do you want with my wife?'

The Agha's son became the colour of his famous boots. He hastily pulled a five-lira note out of his pocket and thrust it into Osman's hand.

'Take this,' he mumbled and hurried away.

'But you're a great big Agha's son!' cried Osman after him. 'Why do you want to drive her away? What harm has she done you? You're a great big . . .'

He was crushed. He stumbled away towards Huru's house, the five-lira note still in his hand.

At the sight of Osman, Huru blew her top.

'What are you doing here, you feeble-minded ass?' she shouted. 'Didn't I tell you not to come back until you'd finished all the ploughing? Do you want to ruin me, you idiot?'

'Wait, Mistress,' stammered Osman. 'Listen . . .'

'Listen, he says! Damn the fool!'

'Mistress,' he pleaded, 'let me explain . . .'

Huru glared at him.

'Mistress, you haven't heard. You don't know what the villagers are going to do to me. They're going to throw me out of this village. Stumpy Veli said so. He said the police . . . He said papers . . . We haven't got any papers. Fadik hasn't and I haven't either. He said the gendarmes would carry Fadik away and do things to her. He said I must repudiate her because my house is a brothel. That's what he said. I said the Mistress knows these things . . . She paid the hundred liras . . .'

Huru was dancing with fury. She rushed out into the village square and began howling at the top of her voice.

'Bastards! So she's a thorn in your flesh, this poor fellow's wife! If you want to drive whores out of this village why don't you start with your own wives and daughters? You'd better look for whores in your own homes, pimps that you are, all of you! And tell your sons to leave poor folks' women alone . . .'

Then she turned to Osman and gave him a push.

'Off you go! To the fields! No one's going to do anything to your wife. Not while I'm alive.'

The villagers had gathered in the square and had heard Huru out in profound silence. As soon as she was gone, though, they started muttering among themselves.

'Who does that bitch think she is, abusing the whole village like that? . . .'

The Agha, Wolf Mahmut, had heard her too.

'You just wait, Huru,' he said grinding his teeth. 'If you think you're going to get away with this . . .'

The night was dark, a thick damp darkness that seemed to cling to the face and hands. Huru had been waiting for some time now, concealed in the blackest shadow of the barn, when suddenly she perceived a stirring in the darkness, and a voice was calling softly at the door.

'Fadik! Open up, girl. It's me . . .'

The door creaked open and a shadow glided in. An uncontrollable trembling seized Huru. She gripped her stick and flung herself on the door. It was unbolted and went crashing back against the wall. As she stood there trying to pierce the darkness, a few vague figures hustled by and made their escape. Taken by surprise, she hurled out a vitriolic oath and started groping about until she discovered Fadik crouching in a corner. She seized her by the hair and began to beat her with the stick.

'Bitch!' she hissed. 'To think I was standing up for you . . .'

Fadik did not utter a sound as the blows rained down on her. At last Huru, exhausted, let go of her.

'Get up,' she ordered, 'and light some kindling.'

Fadik raked out the dying embers and with much puffing and blowing managed to light a stick of torchwood. A pale honeyed light fell dimly over the stacked hay. There was an old pallet in one corner and a few kitchen utensils, but nothing else to show that the place was lived in.

Huru took Fadik's hand and looked at her sternly.

'Didn't you promise me, girl, that you'd never do it again?'

Fadik's head hung low.

'Do you know, you bitch,' continued Huru, 'what the villagers are going to do? They're going to kick you out of the village. Do you hear me?'

Fadik stirred a little. 'Mistress, I swear I didn't go after them! They just came in spite of everything.'

'Listen to me, girl,' said Huru. 'Do you know what happened to Esheh? That's what you'll come to if you're not careful. They're like ravening wolves, these men. If you fall into their clutches, they'll tear you to shreds. To shreds, I tell you!'

'But Mistress, I swear I never did anything to—'

'You must bolt your door because they'll be after you whether you do anything or not, and their pimps of fathers will put the blame on me. It's my hundred liras they can't swallow. They're dying to see it go to pot . . . Just like Esheh you'll be. They had no one in the world, she and her man, and when Ali was thrown into jail she was left all alone. He'd lifted a sheep from the Agha's flock and bought clothes and shoes for their son. A lovely child he was, three years old . . . Ali doted on him. But there he was in jail, and that yellow-booted good-for-nothing was soon after Esheh like the plague. She kept him at arm's length for as long as she could, poor Esheh, but he got what he wanted in the end. Then he turned her over to those ravening wolves . . . They dragged her about from village to village, from mountain to mountain. Twenty, thirty good-for-nothings . . . Her child was left among strangers, the little boy she had loved so. He died . . . Those who saw her said she was like a consumptive, thin and grey, but still they wouldn't let her go, those scoundrels. Then one day the village dogs came in all smeared with blood, and an eagle was circling over the plain. So the men went to look, and they found Esheh, her body half devoured by the dogs . . . They'd made her dance naked for them . . . They'd done all sorts of things to her. Yes, they as good as killed her. That's what the police said when they came up from the town. And when Ali heard of it, he died of grief in jail. Yes, my girl, you've got Esheh's fate before you. It isn't my hundred liras that I care for, it's you. As for Osman, I can always find another woman for him. Now I've warned you. Just call me if they come again. Esheh was all alone in the world. You've got me, at least. Do you swear to do as I'm telling you?'

'I swear it, Mistress,' said Fadik.

Huru was suddenly very tired.

'Well, I'm going. You'll call me, won't you?'

As soon as she was gone, the youths crept out of the darkness and sneaked into the barn again.

'Hey, Fadik,' they whispered. 'Huru was lying to you, girl. Esheh just killed herself . . .'

There was a stretch of grass in front of the Agha's house, and on one side of it dung had been heaped to the size of a small hillock. The dung steamed in the early morning sun and not a breath stirred the warm air. A cock climbed to the top of the heap. It scraped the dung, stretched its neck and crowed triumphantly, flapping its wings.

The group of villagers squatting about on the grass silently eyed the angry Agha. Wolf Mahmut was a huge man whose shadow when he was sitting was as large as that of an average man standing up. He was never seen without a frayed, checked overcoat, the only one in the village, that he had been wearing for years now.

He was toying irritably with his metal-framed glasses when Stumpy Veli, who had been sent for a while ago, made his appearance. The Agha glared at him.

'Is this the way you get things done, you fraud?' he expostulated. 'So you'd have Hollow Osman eating out of your hand in no time, eh?'

Stumpy Veli seemed to shrink to half his size.

'Agha,' he said, 'I tried everything. I talked and talked. I told him the villagers would drive them both out. I warned him of the gendarmes. All right, he said, I'll send her away. And then he didn't . . . If you ask me, Huru's at the bottom of it all.'

The others stirred. 'That she is!' they agreed.

Mahmut Agha jumped up. 'I'll get even with her,' he growled.

'That, you will, Agha,' they assented. 'But . . .'

'We've put up with that old whore long enough,' continued the Agha, sitting down again.

'Yes, Agha,' said Stumpy Veli, 'but, you see, she relies on her son-in-law Ali, the tax-collector. They'd better stop treading on my toes, she said, or I'll have Ali strip this village bare . . .'

'He can't do anything,' said the Agha. 'I don't owe the Government a bean.'

'But we do, Agha,' interposed one of the men. 'He can come here and take away our blankets and rugs, whatever we have . . .'

'It's because of Huru that he hasn't fleeced this village up to now,' said another. 'We owe a lot of money, Agha.'

'Well, what are we to do then?' cried Mahmut Agha angrily. 'All our youths have left the plough and the fields and are after the woman night and day like rutting bulls. At this rate, the whole village'll starve this year.'

An old man spoke up in a tremulous voice. 'I'm dead, for one,' he wailed. 'That woman's ruined my hearth. High morning it is already. Go to the plough, my son, I beg the boy. We'll starve if you don't plough. But he won't listen. He's always after that woman. I've lost my son because of that whore. I'm too old to plough any more. I'll starve this year. I'll go and throw myself at Huru's feet. There's nothing else to do . . .'

The Agha rose abruptly. 'That Huru!' He gritted his teeth. 'I'll settle her account.'

He strode away.

The villagers looked up hopefully. 'Mahmut Agha'll settle her account,' they muttered. 'He'll find a way . . .'

The Agha heard them and swelled with pride. 'Yes, Mahmut Agha'll settle her account,' he repeated grimly to himself.

He stopped before a hut and called out.

'Hatije Woman! Hatije!'

A middle-aged woman rushed out wiping her hands on her apron.

'Mahmut Agha!' she cried. 'Welcome to our home. You never visit us these days.' Then she whirled back. 'Get up, you damned lazybones,' she shouted angrily. 'It's high morning, and look who's here.'

Mahmut Agha followed her inside.

'Look, Agha,' she complained, pointing to her son, 'it's high morning and Halil still abed!'

Startled at the sight of the Agha, Halil sprang up and drew on his black shalvar-trousers shamefacedly, while his mother continued with her lamentations.

'Ah, Mahmut Agha, you don't know what's befallen us! You don't know, may I kiss your feet, my Agha, or you wouldn't have us on your land any longer . . . Ah, Mahmut Agha! This accursed son of mine . . . I would have seen him dead and buried, yes, buried in this black earth before . . .'

'What are you cursing the lad for?' Mahmut Agha interrupted her. 'Wait, just tell me first.'

'Ah, Agha, if you knew! It was full day when he came home this night. And it's the same every night, the same ever since Hollow Osman's woman came to the village. He lies abed all through the livelong day. Who'll do the ploughing, I ask you? We'll starve this year. Ah, Mahmut Agha, do something! Please do something . . .'

'You go outside a little, will you, Hatije,' said the Agha. Then he turned to Halil, stretching out his long, wrinkled neck which had become as red as a turkey's. 'Listen to me, my boy, this has got to end. You must get this whore out of our village and give her to the youths of another village, any village. She's got to go and you'll do it. It's an order. Do you hear me?'

'Why, Agha!' Halil said ingratiatingly. 'Is that what's worrying you? I'll get hold of her this very night and turn her over to Jelil from Ortakli village. You can count on me.'

The Agha's spirits rose.

'Hatije,' he called out, 'come in here. See how I'm getting you out of this mess? And all the village too . . . Let that Huru know who she's dealing with in the future. They call me Wolf Mahmut and I know how to put her nose out of joint.'

Long before dawn, piercing shrieks startled the echoes in the village.

'Bastards! Pimps!' Huru was howling. 'You won't get away with this, not on your life you won't. My hundred liras were too much for you to swallow, eh, you fiends? You were jealous of this poor fellow's wife, eh? But you just wait and see, Wolf Mahmut! I'll set the tax-collector after you all in no time. I'll get even with you if I have to spend my last penny! I'll bribe the Mudir, the Kaymakam, all the officials. I'll send telegrams to Ankara, to Ismet Pasha, to the head of the Democrats. I'll have you all dragged into court, rotting away in police-stations. I'll get my own back on you for Fadik's sake.'

She paused to get her breath and was off again even louder than before.

Fadik had disappeared, that was the long and the short of it. Huru soon found out that someone else was missing too, Huseyin's half-witted son, The Tick.

'Impossible,' she said. 'The Tick ravishing women? Not to save his life, he couldn't! This is just another trick of those good-for-nothings . . .'

'But really, Huru,' the villagers tried to persuade her, 'he was after her all the time. Don't you know he gathered white snails in the hills, threaded them into a necklace and offered it to Fadik, and she hung it up on her wall as a keepsake? That's the plain truth, Huru.'

'I don't believe it,' Huru said stubbornly. 'I wouldn't even if I saw them together with my own eyes . . .'

The next day it started raining, that sheer, plumbline torrent which sets in over the Chukurova for days. The minute the bad news had reached him, Osman had abandoned his plough and had rushed back to the village. He was standing now motionless at Huru's door, the peak of his cap drooping over his eyes. His wet clothes clung to his flesh, glistening darkly, and his rawhide boots were clogged with mud.

'Come in out of the rain, Osman, do!' Huru kept urging him.

'I can't. I don't know . . .' was all he could say.

'Now, look here, Osman,' said Huru. 'She's gone, so what? Let them have that bitch. I'll find you a good woman, my Osman. Never mind the money. I'll spend twice as much on a new wife for you. Just you come in out of the rain.'

Osman never moved.

'Listen, Osman. I've sent word to Ali. Come and levy the taxes at once, I said. Have no mercy on these ungrateful wretches. If you don't fleece them to their last rag, I said, you needn't count on me as a mother again. You'll see what I'm going to do to them, my Osman. You just come inside . . .'

The rain poured down straight and thick as the warp in a loom, and Osman still stood there, his chin resting on his staff, like a thick tree whose branches have been lopped off.

Huru appealed to the neighbours. Two men came and pulled and pushed, but he seemed nailed to the ground. It was well in the afternoon when he stirred and began to pace the village from one end to the other, his head sunk between his shoulders and the rain streaming down his body.

'Poor fellow, he's gone mad,' opined the villagers.

A few strong men finally carried him home. They undressed him and put him to bed.

Huru sat down beside him. 'Look, Osman, I'll get you a new woman even if it costs me a thousand liras. You mustn't distress yourself so. Just for a woman . . .'

The next morning he was more his normal self, but no amount of reasoning or pleading from Huru could induce him to go back to the field. He left the house and resumed his pacing up and down.

The villagers had really begun to feel sorry for him now.

'Alas, poor Osman!' they murmured as he passed between the huts.

Osman heard them and heaved deep, heart-rending sighs. And still he roamed aimlessly round and round.

Wolf Mahmut should have known better. Why, the whole village saw with half an eye what a rascal Halil was! How could he be trusted to give up a woman once he had got her into his hands? He had indeed got Fadik out of the way, but what he had done was to shut her up in one of the empty sheep-pens in the hills beyond the village, and there he had posted The Tick to guard her.

'Play around with her if you like,' he had told him contemptuously. 'But if you let her give you the slip—' and he had seized The Tick's wrist and squeezed it until it hurt— 'you're as good as dead.'

Though twenty years old, The Tick was so scraggy and undersized that at first glance people would take him to be only ten. His arms and legs were as thin as matchsticks and he walked sideways like a crab. He had always had a way of clinging tenaciously to people or objects he took a fancy to, which even as a child had earned him his nickname. No one had ever called him by his real name and it looked as though his own mother had forgotten it too . . .

Halil would come every evening bringing food for Fadik and The Tick, and he would leave again just before dawn. But it was not three days before the village youths found out what was going on. After that there was a long queue every night outside the sheep-pen. They would take it in turns, heedless of Fadik's tears and howls, and at daybreak, singing and firing their guns as though in a wedding procession, they would make their way back to the village.

Night was falling and Fadik began to tremble like a leaf. They would not be long now. They would come again and torture her. She was weak with fear and exhaustion. For the past two days, her gorge had risen at the very sight of food, and she lay there on the dirt floor, hardly able to move, her whole body covered with bruises and wounds.

The Tick was dozing away near the door of the pen.

Fadik tried to plead with him. 'Let me go, brother,' she begged. 'I'll die if I have to bear another night of this.'

The Tick half-opened his eyes. 'I can't,' he replied.

'But if I die, it'll be your fault. Before God it will . . . Please let me go.'

'Why should it be my fault?' said The Tick. 'I didn't bring you here, did I?'

'They'll never know. You'll say you fell asleep. I'll go off and hide somewhere. I'll go back to my mother . . .'

'I can't,' said The Tick. 'Halil would kill me if I let you go.'

'But I want to go to my mother,' she cried desperately. 'You must let me go. Please let me go . . .'

It was dark now and the sound of singing drifted up from the village.

Fadik was seized with a violent fit of trembling. 'They're coming,' she said. 'Let me get away now, brother. Save me! If you save me, I'll be your woman. I'll do anything . . .'

But The Tick had not been nicknamed for nothing.

'They'd kill me,' he said. 'Why should I die because of you? And Halil's promised to buy me a pair of shoes, too. I'm not going to go without shoes because of you.'

Fadik broke into wild sobbing. There was no hope now.

'Oh, God,' she wept, 'what shall I do now? Oh, Mother, why was I ever born?'

They lined up as usual at the entrance to the pen. The first one went in and a nerve-racking scream rose from Fadik, a scream that would have moved the most hardened of hearts. But the youths were deaf to everything. In they went, one after the other, and soon Fadik's screams died down. Not even a moan came out of her.

There were traces of blood on the ground at the back of the sheep-pen. Halil and the Agha's son had had a fight the night before and the Agha's son had split open Halil's head.

'The woman's mine,' Halil had insisted. 'I've a right to go in first.'

'No, you haven't,' the Agha's son had contended. 'I'm going to be the first.'

The other youths had taken sides and joined the fray which had lasted most of the night, and it was a bedraggled band that wended back to the village that night.

Bowed down with grief, Hatije Woman came weeping to the Muhtar.

'My son is dying,' she cried. 'He's at his last gasp, my poor Halil, and it's the Agha's son who did it, all because of that whore of Huru's. Ah, Muhtar, if my son dies what's to become of me? There he lies struggling for life, the only hope of my hearth. But I won't let the Agha get away with this. I'll go to the Government. An old woman's only prop, I'll say . . .'

The Muhtar had great difficulty in talking Hatije out of her purpose.

'You go back home, Hatije Woman,' he said when she had calmed down a little, 'and don't worry. I'll deal with this business.'

He summoned the Agha and the elders, and a long discussion ensued. It would not do to hand over the woman to the police-station. These rapacious gendarmes! . . . The honour of the whole village was at stake. And if they passed her on to the youths of another village, Huru was sure to find out and bring her back. She would not rest until she did.

After long deliberation, they came to a decision at last. The woman would be returned to Osman, but on one condition. He would take himself off with her to some distant place and never appear in the village again. They had no doubt that Osman, grateful to have Fadik back to himself, would accept. And that would cook Huru's goose too. She would lose both the woman and Osman. It would teach her to insult a whole village!

A couple of men went to find Osman and brought him back with them to the Muhtar's house.

'Sit down,' they urged him, but he just stood there grasping his staff, staring about him with bloodshot eyes. His clothes hung down torn and crumpled and stained yellow from his lying all wet on the hay. His hair was a tangled, clotted mass and bits of straw clung to the stubble on his chin.

Wolf Mahmut took off his glasses and fidgeted with them.

'Osman, my lad,' he remonstrated, 'what's this state you're in? And all for a woman! Does a man let himself break down like this just for a woman? You'll die if you go on like this . . .'

'I don't know,' said Osman. 'I'll die . . .'

'See here, Osman,' said the Agha. 'We're here to help you. We'll get your woman back for you from out of those rascals' hands. Then you'll take her and go. You'll both get away from here, as far as possible. But you're not to tell Huru. She mustn't know where you are.'

'You see, Osman,' said Stumpy Veli, 'how good the Agha's being to you. Your own father wouldn't have done more.'

'But you're not to tell Huru,' the Agha insisted. 'If you do, she'll never let you go away. And then the youths will come and take your woman away from you again. And how will you ever get yourself another woman?'

'And who'll wash your clothes then?' added Stumpy Veli. 'Who'll cook your bulgur pilaff for you? You mustn't breathe a word to Huru. Just take Fadik and go off to the villages around Antep. Once there, you'll be sure to get a job on a farm. You'll be much better off than you ever were with Huru, and you'll have your woman with you too . . .'

'But how can I do that?' protested Osman. 'The Mistress paid a hundred liras for Fadik.'

'We'll collect that much among us,' the Agha assured him. 'Don't you worry about that. We'll see that Huru gets her money back. You just take the woman and go.'

'I don't know,' said Osman. His eyes filled with tears and he swallowed. 'The Mistress has always been so good to me . . . How can I . . . Just for a woman . . .'

'If you tell Huru, you're lost,' said the Agha. 'Is Huru the only mistress in the world? Aren't there other villages in this country? Take the woman and go. You'll never find another woman like Fadik. Listen, Veli'll tell you where she is and to-morrow you'll take her and go.'

Osman bowed his head. He thought for a long time. Then he looked up at them.

'I won't tell her,' he said at last. 'Why should I want to stay here? There are other villages . . .'

Before dawn the next day, he set out for the sheep-pen which Stumpy Veli had indicated.

'I don't know . . .' he hesitated at the door. 'I don't know . . .' Then he called out softly. 'Fadik? Fadik, girl . . .'

There was no answer. Trembling with hope and fear, he stepped in, then stopped aghast. Fadik was lying there on the dirt floor with only a few tatters left to cover her naked body. Her huge eyes were fixed vacantly on the branches that roofed the pen.

He stood frozen, his eyes filling with tears. Then he bent his large body over her.

'Fadik,' he whispered, 'are you all right?'

Her answering moan shook him to the core. He slipped off his shirt and helped her into it. Then he noticed The Tick who had shrunk back into a corner, trying to make himself invisible. Osman moved on him threateningly.

'Uncle Osman,' cried The Tick shaking with fear, 'I didn't do it. It was Halil. He said he'd buy me a pair of shoes . . . And Fadik would have died if I hadn't been here . . .'

Osman turned away, heaved Fadik on to his back swiftly and threw himself out of the pen.

The mountain peaks were pale and the sun was about to

rise. A few white clouds floated in the sky and a cool breeze caressed his face. The earth was wet with dew.

The Tick was scurrying off towards the village.

'Brother,' Osman called after him, 'go to the Mistress and tell her I thank her for all she's done for me, but I have to go. Tell her to forgive me . . .'

He set out in the opposite direction with Fadik on his back. He walked without a break until the sun was up the height of two minarets. Then he lowered Fadik to the ground and sat down opposite her. They looked at each other for a long while without speaking.

'Tell me,' said Osman. 'Where shall we go now? I don't know . . .'

Fadik moaned.

The air smelled of spring and the earth steamed under the sun.

(TRANSLATED BY THILDA KEMAL)

The House on the Border

by AZIZ NESIN

We had moved into the house the day before. It was a nice place. That morning, when I walked out, our next-door neighbor, an old man, was watching the street with avid curiosity and called us from his window.

"You shouldn't have rented that place," he cackled.

I stared at him coldly.

"Is this a new way of greeting neighbors?" I growled. "What do you mean we shouldn't have moved in there?"

He was not fazed.

"Thieves break into that house often," he announced with relish. "It's my neighborly duty to warn you."

As if the thieves couldn't break into his house too! Why should robbers favor only ours?

Rather annoyed, I entered the grocery store at the corner to buy cigarettes.

"There are such characters around," I mumbled.

"What's the matter?" asked the grocer.

"Some old goat told me that thieves usually rob the house we just moved into," I complained.

The grocer nodded. "Well, the old goat was right. You shouldn't have rented that house. It's robbed frequently."

I was furious. Without answering him, I walked out of the store. The whole day was ruined, naturally. I fumed till evening.

That night a couple from our block visited us. They were nice people. We talked about this and that till midnight. When they were about to leave, the husband turned and looked at us strangely.

"It's a beautiful house," he said, "but thieves never leave it alone."

Since they were already out of the house I couldn't ask him: "Why is this house supposed to be irresistible to thieves? Why shouldn't they honor your home too?"

Seeing my ferocious scowl, my wife started to laugh.

"Dearest," she said, "don't you understand? God knows, they have thousands of tricks for scaring tenants away. This must be the newest one. They will drive us out and, since the rent is low, either they will move in themselves or bring in one of their relatives."

It was possible. But I couldn't sleep a wink that night. It was as if I had a date with the thief. I waited for him breathlessly, whispering to myself: "He will be here any moment."

I must have dozed off. I jumped up at a slight noise and grabbed the gun I had hidden under my pillow.

"Don't move or I'll shoot," I yelled into the darkness.

As I told you, we had moved in the day before. Now confronted with a nocturnal visitor, I forgot where the light switch was. Groping in the dark, I got entangled in every conceivable object and bumped into the walls in search of a switch. As if this was not enough, some darned thing coiled around my ankles and, with a resounding crash, I found myself on the floor. "The dirty—" I muttered under my breath. "He tripped me." I decided to pump his stomach with lead, quite cold-bloodedly. Unfortunately, during my solo flight to the floor, the gun had fallen from my hand and bounced away.

The darkness was suddenly filled with a horrible laughter: "Heh! Heh! Heh!"

"Are we shooting a domestic horror movie?" I shouted. "If you are a man, show your face, you . . . you villain!"

"I suppose you were looking for the switch," a voice said in the darkness. "It's amazing how all the new tenants make the same mistake."

"Do you know what I'm going to do to you?"

"No," said the man in the darkness. "I don't know. Now, may I turn on the lights and help you?"

I heard the click of the switch and the room was flooded with light. Apparently, when I had crashed down, I had rolled under the table. As for my wife, she was securely lodged under the bed.

There in the middle of the room stood a man larger than life—twice my size, I mean.

I knew that if I emerged from my hiding place I couldn't scare him. I decided he wouldn't be able to size me up if I stayed there.

Imitating a basso profundo to the best of my ability, "Who are you?" I asked. It was a deep-chested growl.

"I'm the thief," he answered calmly.

"Oh, yeah?" I said. "If you think I'm a fool, you're mistaken. You're not a thief. You're trying to scare us away and move in here. Look at me, look closely. Do I look like an idiot?"

He didn't answer my question. "You'll see whether I'm a thief or not," he said instead.

You'd have thought it was his own father's house. He started to rummage through the drawers, picking out what items he fancied and talking to us all the while. I have to admit that he was quite friendly.

"So you turned this into a bedroom . . . the family before you used it as a study. The ones before them too . . ."

"Now look," I said. "You're robbing me. I'll report you to the police."

Without stopping, "Please do," he replied. "Go to the Precinct. And don't forget to give them my best regards."

"But you'll run away while I'm gone."

"I won't."

"You will! You will clean up the whole house and steal away." It was a dilemma. "I have an idea," I said. "First I'll tie you up, then I'll go to the police."

"Help!" shrieked my wife suddenly.

Were all the neighbors waiting on our doorstep, I wonder. As if on cue, they stampeded into the house, chattering excitedly. But did they look at us or offer sympathy? No. They were full of curiosity and in good spirits.

"Another robbery," they said.

"What, again?"

"Who is it this time?"

"Let's see."

Some of them were downright friendly with the thief. They even asked him how he was, while he calmly went on packing our things.

"Help!" I croaked. "Help! I must bind him up. I'll go to the Precinct."

One of the neighbors shook his head.

"It won't do you any good," he said. "But I never stop people from doing what they want . . . go ahead."

What kind of a neighborhood was this anyway?

Suddenly emboldened, my wife brought me the clothesline. The thief didn't resist while I tied him up securely. We carried him into another room and locked the door.

We ran to the police. My wife considered herself the spokesman of the family and told the story to the Chief. He asked for our address.

"Aha," said the Chief. "That house."

"Yes," I answered, "that house."

"We have nothing to do with that house," he informed us. "It's not in our jurisdiction."

"What are we going to do now? Did we tie that poor fellow up for nothing?"

"If you lived in the house next door, we could have done something," the Chief said. Then, as if addressing a couple of morons, he added, "You would have been in our jurisdiction."

"That house was not vacant," my wife explained patiently. "So we moved into this one."

We learned that our house was right on the border between areas under the jurisdiction of two Precincts.

"The other Precinct should look into the matter," said the Chief.

The other Precinct was quite far away. By the time we reached it, the sun was already high in the sky. We told our story again, and again they asked our address.

"That house," said one of the cops.

"That house," I said.

"If you lived next door, we would have done something. Your house is not within our jurisdiction."

"Poor man," murmured my wife. "We tied him up."

"Tell me," I cried out impatiently. "Tell me one thing. Under whose jurisdiction are we? Who is supposed to look after us?"

"The State Gendarmerie," said the cop. "Your house is under their jurisdiction. The Police has nothing to do with it."

We left the cops.

"Let's go home first," suggested my wife. "I'm worried about the thief. He might die, you know."

She was right, of course. What if the thief should die of hunger? Or heart failure? After all, he was trussed up like a chicken. What if the ropes would impede the circulation of his blood? What if . . .

We went home. The thief was where we had left him.

"How are you?" I asked anxiously.

"Fine, fine," he answered. "But I'm hungry."

My wife ran to the kitchen. Alas, we had spinach and, would you believe it, it was the only dish the thief detested. My wife dashed to the butcher, bought some steaks and fed the thief.

This time we went to the Gendarmerie. After listening to our story, the Commandant asked for our address.

"Aha," he said. "That house."

Apparently we had rented a famous place.

The Commandant shook his head. "This is not a case for the Gendarmerie. You should call the Police."

"Now look," I cried. "We went to the Police. They sent us here. Now you say we must call the cops. Is this a run around? Isn't there anybody to look into the case?"

The Commandant pulled out a map.

"I hope you know how to read a map," he said. "Here, it gives the height. See? 140 feet. This is the water tower—116 feet—and here is the hill. Now, this area is under the jurisdiction of the Gendarmerie. If your house were built further up, say about two yards towards Northwest, you would have been in our area."

"All this for two lousy yards," I said. "Do something, man! What would happen if you helped us now?"

The Commandant pursed his lips. "What would happen?"

he repeated. Then he nodded his head sagely. "Only we know what would happen . . . Only we know." Again he put his finger on a spot on the map. "Look, this is your house. Right on the line that separates our area from the Police's. See? Of course, a part of your garden is under our jurisdiction. But the robbery didn't take place there, did it?"

There was nothing we could do but go to the Police again.

"Let's first see how the thief is doing," my wife suggested. "God help us if something should happen to him."

So we went home.

I almost clasped the thief to my bosom. "How are you?" I panted.

"Water! Quick!" he cried out. "I'm thirsty!"

After drinking the water, he looked at us sternly.

"Listen," he said. "Don't say that I didn't warn you. You have no right to hold me here. You are restricting the freedom of a citizen. I have a good mind to sue you."

"But what can we do?" I cried. "We don't know who is supposed to look after us. Apparently, we are in the middle of nowhere. Why they built this house right on the border line is beyond me."

"Didn't I tell you? . . . Now, let me go. Otherwise I'll drag you through the courts for restricting my freedom."

"Give me time," I begged. "Give me till tonight. I want to go to the Police again."

"By all means," he replied affably. "Go and see anyone you wish. But it's futile. I've been aware of the situation for a long time now. They have to decide whether to include your house in one of the areas or change the borders. Till then . . ."

Again we went to the Precinct. This time the Chief brought out a map too.

"Look," he sighed, "this area is under the jurisdiction of the Gendarmerie. Your garden and a small part of the house is within their area. Only a fraction of the house is under our jurisdiction."

"The bedroom is in your area," I pointed out. "And the robbery took place there."

He looked at me owlishly. "Quite. First, this must be definitely established. Then, there is another problem: the thief didn't fly in through the window, did he? He crossed the garden and then entered your house. Right? And the garden is under the jurisdiction of the Gendarmerie. Yours is not a new problem. It is already under discussion. First they have to reach a decision, then they have to inform us of their decision concerning the area your house is supposed to be in. Then we can act accordingly."

We returned home. Our elderly next-door neighbor was at the window as usual.

"So they broke into the house again," he cackled.

"Yes," I nodded.

"No one stays there long," he said cheerfully. "That's why the rent is low. Neither the owner nor the tenants could live there. He decided to pull down the house and rebuild it two yards further up. But then he found you fools—I mean he found you and rented the place."

His wife was looking at us sadly. "It's not your fault," she informed us. "It's the owner's. When they build a house they think of water, gas, electricity and the view. But do they think of the jurisdiction? No! What sort of a fool would build a house right on the border?"

I couldn't answer that question even if I wanted to.

Since we had paid the whole year's rent in advance, to move away was out of the question. So we went home and untied the thief. Then we settled down comfortably in the study and discussed the world situation for a while. The thief dined with us that evening.

"So long," he said after the meal. "I'll be back tonight."

Now we have five or six resident thieves. All our neighbors are familiar with them. We collaborate with the thieves too. That is to say, we help them to defend our home against other unfriendly thieves, who are, after all, strangers to us.

I don't know what will happen eventually. Either all eight of us, my wife and I and the six thieves, will spend the remainder of the year there, or they will include the house in one of the areas, thus enabling me to complain to the authorities. But we are now used to our friends, the thieves. And to report them would be rather embarrassing—after all they share the household expenses now.

(TRANSLATED BY GÖNÜL SUVEREN)

POETRY

MELIH CEVDET ANDAY

On the Nomad Sea

I

You I and our flowerpot on the balcony,
Busy Elizabeth. The building's first triangle.

Neither old nor new. As if the most lucid
Moment of our destiny is quivering

On the nomad sea. We're unaware of it.
The sound of the rock is like the human voice.

At a glimpse you discover: the flowerpot
On the balcony has replaced the cloud. Clouds

Turn into horses in all that foam.
You and I running, running. Ahead of us

A red bird shakes the ancient elder tree
A blind child stared at just now.

Then cloud becomes flowerpot again,
Horses start to heave; we rest. In our ears

A murmur survives like indecipherable words
The walls spoke. Out of this day, this morning.

II

Neither remembrance nor oblivion. Edges meet
In the heavy slow symbols of our gaze

Growing like the trills of a crippled nightingale
Mingled with the crimson smells of shores.

And I migrate to you, moment by moment.
I return in an exodus, like a pulsation,

Seeking your lips' rocks,
Seeking your name I wrote in rain.

Now you vanish in the rifts of your own valley.
Now you gush out

Over your vanished valley.
Time and again I am lost to myself.

This is all there is to it. Neither old nor new
Like the most lucid moment of our destiny.

Countless blues shifting to a thought
Unused as words that can't exist alone,

That rise from nowhere.
The soul's a coal-crystal, emerging from the dark

Like a scarlet moon watching over night.
Adumbrating figure-like forms,

Like a carnivorous plant it closes in
On all things that are scattered and come together.

Scattering is only coming together.
The sexual fluid breaking out of its shell,

The sun's bow, taut, then loosened; earliest images
Of the glitter of starry oysters;

The sky's wing turning red, then pale;
All sorts of fruit with sealed feet on branches,

Sprouting frantic to new infinity, then falling;
The soil whose sea-lion panting

Moves us deep down, heavy with bleached bones.
Neither old nor new. That's all there is to it.

That's all. You I and our flowerpot on the balcony.
Alone in the flutter of heavy symbols.

III

There. I sprinkle words in handfuls
To the birds, to the roots of roses,

To the sun's lip, to the skirt
Of prancing morning, to rocks' red velvet,

To the moon's horns, to the honeysuckle
Hanging from your hair's trellis . . .

All by myself I cast my image over all shapes
And over the squint-eyed ocean-beds.

IV

Henry Moore's on the beach picking pebbles,
Small pebbles, fertile, some with holes in the middle,

Some like women's nipples, like figs,
Dreams on their shoulders.

The heart's meant for the wisdom no form
Is doomed to suffer.

Rocks that ennoble the world with lodes, slab by slab,
Wave like flags that have wiped

The blood-stains of living.
Bones, all those human, all those animal bones,

The daintiest and grandest wreaths
Of the passage of mutation.

And the seashells with insides carved out
Smell of shadows like a billygoat's brow.

Delight was meant to cross-breed
Beasts and grass.

If the eye that sees is the eye that is seen
Then I am someone else.

This frame belongs neither to yesterday nor tomorrow.
Tomorrow's an image. So is yesterday.

Sea, bird, rain, wind,
Belong to this day, this morning.

V

Freud is seated in the tree's subconscious.
He keeps poking the earth's dreams.

Poppies brighten these dreams.
Sea, bird, rain, wind.

The dream is a delayed star distilled
From action's bed of milky figs,

Late or early, the fish that suddenly leaps
Out of yesterday's waters;

A scarlet commotion that has turned daylight inside out,
The face of a cramped well asleep and awake.

Epochs seem hidden in seeds,
Swings creaking in the soil.

Sea, bird, rain, wind.
And I found myself crucified

Between past and future, like a dream.
Neither old nor new. As if the most lucid

Moment of our destiny is trembling
In seas which are laid waste.

All those tree-trunks
Covered with graffiti like asylum walls . . .

The locked gem of birds
Transforming the dead into stars.

Man craved more, so much more.
Still more. Neither old nor new.

Perhaps a giant dies and is resurrected
Time and again or a goddess frightened to death

These mute monuments blooming flower-like
With lines helter-skelter to the eye.

The eye is the god of its own harmony,
Slice by slice, against and opposite the whole.

Shape turning into shape, the present's
Sounding water, life's alarm clock;

The enigmatic masts of change, the shriek,
The diamond of action, woman, noun and verb.

As they chase out a bull that rips through a village
I drove away whatever you possessed.

Now I know how hard it is to strip oneself
Of a raid in two tenses and live in a blue moment.

(TRANSLATED BY BRIAN SWANN
AND TALAT S. HALMAN)

FAZIL HUSNU DAGLARCA

Madman

No white
In his eyes—
In his eyes
No faith.

In the Beds

Night seizes
From you starknaked
All you loved
And shall love.

Beauty and Mind

If you understand,
Love me.
Know more if you are lovely
And love more.

Glimmer

Darkness
Is sensed a little
When the mind
Of the bat strikes.

Soft

The mouth
Of a hungry man
Makes the bread
Come alive.

First Crime

The mountain stabs
At dawn
The beauty
Of the night.

Elegy for the Bluebird

He pulled the trigger.
Maybe you were asleep on a branch
And didn't get shot.
There you kept quiet about evil.

Of a Cat

Widows
While closing the door

Always hear
A cat going up the stairs.

Shriek

Each day,
Each night,
As soon as it sees me—
The sky is God's shriek.

In Figures

While two
Renews one,
Three
Is what two sees.

Bloodless

When you say two,
Don't be so happy.
Two exists
By killing one time and again.

Telling It Right

Two men dupe each other—
A village rises there.
Nations lie to each other—
States fill our world.

Twosome

A child is an apple
Cut in two—
Green to the earth,
Red to the sky.

Belief

The sun
Has faith
In water.
Water, in you.

At the Temple

Whatever I do,
He is.
Whatever I say,
He isn't.

The Faithless

When quiet,
They have no tongues.
When talking,
They have no mouths.

Narrow White

No man
Can fit into one house.

No man can fit
Into one death.

Loving You

If one loves you,
He strips to the moon,
And he loves
Until his corpse.

Teeming Street

Why do you wake up
At night and shudder?
Death can destroy what you might live,
Not what you have lived.

In Forgiveness of Eternity

Night
Is
God's gift
to the blind

Our Losses

First the mammoths vanished
From the earth
Now the birds are vanishing
From the sky

Howl

What dogs
Can't exhaust for all their barking
Is the silence
Of the earth

Old Door

Is what women want
To be blue
Or the night
Husbands grow old and never find out

(TRANSLATED BY TALAT S. HALMAN)

NAZIM HIKMET

About Mount Uludag

For seven years now Uludag and I have been staring each
    other in the eye.
It hasn't moved an inch,
        and neither have I,
yet we know each other well.
Like all living things, it knows how to laugh and how to
    get mad.

Sometimes,
        in winter, especially at night,

when the wind blows from the south,
with its snowy forests, plateaus, and frozen lakes
    it turns over in its sleep,
and the Old Man who lives way up there at the very
    top—his long beard flying,
        skirts billowing—
    rides howling on the wind down into the valley . . .

Then sometimes,
    especially in May, at sunup,
    it rises like a brand-new world—
        huge, blue, vast,
        free and happy.

Then there are days
    when it looks like its picture on the pop bottles.
And then I understand that in its hotel I can't see
    lady skiers sipping cognac
    are flirting with the gentlemen skiers.

And the day comes
when one of its beetle-browed mountain folk, having
butchered his neighbor at the altar of sacred property,
    comes to us as a guest in his yellow homespun
    trousers
    to do fifteen years in cellblock 71.

Since I Was Thrown Inside

Since I was thrown inside
    the earth has gone around the sun ten times.
If you ask it:
    "Not worth mentioning—
    a microscopic span."
If you ask me:
    "Ten years of my life."

I had a pencil
    the year I was thrown inside.
It was used up after a week of writing.
If you ask it:

"A whole lifetime."
If you ask me:
"What's a week."

Since I've been inside,
Osman, who was in for murder,
did his seven-and-a-half and left,
knocked around on the outside for a while,
then landed back inside for smuggling,
served six months and was out again;
yesterday we got a letter—he's married,
with a kid coming in the spring.

They're ten-years-old now,
the children who were conceived
the year I was thrown inside.
And that year's foals—shaky on their long, spindly legs—
have been wide-rumped, contented mares for some time
now.

But the olive seedlings are still saplings,
still children.

New squares have opened in my faraway city
since I was thrown inside.
And my family now lives
on a street I don't know,
in a house I haven't seen.

Bread was like cotton—soft and white—
the year I was thrown inside.
Then it was rationed,
and here inside people killed each other
over a black loaf the size of a fist.
Now it's free again,
but it's dark and has no taste.

The year I was thrown inside
the SECOND hadn't started yet.
The ovens at Dachau hadn't been lit,
the atom bomb hadn't been dropped on Hiroshima.

Time flowed like blood from the slit throat of a child.
Then that chapter was officially closed—
now the American dollar is talking of a THIRD.

But in spite of everything the day has gotten lighter
    since I was thrown inside.
And "at the edge of darkness,
   pushing against the earth with their heavy hands,
    THEY've risen up" halfway.

Since I was thrown inside
  the earth has gone around the sun ten times.
And I repeat once more with the same passion
    what I wrote about Them
      the year I was thrown inside:
"They who are numberless like ants in the earth,
      fish in the sea,
        birds in the air,
who are cowardly, brave,
    ignorant, wise,
      and childlike,
and who destroy
  and create, they—

our songs tell only of their adventures."
    And anything else,
      such as my ten years here,
      is just so much talk.

Angina Pectoris

If half my heart is here, doctor,
  the other half is in China
with the army flowing
  toward the Yellow River.
And every morning, doctor,
every morning at sunrise my heart
  is shot in Greece.
And every night, doctor,
when the prisoners are asleep and the infirmary is deserted,
my heart stops at a run-down old house
    in Istanbul.
And then after ten years
all I have to offer my poor people
is this apple in my hand, doctor,

one red apple:
   my heart.
And that, doctor, that is the reason
for this angina pectoris—
not nicotine, prison, or arteriosclerosis.
I look at the night through the bars,
and despite the weight on my chest
my heart still beats with the most distant stars.

On Living

I

Living is no laughing matter:
   you must live with great seriousness
      like a squirrel, for example—
I mean without looking for something beyond and above
   living,
      I mean living must be your whole occupation.
Living is no laughing matter:
   you must take it seriously,
   so much so and to such a degree that,
for example, your hands tied behind your back, your back
   to the wall,
or else in a laboratory
   in your white coat and thick glasses,
   you'll be able to die for people—
even for people whose faces you've never seen,
even though you know living
   is the most real, the most beautiful thing.
I mean you must take living so seriously
that even at seventy, for example, you will plant olives—
and not so they'll be left for your children either,
but because even though you fear death you don't believe
   it,
because living, I mean, weighs heavier.

II

Let's say we're seriously ill, need surgery—
which is to say there's a chance we won't get up
      from the white table.

Even though it's impossible not to feel sad about going a
    little too soon,
we'll still laugh at the jokes being told,
we'll look out the window to see if it's raining,
or we'll still wait anxiously
        for the latest newscast . . .
Let's say we're at the front,
        for something worth fighting for, say.
There, in the first offensive, on that very day,
        we might fall on our face, dead.
We'll know this with a curious anger,
        but we'll still worry ourselves to death
        about the outcome of the war, which might go on for
        years.

Let's say we're in prison
and close to fifty,
and we have eighteen more years, say, before the iron doors
    will open.
We'll still live with the outside,
with its people and animals, struggle and wind—
        I mean with the outside beyond the walls.
I mean, however and wherever we are,
        we must live as if one never dies.

III

This earth will grow cold,
a star among stars
        and one of the smallest—
a gilded mote on the blue velvet, I mean,
        I mean *this,* our great earth.
This earth will grow cold one day,
not like a heap of ice
or a dead cloud even,
but like an empty walnut it will roll along
        in pitch-black space . . .
You must grieve for this right now,
you have to feel this sorrow now,
for the world must be loved this much
        if you're going to say "I lived" . . .

The Strangest Creature on Earth

You're like a scorpion, my brother,
you live in cowardly darkness
    like a scorpion.
You're like a sparrow, my brother,
always in a sparrow's flutter.
You're like a clam, my brother,
closed like a clam, content.
And you're frightening, my brother, like the mouth of an
    extinct volcano.
Not one,
    not five,
you are millions, unfortunately.
You're like a sheep, my brother.
    When the cloaked drover raises his stick,
        you quickly join the herd
and run, almost proudly, to the slaughterhouse.
I mean, you're the strangest creature on earth—
stranger, even, than that fish
    that couldn't see the ocean for the water.
And the oppression in this world
        is thanks to you.
And if we're hungry, if we're tired, if we're covered with
    blood,
and if we're still being crushed like grapes for our wine,
        the fault is yours
—I can hardly bring myself to say it—
but most of the fault, my dear brother, is yours.

Some Advice to Those Who Will Serve
Time in Prison

If instead of being hanged by the neck
    you're thrown inside

for not giving up hope
in the world, in your country, in people,
    if you do ten or fifteen years
    apart from the time you have left,
you won't say
      "Better I had swung from the end of a rope
                      like a flag"—
you'll put your foot down and live.
It might not be a pleasure exactly,
but it's your solemn duty
    to live one more day
        to spite the enemy.
Part of you may live alone inside,
    like a stone at the bottom of a well.
But the other part
    must be so caught up
    in the flurry of the world
    that you shiver there inside
when outside, at forty days' distance, a leaf moves.
To wait for letters inside,
or to sing sad songs,
or to lie awake all night staring at the ceiling
    is sweet, but dangerous.
Look at your face from shave to shave,
forget your age,
watch out for lice,
    and for spring nights;
and always remember
    to eat every last piece of bread—
also, don't forget to laugh heartily.
And, who knows,
the woman you love may no longer love you.
Don't say it's no big thing—
it's like the snapping of a green branch
                      to the man inside.
To think of roses and gardens inside is bad,
to think of seas and mountains is good.
Read and write without stopping to rest,
and I also advise weaving,
and also making mirrors.
I mean it's not that you can't pass
    ten or fifteen years inside,
        and more even—

you can,
as long as the jewel
in the left side of your chest doesn't lose its luster!

Awakening

You woke up.
Where are you?
At home.
You're still
    not used to waking up
    in your own house.
This is the kind of daze
    thirteen years of prison leaves you in.
Who's sleeping next to you?
It's not loneliness—it's your wife.
She's sleeping peacefully, like an angel.
Pregnancy becomes the lady.
What time is it?
Eight.
You're safe till night.
Because it's the custom:
    the police don't raid houses in broad daylight.

Evening Walk

You no sooner got out of prison
than you made your wife
    pregnant;
she's on your arm,
    and you're out for an evening walk around the neigh-
borhood.
The lady's belly comes up to her nose.
She carries her sacred charge coyly.
You're respectful and proud.
The air is cool
—cool like baby hands.
You'd like to take it in your palms

and warm it up.
The neighborhood cats are at the butcher's door,
and upstairs his curly wife
has settled her breasts on the window ledge
          and is watching the evening.
Half-light, spotless sky:
smack in the middle sits the evening star,
          sparkling like a glass of water.
Indian summer lasted long this year—
the mulberry trees are yellow,
          but the figs are still green.
Refik the typesetter and the milkman Yorgi's middle
     daughter
          have gone out for an evening stroll,
          their fingers locked.
The grocer Karabet's lights are on.
This Armenian citizen has not forgiven
          the slaughter of his father in the Kurdish mountains.
But he loves you,
because you also won't forgive
          those who blackened the name of the Turkish people.
The tuberculars of the neighborhood and the bedridden
          look out from behind the glass.
The washwoman Huriye's unemployed son,
          weighed down by his sadness,
               goes off to the coffeehouse.
Rahmi Bey's radio is giving the news:
in a country in the Far East,
moon-faced yellow people
          are fighting a white dragon.
Of your people,
          four thousand five hundred Mehmets
               have been sent there to murder their brothers.
You blush
          with rage and shame
and not in general either—
     this impotent grief
     is all yours.
It's as if they'd knocked your wife down from behind and
     killed her child,
or as if you were back in jail
and they were making the peasant guards
                              beat the peasants again.

All of a sudden it's night.
The evening walk is over.
A police jeep turned into your street,
your wife whispered:
    "To our house?"

Things I Didn't Know I Loved

it's 1962 March 28th
I'm sitting by the window on the Prague-Berlin train
night is falling
I never knew I liked
night descending like a tired bird on the smoky wet plain
I don't like
likening the descent of evening to that of a tired bird

I didn't know I loved the soil
can someone who hasn't worked the soil love it
I've never worked the soil
it must be my only Platonic love

and here I've loved the river all this time
whether motionless like this it curls skirting the hills
European hills topped off with chateaus
or whether it stretches out flat as far as the eye can see
I know you can't wash in the same river even once
I know the river will bring new lights that you will not see
I know we live slightly longer than a horse and not nearly
    as long as a crow
I know this has troubled people before
        and will trouble those after me
I know all this has been said a thousand times before
        and will be said after me

I didn't know I liked the sky
cloudy or clear
the blue vault that Andrei watched on his back on the bat-
    tlefield at Borodino
in prison I translated both volumes of *War and Peace* into
    Turkish
I hear voices
not from the blue vault but from the yard
the guards are beating someone again

I didn't know I loved trees
bare beeches around Moscow in Peredelkino
they come upon me in winter noble and modest
beeches are counted as Russian the way we count poplars
    as Turkish
"the poplars of Izmir
losing their leaves . . .
they call us The Knife—
        lover like a young tree . . .
we blow stately mansions sky-high"
Ilgaz forest, 1920: I tied a linen handkerchief edged with
        embroidery to a pine bough

I never knew I loved roads
even the asphalt kind
Vera's behind the wheel we're driving from Moscow to the
    Crimea Koktebele
        formerly "Göktepe ili" in Turkish
the two of us inside a closed box
the world flows past on both sides distant and mute
I was never this close to anyone in my life
bandits came upon me on the red road between Bolu and
        Gerede and I am eighteen
apart from my life I don't have anything in the wagon that
    they can take
and at eighteen our lives are what we value least
I've written this somewhere before
wading through the dark muddy street I'm going to the
    Karagöz
Ramazan night
the paper lantern leading the way
maybe nothing like this ever happened
maybe I read it somewhere an eight-year-old boy going to
    the shadow play
Ramazan night in Istanbul holding his grandfather's hand
    his grandfather has on a fez and is wearing the fur coat
        with the sable collar over his robe
    and there's a lantern in the servant's hand
    and I can't contain myself for joy
flowers come to mind for some reason
poppies cactuses jonquils
in the jonquil garden in Kadiköy Istanbul I kissed Marika
fresh almonds on her breath

I'm seventeen
my heart on a swing touched the sky
I didn't know I loved flowers
friends sent me three red carnations in prison
I just remembered the stars
I love them too
whether I'm floored watching them from below
or whether I'm flying by their side

I have some questions for the cosmonauts
did they see the stars much larger
were they like huge jewels on black velvet
         or apricots on orange
does it make a person feel proud to get a little closer
               to the stars
I saw color photos of the cosmos in Ogonek magazine
now don't get upset friends but nonfigurative shall we say
      or
abstract well some of them looked just like such paintings
which is to say they were terribly figurative and concrete
my heart was in my mouth looking at them
they are the endlessness of our longing to grasp things
looking at them I could think even of death and not feel
      one bit sad
I never knew I loved the cosmos

snow flashes in front of my eyes
both heavy wet steady snow and the dry whirling kind
I didn't know I liked snow
I never knew I loved the sun
even when setting cherry-red as now
in Istanbul too it sometimes sets in postcard colors
but you aren't about to paint it like that
I didn't know I loved the sea
         or how much
—putting aside the Sea of Azov

I didn't know I loved the clouds
whether I'm under or up above them
whether they look like giants or shaggy white beasts

moonlight the most false the most languid the most petit-
      bourgeois

strikes me
I like it
I didn't know I liked rain
whether it falls like a fine net or splatters against the glass
my heart leaves me tangled up in a net or trapped inside a
    drop
and takes off for uncharted countries I didn't know I loved
rain but why did I suddenly discover all these passions sit-
    ting
by the window on the Prague-Berlin train
is it because I lit my sixth cigarette
one alone is enough to kill me
is it because I'm almost dead from thinking about someone
    back in Moscow
her hair straw-blond eyelashes blue

the train plunges on through the pitch-black night
I never knew I liked the night pitch-black
sparks fly from the engine
I didn't know I loved sparks
I didn't know I loved so many things and I had to wait un-
    til I
was sixty to find it out sitting by the window on the
Prague-Berlin train watching the world disappear as if on
a journey from which one does not return

(TRANSLATED BY RANDY BLASING
AND MUTLA KONUK)

ORHAN VELI KANIK

Toward Freedom

Before dawn,
While the sea is still snow-white, you will set sail;

The lust of the grip of the oars in your palms,
And in your heart the joy of toil and vigor,
You will go.
In the roll and sway of nets, you will go.
For welcome, fishes will appear on your course
Delighting you.
As you shake the nets,
Scale by scale, the sea will journey into your hands.
When silence pervades the souls of seagulls
In the cemetery of rocks,
All of a sudden,
All hell will break loose on the horizon:
Mermaids will scuttle and birds will scurry . . .
Saturnalia and festivals, orgies and carnivals,
Bridal processions, masquerades, revelries, carousals . . .
Heeeyy!
Whaddya waitin' for, pop, jump in the sea!
Forget who's waitin' for you back there.
Don't you see: Freedom is all around you.
Be the sail, the oar, the rudder, the fish, the water
And go, go wherever you can.

(TRANSLATED BY TALAT SAIT HALMAN)

DRAMA

In Ambush

by CAHIT ATAY

Characters

AGHA, a big landowner, whose real name is Yilanoglu
DURSUN, a farmhand
YASHAR, a young attorney fresh out of law school

The action takes place in rural Turkey around the middle of the twentieth century.

A desolate spot by a bumpy country road. Across from it, a small mound covered with bushes and brambles. Fields stretch to the mountains in the background.
A sunny morning. Yilanoglu enters left. His thick eyebrows, big mustache, and enormous watch-chain immediately catch the eye. He is the typical agha *(big landowner; minor feudal lord in Anatolia) with his shiny boots, velvet riding trousers, navy-blue vest, and double-breasted jacket. He wears his faded felt hat slightly slanted to the left. He appears annoyed and anxious as he looks down the road. He dips his hand into his vest pocket and takes out his watch. He gets so impatient and jittery that he becomes almost mechanical as he glances, in quick succession, at the watch, then to the left and the right side of the road. It is apparent that he is in a great hurry— and waiting for someone. Another glance to his left, and his funny mechanical motions stop. Greatly relieved, he sticks his watch back into the vest pocket. With his hands clasped behind his back, he stands and waits, as if that nervous man is gone and has been replaced by someone who is hard as rock and cold as ice.*
In a moment Dursun enters, panting and sweating. Every-

thing he is wearing is tattered. Except for the occasional glimmer of the double-barreled hunting shotgun hanging from his shoulder, he looks shabby and dismal from top to toe. He is a young man with a stupid look in his eyes. There are big patches on the haunches and knees of his trousers, and the cuffs have been tucked into his embroidered wool socks. He has old large army boots on. His shirt is filthy. On his head, he has an old straw hat with the brim practically all gone. Over his left shoulder hangs a makeshift hunting bag made of cloth.

AGHA: Dammit, where have you been?

DURSUN *(Frightened):* I'm real sorry, boss . . . I was doing . . . I mean . . . in the field . . .

AGHA: Never mind the field!

DURSUN *(Guilelessly):* Don't say that, boss . . . The field is all I got.

AGHA: Damn you, what did I tell you?

DURSUN *(Cheers up):* You sure told me. When you asked me to get my double-barrel and come here, I figured it all out anyway. I said to myself we're going partridge hunting. *(Suddenly.)* Let's go up to Forkhill! How about it, boss? Right now, all those bushes must be teeming with partridges. *(Eyeing Agha.)* Now, you ain't gonna hunt with these clothes on, are you? Besides, where's your gun?

AGHA: Well, you got yours, right?

DURSUN: Sure thing. Gee, I'm stupid. The boss ain't gonna run up and down hills and valleys, is he now? Boss, just don't give it another thought. Come, sit under the tree. Make yourself at home. Meanwhile I'll take a look around. Believe me, if I want to, I can wipe out all the partridges around here. Look, you want me to come back with enough of them for you and your drinking buddies to eat for a whole week? Man, I tell you, I can fill this bag with partridges in no time. Just wait and see, boss. You're gonna be so proud of your farmhand Dursun.

AGHA *(Imperiously):* Go behind that mound over there.

Dursun does as he is told.

AGHA *(Walks over to the right side of the road, turns around, and taking slow steps towards the mound):* Aim! Take aim at me!

DURSUN *(Stunned):* At you, boss? God forbid!

AGHA: Look, I didn't say shoot, did I? Save your appetite for later.

DURSUN: What is this? You testing me?

AGHA: Idiot. We're just rehearsing a plan.

DURSUN: Come off it. Nothing is easier than shooting a man from here. Man, every day I shoot five, ten crows in the field.

AGHA *(Looks to the right of the road. Then walks over to Dursun):* Come out. *(Kneels by the mound. Takes out his cigarette case, taps it on the side and opens it. To Dursun):* Go on, kneel.

Dursun crouches reluctantly, rests the shotgun on his lap. Frightened, eyeing Agha, he waits for him to speak.

AGHA *(Rolling a cigarette, talks sternly):* You're gonna lie there—behind the mound. *(Brusquely.)* Get it?

DURSUN *(Without having understood anything):* Yeah. I get it all right.

AGHA: Atta boy! *(Holding out the cigarette case as if doing a great act of kindness.)* Take it. Roll one.

DURSUN *(Does not dare):* No. You mind if I don't?

AGHA: I'm telling you to roll one.

Dursun takes the case as if he is holding fire. Looking incredulous, he starts to roll the cigarette with shaky hands.

AGHA *(Sticks his cigarette into his amber cigarette holder and lights it):* You're gonna hold the gun—and fire. . . . That's all.

Dursun looks absent-minded as he struggles with the cigarette as though rolling a cigarette with tobacco from Agha's case has made him deaf.

AGHA *(Blares):* Tell me, is there anyone bigger than me in this town?

DURSUN *(Stops rolling):* No such thing.

AGHA *(Challenging):* Can anyone dare take a stand against me? Is anyone brave enough?

Dursun gets frightened. Gives up his struggle to roll a cigarette, which he is unable to do anyway. Hands the cigarette case back to Agha.

AGHA: And how about you, man? What's with you? *(Angrily, puts the case in his pocket.)*
DURSUN *(Cringes. Still thinking of the cigarette case):* I . . . I just couldn't roll it.
AGHA: Man, try to make something of yourself. What can you expect from being a farm worker? *(Like an orator.)* Listen here, you scum! Have you no sense of honor? Have you no integrity? Have you no dignity? You, and the rest of you poor bastards, you people are like sheep, you know!
DURSUN *(Inching away from where he was crouching):* God knows, boss . . .
AGHA: You ever go to the coffeehouse?
DURSUN: Uhh . . . After a day's work on the field . . .
AGHA: Well, let's say you went to the coffeehouse. Who gives a damn: You're nobody. Working on that field, you've turned into a scarecrow. You know, no one in the coffeehouse will even look at you. Man, you're no better than the butcher's dog. *(Pause.)* But me?
DURSUN: They're scared of you, boss. Most of those people haven't got the guts to come near you.
AGHA: You bet your life, that's the way it is. But why?
DURSUN: Your name is Yilanoglu. You got a name. You're the lord here.
AGHA: That mantle didn't fall on my shoulders from heaven, did it now? We earned it all with hard work, with the sweat of our brow. You better get that straight. We toppled a couple of fellows, that's how. Just mowed them down in the street, at the marketplace. I've committed enough crimes to last my family for seven generations. My sons, and their sons can just lie on their backs and enjoy themselves. No one will dare come near them, let alone touch them. *(Pause.)* How about you?
DURSUN *(Dejected):* You're absolutely right. Nobody gives a damn about me. Like you said, just a scarecrow. . . . Crows mock me—they're not afraid or anything—they come and sit on the scarecrow . . . all the time.
AGHA *(Pointing to the shotgun):* But once you fire that! See, that's why I wanted to do you a big favor.

DURSUN *(Full of hope):* I knew it, I knew it. The Great Yilanoglu . . . I said to myself if Yilanoglu, whose fame has spread all over these parts, calls me in, there's got to be something to it.

AGHA *(Giving him advice):* This is the opportunity of a lifetime. Use your head, man. Get it into your head that someone is fond of you. There's a whole bunch of guys in this town who'd love to volunteer for this job. If I have an announcement made on the PA system at the public square, you couldn't even get on the waiting line. That's why I didn't let anyone know. I swear to God I just wanted to give a poor fellow a little boost.

DURSUN *(As if Agha has made him a gift of a whole farm):* How can I thank you enough?

AGHA: Well, you can get a good rest in the pen. Five years, maybe ten. It's like a school. You'll learn how to write petitions. And you'll get a chance to talk to people.

DURSUN: What do you mean—"pen"?

AGHA: No, no, no. You're not going to have any thoughts of escaping. A real man never escapes. If you do something, make sure it's perfect, my son. Escape? That's what a woman does. Now, what was that you were saying?

DURSUN: You know best.

AGHA: Besides, your old lady—instead of staying home and going to waste, she can work on the field, and open up a little bit. Once you come out of the pen . . . Oh boy, when you are released, the minute you walk into that coffeehouse, just imagine all the wonderful things that'll happen to you. God knows, they'll lead you to the best table. Just name all the things you want. Tea and coffee will flow like anything. All those girls walking by this road here—they'll fall all over Dursun. I bet you could even marry into one of the town's wealthy families. You want me to keep telling you about all the benefits? You're gonna own orchards and gardens, fields and lots. Man, maybe you'll get a horse, too.

DURSUN *(Dreamily):* You don't say, boss?

AGHA: You bet your life. *(Looks at the road.)*

DURSUN *(With great excitement, grabs Agha's hand and kisses it):* You're a great boss . . . the best . . . I knew it, I knew there was something in all this. Great Yilanoglu. You want me to be your slave? I'll be your slave for life. You know, there are guys who say, "Yilanoglu is cruel." Goddam liars!

AGHA *(Does not hear. Keeps watching the road):* Tell me, lad, how harmful are those crows for your field? *(Pointing to the road.)* That son of a bitch is bad for the whole town. Upstart, that's what he is. You follow me? Look here, anyone can shoot partridges and crows. *(Pause.)* He'll come this way in just a short while. You know him. Yashar . . .

DURSUN: The son of the Kulaksiz family?

AGHA: That's him.

DURSUN: Sure, I know him. He grew up in our neighborhood. *(Trying to find a grudge against Yashar.)* We used to play knucklebones, and he used to beat me.

AGHA: There you are. You ought to hold that against him.

DURSUN: Did he go to school, boss?

AGHA: He did, dammit. I wish he hadn't. His uncle took care of his education.

DURSUN: I know him too: Blind Ibrahim.

AGHA: We told him: "Man, don't send this youngster to school. Have him work for you." But how can you talk to the blind about colors? He sold his land and orchards, and put the lad through school. A big school, one of the top schools, too. Now, they say Yashar is going to open a law office in town. There you are. *(Angrily.)* And they say he's going to marry Zehra. You know, the widow's daughter. He's going to squander everything she owns. Well, we did our best to warn them, but what do they know? They're waiting for that son of a bitch. Zehra's mother—they say—bought God knows how many pounds of meat from the butcher. A huge amount. Hey, wake up.

DURSUN: Oh, my God!

AGHA: All for him—get it? You know, you're gonna do a great service. Because once he feels he's on top of the world, no one can hold him back, I tell you. *(Pointing to the rifle.)* That is different, though. *(Pointing at the mound.)* Lie back there, like before. Remember the way I was walking toward the mound? Yeah, like that. . . . *(Taps Dursun on the shoulder, then looks at his watch.)* He must be on his way. My horse is back there by the big plane tree. I better go there and take a nap. When I hear the shots, I'll come running. You have nothing to worry about. I'll take care of the rest.

DURSUN *(Proudly):* With God's permission, I'm gonna do it, boss.

AGHA: Well, so long for a while. *(Comes back before exiting.)* In military service, they make you repeat your orders. I was a sergeant. *(Sternly.)* What'll you do?

DURSUN *(Instinctively stands at attention):* I mean . . . like . . . well—

AGHA: That won't do. You're supposed to say: "I lie in ambush behind the mound, and fire at the Kulaksiz boy, sir!"

DURSUN: Just don't worry about it.

AGHA: All right, then.

DURSUN *(Imagines himself as big as Agha):* Goodbye, Yilanoglu.

AGHA *(Returns):* Did you say Yilanoglu? Only two people call me Yilanoglu: Rifat, my friend who owns the Club, and my wife. Dammit, in no time you grow too big for your breeches. You're gonna do a measly little thing, that's all. In the middle of nowhere, you're gonna take a couple of shots from an ambush.

DURSUN *(Cowering):* Forgive me . . . I mean . . . I was gonna say "Boss."

AGHA: Everyone should know who he is and what his place is in life. *(Rubbing it in.)* You're quite a fella, you know. *(Forces a smile.)* Hold the rifle over to the other side, will you, sonny. . . . *(Points to the road.)*

DURSUN *(Stares behind him. After he is sure that Agha is gone):* God must be on my side. What a windfall. . . . I used to wrack my brains about this son of a gun. Now look what happens. Who would have thought—Yilanoglu spilling his secrets to Dursun the farmboy. *(Strokes the rifle and grins stupidly.)* So, this is the way it is, eh? Well, this is the only life I'm gonna live. *(Facing the side where Agha made his exit.)* It's a godsend for sure. . . . Son-of-a-gun really sang this time. *(Suddenly grimaces; holding his groin, he writhes in pain.)* Oh, my God . . . *(As if weeping.)* You reap what you sow. When you work like a dog and get no rest, you sure get a lot of bellyache. I better lie down for a moment. *(Remembers Yilanoglu.)* I know, boss, I know. *(Pulls himself together, but when the pain starts again he sits*

*down by the mound, holding on to the shotgun.
Yawns.)* It's killing me—all this hoeing, all this farm-
work. I tell you, I'm finished. *(His eyes droop. He falls
asleep. The gun slides out of his hands.)*

*In a moment, Yashar enters off the road, on the right.
He has spectacles. He is a young man with a bright,
breezy face and kindly expression. He is wearing a sport
shirt and casual trousers. There is a handkerchief around
his neck—presumably to keep perspiration away. He
carries a small suitcase. Notices Dursun.*

YASHAR *(Walks over to Dursun and takes a close look):* Ah,
this is my friend Dursun.

*Without making any noise, Yashar takes the gun away.
Moving impishly and tiptoeing, he goes over to the bushes
and hides the gun. Then he crouches beside Dursun and
whistles in his ear the tune of their school-song. Dursun,
in his sleep, begins to mumble the tune. Yashar whistles
the tune louder. Dursun sings it louder.*

DURSUN *(As if dreaming):* Oh, boy, we really sang that
song. All of us together. The big house next to the
school used to echo when we sang. Women and girls
would rush to the windows. *(He opens his eyes; he looks
in the direction of Yashar, who is still whistling.)* My
God. *(His eyes bulge.)* Yashar? *(Still reminiscing.)*
They used to kick me out of school, saying I was too
dumb. And boys always made fun of me. *(To Yashar.)*
When you wanted to play hooky, you always made me
take your place during roll call. Remember, pal?

Yashar nods and goes on whistling.

DURSUN *(Nostalgically):* Yeah, man. In those days, you used
to whistle just like now. Your nickname was "Whistling
Boy." Remember how that religious guy once chased
you with a big stick?
YASHAR *(Laughs):* I sure do. He kept saying, "Whistling Boy
attracts all the demons to the neighborhood!" *(Gets up
and opens his arms.)* Come, my friend. You are my
childhood, my carefree, colorful childhood.

DURSUN *(With great excitement, rises to his feet and embraces Yashar):* Hey, friend! My one and only Yashar.

Dursun is suddenly embarrassed about his tattered clothes, lets his arms drop to his sides. Yashar insists on hugging.

DURSUN *(Hesitant, and his eyes filled with tears, he breaks away):* So that's the way it goes, huh? You've become a gentleman. But me . . . *(Angrily.)* I'm a measly little farmhand. . . . *(Suddenly starts looking around.)* Where the hell is my gun?

YASHAR: What gun? Are you out hunting, Dursun?

DURSUN *(Keeps looking about):* That gun is all I got. Without it . . , my hands will be tied. Crows will ravage the field. *(Turns around and glares at Yashar.)* Never mind the field . . .

YASHAR: Don't worry, Dursun. *(Walks over and takes the gun from where he had hidden it.)* I put it away. Just a joke. *(Returns the rifle to Dursun.)*

DURSUN *(Grabs the gun and immediately takes his position behind the mound. Aiming at Yashar):* Hope you don't mind, pal, but I gotta shoot you.

YASHAR *(Laughs incredulously):* Shoot me? Why?

DURSUN: What do I know? I take a shot at a flock of crows, and one crow falls dead.

YASHAR: Well, maybe there is good reason to shoot crows.

DURSUN: Say what you want. I gotta kill you.

YASHAR: Dursun . . .

DURSUN: Go on, tell me.

YASHAR: Are you serious? *(Gently.)* Oh, Dursun . . . You're being a kid all over again. At this age, you're playing cops and robbers, huh?

DURSUN *(Harshly):* It sure breaks my heart, but it's gotta be this way.

YASHAR: Which means . . . you . . . Well, then, what's the reason?

DURSUN *(On the verge of tears):* Goddam. Am I supposed to stay this way forever? Tell me, should I creep and crawl all the time? Like the butcher's dog. I shouldn't even afford to go to the coffeehouse, huh? I shouldn't have my own field and tools, my own horse, is that it? Shouldn't I get married? *(Timidly.)* Now, if I—I mean—if I do this to you . . . if I shoot you—excuse me, pal—people will think highly of me, you see.

YASHAR: I get it, Dursun, now I know. It's always this way. In order for one person to amount to something, another person has to be done away with. What a shame.

DURSUN: Why must you hammer it in? I told you, one crow will fall dead.

YASHAR: One crow falls. All right, dear friend, shoot. But something must have gone wrong between the two of us. *(Tries persuasion.)* I will probably feel sorry for you. Dursun, the killer feels more pain than the victim does. When you go into the coffeehouse, a voice will rise above that din and ask you: "What had he done to you?"—right? Let's say you're all settled; you have your land and house and your wife, and you are about to dip your spoon into your soup, and you suddenly hear that voice asking you: "Crows had to be killed, because they were digging up all the seeds. But Yashar? How about Yashar?"—Tell me, when you hear that question, aren't you going to drop your spoon? Will you be able to walk by these thickets of red berries and remain calm? Will you be able to rip open the cool blood-red watermelon? Tell me.

DURSUN: You used to beat me at knucklebones.

YASHAR: But who saved you from drowning in the lake?

DURSUN: Yeah, man, you're right. I'd forgotten that. *(Walks up to Yashar.)* You're a good kid, Yashar. *(Begging him.)* Let's find something, huh? We got ages till nighttime. *(Keeps begging.)* Please, Yashar, please.

YASHAR: Let's find something.

DURSUN: You know how dumb I am. You went to school and all. Come on, prove yourself.

YASHAR: I'll do my best, Dursun. *(Pondering.)* Is there a blood feud between us?

DURSUN *(Hopefully):* Is there?

YASHAR: I can't think of anything like that.

DURSUN: You're right, dammit. *(Pause. Dursun keeps pulling his pants up, and ponders anxiously.)*

YASHAR *(Stretches, looking at the sun):* Oh, such a marvelous day.

DURSUN *(Annoyed):* This is no time to talk about the weather, is it, pal? *(He, too, cannot help yawning and stretching).* Wouldn't it be just great to take a nap under the plane trees. (*As he is about to lie down, he remembers Yilanoglu and straightens up.*) He wouldn't come to us. Who are we, after all? He is the big man around here.

YASHAR: Well, OK, but there has to be a reason for what you're talking about. If it's wartime, that's different: You'll drop your hoe, I'll throw away my pen—we'll both go. When the sky is as ruthlessly blue as it is now . . . Instead of dying like this, we would try to kill, or even to die for that matter. But in wartime there would be plenty of reasons: That's when we pull the trigger to get rid of the infidel and the enemy. (*Emphatically.*) Are there any such orders, Dursun?

DURSUN (*Evasively*): No.

YASHAR: Then, what are we supposed to do? We have no old grudge. (*Suddenly.*) How about it? Let me insult you . . . spit in your face . . .

DURSUN: What's the matter with you, man?

YASHAR: Just trying to find a good cause. I feel I'm letting you down, and it breaks my heart to do that. You see, I am a humanist.

DURSUN (*Aims at him at once*): Now say that again.

YASHAR: Say what?

DURSUN: You said something, remember?

YASHAR: Humanist.

DURSUN: Man, I used to think of a communist like an eagle or an owl. So you are one of those types, huh? Well, buddy, you gave yourself away. You're a communist, and you expect me not to shoot you?

YASHAR: Don't mix them up. Some of our educated people mistake one for the other. But must you? Humanist, not communist. Also, I admire the Greeks.

DURSUN: My, my! He fell into his own trap again. He is a friend of the Greeks!

YASHAR: Of the ancient Greeks.

DURSUN: If you think you can put me on . . . There's no such thing as an old infidel and a new infidel. You're not playing this game right, you know. I got things to do.

YASHAR: And how about me? (*Dreamily.*) I am going to open a law office, and start serving the townsfolk.

DURSUN: I swear to God, they'll make life miserable for you. They're such a bunch of swindlers . . . Remember the Mayor. No matter how hard he tried, he couldn't make a go of it. In the end he hanged himself. You better listen to what I say, brother: You'll get sick and tired, you'll go searching for some other place where you can die in peace. Forget it, huh? You were doing all right with that Greek stuff. What do you say?

YASHAR: That's fine. Let's leave everything until the day I'll go search for a place where I can die in peace.

DURSUN (Offended, he lowers his gun; like a child): Oh, it's just dandy, ain't it? I'll remain the scum of the earth, working as a farmhand, and day in day out, I'll look into your eyes, asking you, "You wanna die?" so that I'll lead a better life at long last. No, buster, I won't go in for that stuff. (All of a sudden screams.) Yippee. I got an idea. (To Yashar.) Some years back, your father caused my father to get a beating. My mother used to tell the story. I understand they went to court. Now, what have you got to say to that? (Aims the shotgun.)

YASHAR (Shaking his head): No. I heard it from my uncle. The way it happened, Yilanoglu arranged the whole thing, and then tried to blame it on my father.

DURSUN: Yilanoglu doesn't go in for beatings . . . He wipes the guys out.

YASHAR: Well, buddy, you can take a look at the court records.

DURSUN (Lowers the gun): Let's go, then.

YASHAR: Actually, my father was acquitted.

DURSUN (Just as they are about to exit): Shucks . . . You know what? The government building burned down the other day—and all the court records with it.

YASHAR: That's true: I read about it in the papers. They claim one of the big shots had it burned down.

DURSUN: Honest?

YASHAR: What do you expect? Someone from Yilanoglu's party.

DURSUN: Man, I wish that son of a bitch were here instead of you.

YASHAR: You mean Yilanoglu?

DURSUN: (Fearfully): Are you kidding? Who is brave enough to pull a gun on Yilanoglu? You don't think bullets could go through that son of a bitch, do you? (He seems obsessed with the idea.) The man who shoots Yilanoglu is bound to become famous all over the world.

You know they'd write ballads about him—ballads sharp
as knives, bitter as poison.

YASHAR *(Emotionally):* I don't care for those songs. They
oppress the heart. How can you listen to them, Dursun,
when ballads come out saying, "They shot Yashar on the
way to the railroad station." Do you think you can listen
to a song like that?

DURSUN *(Saddened):* I just couldn't. Man, it would tear my
heart out. Remember the ballad about that poor young
man—"They shot Recep by the bridge." His fianceé
wrote that song.

YASHAR: You know, Dursun, I have a fianceé, too—Zehra.

DURSUN *(Pulling himself together):* You don't think the
widow's daughter is gonna sing a song of lament for
you, do you? No, brother, don't eat your heart out. You
needn't worry about her.

YASHAR: Why's that?

DURSUN: Never mind. Just listen to what I'm saying.

YASHAR: Oh. Zehra is free and open. She's on her own. Sings.
She's not like some of the girls who used to be kept behind lattices and veils. But the townspeople . . .

DURSUN: Well, each person's sins . . .

YASHAR *(Sensitive about all matters relating to Zehra):* I
don't follow.

DURSUN: I hear she's flirting with Riza, the hosiery guy.

YASHAR: As I said, it's all gossip. When Zehra goes into
Riza's shop to buy socks, people think something goes
on in there. Those are narrow-minded people.

DURSUN *(Aims the gun at Yashar and talks in a harsh voice):*
What have you got to say about Yilanoglu?

YASHAR *(Emphatically):* Did Yilanoglu stick his nose into
this, too?

DURSUN: The man is the lord of this region. He does whatever he damn pleases. What can you do about it?

YASHAR: Zehra and Yilanoglu. *(Laughs as if he is anxious to
chase bad thoughts away.)* My Zehra is like a sunflower,
Dursun. The sunflower always follows the sun or the
moon or wherever there is light. *(Contemptuously.)*
What would she do with that man who is like the
darkest night?

DURSUN: Whatever Yilanoglu wants, Yilanoglu gets. I hear
even his wife says she likes the girl.

YASHAR: Did you say his wife? Yilanoglu's wife?

DURSUN: I said his wife, all right. I am told that the wife says Zehra is going to be Yilanoglu's second wife. That woman is such a pig. She knows what she's doing. She claims she's gonna arrange the second marriage herself. You get it, don't you? She's doing it, because when Yilanoglu takes Zehra he'll come home instead of spending his nights away from home. The woman knows she is washed out.

YASHAR *(Almost mumbling to himself):* It's frightful. Even talking about it is horrendous. A wife who arranges for a second wife for her own husband. My God, it's so disgusting. It's impossible to live a life like this.

DURSUN *(Aims the gun):* You said it. Buddy, you've come around to my view, haven't you?

YASHAR *(Pensively):* That couldn't be. There is such a thing as conscience and justice.

DURSUN *(Misunderstands him):* You said it's impossible to live, right?

YASHAR *(Doesn't hear; absorbed in thought):* Give me that thing.

DURSUN *(Gleefully handing him the gun):* That's what I call a hero. You're gonna do it yourself, huh?

YASHAR *(Looks at the gun with contempt):* This double-barrel . . . Cold steel . . . Gunpowder . . . buckshot.

DURSUN: Yeah, all that.

YASHAR *(Takes aim at Dursun and keeps talking):* The gun that was aimed at me. . . .

DURSUN *(Frightened):* Heaven help me, am I the target now?

YASHAR: Remember the enmity between us?

DURSUN *(Trembling):* For heaven's sake, Yashar, my best friend Yashar, we couldn't find any reason for a grudge . . .

YASHAR *(Continues):* Treachery . . . Animosity . . . Blood . . . Death.

DURSUN *(Imploring):* You're already the man you always wanted to be, Yashar. And now you're gonna kill me and you're gonna add honor to all the honor you already got, is that it?

YASHAR *(Goes on):* The hand that tries to grab your field, someone else's orchard, another man's house . . . that hand now tries to grab Zehra, huh?

DURSUN: I swear to God, it ain't me. It's Yilanoglu.

YASHAR: He is all the evil things I've been talking about. He is—the pistol on the hip . . . the knife . . . the hatred . . . Yes, that gun, too. *(Flings the gun away.)* Don't take it in your hands, Dursun. You ought to hold on to friendship and love and affection. *(Hugs Dursun and kisses him on the cheeks.)* There's nothing like the smell of the soil, of human warmth, of friendship.

DURSUN *(Cheerfully, with one eye on the gun):* Never mind what the townsfolk say. They'll say anything. Oh, you know what? I hear the widow and her daughter are expecting you. They've bought a lot of meat, too. They're sure waiting for you.

YASHAR: I know. *(Looks with emotion in the direction of the town.)* I hope the town is waiting for me, too. There are so many things I want to do there. *(Enthusiastically picks up his suitcase.)* I better get going. Dursun, you have to come to my wedding. *(Spiritedly walks left.)*

DURSUN: *(Quickly picks up the gun):* What will Yilanoglu say to me? *(Gets hold of himself, aims at Yashar's back.)*

YASHAR: So long. . . . *(Looks back as he is about to exit.)* Dursun, what's going on? Is it Yilanoglu again?

DURSUN *(Embarrassed, aims in the air):* I was going after the crows . . . I mean . . . like . . . I wanted to fire in the air.

YASHAR: Go ahead. Pull the trigger in our own honor, to announce our friendship. *(Yashar waits. Dursun pulls the trigger, and suddenly there is a downpour of confetti all over the stage. Astounded, they first look up, then gaze at each other. Yashar gets hold of himself. Extending his free hand, he cheerfully walks over to Dursun.)* Confetti . . .

DURSUN: What fatty? God in heaven . . . These are flowers, man, apricot flowers. *(Holding his hand under the confetti.)*

YASHAR: You said it, Dursun—flowers. *(Pointing to the sky.)* Heaven's answer . . . flowers of happiness from the huge blue tree . . . *(Deliriously.)* You weren't going to be able to shoot me, Dursun. You couldn't have done it.

DURSUN *(Bewildered):* I stuffed the buckshot into this damn thing myself—and the gunpowder.

YASHAR *(Triumphantly):* It turned into paper. Tiny round pretty pieces of paper. . . . When you come to my wedding, bring your gun along. You can fire as much as you like. The whole place will light up, will be filled with the loveliest colors. *(Runs out happily.)*

DURSUN *(Opens and shuts the gun):* The Devil has gone into this. God Almighty! He has strange ways. *(Not having noticed Yashar's exit.)* Buster, you say I wasn't gonna be able to shoot you, huh? God doesn't want it.

AGHA *(Enters at lightning speed):* Damn you, butcher's dog. Damn coward! You let the bastard go!

Dursun, frightened, jumps behind the mound.

AGHA: Stupid bastard! Now you hide, huh? What were you doing a couple of minutes ago? Couldn't hit the target, is that it?

DURSUN *(Feels guilty):* I couldn't have, boss.

AGHA *(Stands in the middle of the road facing Dursun with all of his awesome bulk):* Why didn't you tell me before? See how you messed everything up. You're such a coward.

DURSUN: This thing doesn't shoot, boss.

AGHA: What thing?

DURSUN: The shots turn fatty or something . . . like paper, you know. I've never seen anything like it.

AGHA: You're raving mad. What does that mean?

DURSUN: I still can't get it.

AGHA: How can something like that happen?

DURSUN: It can. I'll swear on anything. Tiny pieces of paper . . . like snowflakes. May God strike me dead if I'm lying.

AGHA: Shut up, you dog.

DURSUN: I swear to God, I'm telling the truth. *(In a daze, points the barrel at Agha.)* If you don't believe me, let's try it once. I'll fire the left cartridge, and you'll see for yourself.

AGHA: You bastard, you're gonna shoot me, huh?

DURSUN: Have no fear. Nothing will go wrong. Those aren't buckshots in there—just paper. . . . *(Fires.)*

AGHA *(Takes one step):* You dog . . . *(Tumbles at the bottom of the mound.)*

DURSUN *(Stunned, he can't believe what has happened. After a brief pause):* You're putting me on, boss. This thing doesn't kill a man. *(Listens, then straightens up fear-*

fully, walks over to Agha's corpse.) God Almighty!
Yilanoglu is full of holes. *(Scared.)* I swear, I . . . I'm
not guilty. I just wanted to give it one more try. *(Talking to the corpse.)* Boss . . . Boss . . . My one and only
boss. Get up, for heaven's sake. You sure scared me.
(Panic-stricken, he looks around.) He's dead . . . Great
Yilanoglu . . . *(Wants to run away.)* Yilanoglu is dead!
(He dips into his hunting bag, and looks into it.) We
came to hunt partridges, and just look at all the things
that happened to us, man. Dursun the farmhand finished
off Yilanoglu, huh? *(Suddenly looks proud of himself.)*
Why the hell shouldn't I finish him off? Isn't Dursun a
real man? Don't I have my own reputation? Can't I go
into the coffeehouse? *(Posing like a hero.)* Dursun, my
boy, you felled Yilanoglu like a pinetree, didn't you?
(Standing tall.) That's the way I am, pal, I shoot them
down. And that's no joke, I mean business. Anyone can
kill Yashar, that's easy. *(Leans over Agha's corpse. Removes Agha's watch with its chain, his cigarette case
and holder, and stuffs them into his hunting bag. Throws
his hat away, and puts Agha's enormous hat on his own
head, pulling it all the way down until it covers his
ears.)* I swear I'm not lying, pal. *(As if showing the bag
to someone.)* The watch, and the cigarette case . . . all
of them belonged to Agha. You want witnesses, you
want evidence—here they are. *(The hat practically covers his eyes. With the double-barreled gun hanging down
his shoulder, walks left, standing erect.)* If you don't believe me, go to the road that leads to the railway station.
There, by the mound, you'll find his carcass. *(Walks out
like a hero.)*

CURTAIN

(TRANSLATED BY TALAT S. HALMAN)

BIOGRAPHICAL NOTES

Abdau-Sabour, Salah (1931–   ), born in Egypt, has worked on the newspaper *Al-Ahram*. In addition to criticism and poetry, he has written a play on the martyrdom of Al-Hallaj and on the life of Leila Majnoun. Along with Lewis Awad, he is a leader in the free-verse movement in contemporary Arab poetry. Among his best works are his first volume of poetry, *People in My Country* (1952), containing socially committed verse about village life, and his *Meditations on a Wounded Age* (1971), which articulates a more personal vision.

Adonis (1930–   ), the pen-name of Ali Ahmad Saed, who was born in Syria and educated at the University of Damascus. He moved to Beirut in 1956 and became the noted editor of the poetry review *Sh'ir*. The author of a two-volume anthology of classical Arab poetry, he is an influential voice in the social and intellectual movements of the Arab world. *The Blood of Adonis*, translated by the poet Samuel Hazo, is available to readers of English.

Akbal, Oktay (1923–   ) is a prolific writer of fiction and one of Turkey's most widely read columnists. He has won his country's top literary awards for fiction. Among his publications are collections of his essays, two volumes of his diaries, and a collection of profiles featuring his literary friends. His fiction is distinguished by a simple staccato style and a Kafkaesque sense of despair.

Alavi, Bozorg (1907–   ), a political radical and co-founder of the Tudeh Communist party of Iran, was jailed during the thirties for his political views. Since 1941 he has lived in East Germany, where he has both literary and academic standing. His work includes three collections of essays and short stories: *Suitcase* (1934), *Torn Sheets from Prison* (1941), and *Letters* (1952). He has also written a novel entitled *Her Eyes* (1952) and, in Ger-

[494]

man, a history of Persian literature. The translator of "The Lead Soldier" regards it as the best short story in Persian. Alavi is typical of a large number of Iranian writers who have been driven into exile by political circumstances.

Amichai, Yehuda (1924–   ), poet and novelist, was born in Germany but came to Palestine as a child. The Hebrew name he adopted means "My people lives." He has written four books of poems, two novels (the latest published in 1977 by Harper and Row), a collection of short stories called *In This Terrible Wind* (1973), and a number of radio and stage plays. His work has been translated into twenty languages.

Ananyan, Vakhtang (1905–   ) was born in the mountain village of Shamakhyan in the Caucasus. He spent his first eighteen years as a shepherd, absorbing the songs of the blind *ashugs* (wandering minstrels) and listening to stories of fearless hunters who would brave a bear single-handed. He writes about the life he knows so well, the animals that were childhood companions, and his hunting experiences in older years, often embellishing reality with intricate fancy and permeating all with the poetry of steep mountain paths. His *Stories of a Huntsman, Prisoners of Snow Leopard Gorge*, and *Steep Paths* won him acclaim among Armenian and Russian readers.

Anday, Melih Cevdet (1915–   ), one of the more prominent figures of contemporary Turkish literature, is a poet, playwright, novelist, essayist, translator, and critic. His work has been published extensively in Europe and throughout the Soviet Union, as well as in England and the United States. In 1971, UNESCO called him "one of the world's foremost literary figures" and published a volume of his selected poems in French.

Atay, Cahit (1925–   ), who was born in Corum, is regarded as the most talented contemporary Turkish playwright. After studying at the meteorological institute in Ankara, he chose writing as a career. His plays, such as *In the Forest, Mrs. Mother, Miss Daughter,* and *Memets of Karalar Village,* depict the plight of the peasants, often using absurdist techniques.

Avidan, David (1934–   ) was born in Israel to parents who had immigrated from eastern Europe. One of the few modern Israeli poets extensively available to readers of

English, he believes that a poet should translate his own poems. Among his books are *Megaovertone*, from which the poems in this collection are taken, and two plays, *Tomorrow, You're Dead* and *Carambole*. He has recorded his poetry in both Hebrew and English.

Baalabaki, Laila (1936–) was born in Lebanon into a Shi'ite family. She gave up her education to work as a secretary in the Lebanese parliament. She has written two novels, *I Live* and *The Two Monsters,* and is completing a third. Her collection of stories, *A Spaceship of Tenderness to the Moon,* aroused the authorities because of its outspokenness.

Bakir, Amin (————), lives in Cairo and writes in English for the Egyptian stage.

Baraheni, Reza (1925–) was born in Tabriz in the northwest of Iran and educated at the Universities of Tehran and Istanbul. Until he chose exile in the United States, he was a professor of comparative literature at the University of Tehran. The author of more than a dozen books of poetry, fiction, and literary criticism, he has supervised the translation of his work into Arabic, Armenian, English, French, German, Russian, and Turkish. In 1975 he published *God's Shadow,* a book of poems based on his prison torture at the hands of SAVAK, the Iranian secret police; and in 1977 he published *The Crowned Cannibal,* prose and poetry about repression in Iran. He presently lives near Baltimore with his wife and children and teaches at the University of Maryland. The present selection is the first chapter of his novel *The Infernal Times of Agha-ye Ayyaz,* which circulates underground in the Persian language in Iran. In 1977, Random House published *The Crowned Cannibals,* a collection of prison writings.

Basmadjian, Garig (1947–), poet, critic, and translator, was born in Jerusalem. The author of three books of poetry, he also has translated widely from English into Armenian and from Armenian into English. He lives in Paris.

Al-Bayati, Abdul Wahab (1926–) was born in Baghdad, Iraq, where he has worked as a teacher and as a journalist. His exile for Communist leanings led him to Egypt, Lebanon, Syria, Austria, and the Soviet Union, where in 1958 he served as the Iraqi cultural attaché. Bayati has been influenced by Mayakovsky, Nazim Hikmet (who became a friend), Aragon, Lorca, and Neruda. One of his latest collections of verse is *Love Poems on the Seven Gates of the World* (1971). He is regarded as the most committed poet of the Arab world.

Carmi, T. (1925–), Carmi Charney, was born in New York and educated there and in Palestine. He has been living in Israel since 1947. He is the author of five volumes of poetry and of many translations, two of which are available to readers of English: *The Brass Serpent* and *Author's Apology*. He presently works as an editor for a leading Israeli publishing house.

Chalfi, Raquel (1923–) has written plays and film documentaries and presently teaches film and television at the University of Tel Aviv. Her poems included here are taken from "Submarine Cycle" of her first, recently published book of poetry, *Submarine and Other Poems*.

Cossery, Albert (1913–) was born in Egypt and now lives in Paris. The present story comes from his first collection of tales, *Men God Forgot*, which Henry Miller called "a classic." Other books of his which have been translated from French into English are *The Danger of Fantasy, The House of Certain Death,* and *The Lazy Ones*. His characters are the despised and rejected; unemployed actors, tinkers, beggars; and the drug addicts who inhabit. in the words of a critic, "a submarine world where poverty looms gigantic and real."

Daglarca, Fazil Husnu (1914–), a champion of popular causes, was born in Istanbul and followed a military career until 1950. His first book of poems appeared in 1935, and since that time he has published more than five thousand poems, most of them contained in thirty-one volumes. Named "Turkey's leading living poet" by a jury of Turkish men of letters in 1967, he now operates a bookstore and edits a literary periodical called *Turkce* ("Turkish").

Darwish, Mahmud (1942–) is a Palestinian poet, born in al-Bawra, a village east of Acre. Until his departure for Egypt to champion the cause of the displaced Palestinians, he lived in Haifa and edited the newspaper *al-Ittihad*. Of leftist opinions, he won a Soviet prize in 1969 with poems that are charged with the imagery of wounds and martyrdom. His *Selected Poems* are available in English. He now resides in Beirut.

Emin, Gevorg (1919–   ) was born in the village of Ashtarak in Armenia and moved to Erivan, the capital city, at an early age. Graduated in 1940 from the Polytechnic Institute, he edited the magazine *Armenian Literature* and published many volumes of poetry in Armenian, and in Russian translation. He is one of Armenia's most popular poets and attracted large audiences during his visits to the United States.

Faik, Sait (1906–1954), a popular writer of short stories, was born in Adaparazi, near Istanbul. After studying in France, he returned to try his hand, unsuccessfully, at business and teaching school. Thereafter he was supported by the meager income from his writings in journals and newspapers and from property left by his father. The settings of his stories have a strong Turkish flavor: coffee shops, working-class taverns, the Galata Bridge over the Golden Horn, trams, boat landings, seaside cafes, and, above all, the sea itself. His characters are shopkeepers, peddlers, fishermen (most Greek), and unemployed workers.

Farroukhzad, Forugh (1934–1966) was born in Tehran, the daughter of an army colonel. Her formal education, which stopped short of a high-school diploma, was exclusively in girls' schools. At sixteen, she married a government employee, and a year later, in 1952, her first collection of verse, called *The Captive*, appeared. After moving to Ahvaz, she divorced her husband (who got custody of their son) and returned to Tehran. *The Wall, Rebellion,* and *Let Us Have Faith*—the latter published after her untimely death in an automobile accident—established her as the foremost poet of contemporary Iran, despite accusations of immorality and indecency from some readers shocked by her candor.

Farzan, Massud (19 –   ), poet, critic, short-story writer and translator, has taught comparative literature at Harvard, Columbia, and Pahlavi University (Shiraz), and has published widely in a number of English and American journals. At present he divides his time between Iran and the United States, where he has been active in introducing Persian writers to American audiences and American writers to Persian audiences.

A new edition of his poems and translations, *Kashan to Kalamazoo*, has just appeared.

Gaboudikian, Sylva (1919–) was born in Erivan. She studied at the Faculty of Philology at the State University and for two years at the Gorki Literary Institute in Moscow. Her first book of poems was published in 1945, followed by others over the years. Her poems have been translated into a number of the Soviet languages, making her perhaps the best-known Armenian poet of our time.

Golshiri, Hushang (1938–), born in Isfahan, is the author of poems, translations, and a powerful novel, *Shazdeh Ehtejab* (1968), which show literary craftsmanship of a very high order. He presently lives in Teheran.

Al-Haidari, Buland (1926–), An Iraqi Kurd, was educated in Baghdad and has lived in Lebanese exile since 1963. He has worked there as an editor and has published nine volumes of verse on themes of personal experience and social conscience.

Al-Hakim, Tewfiq (1902–) was born in Alexandria and studied law in Cairo and Paris before winning a reputation as the Arab world's leading playwright. His novel *The Maze of Justice* is available in English, as is the collection of dramas from which the present play is taken (*The Fate of a Cockroach*.)

Hedayat, Sadeq (1903–1951), the leading figure in modern Persian literature, was born to an aristocratic Tehran family. During his service in several Iranian ministries, he traveled in Europe, India, and Soviet Asia. On April 19, 1951, having hermetically sealed the room in which he lived in Paris, he asphyxiated himself by turning on the gas. Noted both as a critic and a short-story writer who fused the Persian literary heritage with European influences, he is most famous for his existential novel, which has been translated into English under the title *The Blind Owl* (1957).

Hikmet, Nazim (1902–1963), one of the first Turkish writers to achieve an international reputation, was born in Salonika, then a province of the Ottoman Empire. After studying at the naval college in Istanbul, he completed his education in Moscow and became a confirmed Marxist. He returned to Turkey and soon was sentenced to thirty-five years in prison for allegedly influencing students toward Communism. He was released in 1951 when the world's intellectuals campaigned for his freedom. Though he also wrote novels and plays, he is best known for his deeply compassionate, lyrical yet idiomatic poetry, available to readers of English in *The Moscow Symphony and Other Poems,* and *Things I Didn't Know I Loved* (Persea Press). The Persea Press also published in 1977 his *Epic of Sheik Bedreddin,* based on an early fifteenth-century uprising of the Turkish, Greek, and Jewish peasants against the feudal lords of the Ottoman empire.

Husain, Rashid (1930–   ) has translated Arabic folk poems into Hebrew with Natan Zach and published some of them in *Stand,* a London periodical, and a collection of them with a Tel Aviv publisher.

Idriss, Yussef (1927–   ) was born in an Egyptian village, studied and practiced medicine for a while, was several times imprisoned for his political activism in the fifties, and now devotes himself entirely to writing. Regarded as Egypt's foremost craftsman in the short story, more recently he has been writing for the stage—comedies in colloquial Arabic with political overtones. In his psychologically penetrating stories, death and forbidden erotic love are favorite subjects, the latter often handled in a poetic, almost surreal style.

Ikhlassi, Walid (1935–   ), a Syrian writer who has published stories, novels, and plays, was born in now Turkish Alexandretta and lives in Aleppo. He lectures at Aleppo University on agricultural economy.

Issahakian, Avedik (1875–1957) was born in Alexandropol (now Leninakan) in Armenia and completed his studies at the University of Leipzig. His first volume of poetry, published in 1898, brought him immediate fame as a lyric poet. In 1911, he went abroad, living in Paris, Berlin, and Venice, and returned to Armenia in 1936. His books of poems, ballads, legends, and tales, especially the stanzaic *Abou Maharri,* have been published many times and in many languages. Ilya Ehrenburg spoke of him as one of the leading contemporary poets of the Western world.

Jabra, Jabra Ibrahim (1919–   ) was born in Palestine and studied at Cambridge and Harvard. He now lives in Iraq, where he has established himself as a distinguished novelist, critic, poet, and painter. He translates his own poetry *(Tammuz fi al-Medina* or *July in the City* and *al-Madar al-Mughlaq* or *The Closed Circuit).* He has also translated Faulkner and Shakespeare.

Kanafani, Ghassan (1936–1972) was born in Acre, Palestine, and worked for a time in Kuwait. He edited a daily paper in Beirut until he was killed by a bomb placed in his car. His novels, short stories, and one play deal with the problems of the Palestinian refugees.

Kanik, Orhan Veli (1914–1950) was a major innovator in Turkish letters and remains today one of Turkey's most read poets. The two poems that appear in this book come from his most important book, *I Am Listening to Istanbul,* translated by Talat S. Halman.

Kemal, Orhan (1914–1970), the pseudonym of Hemit Rasit, ranks as one of the greatest authors of Turkey in the period following the Second World War. As a socialist, he concentrated on the problems of the proletariat in almost all of his vast body of fiction (close to forty volumes). He has been translated into many languages.

Kemal, Yashar (1922–   ), a leading candidate for the Nobel Prize, is Turkey's greatest living writer. Brought up among the desperately poor Anatolian peasants, he has devoted himself to describing their plight in *Memed My Hawk* (translated into more than fifteen languages), *The Wind from the Plain, Anatolian Tales, They Burn Thistles,* and *Iron Earth, Copper Sky.* He has joined the Turkish Workers' Party to lend his help and prestige to what he believes is the most compassionate and sensible political movement in Turkey. His latest book is *They Burn the Thistles* (1977).

Al-Khalili, Jafar (–   ) is an Iraqi writer whose stories have been published in Baghdad. He has been inexcusably neglected in English.

Khanzadian, Sero (1915–   ), the son of a peasant, was trained as an elementary-school teacher and taught in mountain villages until he was called to the service in 1941. He was wounded in action several times and decorated for valor. His first book, *The People of Our Regiment* (1949), is about the courageous defenders of Leningrad. It won immediate acclaim. Since then he has published several novels and short-story collections.

Kishon, Ephraim (1924–   ) attended the University of Budapest before moving to Israel in 1949, where he now

lives in Tel-Aviv with his wife and two sons. He has
won numerous awards for his films and plays, which
poke gentle fun at Israeli foibles and institutions, while
quietly pointing up acute social problems that the country faces, as in the present selection from *Look Back,
Mrs. Lot.* Among his better-known plays are *Black on
White* (1955), *Seven Columns in Carawvanville* (1960),
The License (1962), *His Friend at Court* (1963), and
Sallah (1964).

Mahari, Gourgen (1903–1969) was born in Van in Western
Armenia (now Turkey). He was four when his father was
killed, and in 1915, together with thousands of Armenian refugees fleeing from the massacres, he made his
way to Eastern (now Soviet) Armenia, where he was
sheltered in various orphanages until he began attending
the newly opened State University of Erivan. His first
book of poems appeared in 1923, followed by other poetry, novels, and memoirs. During the Stalinist purges he
was sent to Siberia and lived to write about it after
Stalin's death. The present story appeared in *Gragan
Tert.*

Matevosian, Grant (1935–   ) was born in the village of
Agnidzor in Soviet Armenia and educated at a teachers
college in Yerevan. For a while he worked as a staff editor of *Gragan Tert.* He has established himself, within
the last decade, as a writer of great sensitivity and poetic
vision, the singer of Armenian rural life. He has edited
We of the Mountains, a collection of Armenian stories,
and recently published his own short stories and novellas
in *The Orange Herd.*

Megged, Aharon (1920–   ), novelist and playwright, was born
in Poland and went to Palestine at the age of six. After completing his secondary education, he worked as a
dock laborer, a stone quarrier, a farmer, and a fisherman. He now edits several literary reviews and has written another novel, *The Richter File,* from which this
previously unpublished translation, "Leah Berlin," is
taken. His other books include *The Spirit of the Sea,
Hevda and I, The Escape,* and *The Fortune of Fools.*

Murad, Gowhar-e—see Saedi, Gholamhosein.

Nesin, Aziz (1915–   ), Turkey's foremost humorist, has been
highly acclaimed and widely translated. He has written

under numerous pen names in Turkish magazines and newspapers. Other examples of his satire may be found translated in *The Literary Review* (Summer 1972) and *Literature East and West* (XVII, No. 1). In 1977, the University of Texas Press published Part I of his autobiography, *Istanbul Boy.*

Oz, Amos (1939–   ) was born in Jerusalem, the son of Yehuda Arieh, the writer. He attended Oxford (B.A., 1970) and returned to Israel to participate in the military campaigns on the Golan Heights and in the Sinai. He caught the attention of American readers with *Crusade,* translated for *Commentary.* His other books are *Where the Jackals Howl* (1965), *My Michael* (1972), and *Elsewhere, Perhaps* (1973), from which the present selection is taken. *My Michael* is available in paperback.

Qabbani, Nizar (1923–   ) was born in Damascus and studied law at the university there. After serving his government as a diplomat in Beirut, Cairo, London, Peking, and Madrid, he resigned in order to establish his own publishing house in Beirut. He has increasingly turned away from his early themes of romantic love toward social and political concerns, expressing them in a direct and effective free verse. Emile al-Khouri has described him as "the greatest writer of his generation" and he is probably the most widely read Arab poet among women audiences. His works include *Habibati (My Beloved), Qalat li al-Samra (The Dark Girl Told Me),* and *Fath (The Palestinian Commandos).* His *In the Margin of the Book of Defeat* is a bitter and sweeping condemnation of Arab leadership after the Six-Day War.

Rashid, Harun Hashim, is among the most noted of the Palestinian poets living in Israel. He has published several volumes of political poems: *Saphinat al-Ghadab (The Ship of Anger), Ma'al Ghuraba (With the Strangers),* and *'Awdat al Ghuraba' (The Return of the Exile).*

Rass, Rebecca (1923–   ) was born in Tel-Aviv, the daughter of a Polish immigrant who founded a kibbutz in Palestine. After graduating from the University of Tel-Aviv, she traveled and taught in Europe (Norway and Germany). Her first novel, *From A to Z* (1959), was written in Hebrew, but her subsequent books are in English:

From Moscow to Jerusalem (1976) and *The Fairy Tale of My Mind* (to be published in 1978). She is completing another novel called *Count Me Out,* from which the present story is an excerpt, and has translated Karen Gershon's *The Pulse in Stone* (1970). She lives in New York City now and teaches at New York University and at Rockland State Community College.

Ravikovitch, Dahlia (1936–   ), a *sabra* or native of Israel, published her first poems at the age of eighteen while serving in the army. Three volumes since have made her one of Israel's leading poets.

Saedi, Gholamhosein (1930–   ), trained as a psychiatrist, became Iran's leading contemporary playwright and renowned writer of short stories, using the pen name of Gowhar-e-Murad. The film based on his play *The Cow* won international awards. He was imprisoned in 1974 for nearly a year for his "dangerous political views." For a time, he edited the distinguished literary journal *Al-ifba.* His story "The Wedding" appeared in the Spring 1975 issue of *Iranian Studies.* He visited the United States in 1978 after a number of writers and editors supported his request for an exit visa.

Saleh, Taieb (1929–   ), was born in the northern province of the Sudan and studied at Khartoum and London Universities. In England, he worked for the BBC's Arabic Service and now is employed by the Sudan Broadcasting Service. His first full-length novel, *Season of Migration to the North* (available in English), is partly set in the same village as the stories in his collection *The Wedding of Zein,* from which the present story is taken. Arab readers rate him among their best authors.

Sayigh, Tewfiq (1923–1971), was born in Syria, moved to Palestine, and studied at the American University of Beirut and at Harvard. He has taught at Cambridge, London, and Berkeley. A distinguished scholar and poet, he wrote the poem in this collection originally in English and later translated it into Arabic. The present version, however, is by another hand and from the Arabic text. He has been influenced by the free-verse techniques of Jabra Ibrahim Jabra.

Al-Sayyab, Badr Shakir (1926–1964), was one of the most influential voices in the Arab literary world and a leader in the free-verse movement. Having gone through a Romantic and then a realistic phase, he turned to Arab nationalism and to a preoccupation with myth (Tammuzism), blending Moslem, Christian, and ancient Near Eastern mythologies.

Sepehri, Sohrab (1928–   ), was born in Kashan and is considered by some Iranian critics the most gifted poet now writing in Persian. His work reveals the influence of the Sufi poet Rumi as well as Far Eastern models, and perhaps even Walt Whitman. He is also a talented painter. Author of six volumes of poetry, he most recently has published *Hajm-e Sabz (Green Space)*.

Sevag, Paruir (1924–1971), was born in the village of Chanakh-chee (now Sovetashan) in Armenia. At the university he specialized in ancient and medieval Armenian literature and for a time was senior lecturer at the Gorki Institute in Moscow. From 1963 on, he was a senior scholar at the Literary Institute of the Armenian Academy of Sciences. He published many books of poetry in Armenian and other languages. An automobile accident put an end to his brilliant career.

Shamlu, Ahmad (1926–   ), whose pen name was A. Bamdad, was born in Tehran and presently lives in New Jersey. A former editor and professor, he is acknowledged as one of modern Persia's finest poets. Translations of his lyrics have appeared in *The Literary Review* (Fall 1974), *Poesie Vivante* (No. 28), and *Literature East and West* (XI, No. 2).

Tamir, Zakaria, considered the leading modernist of Syrian fiction, was born in Damascus. He educated himself while working as a locksmith, and published his first book, *The Neighing of the White Steed*, in Beirut. During the sixties, he worked for a time with the Saudi Arabian television service in Jeddah. After returning to Damascus to work as a journalist, he published three volumes of short stories. The present selection, possibly because it deals with a sensitive sexual problem in a society where sex is still under strong taboo, has been left out of his collections of stories.

Yehoshua, Abraham (1936–   ), a dean of students at Haifa University, where he teaches world literature, is the author of a collection entitled *The Death of the Old Man* (1962) and of four longer works brought out together under the name *Three Days and a Child*, from which

"Facing the Forests" is taken. A relative dove in politics, he has urged, in his searching essays, that Israelis seek alternatives to armed confrontation with the Arabs.

Zahrad (1924–   ), is the pen name of Zareh Yaldizciyan, who was born in Istanbul and has lived there ever since, earning his livelihood as a businessman and writing poetry in his free time. His poems have been translated into English by A. J. Hacikyan for *Ararat* magazine and by Ralph Setian. He is an unmistakably contemporary poet whose work is marked by a captivatingly simple, visual style which allows him to suggest, behind the mask, a man who has a love-hate relationship with his surroundings.

Zaroukian, Antranik (1912–   ), is a poet, novelist, and the most brilliant literary critic writing in Armenian today. His first novel, *Men without Childhood*, is about the massacres of 1915. His first poems appeared while he was in his twenties, but in 1946, his "Letter to Erevan" brought him worldwide fame. His last novel was written during the Lebanese Civil War, while the publication of *Nayiri*, the Beirut-based literary weekly, was suspended.